Before leaving for Deauville, Rudolph Valentino visited the Joinville Studio in Paris on August 21, 1923. He visited the studio during the filming of René Clair's, "Paris Qui Dort" (The Crazy Ray) Left to right, Antoine Stacque-actor, Madeleine Rodrigues-actress, Rudolph Valentino, Louis Pré Fils-actor, René Clair-director, Henri Rollan-actor

Published by:
Viale Industria Pubblicazioni
Torino, Italy – A.D. 2021
viplibri@libero.it

In Deposito Legale presso SBN
http://www.sbn.it/opacsbn/opac/iccu/free.jsp

ISBN: 978-0-9987098-5-7

The
Rudolph Valentino
Case Files

The Research Discoveries
of
Evelyn Zumaya & Renato Floris

Dedicated to

Luigi Floris

Beloved brother,
who always sought truth in life

Image from the Iconographic section of the Cinémathèque Française
Valentino with his Isotta Fraschini 8A in front of his residence in New York, 6 W. 48 Street, 1924

A Foreword from Renato Floris

For most of my life I had a limited knowledge of Valentino, like most Italians it was a minimal awareness. For me Valentino was an emigrant expelled from a ruthless homeland which offered him no means of survival. I believed like most other people that his success was due to the terrible sufferings he endured, his great dignity and a stubborn will. Most Italians, including myself know something about how Valentino became one of the most loved and acclaimed, yet envied movie stars in Hollywood history.

I first entered the world of Rodolfo Valentino in 1997, on the occasion of the filming of a documentary about him titled, "Lo Sguardo di Valentino". While shooting various scenes and interviews for this documentary, I realized there was not just one Valentino, but many. Everyone had clear and individual ideas about their "own "Valentino.

Valentino then left my life only to return twelve years later on the occasion of a conference organized in his honor by the University of Turin. At that time I had the opportunity to reunite with a friend I met while filming the documentary, Michael Morris, the author of *Madam Valentino*. Michael was one of the few people who had not created his "own" Valentino and his serious research was supported by an adamant intellectual honesty.

At the Valentino conference in Turin, Michael Morris introduced me to his friend, Evelyn Zumaya, a researcher conducting difficult and complex investigations into the life of the star. A formidable harmony immediately took off between Evelyn and myself. Perhaps guided by the spirit of Rodolfo, we began to collaborate to try to understand who Rodolfo Guglielmi really was and how he became Rudolph Valentino.

Another twelve years have passed since that evening with Michael Morris in Turin. Evelyn and I are still hard at work separating the wheat from the chaff, the good from the bad and above all, the true from the false. We entered a labyrinth of research together, a challenging operation with countless obstacles to overcome and pitfalls to avoid.

Our work on Valentino has at times reminded me of carnival fairgrounds, houses haunted by evil spirits, halls of mirrors arranged to confuse and deceive. But we, being obstinate, want just to discover the truth, solve the mysteries and share it all. Leaving the carnival haunted houses behind, we emerge from the gloomy darkness, with this book. It is a sort of library of many individual books, or files, sharing our Valentino research and discoveries. This book is the result of our years of discussion, debate, changes of opinion, research and investigation. Yet, the question remains... what will happen during the next twelve years?
Enjoy,
Renato Floris
Turin June 2021

Rolf De Maré, owner of the Théâtre des Champs-Élysées in Paris
and director René Clair pay a visit to Rudolph Valentino,
in Deauville, on August 26 and 27, 1923

The Case Files

Photo Courtesy of Vincenzo Filomarino, All Rights Reserved.
Left to right: Luisa Caterina Filomarino, Ernesto Filomarino, Rose Caruso
Filomarino & Ernesto Filomarino, Jr.

Uncle Ernesto

A seemingly insignificant notation, "friend Ernesto Filomarino" entered on Rudolph Valentino's 1913 arrival manifest record, served as inspiration for a revision in his history. This entry presented evidence of a wealthy Italian benefactor hosting Valentino on his arrival in America that December.

Excerpt of Manifest of Alien Passengers Aboard the S. S. Cleveland - Port of Arrival, New York – Line # 11.

During our previous research, we learned "Filomarino" was the surname of Alberto Valentino's wife Ada's mother. As we were then in communication with the Filomarino family, upon seeing this entry we contacted Ernesto Filomarino's great-nephew, Vincenzo Filomarino. He confirmed Ernesto Filomarino was the brother of Ada's mother, Erminia.[1] Vincenzo Filomarino also confirmed Ada's "Uncle Ernesto" hosted Rudolph Valentino in New York when he arrived a few days before Christmas on December 22, 1913.

The inclusion of Uncle Ernesto's name and address in the entry for "Rodolfo dei Marchesi Guglielmi" in the "List or Manifest of Alien Passengers for the United States Immigration Officer at Port of Arrival", supported my assertion in *Affairs Valentino* revealing Valentino did not arrive in America impoverished to spend Christmas wandering the city alone in despair. This studio-generated version of Valentino's arrival was further disproved with the discovery of Ernesto Filomarino.

I presented my original claim regarding Valentino's arrival after I located the family of Valentino's godfather Francesco "Frank" Mennillo. During my interviews with them, they shared the details of his affiliation with Valentino for the first time. My reporting Mennillo's role as Valentino's "padrino" and underwriter, challenged the commonly held belief that Valentino, on arrival, was without funds, knew no one and spoke not a word of English. Mennillo's story was the initial proof this was not factually true.

---

1   Erminia Filomarino Del Mazzone – Information documented in city archives of Turin, *Anagrafe della Citta di Torino, Popolazione Stabile, Femmine.*

Through the discovery of the entry of the name "Ernesto Filomarino" in Valentino's arrival manifest, a second family's testimony confirmed the fact that wealthy, successful patrons greeted young Rudolph in the new world. Ernesto's great-nephew Vincenzo opened his family archive of documents and images to us and through his generosity we learned much more about this enigmatic yet key figure in Valentino's story.

Ernesto Filomarino was born in Genoa on October 2, 1871.[2] His family resided in Genoa at the time of his birth because his father Luigi was an officer with the port authorities. Ernesto's father, Luigi was transferred frequently and worked in Crotone, Naples, Bari and other Italian ports. Father Luigi and mother Camilla Felice died in Taranto, leaving their children residents of the city.

Ernesto Filomarino emigrated to America in 1897, at twenty-six years of age. He prospered, as did Frank Mennillo, by catering to the burgeoning Italian-American population. By 1912, Ernesto was a successful businessman, administrating his own diverse organization with the publishing and selling of books to the Italian community being his most established enterprise. Ernesto accommodated those Italians who could not read by selling stereoscopic viewers with educational and historical visual cards. All of his products were marketed nationally by means of a full catalog of his inventory.

Ernesto's printing presses and distributing operation employed many Italian immigrants in his Spring Street home and headquarters. As a pioneer in providing affordable books to the Italian community in America, he advertised in Italian newspapers coast to coast. In addition to publishing and distributing books, Ernesto also operated a travel agency from his Spring Street offices; booking primarily passages on steamships. Initially, he partnered with the firm of Olivetti, but by 1915 he was sole proprietor of his Elite Art Printing Company.

Ernesto Filomarino was an accomplished artist and his great-nephew Vincenzo relates he painted many portraits of his family. Documents in the Filomarino family archive reveal Ernesto was naturalized on April 9, 1902 and married Maria Rosina Caruso, known as Rose. Ernesto and Rose had two children, a son Ernesto and a daughter Luisa Caterina.

Ernesto and Rose were ideal hosts, with their ability to offer family members and friends arriving in New York a familial and comfortable boarding and employment. Rudolph Valentino was not the only family member to find his way to Ernesto and Rose's welcoming and gracious home at 215 Spring Street. Three years later, a second family member, Federico Rizzo arrived in America on June 1, 1916, and also cited

---

2   Filomarino family archives, Ernesto Filomarino Birth Registry.

Ernesto's address as his place of destination in New York. [3]

Despite this documentation and the clear entry of Uncle Ernesto's name and address in Valentino's port of entry records, the image of Valentino arriving to be hosted by a wealthy family member is not found in the studio-generated version of his life story. This one aspect of Valentino's story was critical for his employers in Hollywood to fictionalize. They felt it imperative to portray Valentino as the rags to riches Horatio Alger hero who arrived in New York desperately poor, not speaking a word of English and knowing no one. Presenting Valentino in this fictional context inspired his Italian-American audiences; a mostly poor working class who idolized Valentino as the embodiment of the American dream to which they aspired.

If Valentino held to the fiction of his starvation during his earliest days in America, it was because he bowed professionally to his employers and publicity agents. They were adamant his popularity would dissipate if his public knew he arrived privileged to spend his first day with Mennillo's tailor and his first night sleeping in Uncle Ernesto's comfortable home. The cinematographic image of Valentino, as having not eaten in days, shuffling along the streets of New York shivering in the cold is false in light of the existing documentation about Uncle Ernesto, his reputation and his financial and social status in the Italy-Americano community.

Valentino arrived in New York in December of 1913, with $4,000.00 U.S. dollars, which by today's exchange would be the equivalent of $104,000.00. The Guglielmi and Filomarino families held pride in their ancestral lineages and were not economically impoverished. They did not send Rudolph to begin a new life with pennies in his pocket and to live destitute in a place where he knew no one. Likewise, the Filomarino family did not leave Rudolph alone for Christmas. Knowing the financial status of Ernesto Filomarino at the time and in speaking with the Filomarino family, we now know Valentino was not relegated to a boarding house where, as the studio-generated version of the story goes, his suitcases were confiscated until he paid for his room.

Rudolph was welcomed as family, because he was family by virtue of his brother Alberto's marriage to Ada. Despite his struggles to find his way on his own, Valentino danced with stars, made love to wealthy ladies such as Blanca DeSaulles and left New York City with the "Masked Model" road show as a star with billing. With the testimony of the Mennillo family and the Filomarino family and the subsequent documentation discovered, the story was corrected and confirmed.

During our research we also discovered one more voice from the past to support the documentation of Valentino's being hosted by Ada Valentino's, Uncle Ernesto. We found an interview given by one of Ernesto's employees at the time of Valentino's arrival; an Italian emigrant William Bianchino, a native of Coggiola in the province of Biella. He arrived in the United States with his parents when he was only five years old. [4] William Bianchino recalls:

---

3   List of Alien Passengers on the *S.S. Duca Degli Abruzzi,* June 1, 1915
4   *The News*, Paterson, New Jersey, December 20, 1969, "N. Haledonite Helped Shape Valentino's Career"

"When Valentino came to this country from Taranto, Italy, he came directly to our office because my boss, Mr. Filomarino was a good friend of Valentino's mother".

Mr. Bianchino relates how Rudolph, while working as a dancer, earned $75.00 dollars a week, (equal to the current $1,963.47). To this we add a weekly remittance sent to Valentino from his mother Gabrielle of $5.00 dollars, (equal to $130.90 today). According to William Bianchino, Valentino enjoyed a comfortable income. Bianchino explains:

"I recall Valentino told me he made only $75.00 a week by dancing and on that salary he had to change clothes three times a day to meet reporters and his money was spent like that".

"...when he (Valentino) said he purchased a railroad ticket to Tulsa, Oklahoma, to engage in that profession (dancing), I repeatedly tried to talk him out of it."

The article continues,

"Bianchino said he told Valentino not to go to Oklahoma because, 'a fellow like you doesn't belong down there. Stay in New York. That's where the money is. The moment you leave here you won't make any money.' "

Ernesto Filomarino died on March 11, 1921[5] and would not live long enough to see Rudolph become a famous movie star. His wife Rose died two years later on April 29, 1923.

5   Filomarino family archives, "Department of Health of The City of New York, Bureau of Records, Standard Certificate of Death #7016"

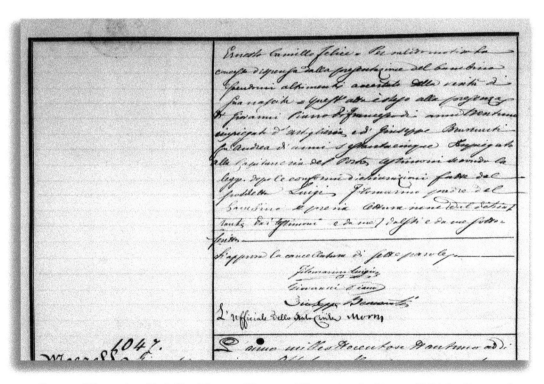

Ernesto Filomarino Birth Certificate - Vincenzo Filomarino Archives - All Rights Reserved

Eldredge, F. M., Printing Co., Inc., 736 Flushing av., Brooklyn; tel. Williamsburg 3176. Job printers.

Electric Bond & Share Co., 71 Broadway; tel. Rector 7930.

Electric Press, Inc., 25 Elm; tel. Worth 4710. Frank Klinzing, pres.; George E. Manardy, treas. Catalogue and job printers.

Electro Dynamic Co., see Dudley-Curry Co.

Electro Light Engraving Co., Inc. (est. 1881), 409-415 Pearl; tel. Beekman 2350. Benj. W. Wilson, pres. and sec.; Albert W. Morley, Jr., v.-p.-treas. Manufacturing photo-engravers.

El Heraldo (Spanish), see D. C. Divry.

Elias, Samuel, see Harlem Printing Shop.

Elish, H. M., & Co. (est. 1917), 47 Great Jones; tel. Spring 131-132. Harry M. Elish, prop. Paper dealers.

ELISH, M. M., & CO., Inc. (est. 1898), 29 Beekman; tel. Beekman 29. Maurice M. Elish, pres.-treas.; A. M. Elish, sec. Paper dealers.

Elite Art Printing Co., The (est. 1915), 215 Spring; tel. Spring 7965. Ernesto Filomarino, prop. and buyer. Job printers.

Elite Press, The (est. 1907), 71 Suffolk; tel. Orchard 3753. Harry A. Horowitz, prop. and buyer. Job printers.

Elite Print, 529 Sutter av., Brooklyn; tel. East New York 6397. Alex. Sheftel, prop. and buyer. Job printers.

Elkeless Cigar Box Co., 79th and E. End av.; tel. Lenox 4485.

Elkin, N., see Alpha Press., Inc.

Ellery, Jos. E., 381 Fourth av.; tel. Madison Square 1863. Jos. E. Ellery, prop. and buyer. Printers and novelty manufacturers.

Elliness Press, The, Inc. (est. 1916), 13 E. 30th; tel. Madison Square 5178. Harry N. Levinson, pres.; Etta Levinson, sec.-treas. Job printers.

Elliot, H. R., & Co. (est. 1877), 13 Stone; tel. Broad 2105-2106. Partnership. H. R. Elliot and A. L. Bouyon, both buyers. Job printers and manufacturing stationers.

Ellison & Wood (est. 1902), 25 Cliff; tel. John 3677-3678. Partnership. Thos. W. Ellison and N. H. Wood. Printers and stationers.

Ellsworth, Richard C., see The Brooklyn Daily Times.

Elore Union Printing (est. 1912), 5 E. 3d; tel. Orchard 8390. M. Revjor, sec.; Joseph L. Sugar, treas. and buyer. Printers and publishers Elore Hungarian Daily and Elore Hungarian Illustrated Weekly.

ELSINORE PAPER CO., Inc. (est. 1900), 131 W. 24th; tel. Farragut 4080. M. Williamson, pres.; L. Hecht, v.-p.; A. George Lutz, sec.-treas. Paper dealers.

Elson, Louis I., see Star Paper Box & Tube Co.

Embossograph Process Co., The, Inc. (est. 1915), 251 William; tel. Worth 2379. S. Lipsius, pres.-treas. Patented process for embossing without dies.

Ernesto Filomarino as owner of Elite Art Printing Company

Ernesto Filomarino Advertisements

Ernesto Filomarino's Death Certificate - Vincenzo Filomarino Archives - All Rights Reserved

N. Haledonite Helped Shape Valentino Career

By GUS LEVENDUSKY

NORTH HALEDON — Had it not been for the strong persuasiveness of a man now living in North Haledon, the entire world, particularly the female population, might have been denied the romantic charms of the screen's greatest lover of all time, the late Rudolph Valentino.

William Bianchino, 79, now residing at 100 Ballantine Drive, in the borough, first met Valentino in 1913 while Bianchino was employed by the Olivetti Company, New York City, a combination mail order house, steamship and bankers' agency.

The North Haledonite recalled, "When Valentino came to this country from Taranto, Italy, he came directly to our office because my boss, Mr. Filomarino was a good friend of Valentino's mother."

Bianchino remembered how Valentino, who then used the name Guglielmi (this real last name was Guglielmo), worked in the nearby theaters as a professional dancer specializing in the Argentine tango at a salary of $75 a week.

Makes $75 A Week

"I recall when Valentino told me," Bianchino remarked, "that he made only $75 a week by dancing and on that salary he had to change clothes three times a day to meet reporters and the money went like that." The only other income he had was the weekly $5 that his mother sent over from Italy, according to Bianchino.

"He went to several colleges in Europe, and received his degree in landscape gardening," Bianchino recalled, "and when he said he had purchased a railroad ticket to engage in that profession, I repeatedly tried to talk him out of it."

Bianchino said he told Valentino not to go because, "a fellow like you doesn't belong down there. Stay in New York. That's where the money is. The moment you leave here you won't make money."

Valentino finally agreed to stay in the East. He continued with show business for a while until one day Mr. Filomarino told Valentino to try the cinema, for he had the qualifications needed for the movies

Left for California

It was then that Valentino left New York to go to California and try for a movie career, and the rest is history. Valentino went on to fame in the silent screen with such films as "The Four Horsemen of the Apocalypse," "Camille," "Blood and Sand," and "The Sheik," which gained him his greatest popularity. His last two pictures were, "The Eagle" and "The Son of the Sheik."

In 1926, while visiting New York City for the premiere of his last picture, Valentino was suddenly taken ill and following an operation, died. He was only 31 years old.

His death at that time was ironic—for if female hearts had violently fluttered at his romantics on the silent screen, how much more would those same hearts have throbbed if they could not only see Valentino but hear him talk as well. Just one year later, in 1927, the first talking picture, "The Jazz Singer," starring Al Jolson, was made.

Knew Him 6 Months

"I only knew him six months and never saw him after he left New York," Bianchino recalled. He added, "Perhaps by talking Valentino out of the Tulsa trip, probably I might have been responsible for his success, I don't know."

Bianchino described Valentino as the executive type, a conservative who was a serious thinker and very precise when speaking.

"He was never the laughing type, always serious, but when he did smile it was a little crack that sort of resembled a Mona Lisa smile," the former Olivetti employee recalled.

Bianchino is married to the former Rena Lova of Paterson. They have one daughter, Mrs. Peter Germaine Catania, of North Haledon, and one grandson, Peter Catania, a sailor on the carrier Oriskany, that served in Vietnam and is now in San Francisco for repairs.

The Bianchinos were married 50 years on Nov. 22 but withheld a family celebration until their grandson can come home. Bianchino was last employed as an electrical appliance salesman for several companies before retiring in 1955.

TWO SETS OF MEMORIES — William Bianchino of North Haledon, and his wife, Rena, reminisce over an old Paterson News clipping of 16 years ago about Rudolph Valentino who won fame as the world's greatest screen lover of all time. Bianchino's thoughts take him back to 1913 when he personally knew Valentino before "The Sheik" became famous, and of the days when he talked Valentino out of becoming a landscape gardner.

The William Bianchino interview

9

Ernesto Filomarino Stereoscopic advertisement

Gerry

Douglas Gerrard

The Admirable Douglas Gerrard

Douglas Gerrard was Rudolph Valentino's loyal friend, mentor, sponsor and acting manager from 1921 until 1923. He was a highly-respected and influential Hollywood director and actor, having achieved fame and fortune on the English, Irish and Australian theatrical stages. With his royal Irish lineage and Shakespearean stage experience, the Irishman commanded an impressive social status among Hollywood's elite and was known affectionately as, "The Admirable Gerry". Despite his success, Doug Gerrard's professional career would decline after August 27, 1922; the day he fired four shots into the night in the woods of upstate New York.

Doug Gerrard as "David Rossi"

The shooting took place while Gerry was in the Adirondack mountains with Valentino and Natacha Rambova visiting her father's estate, Foxlair. Valentino was then, as one headline of the day described him, "Very, very unhappy", because his employer Famous Players-Lasky Corporation interfered in his personal life and ordered him to live separately from Natacha for one year.

This order, received as a barbaric intrusion by Rudolph and Natacha, was officially handed down by the studio and the L.A. District Attorney after the Valentino's

The Valentino's Mexicali Wedding, Gerrard on right

Mexican marriage the previous May was declared illegal. Natacha was exiled from Hollywood to avoid any further bad publicity, their Mexican marriage annulled, Valentino narrowly avoided a fifteen year prison term for bigamy and they were ordered to wait one year before they could cohabit or remarry.

Valentino vowed never to work another day for a studio wielding such control over his personal life and in the summer of 1922, he took to the woods with Douglas Gerrard to spend time with Natacha. The studio responded by dispatching a detective to spy on their top box office star who had just notified them he was breaking his contract, going on strike and accepting no further studio paychecks.

At the time, Douglas Gerrard was also employed by Famous Players-Lasky and his shooting the studio detective, he believed to be a prowler, would compromise his position of prestige in Hollywood society and end his working relationship with Famous Players-Lasky. The fallout from those gunshots instigated his catastrophic fall from grace.

Previous to this unfortunate event, Gerrard acted and directed in major film vehicles while working for some of the biggest movie studios such as Universal, Kalem and Famous Players-Lasky. After he met Rudolph Valentino, he acted as his sponsor, with one article referring to him as the "appointed counselor" by loaning Valentino money, dress clothes and inviting him to high society galas attended by his influential friends in the motion picture industry. During Valentino's early years in the motion picture business, Gerry acted as a sort of fatherly personage. Yet there was a minimizing of Gerrard's contribution to Valentino's success.

Rudolph Valentino & Doug Gerrard @1922

We find familiar images of Gerrard and Valentino engaged in a great deal of camaraderie; such as the video clip of them sparring with Gerry feigning a black eye. They ride horseback together and Gerrard appears as just another member of Valentino's inner circle of friends. But much more was going on professionally and when Rudolph fell in love with Natacha Rambova it is apparent she and Gerry became close friends also.

There are rumors Gerrard, being energetic and tremendously social, could have been banished by Natacha. This because he and Rudolph's other single friends often took him out for nights of partying, bootleg wine, whiskey and women and for Natacha this was intolerable behavior.

Gerrard acted as a witness to the Valentino's first wedding in Mexico which resulted in Valentino being charged with bigamy and thrown in jail for a night while his friends raised bail.

D. Gerrard, Valentino & June Mathis

Gerrard and screenplay writer June Mathis met the press with Valentino outside the jail upon his release and here Douglas Gerrard is seen in his managerial role. It was in great measure due to Gerrard's testimony, the charges of bigamy against Valentino were dismissed. Gerrard acts clearly in a managerial role as Natacha writes about his negotiating with their attorney and she directly refers to his advising them. Subsequent to the shooting at Foxlair and the onset of Valentino's strike, we see an immediate disappearance in the

14

roles Gerrard then received in Hollywood. The shooting at Foxlair was extensively covered by the press and became synonymous with the details of Valentino's legal filing against Famous Players. The two events were not unique from each other and this was not good news for Douglas Gerrard.

By May of 1923, Gerry is still acting as a spokesman for Valentino. For example, in a syndicated article titled, "Has Valentino Made Peace with Enemies?" Gerrard gives the press a statement explaining how Valentino has received offers in regards to the settlement of the strike. It is unclear who initiated the boycott of all things Douglas Gerrard. Was it Natacha fearing another telling of the shooting in the press?

It is not until after Rudolph and Natacha's separation in August of 1925, some three years almost to the day from the shooting at Foxlair, when Gerry reunites with Rudolph Valentino and is again a regular guest at Falcon Lair.

By August of 1926, Valentino dies suddenly and Doug Gerrard acts as a pallbearer at the Los Angeles funeral. By 1926, Gerrard makes a comeback with Warner Brothers. Gerry died as a result of a fall while walking in Los Angeles and an investigation into his death was initiated with the determination being he suffered a heart attack which caused his fatal collapse.

Biographical information and images courtesy of the Liam Muldowney Archive. All Rights Reserved.

Douglas Gerrard directs and acts in the movie, "Polly Put the Kettle On", in 1917, starring with Ruth Clifford

The Friend Douglas Gerrard

By

Baltasar Fernández Cué

First published in Spanish in *Cinemundial* in February 1927

Translation by Renato Floris

Thanks to the Warner Brothers company, it seems the rehabilitation of the Irish actor Douglas Gerrard is already underway. It is, therefore, more than likely the many friends of the admirable Gerry - as he is familiarly known in Hollywood - have the satisfaction of seeing him crown his lengthy artistic career, so full of vicissitudes. Douglas Gerrard did not suffer for lack of preparation, like so many thousands and thousands of the deluded. He is, without any doubt, the most prepared artist who ever came to Hollywood.

While in England, he gradually rose through the challenging yet great Shakespearean theater, to the point of being cast in the role of Marc Antony in the last *reprise* of Julius Caesar; with which the illustrious actor and businessman Sir Herbert Beerbohm Tree delighted London society a few years before his death. And in Germany, where he learned the language so perfectly he became an actor in German theater, Douglas Gerrard also acquired many of his artistic skills.

On his arrival in the United States, he immediately devoted himself to the cinema. Gradually, while ascending as an actor, he also became a director in the studios of Famous Players-Lasky. But suddenly, within a few moments, he rolled down the slope he had climbed with so much difficulty. He was again on the level from where he started, although this time, with the added and aggravating circumstance of having nothing less than the powerful Famous Players-Lasky Corporation working against him.

When we experience such a loss, we realize something about us was amiss. For Gerrard, he had too much heart and lacked the willpower to ever be disloyal or in the least, indifferent. When his friend Valentino went on strike from Famous Players, Gerry supported the then weakened comrade, standing with him against his own formidable superiors. For this Gerry lost his job, acquired a stigma, and suffered far more severely than Valentino himself as a result of the consequences of an action which he himself generated.

With admirable stoicism, Gerry returned to restart his career without sacrificing any of his noble sentiment and with the tenacity which characterizes the strong men of his ethnic background. Even today, after the vicissitudes he experienced and after having suffered many an ingratitude and disloyalty, Gerry maintains the brave and loyal heart he had long before in his beloved Ireland. For these reasons he is one of the best friends you can find in Hollywood.

For him, his friends are sacred. Poor and rich, big and small. They are all, from the point of view of Gerry, as a democracy in which all are equal whether millionaires, directors, stars or starlets.

In Douglas Gerrard's heart, humanity is divided mainly into two classes: friends and not friends. For the friends, he gives everything. For the not friends, the right to become friends. Both classes are divided into two sub-classes: women, on one hand and on the other, men. I must add how the manly Douglas Gerrard violates his democratic rules somewhat in giving preference to women. But among them, it is rare for the Irish artist to have a predilection.

It is true he had unique and unforgettable loves. You just need to look at the huge museum of images displayed on the walls of his living room. Among the countless, affectionate dedications from the most famous personalities from all over the world, there are some which confirm mutual passion. Above all were those inscribed with firm strokes written across the various portraits of Anna Pavlowa as she revealed the passionate love affair which linked her heart to Douglas Gerrard's.

Typically, the admirable Gerry is in love with the beautiful sex as a class, and bestows his love on an individual woman considering her as the representative of all the beautiful sex. (This representative, anyway, could change every day). This is, in our humble opinion, true manly love; and the rest is, at least, just pathological obsession.

But even regarding the beautiful sex, the admirable Gerry does not know how to be selfish. If he laid his eyes, with or without the usual humorous monocle, on a juicy fruit but realizes that this fruit is pleasing even to the humblest of his guests, his great respect for hospitality imposes on him the greatest self-denial and immediately. He will generously leave the rich fruit to the guest, and then reach out to the nearest bowl in search of some other fruit to satisfy his tastes.

His home is, therefore, like a rare oasis in the middle of the wasteland of selfishness which is all Hollywood.

Outwardly, it is one of many similar bungalows, which are irregularly situated in a private garden not far from the Cinelandia studios. Next to the staircase by the entrance, a small and insidious pond trembles and shines. There, every so often and late at night, the admirable Gerry, or one of his companions, dives in for having mistaken the sidewalk for a step of the stairs. Inside, the little house is a bohemian temple whose great priest, the admirable Gerry, is always ready to celebrate some relevant ceremony.

One directly enters his living room. From the four walls, the most beautiful saints of the silent art smile. Here and there, chairs, sofas, shelves, ashtrays, forgotten glasses are scattered. And then there is the indispensable gramophone and the radio set. A few steps from the entrance, the staircase leading to the upper floor: bedrooms and bathroom. And there, the friendly "secretary" for the external relations of Gerry: his tireless automatic telephone. In the middle of the room, a gas heater. But for more solemn occasions, in the background there is the classic fireplace where the rough logs sizzle; both to remember those homey gatherings of remote Ireland as well as to offer his friends the suggestive hospitality of a family atmosphere.

Hanging in the corner of his living room, an American flag flutters as if blown by a faint hidden breath. It reminds us of a heroic feat by Gerry when one day, he was surprised by a stern prohibition officer. After browsing around every corner of that bohemian temple, he left the kitchen with all the bottles he could carry. He was already approaching the room when he casually discovered the fluttering emblem of the Republic of North America. The prohibition officer became more friendly and with tears in his eyes he set the bottles on the silent gramophone, saying in a trembling voice to Gerry:

"A foreigner who loves my country in such a way does not deserve to have his drinks confiscated, god is my witness!"

"Certainly, I love this great Republic," Douglas Gerrard immediately replied and added, "But bear in mind that flag is not there just for such a sentimental reason. The purpose of this flag is also to shine an opportunity to free my life from the impertinent espionage of the prohibition officers."

The officer grabbed all the bottles and the Gerry remained dry for the sake of truth.

We rarely find Douglas Gerrard alone. For him, living involves presiding over a jovial meeting, crowning the chatter of friends with his strong and characteristic laughter and his essential intelligence, which is not just an elegant gadget but one aspect of his multifaceted humor.

But we have found how once or twice a year it occurs to him to rest and alone. However, when we find him unaccompanied, it was almost always because even the comrades he liked were not about. We took advantage of those exceedingly rare occasions for serious chats. He mainly spoke to us about theatrical and cinematographic issues. In brief moments, he made the spirits of the great artists of contemporary English theater come alive in his bohemian temple. Henry Irving, Herbert Beerbohm Tree, Wilson Barret, Forbes Robertson, all scrupulously imitated by Douglas Gerrard both in diction and in movements, thus highlighting the characteristic details of each of those actors. Other times he told us anecdotes about movie stars. Douglas Gerrard thus became a professor of theater art and a speaking chronicler of the life of Cinelandia.

It was on one of those rare occasions Gerry was alone when his great friend Rudolph Valentino sadly entered the bohemian oasis. Douglas was unusually concerned when he saw his companion's unhappy face. Without preamble, Valentino said:

"Gerry, I just separated from Natacha."

In response, Gerry comically removed his monocle and gave a thunderous laugh which shook the walls of the building. He then continued his rowdy commentary until the smile returned to Rodolfo's lips. In his own way, Gerry did his friend a favor.

Incidentally, he also mentioned his ideas about marriage. Subsequently, he listened in silence to the cause of the famous separation; a dozen bitter words which humiliated the conqueror of the screen himself, while he was sharing them with his closest friend.

As soon as Rudy finished the brief account, Douglas Gerrard rose solemnly, walked to one of the walls which was covered with portraits and violently ripped up the two photographs Natacha Rambova dedicated to him.

But Douglas Gerrard was born neither for such solemn situations, nor to be alone or with few friends. His usual attitude - if he wasn't already presiding over a friendly dinner - is curling up in the soft armchair next to the phone, taking out a small address book from his pocket and calling, one after the other, all the friends needed to liven up his bohemian house. You must see the ingenuity and humor which he invests in trying to convince them to cancel any commitment preventing them from coming to visit, or in convincing the mothers it is a matter of organizing an important contract which will enrich their daughters, etc., etc. And so it goes yesterday, today, tomorrow...

Fortunately, Douglas Gerrard is enormously strong, muscular and in good health. Therefore, he can enjoy the life which forces him to find reasons for enjoyment every day; which, in the case of Gerry, means an immense expenditure of energy. He is not one of those who are satisfied with cavorting and having fun with only one friend.

Gerry is above all, the chief general of the spree; the soul of the meeting and he who is always engaged by everything. It is he who animates the party if it fades and gives it a further boost when it is already animated; the one who harmonizes the couples in case of disagreement and who hurries them along when they progress too calmly.

In addition to all this, Gerry works all day and into the night - for long periods - in the Warner Brothers studio, where thanks to his efforts, his faculties and his character, he has regained his old position.

Or better still, he has regained a new position more in line with his joviality. Because Douglas Gerrard is no longer dedicated to the "romantic" roles which were once assigned to him. Director Roy Del Ruth has discovered Douglas Gerrard, despite being an important Shakespeare professional, is also a respectable cinematographic comedian. It is as a comedian he invariably uses him now.

Under the direction of Roy Del Ruth, Gerry received acclaim in the company of Louise Fazenda in the comedy, "Widows Footloose"; now under his own careful direction he directs Monte Blue and Patsy Ruth Miller in, "Wolf's Clothing" which will no doubt further elevate his reputation.

Los Angeles, 1926

This looks like the real thing, but it is not. Douglas Gerrard and Francelia Billington are not married. Altho this is "Her Wedding Day," it is only in a Universal picture

During the filming of "The Dumb Girl of Portici" in 1916,
Anna Pavlova (star of the film) and Doug Gerrard fell in love,
engaging in a brief yet passionate love affair.

Left to Right: Fiorello LaGuardia, Rudolph Valentino,
Douglas Gerrard (with bowtie) & Frank Mennillo

Francesco "Frank" Mennillo
The Godfather

VALENTINO'S DYING WORDS
TOLD BROTHER IN SECRET

Last Words Secret.

Then Mennillo, who is a wealthy real estate man and who rode the high and low waves with Rudy for eleven years, whispered to Alberto.

"I must tell you a message from Rudolph. It is for your ears alone. They were the last words spoken by Rudolph."

Then Mennillo and Guglielmi retired into privacy.

The secret of those last words of Rudolph on his dying bed will be buried in his grave.

Mennillo and Guglielmi have solemnly sworn that they will never reveal the words.

As a tribute to his illustrious brother, Alberto has changed his first name to Valentino.

Rudolph Valentino's dying words were shared with his godfather, Frank Mennillo which were then shared only with Alberto Guglielmi Valentino, The Daily News, New York, New York, September 2, 1926

*Frank Mennillo at the White House with President
Calvin Coolidge and the Italian-American League*

Frank Mennillo, Rudolph Valentino & Mae Murray

Rudolph Valentino and the Olive King

In the late 1930's, five hundred miles of irrigation canals were constructed throughout California's Central Valley. Prior to the completion of this feat of engineering, annual droughts and flash flooding devastated crops and livelihoods. During these difficult years, lending institutions considered any investment in the area's farms and canneries risky business. Cash was in short supply and insolvency more often than not the order of the day.

On one of those central valley days in the summer of 1932, cannery owner Frank Mennillo delivered a speech from the flat bed of a truck parked in a tomato field. He paused to study his audience of apprehensive farmers as they leaned against a row of trucks laden with ripe tomatoes. Mennillo mopped sweat from his forehead with a handkerchief before resuming his effort to convince the tomato farmers they should surrender their crops without receiving the usual "cash-up-front" payment.

He explained how he would begin the "pack" or canning process upon receipt of their tomatoes and then pay them handsomely as soon as the cans of tomato juice were delivered to his distributor. When he paused for a response to his proposal, one farmer called out, "Sure Frank, I'll trust you," and then turned to address his fellow farmers saying, "You all know Frank's good for it!" No one argued his point and a consensus was quickly reached. A grateful Frank Mennillo stepped down from his ad hoc podium on the truck bed and sealed the deal by shaking hands with every farmer present. The trucks piled high with hot tomatoes were soon rolling towards his California Tomato Juice cannery in the nearby city of Merced.

It was doubtful the tomato farmers were aware just how strapped for cash the well-spoken cannery owner was that day. Despite his finely-tailored suit, Frank Mennillo was often unable to afford dinner at his residence, The Merced Hotel. He frequently scrounged meals for himself and his son Arnold by purchasing a loaf of bread and some olive oil and then visiting a few tomato farmers to "taste the crop."

By 1932, such hardship was nothing new for Frank Mennillo and in the course of his mighty boom and bust career he had already earned and lost a million dollars several times. The dramatic events of his swashbuckling life did not all transpire on the open fields of California's central valley. He lived in the shadow of great celebrity including two seated U.S. Presidents and silent movie heart-throb Rudolph Valentino.

Frank Mennillo was a private man and not one to boast publicly about his influential friends in Hollywood and the White House. Consequently, the true story of his affiliation with Rudolph Valentino has never been told until now. The details surfaced only as I researched Valentino for my book, *Affairs Valentino*. After interviewing the Mennillo family, Frank Mennillo's daughter-in-law and grandson, and with exclusive access to their archives, I discovered a possible explanation for the current dearth of information about Frank Mennillo in all publications on Valentino. I believe Mennillo's dominating presence in the movie star's life story was eradicated by Valentino's employers in the motion picture industry the moment he became an internationally known movie star and box-office gold. The story of Frank Mennillo's disappearance is one of xenophobia and studio censorship which began in 1913 when Rudolph Valentino first arrived in America.

Rudolph Valentino's Godfather Francesco, "Frank "Mennillo

In 1913, some 200,000 Italian immigrants entered the United States after being processed at New York's Ellis Island. This influx strained job markets and already over-crowded inner city neighborhoods; generating widespread discrimination and xenophobic rhetoric. Many social movements of the day contributed to the situation by specifically capitalizing on the public's resentment of Italian immigrants. Temperance organizations portrayed them as excessive drinkers and fundamentalist Protestants called them "agents of the Pope".

By the time Valentino secured his first movie roles, many members of America's theater going audiences were prejudiced by the glut of anti-Italian propaganda. Hollywood producers perceived the ready, racist Italian stereotypes as precisely those of the quintessential screen villain and cast aspiring young Italian actor, Rudolph Valentino to play the part. From the moment he swaggered onto the screen in his signature role of *The Sheik* in 1921, his villains were received by his audiences as sympathetic action heroes and he was idolized as "The Great Lover". His meteoric rise to fame presented problems for his studio employers when marketing his public image suddenly became a million dollar business.

This effort further complicated when Congress passed a controversial immigration bill in 1921, the same year *The Sheik* premiered in Hollywood. The Emergency Quota Act was enacted into law with only six dissenting votes just as Valentino assumed his lofty position as the nation's first foreign leading man. This discriminatory piece of legislation restricted the admittance of Southern and Eastern European immigrants to three percent of the total population from these countries already living in the United States. It also reduced the number of Italian immigrants to a fraction of the previous year's total.

While studio executives feared a backlash to Valentino's Italian heritage might be reflected at the box-office, racist terms referring to him as a "wop" and "greaser", were freely bandied about in the national press. Conservative organizations protested his influence and voiced their collective opposition to the actor known as "The Sheik". In response to this troubling trend, an apparent course of action was pursued to minimize the rising star's ethic origins and downplay his personal associations with the much-resented population of Italian immigrants.

While Valentino's steamy on-screen performances were lining the pockets of his employers, their public relations offices were carefully crafting all copy written about him before its release for publication. Valentino's legions of fans, as well as his critics, were appeased but remained unaware that a few deliberate omissions were made from his life story. He was cast in the role of a rags to riches hero who wandered the streets of New York on his arrival shivering and hungry and knowing no one. This was far from the truth as he was sponsored by the uncle of his sister-in-law, Ernesto Filomarino.

Yet one of the most notable of the omissions from Valentino's true story in this regard was his godfather, Frank Mennillo. Over the eight decades since Valentino's death, authors of every book or article published about his life and work have primarily referenced the highly-censored and studio-generated accounts in which Frank Mennillo receives meager mention. However, his role and presence in Valentino's story is not insignificant.

The only facts known about Valentino and Mennillo previous to the publication of *Affairs Valentino* are as follows: Valentino lived with Frank Mennillo in New York City during the winter of 1922-1923, Mennillo visited Valentino in the hospital during the movie star's final illness in August of 1926 and then served as a pall bearer at his funeral. These sketchy by-lines represent the extent of the public's knowledge of Frank Mennillo's life when in fact they represent the meekest commentary on a much broader and colorful story.

In 1923, Valentino's ghost-written autobiography was published in serial format in the fan magazine *Photoplay*. The *Photoplay* articles portrayed his initial arrival in New York City as a lonely experience which was followed by his destitution on the streets of Manhattan. This scenario was far from an accurate one as a wealthy Frank Mennillo not only awaited Valentino's arrival but acted as his doting "padrino", or godfather, from the moment young Valentino first set foot in America until his dying breath some thirteen years later.

When Valentino arrived in 1913, it was a common practice for Italian families to solicit a financially well-established sponsor or "padrino" to greet their relatives on their arrival in New York. Although the term literally translates as "godfather", at the turn of the century the word meant simply a sponsor who acted as benefactor, protector and mentor. In this respect, Frank Mennillo was Rudolph Valentino's "padrino" by definition.

A few weeks prior to his arrival, Frank Mennillo received a letter from the Guglielimi/Valentino family in Italy requesting he act as young Rudolph's sponsor.

Frank Mennillo and his brother Ciro amassed their fortunes furnishing New York's Italian community with familiar goods shipped directly from the homeland. The Mennillo brothers were both graduates of the University of Naples and after immigrating to New York in 1904, they became wealthy businessmen importing Italian "ceci" or chickpeas, olive oil and other Italian products while also operating several automobile dealerships in Boston and New York.

Although the Mennillo brothers were highly-respected, leading members of New York's Italian-American community, Frank Mennillo's position of respectability belied a few tumultuous years as a youth in Italy. One family account details his disappearance which instigated a frantic, international search by relatives and friends. Fortunately, the run-away Frank Mennillo left a warm trail and his family members were surprised to learn the teenager traveled across the Mediterranean Sea to Africa. He was located in a remote village where he was living with a devoted concubine. His infuriated family ferried him home to Italy where he followed the straight and narrow by dedicating himself to the family's exporting business with brother Ciro.

Frank would face his own troubled times in his early years in New York. His marriage would fail and result in a contentious custody situation over the couple's son. However, it was not a long adjustment for Frank and by 1913, he was well-known for introducing one particular Italian relish, the olive, to East Coast dinner tables. This distinction earned him the lifelong moniker of "The Olive King." The Olive King founded the American Olive Company and distributed ripe olives throughout the U.S. in addition to personally designing some of the first machinery used in the relatively new canning processes.

When Rudolph Valentino first passed through customs at Ellis Island in New York he was greeted by his wealthy sponsor, Frank Mennillo. Mennillo was then thirty-two and he and his wife Zelinda had by then separated and agreed on an amicable custody of their four-year-old son, Arnold. It would be Frank Mennillo who first escorted a wide-eyed Valentino on a tour of New York City and it was Frank Mennillo who placed the order with his personal tailor for a new suit for Valentino, complete with top hat and spats. Mennillo instructed his handsome young charge in the latest of men's fashion and told him he should never be seen in public without a pair of spotless white spats.

Under the watchful tutelage of the dapper Frank Mennillo and outfitted in a suit befitting a millionaire, Valentino began his life in America commanding a distinct social advantage. Despite his initial difficulties finding his own way in New York City, Frank Mennillo's generous hand was always open and nearby.

Early in 1915, just over one year after Valentino's arrival, Mennillo left New York City and relocated in California. There he invested the profits from his east coast businesses in Los Angeles and San Francisco and purchased a home at 1332 South Hope Street in Los Angeles. He continued in his position as the majority stockholder of the American Olive Company and entered into partnership with businessman Jack

Ruddle to found "Ruddle and Mennillo" at 226 North Los Angeles Street; an agency distributing Fageol tractors and trucks. He also purchased a theater and a seafood cannery on Terminal Island in Los Angeles and traveled north to establish eleven olive canneries and an Italian plum tomato cannery in California's central valley. He received financing for his new California businesses by securing loans from the president of The Bank of Italy, A.P. Giannini.

Meanwhile, three thousand miles away in New York City, a twenty-year old Rudolph Valentino was not faring well in his padrino's absence. Floundering financially as well as socially, he became romantically involved with a high-society married woman. As a result of this indiscretion, he was arrested and narrowly avoided deportation. Over the next year and a half his precarious situation worsened. Valentino left New York and journeyed straight to San Francisco and towards the financial security of Frank Mennillo who was living in the bay area at the time.

Mennillo welcomed Valentino to the west coast by offering him employment in any one of his California businesses and by introducing him to banker A.P. Giannini. Upon Frank's suggestion, Valentino petitioned Giannini for a loan to finance the purchase of a local vineyard. Despite a reputation as an aggressive lender to Italian immigrants, Giannini was not impressed with the proposal and refused the request. Valentino's bid to own a vineyard was not to be and he subsequently headed south to Los Angeles to seek employment in the movies.

For the next year and a half, he eked out a living by securing roles in a string of unimpressive movies. He earned little income for these appearances, accrued substantial debt and survived only through the continued generosity of Frank Mennillo. However, 1919 would represent a turning point in both Mennillo and Valentino's lives.

It was then Valentino's financial reliance on Frank Mennillo abruptly ended when Mennillo went bankrupt. This dire and unexpected turn of events came about after several people in the Midwest died from contaminated canned goods. Although the poisoning did not involve any of Mennillo's products or canning processes, the panic generated by the deadly episode prompted his primary financial backer, A. P. Giannini to call in all of the loans he held on Frank's many businesses. Unfortunately for Frank Mennillo this amounted to $100,000.00; nearly a million dollars by today's currency exchange.

In a desperate effort to raise the capital to repay Giannini, Frank hired a garage mechanic to act as his chauffeur and rigged a Packard touring car with sleeping accommodations. He then embarked on a slow drive from San Francisco south to Los Angeles to liquidate all of his businesses. At the conclusion of this disheartening trek, he was only able to return $84,000.00 to A.P. Giannini. The "most loved and most hated" banker in America was livid with the partial payment and issued a vendetta by saying he would personally see that Frank Mennillo never worked another day in California. Frank responded with a litany of invective and informed Giannini he had "ruined him" based on faulty information. Frank then packed his remaining possessions in six trunks and with his last five hundred dollars in his pocket he boarded a train for New York City.

With his reliable godfather flat broke, Valentino's financial independence in Hollywood assumed an air of urgency. He knew it was imperative he devote himself to becoming a success as an actor and pounded the pavement in search of screen roles. Shortly after Frank's departure for New York early in 1920, Valentino decided to follow suit in the hopes of securing even higher paying roles in better quality movies being filmed on the east coast.

Frank Mennillo arrived in New York City still reeling from the catastrophic events in California. Determined not to return to the importing business with his brother Ciro, he leased a suite at The Roosevelt Hotel and then traveled on to Washington, D.C. to accept a position with the Italian American League.

Through his connections with this organization, Mennillo was appointed Vice-Chairman of the Italian-American National Campaign Committee for the election of Warren G. Harding. While Mennillo was charming his way into the White House and Harding's good graces, Valentino arrived in New York City and secured work in two minor films.

Frank Mennillo - Image courtesy of the Mennillo family - All Rights Reserved

Mennillo was a gifted public speaker and soon left Washington, D.C. on a cross-country tour rallying crowds in Italian neighborhoods and delivering translations of Harding's campaign speeches. About this same time Valentino received notice he had been cast in the lead role in Metro Pictures production of *The Four Horsemen of the Apocalypse*; he was at last about to be rewarded with financial independence and international recognition.

While Valentino returned to Hollywood to begin filming *The Four Horsemen of the Apocalypse*, Mennillo barn-stormed across the country as a member of Warren Harding's entourage. Valentino's legendary success within the following year resulted in a lucrative contract with the Famous Players-Lasky Corporation. Despite this achievement, he grew increasingly unhappy and felt he held the same artistic input in his films as a five dollar a day extra. It seemed to him the gap between his private persona and his studio-generated public persona grew wider by the day. Despite his overly-groomed public image, on the set of Valentino's movie, *Blood and Sand*, his co-workers still referred to him as "that dishwasher" and "that wop". His protests to such denigration went unheeded as his employers continued to reap profits from his popular films.

By the fall of 1922, Rudolph Valentino's depreciating relationship with his employers reached a crisis point when he violated the terms of his contract by walking off the job. After he issued an ultimatum stating he would not return to work until he was granted complete control over all aspects of his films, he was served with a no-work injunction forbidding him from working until his contract expired. As this dispute played out in the courts, Valentino's paychecks ceased and he turned once again to Frank Mennillo for assistance. Without hesitation Mennillo extended his financial support by inviting Valentino to share his Hotel des Artistes apartment on Sixty-Seventh Street in Manhattan.

During the winter of 1922-1923, Valentino lived with Frank Mennillo and a young Arnold Mennillo who pressed his "Uncle Rudy" for instruction in all the latest dance steps, including the tango. Arnold divided his time between his father's New York apartment, his boarding school in Stanford, Connecticut and his mother's apartment in Greenwich Village.

Zelinda Mennillo earned a reputation as a prominent Greenwich Village activist and served as the principal of the Sullivan School as well as working closely with noted New York City philanthropist William Church Osborn and his organization, the Children's Aid Society. As a tireless social reformer of the Progressive Era, she devoted her career to the improvement of conditions for underprivileged children, especially the young offspring of New York's gangsters.

In the wake of President Harding's sudden death in the summer of 1923, Frank Mennillo continued his work with the Italian-American League. Although he traveled with Harding's successor, President Calvin Coolidge he never cultivated the same rapport with "Silent Cal" as he had with Harding. It was also during the summer of 1923, Mennillo met and befriended George Ullman, Valentino's new business manager.

Ullman was a shrewd businessman and quickly negotiated several lucrative screen contracts for Valentino which allowed him to return to work in the movies. Although financial assistance from Frank Mennillo was no longer necessary for Valentino, Mennillo continued in his role as concerned padrino. Despite his guidance and Ullman's business expertise, Valentino's fame subjected him to undue stress as he was relentlessly pursued by rabid fans and prying press. In an effort to cope with this extreme level of public attention, he indulged in excessive quantities of bootleg liquor and imported cigarettes. Frank Mennillo and George Ullman implored him to guard his health and watched with grave concern when their pleas failed to reverse the troubling trend.

Frank Mennillo faced more challenges at this time than worrying over Valentino's deteriorating health. The Mennillo family believes to this day Frank played a role in "Teapot Dome", the scandal which would forever tarnish the Harding administration. For as the details of Harding's corrupt cabinet and circle of friends began unfolding in the press, Frank Mennillo decided it was time to leave politics and return to the canning business in California.

His decision to return to the west coast might also have been prompted by the passage of further restrictive immigration legislation in 1924, the National Origins Act. This law established even more stringent annual quotas and permitted U.S. entry to a mere four thousand Italian immigrants a year. This quota was perceived as discriminatory by many, including members of the Italian American League; as the annual quota for German immigrants that same year was set at fifty-seven thousand. Upon the passage of this bill, eighty-six percent of all immigrants were of British, French and German origins. Frank Mennillo was well-aware of the fact that in the over-crowded inner city neighborhoods of New York, prejudice against Italians, even successful members of the community, was still prevalent. This social climate prompted his return to California and by the summer of 1926, he was actively engaged in his plans to move west.

During that fateful summer, he and George Ullman's worst fears concerning Valentino's health realized when they found themselves standing together at the movie star's deathbed in New York's Polyclinic Hospital. As with Valentino's earliest days in New York, Mennillo assumed his role as the star's godfather during his final hours by summoning two priests to perform final rites. But despite Mennillo's best efforts, on August 23, 1926, Valentino died in his godfather's arms after whispering a final message in his ear. His death profoundly impacted both Frank Mennillo and George Ullman as the two men shared more than the final intimate moments of Valentino's life. They would both be entangled in years of subsequent legal complications resulting from the contentious settlement of the movie star's estate.

During the weeks immediately following Valentino's death, Frank solidified his plans to return to the canning business with the purchase of five acres of land in Merced, California. While raising capital for this venture, Frank received another letter from the Valentino family requesting he sponsor Valentino's only sister, Maria Strada upon her arrival in New York. She was traveling to America with her husband to assist in settling her deceased brother Rudolph's estate. When she and her husband arrived in January of 1927, Frank Mennillo was there to greet them. Over the following days he expedited their business transactions as well as their travel arrangements to California.

While Frank Mennillo escorted Maria Strada and her husband about New York, his name was appearing prominently in the local headlines. It was reported he and a former ambassador from the Republic of Salvador, Count Ramon de Clairmont, were suing each other for libel. Their legal imbroglio originated when the fifty-year-old Count de Clairmont left the under-aged daughter of one of Mennillo's closest friends, the elderly coffee exporter Don Francisco Duenas, in a family way. Don Duenas was furious to learn of his daughter's predicament and further outraged when the beautiful young girl eloped with the middle-aged Count.

The fragile Don Duenas became so upset over his daughter's behavior, he fell gravely ill and turned to his friend. Frank Mennillo. Mennillo investigated the Count de Clairmont and found nothing to support the legitimacy of his claim to any royal title. He also discovered how in 1918 the Count was detained at Ellis Island on suspicion of being a German spy. When confronted with these allegations the ersatz

Count challenged his ailing father-in-law to a duel and Frank Mennillo accepted the flung gauntlet on Don Duenas' behalf. It was then the Count turned his wrath upon Signor Mennillo by publicly accusing him of being a "scoundrel".

As dueling was outlawed in the United States, Mennillo sent word to the Count to meet him at sunrise on any island in the Caribbean and vowed to arrive armed with the Count's weapon of choice. The threats and counter-threats between Frank Mennillo and the Count escalated until the issue was finally deferred to the courts. Mennillo responded to the Count's lawsuit by telling the press, "in these Stati Uniti gentlemen are forbidden by law to avenge insults upon the field of honor. It is regrettable that in this modern day and age a gentleman must seek redress in the courts of law."

(NEWS photo)
RUDY'S BROTHER HERE AMID AUTOPSY DEMAND. — Arriving aboard the Homeric, Alberto Guglielmi, brother of Rudolph Valentino, was met at pier by delegation demanding autopsy on screen idol's body to ascertain death cause. Above (l. to r.) Frank Mennillo, Guglielmi, and S. George Ullman on board the Homeric.—*Story on page 2*

Late in 1927, the dueling lawsuits worked their way through the legal system and Frank Mennillo finally returned to his California home in Los Angeles. Within a few days of his arrival he met with Valentino's manager and then executor of his estate, George Ullman at The Jonathan Club on South Figueroa Street. They met in the private club's Italian Renaissance Town Club where Mennillo shared details of his plans for his new tomato juice cannery. He also petitioned Ullman for a loan from Valentino's estate which he planned to use to fund the construction of his plant. With Mennillo's years of experience in the canning business, the deal seemed sound to George Ullman and a loan of $40,000.00, dispensed over a few months, was soon negotiated.

Frank Mennillo traveled to Merced in the central valley only to learn that A.P. Giannini had not forgotten his 1919 vendetta. When Mennillo contacted the local Merced bank to request further financial investment in his cannery, he was informed Giannini had sent word his credit was no good in that or any other bank. Mennillo was consequently forced to open his cannery in part with funding received from George Ullman and in part from another loan secured by depositing his personal securities as a guarantee. It was no secret Frank Mennillo hated A.P. Giannini and the rift between the two men grew so fierce that no member of the Mennillo family ever stepped foot inside any of Giannini's banks.

Throughout the leanest years of the great depression, Frank Mennillo struggled to keep his Merced cannery solvent while working with his son Arnold, the cannery's treasurer, at his side. In the spring of 1936, Mennillo closed his California Tomato Juice Company and returned to Los Angeles to work in the produce brokerage business. Only six months after returning to Southern California he was diagnosed with cancer. Surgery was performed to stave off the aggressive disease but Mennillo's post-surgical condition deteriorated rapidly.

Within one week of the surgery, a fifty-four-year old Frank Mennillo passed away with his brother Ciro and son Arnold by his bedside. His many obituaries in Los Angeles, San Francisco and Merced made no mention of his close relationship with Rudolph Valentino but instead praised "The Olive King's" many contributions to the canning business and "his improvements in canning procedure and the development of new processes."

In the vast lexicon of information, misinformation, fact and fiction accepted today as truth about Rudolph Valentino, the contributions of various individuals are acknowledged. But scant mention is made of the magnanimous Frank Mennillo, pioneer in the canning business, barnstorming political speaker and free-wheeling entrepreneur who was also Rudolph Valentino's lifelong and steadfast friend, financial backer and godfather.

This article was written by Evelyn Zumaya with the authorization of the Mennillo family.

The S. George Ullman Papers

by
Evelyn Zumaya

On August 13, 2015, I was privileged to visit with S. George Ullman's daughter, Brenda, "Bunny". Nearly twelve years had passed since I first visited this gracious woman in her scenic hilltop home as a curious reporter working on a biography of Rudolph Valentino. In August of 2015, I walked up the familiar winding path, past the holly bushes and many bird feeders, to be welcomed as a friend. As I sat with Bunny amid the fragrant blooms on her sunny patio, my thoughts wandered back to my visit to her home in 2003. I could not help but feel humbled as I recollected the events awaiting me from that day forward. To encapsulate the saga which transpired after that first interview with Bunny would do little justice to the magnitude of this story.

Bunny reminded me August thirteenth was her brother Bob's birthday. Bob played a critical role in my research and read a final draft of my book, which I titled, *Affairs Valentino* just a few weeks before he passed away in 2005. Bob worked diligently to ensure his father's legacy be reported based on facts and documentation. In gratitude for his contributions, I dedicated the book to his memory.

From 1923 to 1926, Bob and Bunny's father, S. George Ullman held the position of silent film icon Rudolph Valentino's closest friend, mentor and business manager. After Valentino's death in 1926, he was appointed executor of the movie star's estate. Ullman commanded a prominent role in Valentino's story and for this reason I made locating his archive an early objective in my Valentino research .

Without a doubt, the most valuable item in the treasure trove presented to me by Bob and Bunny Ullman was their father's unpublished memoir. He wrote this account revealing more about his behind-the-scenes life with Rudolph Valentino shortly before his death in 1975. This memoir was a biographer's dream discovery. By the time I began my interviews with the Ullmans, I had read nearly every published word about Valentino and was riveted by Ullman's wealth of new and personal anecdotes. The more I read, the more I realized his tales of life with "Rudy" were drastically altering the currently held version of the star's character and his life story.

I received Ullman's copy of his unpublished 1975 memoir as a stack of loose, yellowing pages; some faded and others barely readable. Tucked within these pages, Ullman included a copy of his original managerial contract signed with Valentino in 1923, a personal letter he received from Valentino's attending physician at the time of his death and an article referring to the creation of a children's ward in Valentino's honor in a London hospital. This remarkable memoir remained unpublished and was largely forgotten for thirty years after Ullman's death.

Bob and Bunny Ullman were generous with their time and both assisted me greatly in the creation of their father's first accurate and authorized biography. During my visit with Bunny in 2015, she chose the image of her father for the cover of the first publication of his 1975 memoir. "This one looks the most like him", she told me.

The tragedy which befell their father as a result of his executorship of the Valentino estate, was still a reality during my interviews with Bunny and Bob. Both were bitter about what happened to their family as a result of Alberto and Jean Valentino's legal actions. From Bob's deep disdain for all things Hollywood to Bunny's guarding her privacy from all things Valentino; their anguish of a lifetime was palpable. George Ullman once wrote he should never have tried to settle his friend Rudy's affairs, but he made the decision to do so because he was too idealistic. For this idealism he suffered a tremendous sacrifice.

A final consideration in assessing the role Ullman played as Rudolph Valentino's manager, would be his education in Industrial Engineering. I feel this academic discipline formed the basis for Ullman's success as Valentino's manager and provided him with the ability to endure the business complexities and challenges following Valentino's death.

If it were not for Ullman's clever promotions and hard work in the days and months after Valentino's death, the star might not today be enjoying the degree of international popularity which currently nurtures his legacy. There is no doubt Ullman's background in Industrial Engineering served him well in his efforts in synthesizing the disparate aspects of Valentino's businesses and analyzing the statistical results of his success.

Ullman's scientific application in utilizing these key aspects of Industrial Engineering, resulted in his meticulous book keeping and expertise in sales and public relations. In this effort he forged his own iconic legacy as Valentino's manager. Ullman's broad understanding of the market in which Valentino was employed and his ability to assimilate the principles of corporate management with celebrity management were practical applications he utilized which were decades ahead of his time.

He was recognized and remembered by all who knew him as a man of high integrity.

The Life of S. George Ullman

Although S. George Ullman was a classically trained violinist, he is not remembered for his mastery of the violin. It would be his affiliation with silent movie icon, Rudolph Valentino which would grant him distinction in Hollywood history. Despite the years since Valentino's untimely death in 1926, George Ullman continues to command a dominant role in any film production, publication or discussion of Rudolph Valentino. Although little has ever been known about this pioneer in celebrity management, George Ullman has been portrayed on screen and written about for decades.

S. George Ullman @ 1930

His professional and personal relationship with Valentino was as complex as it was controversial and for Valentino's fans and film history buffs the mere mention of the name George Ullman generates no small amount of heated exchange. One fact, however, is indisputable; during the dawn of Hollywood's Golden Age, S. George Ullman gained international recognition as Rudolph Valentino's trusted mentor, best friend and manager. Ullman's fierce devotion to his friend "Rudy" would ultimately result in his descent from that pinnacle of prestige and professional acclaim and cast him into a thirty year Byzantine legal morass. Ullman's extraordinary story began just before the turn of the twentieth century.

George Ullman was born on September 19, 1893 to Joseph and Anna Ullmann. Perhaps the midwife filing the report of his birth was in error or his parents neglected to record their change of heart. For the name on Ullman's birth certificate reads, Simon Joseph Ullmann. In later years, George eliminated the second "n" in his surname and was known as, Samuel, or "S." George Ullman.

George Ullman's parents were immigrants; his father from Hungary and his mother from Germany. Father Joseph earned his living as a master tailor and included among his clientele some of New York's wealthiest and finely dressed gentlemen. When their son Samuel George was born, Joseph and Anna resided at 1606 Avenue B in New York City.

George Ullman was the third born of the Ullmann's four boys and a bright and scholarly child who demonstrated an early passion for classical music and an aptitude for writing. The precocious boy became so accomplished on his violin, he was soon giving lessons to other aspiring virtuosos in the neighborhood. This inspired George's dream of one day conducting an orchestra.

Joseph and Anna Ullmann never tired of listening to their son practicing the violin and were sure he was destined for a promising future as a violinist with a symphonic orchestra. They never imagined it would be a chance meeting between their dedicated young musician and movie star Rudolph Valentino which would define their son's life and legacy.

On December 8, 1915, a twenty-two year old George Ullmann enlisted for a brief but eventful stint in the National Guard in New York City. The National Guard's New York Field Artillery's Battery D of the First Regiment listed two Ullmann brothers in their ledgers as privates first class. George's younger brother Leo was also on the First Regiment's roster.

George's National Guard record lists his horsemanship as "fair," his character as "excellent," his hair black, complexion dark, height at five feet seven inches and his occupation as "advertising

The Ullman boys – S. George on right

solicitor." In June of 1916, Battery D's First Regiment was mustered into Federal Services and dispatched to Texas and New Mexico to join the Pancho Villa Expedition. President Woodrow Wilson called up some 12,000 troops in an effort to suppress an invasion of U.S. territory led by the rebel general of the Mexican Revolution. For a few months during the summer of 1916, George Ullman and his brother Leo rode the Texas plains with a provisional cavalry division in the campaign to bring Pancho Villa to justice.

In May of 1917, George was honorably discharged from the National Guard by reason of, "dependent relatives." George married his eighteen-year-old sweetheart, Beatrice Mallet, who went by the nickname, Bee. After their marriage, George worked for the Federal Reserve Bank during the day and at night attended law school. Occasionally, George earned extra money by pursuing another one of his passions, boxing. His career in the ring did not last long and by 1918, he left law school to attend night classes at New York University and study Industrial Engineering. He would devote three years to this relatively new field of study. George was eager to establish himself in a reputable career as he had a family to support. On October 18, 1918, George and Bee's first child, Daniel, was born.

S. George Ullman @1917 New York

For the next few years, George worked as a consultant offering his expertise in industrial engineering to businesses in the New York area. In the fall of 1922, he was hired by Scott Preparations, Incorporated, the manufacturers of Mineralava Beauty Clay, to troubleshoot the company's flagging profits. When George proposed a cross-country celebrity promotional tour to boost the company's sales, he was hired to act as road manager for the three months long journey. The celebrity hired to represent Mineralava Beauty Clay was Rudolph Valentino.

At the time, Valentino was on strike from his employer and unable to work as an actor until his contract with the studio expired. He and his wife, Natacha Rambova accepted the Mineralava Company's offer to perform as featured stage dancers in eighty-eight cities and extol the virtues of Mineralava's Beauty Clay. The tour was George's brainchild, the first of its kind and an unqualified success in terms of publicity for Valentino. By the end of the tour in the spring of 1923, George had not only become Rudolph Valentino's close friend and confidant but also his business manager.

George Ullman signs a contract to lease the United Studios in Los Angeles with M.C. Levee & J.D. Williams

On July 6, 1923, Rudolph Valentino and George Ullman appeared in front of a notary public in New York City and signed a contract naming George as Valentino's sole business manager. One month later, on August 13, 1923, Bee gave birth to the Ullman's second son, Robert. Rudolph Valentino would insist on becoming baby "Bobby" Ullman's proud godfather.

As George assumed control of Valentino's business affairs, he discovered neither Rudy Valentino nor his wife Natacha had any interest in managing their finances. George would bring order to their financial household by clearing substantial debt and settling many legal collection processes filed against them. George also negotiated a swift and sweeping victory over Famous Players-Lasky by securing a contract for Rudy which guaranteed his artistic control over his films and an immediate and lucrative return to the screen.

As soon as Valentino completed his contractual obligations with the studio, George negotiated his next contract with Ritz-Carlton Pictures. Since these films would be produced in Los Angeles, the Valentinos left New York to move west. George and his family joined the Valentinos and also headed for the sunnier climes of Southern California.

On November 24, 1924 the Ullman's arrived in Hollywood with six-year-old Daniel and one-year-old Bobby in tow. They rented their first home in Los Angeles but soon purchased a home at 701 Foothill Drive in Beverly

Valentino & Ullman on the set of The Eagle

Hills. The backyard of their Foothill Road home would be the site of fond childhood memories for Dan and Bob Ullman. It was there where their father sparred with his sons and where Uncle Rudy became a frequent and favorite visitor.

As George continued to secure lucrative screen contracts for Valentino, the star grew so dependent on his stalwart friend and manager, he rarely made a move without first consulting him. Today George's multi-faceted position would be filled by a full staff including a business manager, a publicist, a bodyguard, a personal assistant, an accountant and a press agent.

At the time, being Rudolph Valentino's business manager carried substantial weight in Hollywood and in tinsel town's caste system of the rich and powerful George Ullman held considerable rank. By 1926, with Valentino's popularity at its peak, George and Bee Ullman enjoyed a comfortable lifestyle and counted the film industry's elite among their closest friends. They were also frequent guests in the Valentino's home where Rudy and Natacha delighted in their roles of doting aunt and uncle to the Ullman's two little boys.

But George and Bee's glamorous life in Hollywood would be relatively short-lived. Less than two years after their move to California, Rudolph Valentino's sudden death on August 23, 1926 devastated George both personally and professionally. Managing the international response to the movie star's tragic death and the ensuing riots in New York outside of Campbell's Funeral Home left George no time to mourn. It was during this difficult time he organized both of Valentino's funerals and the journey to California by train with Valentino's body and grieving entourage.

George's work did not cease with his friend's death and except for a vague will, Rudolph Valentino did not leave affairs in order. As executor, George was charged with the settlement of the star's heavily-involved estate and only George knew the true extent of Rudy's staggering debt. To complicate matters for George, Rudy's older brother, Alberto, arrived from Italy to contest the will and petition the court to have George removed as executor.

While responding to the barrage of legal exchange with Alberto Valentino, George endeavored to generate income for Rudy's debt-ridden estate. By promoting his last two movies, *The Eagle* and *The Son of the Sheik*, George was able to successfully keep Valentino's production company, Rudolph Valentino Productions profitable. When the court rejected Alberto Valentino's petition to have George removed as executor, George continued to act in his dual role of executor of Valentino's estate and as head of Rudolph Valentino Productions.

Bee Ullman & secretary Clara Trask read condolences after Valentino's death

George asserted his authority to act in this dual role was explained to him personally by Valentino. He was adamant Rudolph left him instructions as to how he wanted his estate settled and these instructions were attached to a second page of the will. Unfortunately for George, when Valentino's will was filed with the Probate Court, any second page of instructions was missing. With no copy of this critical document in hand, George was unclear as to the specifics of Rudy's instructions.

The existing will appointed George executor and stated any profits resulting from his management of Rudolph Valentino Productions should be dispensed, as outlined in those instructions, to Rudy's brother Alberto, his sister Maria and his ex-wife Natacha's, Aunt Teresa Werner. George proceeded in his role as head of Rudolph Valentino Productions, promoting Valentino's last two films, investing any profits and dispersing money to Alberto, his sister Maria and Teresa Werner. In this effort George was successful and he soon earned enough income for the estate to pay off Rudy's nearly $200,000.00 debt and show a profit.

However, Alberto Valentino protested to the court claiming George was basing his actions as executor upon instructions supposedly outlined on a second page of the will which he claimed never existed. When no copy could be found to support George's memory of Rudy's instructions, he had no other option but to accommodate Alberto Valentino's requests and dispense cash advances from Rudolph Valentino Production accounts to not only Alberto, but his sister Maria and Teresa Werner against their future shares of the estate.

While George responded to the steady legal petitions from Alberto Valentino, he continued to manage the post-mortem business of Rudolph Valentino from the office of his own talent agency on Sunset Boulevard, The S. George Ullman Agency. In anticipation of the final settlement of the estate, George founded the business in 1928.

On April 4, of that same year, the Ullman's celebrated the arrival of their third child, a baby girl. At the time, silent screen

The Ullman family @1930

vamp, Theda Bara, lived across the street from the Ullmans and was immersed in the study of numerology and astrology. Her gift to her friends was the divination of their baby's perfect name, Brenda. But since it happened to be Easter, baby Brenda's five year old brother Bobby renamed his sister, Bunny.

Before baby Bunny was a year old, Bee Ullman fell gravely ill with tuberculosis and in a desperate surgical maneuver to save the young woman's life, doctors collapsed and removed one of her lungs. Bee's recovery was long and she would require several surgeries over the next ten years. In one particularly invasive procedure several of her ribs were removed.

As George cared for his ailing wife, he devoted as many hours as possible to rebuilding his career as an artist representative. Although George would never again represent a star with the reputation of Rudolph Valentino, he did represent some stars of note: John Carradine, Francis Lederer, Constantine Shane and character actor, Jack Kruschen. A few of George's clients were his personal friends and visited in his home.

When George represented actor Frank Orth, he and his wife, vaudeville star, Ann Codee, spent many Saturday nights at the Ullmans. Ann Codee was a virtuoso pianist and often accompanied George on his violin.

George would also become a life-long friend of a young radio host, Jack Paar. At one soiree in the Ullman home, one of George's clients, Erich Von Stroheim, fell into the backyard fish pond after one too many cocktails. Decked out in a loaner suit from George, Von Stroheim stumbled back out to the garden party and to the howls of laughter from the other guests he toppled a second time into the shallow pond.

It was a struggle for George to find the time and resources to run his own talent agency as he was also required to spend a great deal of his time and money responding to Alberto Valentino's legal challenges. While awaiting Alberto's approval of his executor's accounts and the settlement of the Valentino estate, George continued dispersing funds to the three people he believed to be Rudy's rightful heirs and invested a portion of Rudolph Valentino Production's profits as secured loans.

Although some of these investments failed to turn a profit, by 1929 George increased the value of Valentino's previously bankrupt estate to nearly $300,000.00. Accomplishing this feat during the first days of the depression was an impressive achievement by any standard. Nevertheless, Alberto Valentino continued his campaign to impugn George's integrity and have him removed from his position as manager of his brother's business affairs.

Teresa Werner's arrival to represent her interest in Valentino's estate - with Bee Ullman

In 1930, he filed a lawsuit against George charging him with fraud and mismanagement of the estate and petitioned the court to dissolve his deceased brother's production company. Pending the outcome of the hearing on these charges and an audit of all executor's accounts, George resigned as executor.

It was at this point George told the press he did so in order to avoid discord clouding the memory of his dear friend, Rudolph Valentino. The court hearing would last until early 1931 with George on the witness stand defending his executor's accounts. During these proceedings a ragged carbon copy of the long sought-after missing second page of Valentino's will, detailing the instructions to George, was presented to the court by the attorney who originally drew up the will. It was entered as evidence and declared by the court to be a valid portion of Valentino's will.

George was vindicated by the smudged paper's appearance which proved he was correct claiming Valentino appointed him to the dual role of managing Rudolph Valentino Productions and executor. But the document revealed one critical piece of information which George failed to recall. According to the newly discovered portion of the will, Valentino's sole heir was his nephew, Jean Valentino. This meant George had unknowingly been advancing estate funds to the wrong heirs, Alberto, Maria and Teresa Werner.

As sole heir, young Jean Valentino held the only legal right to borrow against a future share in the estate. Consequently, as executor, George could be held responsible to repay to the estate the entire amount he dispensed to the three people he believed to have been the rightful heirs.

Despite the fact George did not have access to this missing page of instructions, and despite the fact the court-ordered audit found no evidence of fraud or mismanagement in his book keeping, early in 1932 the court ruled against him. The judgment handed down against George, calculated at a rate of exchange from 1932 to the present, totaled nearly two million dollars at the time. George was ordered to reimburse the estate all monies lost from several failed investments made from the profits of Rudolph Valentino Productions, a portion of his salary as executor, all Rudolph Valentino Production company office and business expenses and every penny he'd advanced to Alberto, Maria and Teresa Werner, totaling some $70,000 (by today's exchange nearly $910,000). George filed his immediate appeal of the decision.

George Ullman with his sons Dan and Bobby @ 1926

In the wake of this crushing legal decision, George filed for bankruptcy, sold his home on Foothill Drive and moved his family into a rented house on Canon Drive in Beverly Hills. His real property was subject to seizure by Jean Valentino and his wages subject to garnishment. While George awaited the decision of the Appeals Court he supported his family with income from his talent agency and focused his professional efforts on keeping keep his family and home secure. Even in his leanest financial times, he took Bee and the children to summer evening concerts at the Hollywood Bowl.

In 1934, the Appeals Court decision was handed down. The court ruled that based upon Valentino's two page will, his estate and Rudolph Valentino Productions were considered one entity in the eyes of the law and as executor George acted properly in this dual role. They found no evidence of fraud or mismanagement and ruled George should not be held responsible for losses incurred from his investments of the production company's profits nor held responsible for any expenses incurred within the course of carrying on the business of Rudolph Valentino Productions.

Citing the decision:

"..when the appellant (George) resigned after having received a practically bankrupt estate, and having thereafter paid all creditors' claims in excess of $190,000.00 and other expenses and having advanced some $66,000.00 to the heirs, he (George) turned over to the petitioner as successor (Alberto Valentino), assets in an appraised value in excess of $300,000.00 and in actual value, as conceded by petitioner (Alberto Valentino) in excess of $100,000.00. With these facts...the District Court of Appeals very naturally and reasonably holds that there was no mismanagement."

The Appeals Court decision allowed George a portion of his salary as executor but was by law required to hold him financially responsible for all of the money he advanced as executor to the unlawful heirs, Alberto, Maria and Teresa Werner. The Appeals Court recognized the "unusual circumstance" of the missing second page of the will by saying it was unclear to the court how it came to be missing or whether George Ullman had ever had a copy in his possession.

S. George Ullman @ 1930

The Appeals Court outlined their recommendation; in light of the unusual disappearance of the second page of the will and the fact George Ullman had not personally benefited from the advances, a fair and appropriate lien should be established against the estate to cover the total amount of the advances. The Appeals Court then deferred any final decision to Jean Valentino when he turned twenty-five and inherited the estate. With the $70,000.00 worth of advances temporarily set aside, the Appeals Court reduced the judgment against George to $26,000.00 by stating,

" ..there is not the slightest scintilla of evidence that...he (George Ullman) was not acting in good faith."

On April 18, 1934 a small article appeared in *The Hollywood Reporter* reading,

"Ullman Exonerated in Valentino Estate Row...The District Court of Appeals yesterday exonerated S. George Ullman of charges of mismanagement of the estate of Rudolph Valentino of which he was executor when it reversed an order by the Los Angeles Probate Court. Ullman's management had been objected to by Jean Guglielmi, nephew and heir to the estate who charged Ullman had made too many cash advances to the other heirs. The Appellate Court praised Ullman for his work "

George made a first payment of $5,600.00, but as he was unable to pay the judgment's principle, the interest soared by tens of thousands of dollars. He took solace in the fact the Appeals Court found him innocent of any fraud or mismanagement and waited to learn whether Jean Valentino would hold him responsible for the repayment of $70,000.00 of advances.

After George resigned as executor, the administration of the Valentino estate was passed on to The Bank of Italy. George left an estate worth $300,000.00, but less than two years later, it was appraised at only $130,000.00. By the time Jean Valentino inherited the estate from The Bank of Italy on his twenty-fifth birthday, August 14, 1939, their lack of management diminished the value of the estate to near insolvency.

Jean's first order of business as he assumed his inheritance was to ignore the Appeals Court's recommendation a lien be established against the estate to recover the money advanced to Alberto, Maria and Teresa Werner. Instead he tacked the entire $70,000.00 back onto the judgment against George. He then instructed his lawyers to keep a watchful eye on George Ullman by offering his legal team a bounty in the form of a percentage of every dime they could collect from George on the revised judgment which then totaled nearly $100,000.00.

By filing notices of wage garnishment and property seizure with the L.A. County Sheriff and scrutinizing the business records of The S. George Ullman Agency, Jean was relentless in his pursuit to collect the very money his father, Aunt Maria and Teresa Werner spent years before. In

Beatrice & S. George Ullman

December of 1952, after years of failing to uncover a single impropriety in George's books, Jean's attorney was asked by the press why his client continued to pursue such a fruitless collection. He replied it was obvious George Ullman could not afford to pay the judgment and admitted George always complied with the court's requests for documentation to prove this fact. But he added, Jean Valentino held out hope that perhaps George Ullman would strike it rich one day.

By 1952, nearly three decades after Rudy's death, Valentino's estate was still filed as an active probate case and it would be 1956 before Jean Valentino would finally dismiss the judgment against George. It was at that time that George sold his home and made a final payment of $2,500.00.

George told his children little about his legal battles with Alberto and Jean Valentino and they grew up unaware he was under such intense legal scrutiny for thirty years. George and Bee Ullman lived the last few years of their fifty-nine year marriage in an apartment at 8450 DeLongpre Avenue in Hollywood. In 1975, George Ullman died, survived by his three children, nine grandchildren and wife Bee. After her husband's death, Bee left Hollywood and moved to northern California to live with her daughter Bunny. There, despite her battle with tuberculosis many years before, she lived to be 89 years old. The Ullman's eldest son Daniel passed away in 1979, Bob died in 2005 and Bunny in 2016.

Rudolph Valentino With the Ullman boys & Bobby Ullman, bottom right, as he appeared in the film, "Lummox" in 1935

Left: Bee Ullman, Right Top: George Ullman and Rudolph Valentino outside the United Artists' bungalow, Right Center: Bobby Ullman with Douglas Fairbanks and father George Ullman behind horse, Bottom Right: George Ullman, Teresa Werner, Valentino and Natacha Rambova

Dead Valentino Still Hero to His Agent

Real Rudolph is Divulged by Man Who Knew Him Best
July 12, 1944
The Los Angeles Herald-Express
By George Ullman
(Film Colony Agent)

Although Rudolph Valentino is almost eighteen years dead, I am still being asked, "What was the real Valentino like?"

Every famous person is more or less the victim of his legend: none more so than the boy born Rodolfo Alfonzo Raffaelo Pierre Filibert Guglielmi d'Valentino d'Antonguolla, who came to be called "The Sheik."

Rudy hated that tag, especially after it became a by-word for what is known as wolfing today. He was never a sheik in the accepted sense of the word; he was a man who sought to love one woman and whose unsatisfied dream was for a real home and children.

Valentino's outstanding characteristic when away from camera was shyness. He hated dance for that reason. His career with Bonnie Glass and later with Joan Sawyer, doing ballroom dances, brought him too close to his audience. He was an eternal boy but understood his capabilities. He knew he registered best in romantic roles. He was a failure when he departed from them, although he was persuaded to do so more than once.

Dodged Book Sets

Valentino was practically a chain smoker. He drank wines, loved good food, ate voraciously, cooked well and liked to cook. He appeared almost ordinary in golf or business clothes, was superb in anything approximating a costume, such as riding clothes, fencing apparel or lounging robes. He kept a large library of books with costume plates which he studied religiously. The remainder of his library was distinguished for rare volumes mostly in foreign languages. He hated sets of books and never bought them.

Al Jolson was instrumental in bringing Valentino to Los Angeles. Norman Kerry, who became a lifelong friend helped him over tough days. Rudy was hopelessly extravagant and died broke. He bought a Mercer with his first permanent salary of $125 a week-spent most of it on repairs. His later cars were Voisons and Isotta Fraschinis. He loved machinery and had a workshop in his garage. Once he took his car apart and put it together again.

Danced for Grauman

Valentino danced in Grauman's Prologues before he made good in movies. Mae Murray gave him his first chance; they were always good friends. He was deeply interested in supernatural things during his marriage to Natacha Rambova; chiefly automatic writing. He had no small superstitions.

He never permitted anyone, even his wife, to see him disheveled. He had no shabby, comfortable old clothes. He spent a fortune on his wardrobe which was always new. He kept himself in superb physical trim, a result of two disappointments. As a boy he was turned down by the Royal Naval Academy because he lacked one inch in chest expansion. The Air Force turned him down in World War One because of his defective vision. His physical routine included sparring with Gene Delmont and Jack Dempsey who was a good friend.

He loved horses; a white Arabian stallion, Ramadan, was his favorite. A harlequin Dane and a Celtic Wolfhound were with him constantly as was a black Cocker Spaniel given to him by Mayor Rolph of San Francisco.

He wore black satin lounging clothes with a scarlet stripe on the trouser leg. His house had a black marble drawing room floor and scarlet velvet drapes. His dining room was in red lacquer and upholstered in black satin. His bedroom was done in black velvet and yellow. He seldom laughed, rarely smiled, had a volcanic temper, quick and intense. He was often profane, even foul before men; never with women. He hated large statuary but had small figurines of jade, ivory and coral. When on his yacht he cooked, scrubbed, trimmed sail and worked like a navy.

Kidded Odd's Tastes

His intimate friends included O. O. McIntyre whom he kidded about his love of loud colors. Valentino always mailed Odd terrible ties. Beltran-Masses, famous Spanish painter, was an intimate of his. Valentino later studied with him. He was planning to take piano lessons when he died.

Other good friends were Lady Cursan, Cora Macy, Vilma Banky, Pola Negri, Prince Mdivani, Schuyler Parsons, Mario Carillo, Frank Mennillo (who was with him when he died), Ronald Coleman, Lady Loughborough, June Mathis, Cora McGeachy and Prince Habib Lotfallah of Egypt. Had Rudy lived he would have made a picture there.

He was married to and divorced from Jean Acker and Natacha Rambova. He romanced with Vilma Banky and Pola Negri but never confided in me about them. Rambova tired of their marriage first; he loved her deeply and she broke his heart.

I am a firm believer in personality as well as handsomeness being vital on the screen. In this, Valentino was a superb showman in his public life and even if he in his private life was as different as the real Valentino was from the Valentino legend.

Valentino As I Knew Him – The Book

According to Bob and Bunny Ullman, their mother, Beatrice, "Bee", told them their father wrote *Valentino As I Knew Him* as a sort of personal eulogy while on board Valentino's funeral train traveling home to California with an entourage of loved ones and press. Ullman was still grieving the loss of his friend at the time and consequently his final 1926 manuscript was not only a biographical narrative but an intimate account of Valentino's last hours of life.

As Ullman kept vigil by Valentino's deathbed and witnessed his death, he felt compelled to share appropriate details with the movie star's public. To quote the 1975 memoir and Ullman's reason for writing *Valentino As I Knew Him* in 1926:

"....In the year that Rudy passed away I wrote a book---rather hurriedly I'm afraid, so that the many thousands of his admirers could have at least an honest, although brief biography quickly because I knew that a great amount of fiction and inaccurate accounts would soon be published, which indeed did happen.

Since that time, erroneous reports have surfaced claiming Ullman's 1926, *Valentino as I Knew Him* was ghostwritten. I state with the authority of Ullman's family that he wrote *Valentino As I Knew Him* in 1926. His friends and his wife Bee, recall seeing him working on this book while on the funeral train riding to California and many pages of the original manuscript, in Ullman's handwriting, are still in existence.

Comparing the stylistic composition of Ullman's 1926, *Valentino As I Knew Him* with his 1975, memoir reveals the same construction of short paragraphs, consisting of long, run on sentences. *Valentino As I Knew Him* did receive editorial embellishments before publication. Despite, the familiar phrasing, compositional and grammatical quirks of George Ullman are evident in both works. Additionally, his free-flowing writing style in the 1975 memoir is the same style we find in *Valentino As I Knew Him,* as he writes with little emphasis upon the chronological order of his narrative.

The final manuscript of his 1926, *Valentino As I Knew Him* was readied for publication with the editorial expertise of Los Angeles writer, Lillian Bell and Raymond Fager, a clerk and typist employed by Rudolph Valentino Productions. George Ullman's *Valentino as I Knew Him* was first published in October of 1926 by Macy-Masius and second and third editions were released in 1927 by the publisher, A.L. Burt. A version of the book translated into French was published soon after.

It was over four decades later, in the 1970's, when Ullman began writing his last memoir, initially as an apparent rewrite of his original publication, *Valentino As I Knew Him.* He soon abandoned this direction to write instead a sequence of anecdotes and personal memories. Although Ullman has been accused of writing his 1970's memoir to exploit Rudolph Valentino, this is a false statement. Ullman was in failing health at the time and his children recall they encouraged him to pen his memoirs about his life with Rudy; as Bunny Ullman said, "More to give him something to do".

As Ullman completed the handwritten pages of his second memoir, his children delivered them to a typist. I learned from Bunny Ullman her father recorded some of the memoir on a reel to reel tape recorder. She recalled how a portion of those tapes included her father swearing in frustration as he tried to figure out how to work the tape recorder.

In his 1926, *Valentino As I Knew Him*, George Ullman created a textbook example of his finest advertising "speak", crafted during the years he was employed as Valentino's business manager. I would not say he misrepresented Valentino in his first book, but rather he omitted elements to stay the course as point man in his efforts to groom the further marketing of Rudolph Valentino. As readers study the differences between both works, they will note Ullman expanded his story considerably in his 1975 memoir.

It is best to appreciate *Valentino As I Knew Him* by considering the date it was published and the daunting task facing George Ullman at the time of his writing. It is my opinion that the 1926 work stands as an advertising tour de force by Rudolph Valentino's business manager who, at that time, was still hard at work polishing Rudolph Valentino's public image. For when Ullman wrote *Valentino As I Knew Him* in 1926, he faced the challenging task of marketing Valentino's last movie, *The Son of the Sheik,* released just prior to the star's death. Ullman also had no choice but to market Valentino and his films, in order to clear the heavily-indebted estate. For this reason, in *Valentino As I Knew Him*, Ullman adheres largely to the studio-generated version of Valentino's life; a story which Ullman himself, at times, personally crafted for public consumption.

In light of the events transpiring in George Ullman's life during the nearly fifty year time span between the writing of his first publication in 1926 and his memoir in the 1970's, Ullman demonstrated remarkable restraint in his latter memoir. His dignified literary demeanor stands as proof of his enduring affection and respect for his friend Rudolph Valentino.

A Review of *Valentino As I Knew Him*

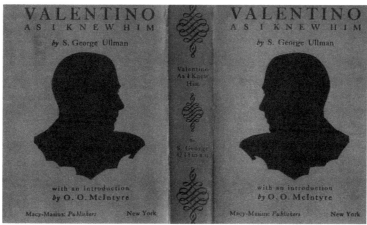

Appearing in the New York Times Sunday Book Review
November 14, 1926

"Business manager, intimate friend, fatherly counselor of the famous moving picture star, Mr. Ullman endeavors to make his biography as interpretation of Valentino's character and an exposition of the reasons why, because of his qualities, he won fame on the screen and the devoted affection not only of his friends but of millions who knew him only by his work in the movies. The author has gathered his material, he says, for this last tribute to his friend "from stories he told me here and there, some related in the great bay window of his Hollywood home, some on horseback riding over the desert at Palm Springs, some on our long railway journeys between California and the East." Valentino apparently told him much about his childhood and youth, and he reconstructs with considerable completeness all that period of the star's life before he came to the United States in 1913-sent hither by his family on a sort of deportation sentence because they began to fear he was going to be no credit to them and they wanted him so far away that the disgrace they believed was inevitable would not touch them. He had a difficult time and many vicissitudes for a good many years after his arrival before his place in the moving picture world began to be assured and adequately paid.

Mr. Ullman tells all this in such detail that the story might well discourage many an aspirant for movie fame. He emphasizes Valentino's own attitude towards his years as a dancer, saying that while he enjoyed and loved dancing for its own sake he abhorred being a professional dancer. He takes pains also to bring out Valentino's essential masculinity of character and tells how deeply he resented the slurs that were sometimes cast upon him because of the parts he played. Mr. Ullman thinks that his life may have been shortened because of his anger and mental suffering over a reference to him in an editorial in a Chicago paper not long before his final illness. The work is written with tender affection and from the viewpoint of one immersed in the moving picture world."

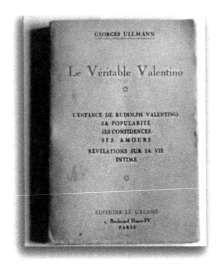

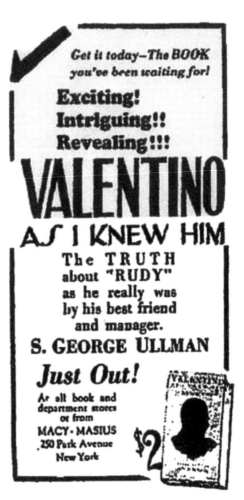

Top & Bottom Left: The French version of "Valentino As I Knew Him"
as "Le Véritable Valentino"
Right: Advertisement for the book at the time of its publication

Shadowing the Sheik

Uncovering the Story of *Affairs Valentino*

by
Evelyn Zumaya

On the morning of July 10, 2005, I boarded a flight in Oakland, California and flew to John Wayne International Airport in Irvine, California. A few minutes after the plane touched down, I hailed a cab on MacArthur Boulevard for the next leg of my journey; a ten minute ride to a gracious home in a secluded neighborhood a few miles south of Irvine. I arrived at my destination that picture perfect Southern California morning to find the familiar entry patio vibrant with potted orchids. I was aware of my host's appreciation for this sensitive bloom and brought along a bouquet of freshly-cut Thai orchids. With my orchids and briefcase in hand, I rapped on the front door, took a deep breath and braced myself in anticipation of the interview before me. For contrary to my radiant surroundings on the patio, I knew the scenario on the other side of the front door was anything but sunny.

I'd stood there many times but on that occasion it was with a lump in my throat and a leaden heart as I knew this would be my final visit with Rudolph Valentino's godson, Robert Warren Ullman. "Bob" was gravely ill. A few days earlier I received his e-mail requesting I travel to Irvine to visit him one more time. He concluded his brief message with a warning, "Better make it sooner than later".

From 1923 to 1926, Bob's father, S. George Ullman was silent film icon Rudolph Valentino's closest friend, mentor and trusted business manager. And it was during the course of researching my book on Valentino titled, *Affairs Valentino,* I interviewed Bob and his younger sister Bunny. Locating George Ullman's surviving children became an early objective in my research as I hoped he left archival materials relating to his affiliation with Valentino. With Ullman occupying a close vantage point of Valentino's personal and professional life, I became determined to pursue this avenue of investigation.

In the rare book library of the University of Southern California, I pored through the archives of Valentino biographer Irving Schulman. On one of his *L.A. Times* article photocopies, he scrawled the words, "A Mystery Indeed." This article reported the story of George Ullman's assertion Valentino's safe was raided after the star's death and a critical portion of his will removed. This turned out to be a mystery I would solve after finding the Ullman siblings and the Ullman archive.

In my effort to locate George Ullman's estate, I subscribed to an internet "people search" engine, purchased a listing of every Ullman in the continental United States and mailed a letter of inquiry to each listing. Within a few weeks I received an e-mail from George Ullman's grandson. He directed me to Ullman's surviving children; Bunny, then seventy-six years old and her older brother Bob, who at eighty was terminally ill with cancer. George's grandson also informed me his father, George's oldest son Dan, died some years earlier.

I forwarded a letter of introduction to Bob and Bunny Ullman and within a few days I received a telephone call from Bob. During this first conversation, he informed me he would be happy to discuss his father's story with me as they had never been contacted regarding his association with Rudolph Valentino. I made plans to travel to Irvine to interview him in person and placed a telephone call to his sister Bunny. Unlike Bob, Bunny lived nearby and I was able to meet with her within a few days. During my first of many interviews with Bunny, she shared a significant cache of unknown documents and artifacts relating to her father and Valentino.

The most important item in this treasure trove was her father's unpublished memoir. Prior to his death in 1975, George Ullman wrote this frank memoir revealing his behind-the-scenes life with Rudolph Valentino. Until Bunny handed me this lost piece of Hollywood history, her father's memoir remained unread and nearly forgotten in the Ullman home for thirty years. Upon first glance, I noticed some of the document's pages were written in Ullman's handwriting while others were transcribed by a typist. Bunny explained how she and her brothers encouraged their father to write the memoir during the last months of his life and ferried his handwritten pages to a typist for transcription.

I then made my first trip to Irvine to interview Bob Ullman and was thrilled when he shared his private collection of family photographs and documents as well as many details of his father's tenure as the executor of Valentino's estate. This was a subject of great interest to Bob as his father told him little about his thirty year involvement in the contentious settlement of Valentino's estate. Bob made it clear to me his father's legal travails as Valentino's executor profoundly affected the Ullman household. I knew this was typically a subject which received scant coverage in books on Valentino and decided that investigating this "after-life" of Valentino might reveal a great deal more about his business affairs and his partnership with Ullman.

Bob informed me how as a result of his father's tenure as Valentino's executor, a $100,000.00 judgment was levied against him; by today's monetary exchange nearly one million dollars. I learned this judgment was handed down after Valentino's only brother, Alberto Valentino, charged Ullman with fraud and mismanagement of the Valentino estate. Although Ullman was exonerated on all charges, the judgment was issued by the court ordering Ullman to reimburse the Valentino estate for cash advances he made as executor.

It was apparent to me during this first interview with Bob that he lamented the dearth of information regarding this painful aspect of his father's life and regretted his being much maligned for his role as Valentino's business manager and executor of his estate. According to Bob, many members of Valentino's inner circle, including his brother, resented George's authority over Valentino during the star's life and many years after. Because of this resentment, he felt his father was accused of unfounded allegations which were never substantiated by any factual documentation. He said this frustration was shared by the entire Ullman family and was further compounded when George Ullman refused opportunities to publicly defend himself against the uncorroborated and denigrating reports.

As I concluded my interview, Bob told me he spent his professional career as a mortgage banker. I had no idea at that moment just how valuable his accounting expertise and inherent stickling for details was about to become to my work. Before I left that day, Bob insisted I locate the probate court records of Valentino's estate settlement before writing a word about this sore subject. Without such authoritative reference, he added, I would just be perpetuating more surmise and speculation. As he had never accessed the documents, he was eager to discover what they might reveal and encouraged me to delve deep for all available supporting primary source material which would reveal the facts of his father's performance as Valentino's executor.

Despite this tall order, I knew Bob was correct. Until I analyzed the court records relating to the settlement of the Valentino estate, I could not authoritatively report the story. I was confidant I could easily locate these records as they would all be on file and available for public review in the Los Angeles County Hall of Records (LACHR). Within the next few days, I found myself sleuthing through the dusty stacks of the LACHR in search of Rudolph Valentino's public records. In light of the thirty years of legal exchange relating to the settlement of his estate, I expected the case file to be substantial in size. Unfortunately, my initial searches were fruitless and I returned to Irvine to share my disappointing news with Bob. He continued to assert that, by law, these records should be housed in this precise location and remained adamant I not write about his father's tenure as Valentino's executor until I found legal documentation of his performance.

More than a little discouraged, I pursued my search for Valentino's missing case file while searching for other available sources of public information to fact check George Ullman's memoir and substantiate his claims. With the assistance of a genealogical search service, I retained a researcher in Italy who successfully located critical Valentino family documents. At the headquarters of the National Archive of Alien Registration, or NARA, citizenship records revealed a wealth of vital supportive data including martial status, ports and dates of entry, occupations, addresses and rare passport photographs.

I logged onto the websites of the historical newspaper archives of both *The New York Times* and *The Los Angeles Times*, PROQUEST, and referenced many previously never-before-accessed press coverage of the day. This was then, in 2003, a relatively new research tool which allowed me to access the historical archives of many major newspapers on the internet merely by merely obtaining a library card to the libraries archiving the PROQUEST database.

For a modest fee, a researcher at the Los Angeles County Library located and copied many documents for me including an unknown file of hand-written index cards referencing further never-before-accessed articles relating to Valentino and George Ullman.

Despite far too many setbacks, my primary goal was always to locate Valentino's case file of public records. I made this my objective not only for the benefit of my work but also for Bob Ullman. With his life slipping away, his time remaining to learn the truth about his father was growing shorter. I returned again and again to the Los Angeles County Hall of Records but continued to come up empty-handed as I was only able to recover a few documents relating solely to the collection processes on the court judgment held against George Ullman.

Clearly stymied, I explained my predicament to the LACHR staff and reminded them they were charged by the public to safe-guard these documents in this location. They offered several possible explanations why Valentino's case file could not be found on the premises. Perhaps, they alleged, the file suffered water damage during a fire in the building years earlier. They explained how all documents compromised in the blaze were freeze-dried and then housed at a separate location. After a time-consuming and thorough search through these freeze-dried records, this proved not to be the case. The LACHR staff then informed me that perhaps Valentino's file might be archived at the facility's auxiliary location; this also proved not to be the case.

At this juncture my research assumed the added dimension of investigative reporting when I realized I had uncovered a crime; Valentino's case file of public records had not simply been misplaced but was in fact stolen. I had inadvertently stumbled onto compelling evidence of the theft of these documents while also exposing a shadowy world of the Valentino family's fiercely-guarded secrets and their practice of controlling Valentino collectors with a currency of their privately owned memorabilia.

Knowing the illegal removal of any records from the LACHR constituted a felony in Los Angeles County, I proceeded to pursue my work in secrecy until I was able to document my suspicions. Whenever I did make this information public, I would be revealing evidence of an unshakable, decades-old Valentino family vendetta and their organized conspiracy which had successfully kept critical information about Rudolph Valentino and the truth about George Ullman cloaked from public access for eighty years.

After searching various depositories, I was at last rewarded in my quest for documentation when I located a case file of some one thousand pages of copies of Valentino's missing probate court documents in a separate, unlikely location; an appeals court law library in San Francisco. This file included Valentino's personal and professional financial statements, official court transcripts of testimony delivered during the lengthy settlement of his estate and extracts from his private household ledgers with entries detailing payments to such things as his personal staff and loyal bootleggers.

The file also included copies of Valentino's studio and business contracts, detailed records of his personal production company's transactions, a precise listing of his debts at the time of his death including such specific items as his oil, grocery and ice bills and pages of a court-ordered audit of all of George Ullman's executor's books. The information contained within these documents allowed me to validate the data in George Ullman's memoir and learn a vast amount of new information concerning Valentino's personal and business affairs and his business affiliation with Ullman. To the best of my knowledge, none of this information had ever been published or referenced in any publication about Valentino.

Perhaps, the most surprising document I found in this recovered case file was that previously "missing" second page of Valentino's will. As I read this mysterious single sheet of paper, the commonly-held version of Valentino's *Last Will and Testament* was overturned. Furthermore, the contents of the document presented an explanation as to why Valentino's court records were stolen from LACHR. The mere existence of this file of copied documents found in San Francisco, in addition to the references contained within, proved definitively that Bob Ullman was right on target; Valentino's original court records were indeed once housed in their rightful location in the LACHR.

During the entire time I conducted my investigation, the staff at LACHR conducted their own internal search for Valentino's records. Upon the conclusion of their appraisal of the situation, Bob and Bunny Ullman received a notarized letter from the Los Angeles County Clerk acknowledging that Valentino's probate records were unavailable for public review at their Los Angeles facility due to the entire case file being "missing". It was then Bob, Bunny and I sat down with the recovered case file of copied documents to read the facts of their father's story.

As I worked my way through the hundreds of pages of old court records, I recognized the name of another key player in this story, Frank Mennillo. Although it was often stated in Valentino publications that Frank Mennillo was his life-long friend, Mennillo received only meager, and as I was about to learn, inaccurate mention. According to the information in the recovered court records, Mennillo played a major role in the settlement of Valentino's estate and with this in mind I pursued yet another angle of the story.

After reviewing the minimal information I could find on Mennillo, I set out to locate the Mennillo estate. I did so by the same means I utilized to locate the Ullman estate; a national mailing. I soon received a response from Frank Mennillo's grandson who informed me no one had ever interviewed their family regarding his grandfather's affiliation with Rudolph Valentino. He put me in touch with Frank Mennillo's daughter-in-law and I then began a series of informative interviews with the Mennillo family.

They eagerly shared family photographs and archives with me and I learned how Frank Mennillo was Valentino's godfather, or benefactor, when he arrived in the U.S., and assisted him throughout his life with his personal and financial problems.

During my interviews with the Mennillo family, I gleaned more information supporting the claims George Ullman made in his memoir and learned more about Valentino's affiliation with not only Frank Mennillo but George Ullman as well. Most significantly, my interviews with both the Ullman and Mennillo families presented me with the first account of Valentino's death from the two people who stood at his deathbed in 1926; George Ullman and Frank Mennillo. Remarkably, even decades after these events, the information I received from the Ullman and Mennillo families was collaborated by the information contained within the court records.

With these significant revelations, the Ullman 1975 memoir and Valentino's probate court records in hand, I began writing an epic tale of unforgivable betrayals, high-stakes courtroom dramas, ruthless power plays and a rash of individuals conspiring to prevent a dark family secret from being revealed.

I credit Bob Ullman's determination for encouraging me to stay the course long enough to achieve my goal of recovering Valentino's court records and thereby document this story. With unfaltering objectivity and devotion, Bob checked and rechecked the details of his father's performance as Valentino's executor, scrutinized the various insurance policies and dividends paid to the Valentino estate and conducted his own line-by-line audit of his father's recovered books and ledgers.

During this arduous process, Bob's failing health inspired me to complete my work as quickly as possible. Despite the pressure of my grim deadline, I kept Bob's desire to complete his contribution to *Affairs Valentino* before he died, foremost in my mind.

My subsequent interviews with him were briefer and the external manifestations of his advancing illness grew more apparent. When I presented his wife with my bouquet of Thai orchids on July 10, 2005, she whispered to me saying my stay should not exceed ten minutes. Despite Bob's fragile condition and failed eyesight, he stood for one brief moment to greet me.

When I took my seat, I spotted a hospice brochure titled, "Final Journey" on a nearby coffee table and felt compelled to flip the pamphlet over. Perhaps in doing so I could dismiss the image of the sunset on the cover and the subject of death. Perhaps Bob and I would then be free to spend the next few hours in animated conversation. We could recall a time during the golden age of Hollywood when he lived with his family in a fabulous home in Beverly Hills and when as a robust toddler he sat upon his god-father, Rudolph Valentino's lap. Perhaps I would hear more stories like the tale of how a drunken Erich Von Stroheim tumbled into the Ullman's fish pond. I might have been regaled with Bob's childhood tales of how he rode on Douglas Fairbanks' horse on a movie set or how Theda Bara's husband Charles Brabin tried to scare the Ullman children into never smoking by blowing cigarette smoke through a white handkerchief.

Instead of sweet reminiscence, this would be a fleeting ten minute visit before his wife gave me the nod. Bob stood once again with effort and gave me a quick hug as sincere as it was feeble. Realizing the weight of that awful moment, we tried to make light of our good-bye forever and I headed for the door. Bunny kept me abreast of Bob's condition and three weeks after my visit I received her telephone call informing me that her brother had passed away.

My interviews with both the Ullman and Mennillo families became the foundation for *Affairs Valentino*. All documents, archives, twists in the plot line and quizzical additions to this life story of Rudolph Valentino, were subsequently discovered as the direct result of the stories of George Ullman and Frank Mennillo's affiliations with Rudolph Valentino.

TO WHOM IT MAY CONCERN:-

MR. S. GEORGE ULLMANN is my sole business busine
manager. I have none other, and any one other than Mr.
Ullmann representing that he is my business manager
does so entirely without my sanction and authority.
The production of this letter by Mr. Ullmann will
evidence his authority from me to act as my said agent. agen ag

Dated, New York, July 6, 1923.

Rudolph Valentino (L.S.)

City, County & State of New York, SS:

On this 6th day of July, 1923, before me personally came RUDOLPH VALENTINO, to me known and known to
me to be the individual described in and who executed the
foregoing authority and he duly acknowledged to me that
he executed the same.

[signature]
Notary Public N.Y. County #193
Comm. Expires Mch 30/1925

On July 6, 1923, S. George Ullman becomes Rudolph Valentino's business manager

ENLISTMENT RECORD.

Name _Samuel G Ullman_ .... Grade _Private 1st cl_

Enlisted _December 8, 1915_ ...., at _New York N.Y_ ..... for _Six_ ...... years.

*In the service of the United States, **under call of the President**, from _June 28, 1916_ to _Nov 15, 1916_

Serving in .... _First_ .... enlistment period at date of discharge.

Previous service .... _None_

Noncommissioned officer ....

Marksmanship .... _None_

Horsemanship .... _Fair._

Battles, engagements, skirmishes, expeditions .... _None_

Knowledge of any vocation .... _Advertising Solicitor_

Wounds received in service .... _None_

Physical condition when discharged .... _Good_

Typhoid prophylaxis completed .... _December 21, 1915_

Married or single .... _Married_

CHARACTER .... _Excellent._

Remarks _Reported at Co fund June 19, 1916 Mustered into Federal Service June 28, 1916 Mustered out of Federal Service Nov 15, 1916_

Signature of soldier ....

Sylvester Simpson.
Captain 1st N.Y.F.A
Commanding _Battery C_

Form No. 525-1, A. G. O.
(For National Guard.)
Ed. Aug. 16-16—200,000.

* Line out if not in the Federal service during enlistment

S. George Ullman's National Guard Enlistment Record citing his "Character" as "Excellent"

65

National Guard,

STATE OF _New York_

To all whom it may concern:

THIS IS TO CERTIFY, That _Samuel G Ullman_

a _Private 1st Cl_ of _Battery "D"_ of the _First_ Regiment

of _New York Field Artillery_ National Guard,

is hereby HONORABLY DISCHARGED from the NATIONAL GUARD of the UNITED STATES

and of the State of _New York_ by reason of _dependent relatives_

per S O # 125 A G O May 18, 1917

Said _Samuel G Ullman_ was born

in _New York_, in the State of _New York_, and when enlisted

was _25_ years of age, by occupation a _Advertising solicitor_,

had _Brown_ eyes, _Black_ hair, _Dark_ complexion, and was _5_ feet

_7_ inches in height.

Given under my hand at _Armory 1988 Bway New York City_ this _twenty-first_

day of _May_, one thousand nine hundred and _seventeen_

Merritt H. Smith

Colonel 1st N.Y.F.A.

Commanding.

_George Ullman's New York State National Guard Honorable Discharge Record
from Battery D, New York Field Artillery in May 1917_

66

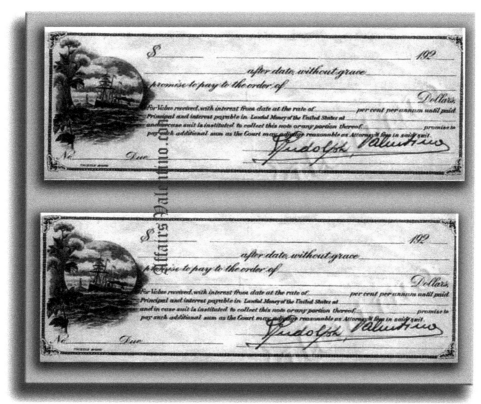

During the litigation brought against S. George Ullman in 1930 by Valentino's brother, Alberto, Ullman presented these two checks to the court. His lawyer argued; if Ullman intended to raid the Valentino estate bank accounts, he could have done so easily by filling out any amount on the blank checks he held in his files which were signed by Rudolph Valentino. The judge refused to admit the checks as evidence ruling Ullman's integrity was never questioned.

These checks stand as proof of S. George Ullman's honesty and intent in regards to the settlement of Valentino's estate.

PARAMOUNT 'DOUBLE DOOR' FANTASTIC BUT THRILLING

Direction, Acting Fine in Weird Yarn

"DOUBLE DOOR"
(Paramount)

Direction ....Charles Vidor
Author ....Elizabeth McFadden
Adaptation ....Gladys Lehman
    and Jack Cunningham
Art Direction..............Hans Dreier
    and Robert Odell
Photography ....Harry Fischbeck
Cast: Mary Morris, Evelyn Venable, Kent Taylor, Guy Standing, Anne Revere, Colin Tapley, Virginia Howell, Halliwell Hobbes, Frank Dawson, Helen Shipman, Leonard Carey, Ralph Remley, Burr Caruth.

The Paramount picture, "Double Door," has very much the same fantastic, incredible, melodramatic plot that used to thrill the readers of those paper-backed novels in the '90's.

It is of the Marie Corelli, Mrs. E.D.E.N. Southworth and Bertha M. Clay school, with villainesses, heroes and heroines that could do nothing less than demand hisses or loud shouts of approval from the audience. Even the preview audience so forgot its accustomed blase detachment as to shout instructions to the heroine and call loudly for her lover when the wicked old woman was about to shut her up in the secret vault.

Were it not for the fact that "Double Door" is superbly directed, stunningly photographed and more than competently acted, it would be a swell burlesque. As it is, it carries considerable pictorial and mechanical weight, which partly makes up for the heavyhanded, leering plot.

Mary Morris plays Victoria Van Brett, the meanest woman in the world, who reigns like a vindictive empress over the immense Van Brett mansion in New York and keeps her sister, Caroline (Anne Revere) and her step-brother, Rip (Kent Taylor), virtually prisoners, semi-hypnotized in the rich, dark old tomb of a house. Things reach a blood-curdling crisis when the old woman, hating Rip's young wife and failing to separate them by means of unusually bitter persecution, attempts to murder the girl by locking her into the air-tight vault in which the family jewels are kept.

Miss Morris turns in an exceptionally strong, vivid performance; Anne Revere, as Caroline, is completely and cleverly convincing as the sister with no will of her own; Kent Taylor is likeable as Rip, who finally dares to defy Victoria, and Evelyn Venable fulfills perfectly the promise she gave in her earlier films. Guy Standing gives a flawless performance in a role that might have passed unnoticed in other hands; Colin Tapley is well cast and appealing as a family friend; Virginia Howell is good as the long-suffering Avery, and Halliwell Hobbes is seen briefly but to advantage.

Charles Vidor's direction is a miracle, considering the story, guiding moments to peaks of real excitement. Elizabeth McFadden is the author, with the idea suggested by Hermine Klepac, and Gladys Lehman and Jack Cunningham made the adaptation.

'Rip Tide' Smash Success in London

London.—"Rip Tide" is doing enormous business at the big Empire Theatre here and is being held over for a second week, with a strong probability that it will run three weeks. The Empire is a grind house.

James M. Cain Buys His MGM Contract

James M. Cain has returned $3,330 to MGM and begged out of writing the screen play for "Duchess of Delmonico," on the ground that he had no desire to go through with the assignment and preferred to work on a novel he had already started.

The William Morris office returned its commission on the deal, having set a contract for $10,000 for the writer, one-third of which was paid down.

Sol Rosenblatt Turns Down Vaude Labor Bd.

New York.—Sol Rosenblatt has refused to take any action at this time on the recommendations of the Vaudeville Actors' Labor Committee. He says that action now would mean the re-opening of the entire code and require open hearings at which all sections of the code would be discussed. This he is unwilling to see happen.

Loretta Young Figures In Double Loan Deal

Due to the postponement of the starting date on "Professional Correspondent," MGM yesterday loaned Loretta Young to Fox. The arrangement was made with Twentieth Century's consent, latter having given MGM a three-picture committment on the actress.

This is said to be the first sub-loan ever put through. Fox gives her an assignment today.

Waycoff with Small

Edward Small yesterday signed Irving Waycoff as production manager on "The Count of Monte Cristo," which Rowland V. Lee directs when it goes before the cameras next month at Pathe. Waycoff was formerly business manager for the Gloria Swanson productions.

Revue For Playhouse

Moe Morton has taken a lease on the Hollywood Playhouse with plans to put on a revue, "Shim Shams of 1934," which Dave Gould will stage.

Too much praise cannot be given to Hans Dreier and Robert Odell for their art direction, and Harry Fischbeck's photography is utterly and beautifully in the mood of this extraordinary story.

This is a page out of the past, a chapter out of an old thriller, and because it is so remarkably well done, it will enjoy a certain popularity as a novelty. It needs cutting badly in the beginning and some toward the end.

New Pictures on B'way This Week

New York.—MGM's "Tarzan and His Mate" and Fox's "Stand Up and Cheer" are the outstanding pictures among the new ones to be seen at the Broadway picture palaces this week. The list comprises:

"I Like It That Way" at the Mayfair Monday; "Modern Hero" at the Strand today; "Stand Up and Cheer" at the Music Hall tomorrow; "Wharf Angel" with Gloria Swanson on the stage, at the Paramount; "I'll Tell the World" at the Roxy, and "Tarzan and His Mate," with radio stars on the stage, at the Capitol on Friday.

Ullman Exonerated in Valentino Estate Row

San Francisco.—The District Court of Appeals yesterday exonerated S. George Ullman of charges of mismanagement of the estate of Rudolph Valentino, of which he was executor, when it reversed an order of the Los Angeles Probate Court.

Ullman's management had been objected to by Jean Guglielmi, nephew and heir to the estate, who charged Ullman had made too many cash advances to the other heirs. The Appellate Court praised Ullman for his work.

Twelvetrees Wins Suit

Rebecca and Silton lost their suit for $236 against Helen Twelvetrees yesterday in Superior Court when Judge Thomas C. Gould sustained a demurrer claiming the court had no jurisdiction because of the amount of the suit.

New Universal Title

Universal has set "Funny Thing Called Love" as the new handle for "Love Life of a Sailor," the Chester Morris-Mae Clarke vehicle which went into work yesterday with Kurt Neumann directing.

Fight to Oust Casey
(Continued from Page 1)

ned to appeal to Washington to have Casey removed from the committee on the ground that it is a violation of the code for a man to sit on a grievance board on any matter involving his own or his company's interests.

"We maintain," says the labor man, "that Casey, who also heads the producers' committee, comes under this head, because it is his job to work for the studios in labor matters. The labor troubles of the studios are Casey's troubles. Therefore, according to Article VI, Part 2, Section 6, he has no right to sit on complaints involving the studios he represents. We are not going to let this thing die. We are going to carry on until we get the committee or Casey out."

President W. C. Elliott, of the IATSE, has written to one of the IATSE locals, stating that he is going to start a battle in Washington to have Casey removed.

Just one more story on Little Pigs—because it has true and "goes to show" good picture shines in the friend of ours, while spending time in Europe, took up and became quite proficient much so, that his instructor to take him on a difficult run around a famous mountain Austrian Tyrol. The instructor the boy to take it easy, fast and follow him at a safe and that, if he watched him all right. So they started and everything was smoothly when the boy instructor frequently turned and evidently saying. Thinking the instructor was other evening, as we were collapse from stage-show big brawny out-of-towner to the usher and loudly demanded his money back. He claimed that when he got to the place, they had promised that the stage show would start a few minutes. He said been two hours ago, that no signs of the show stopped he had paid his money to TURE and, as a final argument cinch matters, he came. "Hell, I'm not scheduled to New York long enough to see the picture!"

It begins to look as though one is going out for Summer again and Ernest Truex will take over the Country Theatre Club in White Plains. His son, Philip, will go with him. So while Peggy and Blume going over whose house damned thing went and but not before Peggy got her throat and lost her voice. Believe it or not frightener who got herself a contract has a husband drawn a sober breath since to Hollywood, and wonders coming back. . . . Wonder make such a fuss over when "Rip Tide" breaks stays three weeks in spite And how did a certain know a picture was going stars before the picture was Add Famous Last Words like you to meet a little just crazy about you, Mr.

In 1934, the lower court verdict against George Ullman was overturned on appeal and he was exonerated on all charges. Within his personal archive, I found this document which stands as his copy of the minimal press his exoneration received.
From the Hollywood Reporter, April 18, 1934.

3, North Castle Wynd.
Edinburgh EH1 2ND,
March 21, 1975

S. George Ullman, Esq.
8450 De Longpre Avenue.
Los Angeles, Calif 90069,
United States of America.

Dear Mr. Ullman,

Thank you for your great kindness
in returning the book on Rudy with your
wonderful comment written below your foreword. I may say this transcends the
greatest ambition I ever dreamt when I
began the book in 1947. When you wrote
the Foreword in 1950, I could scarcely
believe the reality that this had happened,
so unattainable did I regard this, stamping as it did the book with absolute
authority on Valentino second to none
throughout the world, that I would never
have dared to ask you to write of my
own volition.

And now you have affixed your
signature upon the book again to bring it
up to date and perpetuate the challenge
of the truth it contains about Rudy, to vanquish the lies and calumnies that others
might say and write about him; as well
as bringing enlightenment and nostalgic
pleasure to those who will never forget
his noble roles upon the screen/and those

*In 1975, George Ullman contributed, on invitation, a foreword to the Rudolph Valentino
biography written by Norman A. MacKenzie. MacKenzie wrote the above letter in gratitude to
George Ullman.*

69

of the younger generations who will
always find something to admire in the
chivalrous example and romantic magic
of the hero who thrilled their mothers and
grandmothers — and many a grandfather
— as the legendary and immortal
Rudolph Valentino.

Such is the impact your Foreword
and signature has had upon me, and
I am humbly and most deeply honoured
that my name should appear beside
your own upon the book.

The present edition, incidentally, is
almost sold out and the publisher is
already printing its second impression, to
meet continued orders. No fewer than
110 public libraries in Britain now have
the book and at least one American books
importer ordered 53 copies to be sent to
him in the U.S. for his large mail-order
business. The book is catalogued in the big
public lending and reference library in
Edinburgh but is never seen on the shelves
— so keen is the demand that it is always
out on loan, while there is an increasing
number of readers waiting to borrow it on
the reserve list.

I am sorry indeed to learn that you
have been in hospital and sincerely hope
that you will be feeling strong and well again

Dated March 21, 1975

Dear Mr. Ullman,

Thank you for your great kindness in returning the book on Rudy with your wonderful comment written below your Foreword. I may say this transcends the greatest ambition I ever dreamt when I began the book in 1947. When you wrote the Foreword in 1950, I could scarcely believe the reality that this had happened as unattainable did I repair this, stamping as it did the book with absolute authority on Valentino second to none throughout the world, that I would never have dared to ask you to write of my own volition.

And now you have affixed your signature upon the book again to bring it up to date and perpetuate the challenge of the truth it contains about Rudy to vanquish the lies and calumnies that other might say and write about him; as well as bringing enlightenment and nostalgic pleasure to those who will never forget his noble roles upon the screens and those of the younger generations who will always find something to admire in the chivalrous example and romantic image of the hero who thrilled their mother and grandmothers - and many a grandfather - as the legendary and immortal Rudolph Valentino.

Such is the impact your Foreword and signature has had upon me and I am humbly and most deeply honored that my name should appear beside your own upon the book.

The present editor, incidentally is almost sold out and the publisher is already printing its second impression to meet continual orders. No fewer than 110 public libraries in Britain now have the book and at least one American book importer ordered 53 copies to be sent to him in the U.S. for his large mail order business. The book is cataloged in the big public lending and reference library in Edinburgh but is never seen on the shelves-so keen is the demand that it is always out on loan, while there is an unending number of vendors writing to borrow it in the reserved list. I am sorry indeed to learn that you have been in the hospital and sincerely hope that you will be feeling strong and well again by the time you get this. Meantime thank you for your good wishes and please receive mine with my highest regards and gratitude for the privilege of knowing you as Rudy's closest friend.

Yours sincerely
Norman A MacKenzie

71

33 A.

One result of Mrs. Montgomery's broadcast a actually occurred to me.

During _on_ about December 10, 1927, my phone there rang and a man's voice asked whether I was the George Ullman identified with Rudolph Valentino. When I answered affirmatively, he said, "I'm back," this is Rudy" I asked him which Rudy and he said "Rudy Valentino!" Of course I scoffed at this but he insisted that he wanted to see me. I told him that I was too ill to talk to him and to ask him not to annoy me. But he did find his way to our apartment and when my wife opened the door, there was the tall young man who said to her, "Don't you recognize me? I'm Rudy". He asked for me but she told him that I was ill and in bed. She closed the door and when another visitor came he said "Someone left you a present. There, on the carpet of our landing, was an opened raw egg spilled there. This fellow has called phoned several times once at 7 AM! He wrote an abusive letter to me, but I haven't heard from him in about two months.

This isn't the only time men have believed themselves the reincarnation of Valentino; but this one was the most persistent and annoying.

During the last year of his life, George Ullman wrote a second memoir about his life with Rudolph Valentino. His handwritten pages were then typed by a secretary. Here he writes about the Valentino impersonator who threw eggs at the Ullman's front door.

*S. George Ullman,"...the absolute authority on Rudolph Valentino,
second to none throughout the world." Norman A. MacKenzie*

George Ullman's birth certificate as filed in the New York State archives

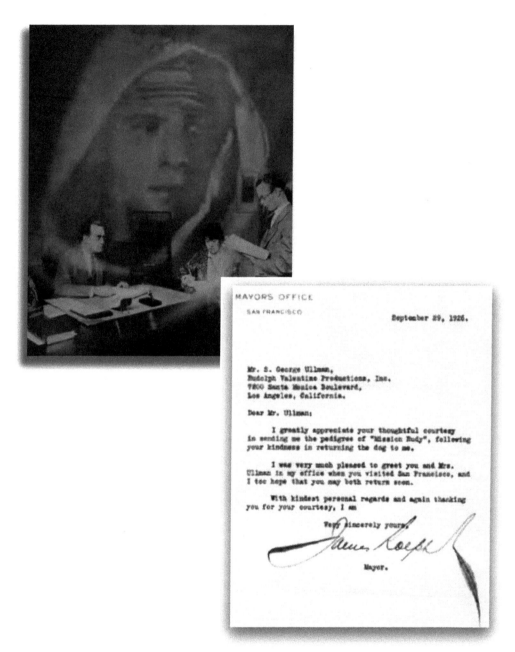

MAYORS OFFICE

SAN FRANCISCO

September 29, 1926.

Mr. S. George Ullman,
Rudolph Valentino Productions, Inc.
7200 Santa Monica Boulevard,
Los Angeles, California.

Dear Mr. Ullman:

I greatly appreciate your thoughtful courtesy
in sending me the pedigree of "Mission Rudy", following
your kindness in returning the dog to me.

I was very much pleased to greet you and Mrs.
Ullman in my office when you visited San Francisco, and
I too hope that you may both return soon.

With kindest personal regards and again thanking
you for your courtesy, I am

Very sincerely yours,

Mayor.

George Ullman photographed in his Sunset Boulevard office after Valentino's death. Below a letter he received from the Mayor of San Francisco thanking him for returning the water spaniel, "Mission Rudy", he and his wife gifted to Rudolph Valentino a few months prior.

Beatrice Ullman & her son Robert Ullman at the Screen Actor's Guild showing of Valentino's movie, The Four Horsemen of the Apocalypse in 1976. Below: her invitation to the event.

The Documented Facts Reversing Alberto Valentino's Claim He Received But Pennies From His Brother's Estate

Among the revelations surfacing with my recovery of one thousand pages of copies of Valentino's probate case file, was the reversal of the fabrication told by Alberto Valentino when he claimed he received only pennies and a few sentimental items from his brother Rudolph's estate. Alberto Valentino repeated this throughout his life, including mentioning it in one of his final interviews in 1977. In every interview he repeated the story and furthered this falsehood by claiming George Ullman was found guilty of embezzling estate money. He blamed Ullman for prolonging the settlement of the estate and for the money being spent lawyers. The documentation in the recovered court records proved this all to be false.

Alberto Valentino & George Ullman - 1926

Alberto remained in Los Angeles after Rudolph's funeral and during the next few years from 1926-1930, he lived large on advances given to him in good faith by George Ullman.

Until the second page of Valentino's will, "Paragraph Fourth" reappeared in 1930, informing Ullman that Alberto was not an heir to his brother Rudy's estate and entitled to no more than a weekly allowance, Alberto supported his star lifestyle on the advances from Ullman. The income Alberto received from Ullman was far more than a few pennies. Additionally, the items Ullman permitted Alberto and his sister Maria to remove from Falcon Lair after their brother's death were itemized by the court. The court records tell the revised account.

Before Valentino's death, as itemized under the *"Baskerville Audits"*, subtitle, *1926 "Gray Book" Household Expenses #3*, Alberto receives a total of $6,050.00 in cash in weekly payments of $500.00 and this from his brother Rudolph between April 7, until July 6, 1926. (today's value calculated x 15 in 2021 = $90,750.00)

After Rudolph's death, as itemized in the court records under the heading of "The Matter of Heirship and Distribution", Maria Guglielmi Strada receives, in cash and personal property, $21,616.33, (today's value, $324,244.95), with the personal property Ullman advanced to her totaling $3,428.00 (today's value, $51,420)

Alberto Valentino received a total in cash advances from Ullman of, $36,949.71 (today's value, $554,245.65). Contrary to Alberto alleging throughout his life that he and his sister only received a "few items of sentimental value and pennies", Rudolph Valentino's siblings received, according to the Appeals Court records, a total of $59,027.33 (today's value, $885,409.95)

This total reflects only the data entered in the courts extracts which I had access to in the court of appeals records and only funds received by Alberto and Maria before 1930.

From the court records, some of the testimony given and data as recorded:

583   Q. Now, will you state to the court what money you have received from the estate? A. I received in March—on March 21, 1927, a draft on the Wilshire National Bank for $5,-000.00 when I was myself in Los Angeles, and for personal property at the same time for $3,-428.00 and when I was back to Italy I received four cashier's check for $1000.00 each on the Pan-American Bank.

Q. The Pan-American Bank of this city?
584   A. Yes.

Q. Will you state what if any property or money other than what you have recited you have received? A. I received never anything else.

Mr. Scarborough: That is all.

[Rep. Tr. p. 626, lines 1 to 26]:

Cross-Examination

By Mr. Wilson:
585

Q. Now, if I understand you correctly, Mrs. Strada, you received only a total of $6000 from the estate?

Mr. Scarborough: No, $9000, Mr. Wilson.

A. $9000.

Q. By Mr. Wilson: Made up of what amounts? A. $5000, a draft on the Wilshire National Bank, and four cashier's checks of $1000 each on the Pan-American Bank of Los Angeles.

Appellant has also made the following expenditures from the assets, which came into his hands, the propriety of which is questioned, since they have not been repaid (see Summary of Objections below)

Cosmic Arts, Inc.—Lambert Process [Supp. p. 247, Item g.]	$ 19,045.21
Loan to Menillo	40,000.00
Loan to Pan American Co. ($50,000, less recovery)	16,000.00
Advances to Menillo, account distributive share of Maria G. Strada	9,100.00
Advances to Maria G. Strada, account distributive share	12,516.33
Advances to Alberto Guglielmi, account distributive share	37,411.00
Advances to Teresa Werner account distributive share	7,617.00
Advances to Appellant, account commissions	22,500.00
Total	$164,189.54

The above tabulations show that Appellant took into his hands property of the value of $490,223.37 (adjusted inventory total above), which increased while in his hands to $889,-037.77 ($330,415.82 (property on hand or turned over to Administrator) plus $389,432.41 (concededly proper expenditures) plus $169,189.54 (allegedly improper expenditures)). Appellant, as will be shown, caused this increase by complying with the directions of testator contained in the will, to continue the business of decedent

394   (Discussion.)

The Court: Now, gentlemen, let us take this view of it. We are losing time here. I want to get on with this hearing. Without determining the matter at this time, I suggest to counsel that where such a large sum is advanced, I think the point should be raised at the earliest possible moment and presented to the court in an appropriate proceeding. As long as I have sep-
395 arated myself from my own court, from any ordinary proceedings of that court, I would just suggest in an advisory way that it could be taken up at the conclusion of the hearing, after the strict hearing on this account, and that would probably be better. I will leave that to you gentlemen to consider.

Mr. Wilson: Your Honor, that would also refer to the amount of moneys which have been advanced and to which objection has been made,
396 to Alberto Guglielmi in the sum of $36,211.00 and those advancements to Mrs. Werner in the sum of $7,617.00, those to Mrs. Maria Strada in the sum of $10,188.00; inquiry into those matters will be left until the conclusion of the hearing?

[Rep. Tr. p. 202, lines 1 to 26]:

Mr. Mann: I believe, if Your Honor please, that the Strada and the Guglielmi advances stand in a little different position.

Direct Examination

514 [Rep. Tr. p. 359, lines 4 to 26]:

Mr. Scarborough: Wait a minute, isn't that—

Mr. Wilson: I think we are not going into that.

A. All right.

Mr. Scarborough I don't believe those parts of the account were to be considered now.

Mr. Wilson: That is right.

515 The Court: Excepting this, that if personal property was turned over, I don't know how you are going to check back—

Mr. Scarborough: All of them have received some personal property.

The Court: Under the "Items Advanced Albert Guglielmi by the executor as transcribed from the records," there are "Bag, Keystone View Company, International News," I don't know what those are. The next one under the
516 subtitle, "Purchases at Auction: Franklin coupe, $2100.00." Was that a part of the property advanced to Alberto Guglielmi? A. Yes, sir.

Mr. Mann I believe, if I am not mistaken, that practically, if not all of this personal property, these various items were purchased by Alberto Guglielmi at the auction and charged to his interest in the estate.

[Rep. Tr. p. 360, lines 1 to 5]:

The Court: If they were purchases in open auction, and the amount that each brought was credited as an advance, is that it?

586   Q.   Now, did you ever receive any—

Mr. Scarborough: I just thought it well, Mr. Wilson, to ask her at that point when she received that $4000.

A.   I received May 4, 1928, being myself in Italy.

Q.   By Mr. Scarborough: You were then in Italy? A. Yes, sir.

Q.   Had returned home? A. Yes, sir.

587   Q.   You got the checks through the mail, then? A. Yes.

Mr. Scarborough: Go ahead, Mr. Wilson.

Q.   By Mr. Wilson: Did you ever receive any personal property, such as coats or things like that? A. Coats?

Q.   Yes, you know what I mean by personal property. A. Yes, I received different little things and some jewels and some pajamas for [Rep. Tr. p. 627, lines 1 to 26]:

588 a total amount of $3428.

Q.   You got that in addition to the other that you just testified? A. Yes, in addition to the $9000.

Q.   Now, did you receive on the 28th day of December, 1927, a check in the sum of $500? A. I did.

Q.   You did? A. Yes. That is in the $9000 there, comprising the $9000.

Mr. Scarborough: I do not believe the witness understood counsel's question.

610   The Court: Are there any witnesses you desire to have remain?

Mr. Wilson: Well, I see some other folks here, Your Honor, but I don't know who they are.

Mr. Haines: They probably won't be witnesses.

Mr. Wilson: We may need Mr. Stewart. I don't know what is coming.

Mr. Hartke: We won't need him.

611   The Court: You are excused, Mr. Stewart. Thank you.

Mr. Mann: I will stipulate that Mr. Alberto Guglielmi received $36,211 as disclosed by detail 8 of the auditor's report, plus an additional sum of $1200 which was paid to him after December 30, 1929, making a total of $37,411.

Mr. Scarborough: You see, Mr. Wilson, the audit report does not cover the supplemental account.

612   Mr. Wilson: I am trying to cover this up to now, and then there are some other checks which Mr. Ulman presented during the trial which are not included in this report.

Mr. Scarborough: This report only covers— the auditor's report merely goes to December 30th.

Mr. Mann: The account of Mr. Ulman went to January 31st. We are willing to stand on the figures in the auditor's account plus $700 dis-

145   146   147

Detail 9

1 Page Only

DETAIL 9—BASKERVILLE AUDIT

Items Advanced Marie Guglielmi Strada

By the Executor

As Transcribed From the Records

Date 1926	Cash	Personal Property
Aviation Coat		5 00
Portable Corona Typewriter		40 00
		32 00
Set Cabachon Emerald & Platinum Cuff Links		775.00
Gold Wrist Watch		400 00
Cabachon Emerald Ring		700 00
Cabachon Saphire Ring		1000 00

148   149   150

	Cash	Personal Property	
Calendar Gold Pencil & Chain		80 00	
Card Case		10 00	
Silica Cigarette Case		16 00	
Pig Skin Wallet		5 00	
Steamer Trunk		100 00	
Stationary Grip		15 00	
Sweater		5 00	
Dressing Robe		10 00	
Japanese Lounging Suit		10 00	
White Gold Cigarette Case		125 00	
Amber & Saphire Cigarette Holder		100 00	
		3428 00	3 428 00
1927			
3/7 Cash	5 058 33		
12/28 "	500 00		
12/8 "	500 00		
	6 058 33		6 058 33

Rudolph & Natacha's Last Kiss
&
The Dissolution of Cosmic Arts, Incorporated

Within the pages of the recovered court records, I learned much more about Rudolph Valentino and Natacha Rambova's last kiss and what would be the last time they saw each other. Until I found this information, it was believed they were just embarking on a "marital vacation".

Within the pages of the court records, I found testimony by George Ullman revealing how the dissolution of Valentino's corporate alter ego, Cosmic Arts, Incorporated took place minutes before the infamous parting scene at the train station. Until the records were recovered, it was believed Natacha Rambova was leaving her husband but I learned it was the other way around. Rudolph was sending Natacha away after eliminating her from his business affairs with the dissolution of said entity.

Natacha Rambova prepared to leave Los Angeles on August 13, 1925

Cosmic Arts, Incorporated was not known about until I shared the contents of the records in this regard. This aspect of Valentino's life came to light because the cost of maintaining the company after Valentino's death by executor Ullman came under scrutiny as it was objected to by Alberto Valentino. The accounting records of Cosmic Arts were included by Ullman in his appeals case.

During the last years of his life, Rudolph Valentino owned and operated Cosmic Arts Incorporated, a scientific research laboratory in New York City. He funded all of the laboratory's expenses including rent, utilities, office supplies, laboratory equipment and the salaries of two scientists, Albert Lambert from Brussels and Jean Gauthier. As owner of the laboratory, Valentino not only paid Gauthier and Lambert's salaries, but also the salary of Richard Ingalls, a sales representative who promoted the two scientist's work.

Whenever the need arose, Valentino loaned the two scientists and Richard Ingalls the services of his New York secretary, Estelle Dick. Albert Lambert and Jean Gauthier discovered a mineral which they registered with the U.S. Patent Office as Lambertite. Their scientific research involved experimentation with Lambertite and the development of a chemical process utilizing this mineral in a revolutionary technology of film processing. Rudolph Valentino not only owned the laboratory, he held the patent on the chemical process called, The Lambert Process.

Valentino purchased The Lambert Process patent in May of 1923 and hoped to resell the patent and pocket a substantial profit if Lambert and Gauthier were ever successful in their experimentation. The prospect of a scientific breakthrough in his laboratory was not the only motivation for the purchase. For several years the laboratory served as his corporate identity, or legal alter ego and a safe shelter for all of his financial transactions.

After purchasing Cosmic Arts, all of Valentino's studio contracts were assigned to the laboratory's ownership and the laboratory, in turn, paid his salary. This business practice was widely used and legal. It would be two years after assuming ownership of the laboratory when George Ullman reorganized all of Valentino's financial holdings, including Cosmic Arts, under the ownership of a newly-created corporate identity, Rudolph Valentino Productions.

By March of 1930, Ullman was still acting as both the executor of Valentino's estate and head of Rudolph Valentino Productions. In this capacity, he was underwriting Cosmic Arts Incorporated as a subsidiary of Rudolph Valentino Productions. He nearly sold The Lambert Process patent for a quarter of a million dollars in June of 1927, but before a final sale could be transacted the deal fell through.

Determined to recuperate some of the years of investment, Ullman continued to issue checks to scientists Lambert and Gauthier in New York and record all of their Cosmic Arts' expenditures in his Rudolph Valentino Productions' accounting ledgers. During the first three and a half years after Valentino's death, Ullman bankrolled Cosmic Arts, Inc. to the sum of just over $18,000.00 dollars. Unfortunately, every item he recorded in his ledgers under the heading of "Cosmic Arts Expenditures" was being added to a lengthy list of transactions coming under scrutiny by Alberto Valentino and his attorneys.

They challenged George Ullman's underwriting of Cosmic Arts, Inc. and believed the laboratory to be an illegitimate expenditure of the estate. They maintained that he, as executor, had no authority to continue financing the laboratory as a subsidiary of Rudolph Valentino Productions.

On August 13, 1925, at 2:00 o'clock in the afternoon, George Ullman met with Natacha Rambova. Rudolph did not attend this meeting. The purpose of the meeting was to affix Natacha's signature to documents which dissolved Valentino's corporate alter ego, Cosmic Arts, Incorporated. With Natacha's signature, she surrendered her ten shares of Cosmic Arts stock which gave her the controlling and only interest in the corporation. From that moment on, Natacha had no business involvement with her husband Rudolph and could make no claim against the business. That day Rudolph established the Rudolph Valentino Production Company as his new corporate alter ego with Cosmic Arts reorganized as a subsidiary.

A few hours after this meeting, Natacha met Rudolph at the train station where they playfully kissed for the press, while stating they were embarking on a "marital vacation". The truth was they would never see each other again and Natacha would go on to France to file for a divorce.

Although Natacha laughs somewhat nervously and out of character for her at the train station good-bye, she wrote later she was devastated, extremely emotional and she cried as the train left the station. Contrary to the popular belief she was eliminated from Rudolph's business by United Artists' Joe Schenck, she in fact held all the power until that day. With Valentino's studio contracts being assigned to Cosmic Arts, and with Natacha the sole stock holder, until August 13, 1925 at 2:00 in the afternoon, she owned and controlled Valentino's contracts.

160   Q. You don't know. Do you know who or-
[Rep. Tr. p. 110, lines 1 to 14]:
ganized the corporation? A. You mean the
attorney, or the—

Q. No, the parties? A. Yes, I do.

Q. Who? A. Rudolph Valentino, his wife,
Natacha Rambova, Mrs. Theresa Werner.

Q. Rudolph Valentino resigned almost immediately when you were elected one of the directors, were you not? A. Yes, sir.

161   Q. From that time on you served as secretary and treasurer of that corporation? A. I
did.

Q. Mrs. Valentino was the president, was she
not? A. I believe so.

[Rep. Tr. p. 113, lines 10 to 21]:

Q. Now, referring to the minutes of a special
meeting of the board of directors of April 21st,
1925, which appear in this record, does the

162 Joseph Schenck contract, dated March 30, 1925,
referred to in those minutes, is that the same as
Executor's Exhibit 1, introduced yesterday? A.
Yes, sir.

Q. The same one? A. Yes, sir.

Q. This resolution speaks of an assignment
from Cosmic Arts, Inc., to Rudolph Valentino
Productions of that contract? A. Yes, it does

[Rep. Tr. p. 115, lines 12 to 26]:

Q. By Mr. Scarborough: Who was Estelle
Dick? A. Estelle Dick was originally Mr.

163 Valentino's secretary, while he was in New York,
before coming out to California the last time to
make pictures.

    *   *   *   *   *   *   *   *

Q. You say "take care of the details"; what
[Rep. Tr. p. 116, lines 1 to 26]:
details; what did Miss Dick have to do? A.
Well, of course, I wasn't there all the time, but
I do know that she did have innumerable con-
ferences with the inventor and others interested
164 in the patents. She had all of the clerical work
to do in the matter of typing, maintaining contact between the patent attorneys and the inventor; also another man who was endeavoring
to place the Cosmic Arts' interests to the best
advantage. She was busy all the time, so far
as I know.

Q. Did anyone else pay any part of her
salary? A. No, sir.

165   Q. You state that you maintained an office
there? A. She had an office there, yes. She
had a desk.

Q. Did you pay the rent? A. The rent was
paid through the Valentino Productions, who
owned the Cosmic Arts.

Q. You mean, in your account there are
items of rent paid out? A. Yes.

Q. I notice in the account various items for
laboratory rent. What was that for? A. That
was an experimental laboratory which was main-

217 terest in consideration for his services. I offer this as Executor's Exhibit No. 2.

   *   *   *   *   *   *   *   *

Q. Who was the owner of Cosmic Arts?

Mr. Scarborough: Objected to upon the ground it is incompetent, irrelevant and immaterial, and calling for a conclusion of the witness. The record on file as Exhibit 3 for identification is the best evidence.

218 The Court: I suppose that is true, Mr. Wilson.

Mr. Scarborough: I have them here, Mr. Wilson.

Mr. Wilson: Will you stipulate how many shares of stock were outstanding?

Mr. Scarborough: Yes. 10 shares of stock, all issued to Natacha Rambova. The records so show.

219 Mr. Wilson: Is it stipulated, if Your Honor please, there were 10 shares of stock actually issued in the Cosmic Arts, Inc., and that all of those stocks, in three separate assignments, one [Rep. Tr. p. 138, lines 1 to 26]:

of eight, one of one and another one of one, were actually issued to Natacha Rambova, who was, on the 23rd day of May, 1923, that being the date they were issued, the wife of Rudolph Valentino; is that right?

463   Q. The board, at that time, passed this resolution? A. Yes, sir.

Q. Was there an assignment of the Schenck contract to the Rudolph Valentino Productions, Inc., other than this resolution? A. No, sir.

Q. This constitutes the assignment itself? A. That does.

Mr. Scarborough: I would like to have it read into the record.

464   Mr. Wilson: There is no objection.

Mr. Scarborough: The following resolution appears in the minutes of the meeting of the board of directors of Cosmic Arts, Inc., held at [Rep. Tr. p. 268, lines 1 to 8]: Los Angeles on August 13, 1925, at 2:00 o'clock p. m., at which there were present Natacha Rambova and S. George Ullman.

465   "Resolved, that, due to the fact that Rudolph Valentino has become dissatisfied with the management of Cosmic Arts, Inc., and is desirous of forming a corporation for the purpose of perpetuating his own name, to be know as the 'Rudolph Valentino Productions, Inc.,' and [Rep. Tr. p. 269, lines 1 to 25]:

Whereas, the incorporators of the Rudolph Valentino Productions, Inc., have agreed to assume the liabilities of the United Studios, that the Schenck contract now held by the Cosmic Arts, Inc., for the consideration above men-

The Recovery of the Second Page
of
Rudolph Valentino's Will

Without a doubt the most narrative changing document within the file of recovered appeals court records was the missing second page of Rudolph Valentino's "Last Will and Testament". While Valentino's brother Alberto was informing interviewers and biographers how he, his sister and Natacha's Aunt Teresa Werner were Valentino's heirs, the second page of the will was missing from all discussion. The second page of Valentino's will was designated by the court as "Paragraph Fourth" and on this codicil Valentino named Jean Valentino his sole heir.

The original document disappeared from Valentino's safe at Falcon Lair during the first few days after his death. A carbon copy was found four years later and recognized by the court as a legitimate part of Valentino's will. Paragraph Fourth designated Ullman as executor and charged him with the continuance of running Rudolph Valentino Production, Company.

The Court of Appeals recognized Ullman acted in good faith in disbursing the funds as he did not have access to the entire will nor this sheet of instructions, Paragraph Fourth. According to the final will, which included Paragraph Fourth, Alberto was not a rightful heir and was to only receive a weekly stipend or allowance until Jean inherited the estate when he turned twenty-five years old.

"To

S. George Ullman.

I have this day named you as executor in my last will and testament; it is my desire that you perpetuate my name in the picture industry by continuing the Rudolph Valentino Productions, Inc., until my nephew Jean shall have reached the age of 25 years; in the meantime to make motion pictures, using your own judgment as to numbers and kind, keeping control of any pictures made, if possible.

Whenever there are profits from pictures made by the Rudolph Valentino Productions, Inc., it is my wish that you will pay to my brother Alberto the sum of $400.00 monthly, to my sister Maria the sum of $200.00 monthly, and to my dear friend Mrs. Werner the sum of $200.00 monthly.

When my nephew Jean reaches the age of 25 years, I desire that the residue, if any, be given to him. In the event of his death then the residue shall be distributed equally to my sister Maria and my brother Alberto.

Sept. 1, 1925

RUDOLPHO GUGLIELMI

Witness:
Leo Mahoney   RUDOLPH VALENTINO."

Paragraph Fourth as included in the Appeals Court Records

Left to Right: Robert Florey, Rudolph Valentino, Unidentified Infant, Jack Dempsey

Robert Florey's
"Unforgettable, Unforgotten - Rudolph Valentino Survives His Legend"

Translation from the French
by
Renato Floris

Rudolph Valentino prepares to fly from London's Croydon Airport to Le Bourget in Paris, August 15, 1923. He shakes hands with the pilot while Robert Florey carries an attache of press releases and photo stills.
Image reproduced from Pictures and Picturegoer, August 1924

A Note on Robert Florey's,
"Inoubliable, Inoublié, Rudolph Valentino-Survit à Sa Légende"

"Unforgettable, Unforgotten, Rudolph Valentino Survives his Legend"

Robert Florey was born in Paris on September 14, 1900. He was just twenty one years old when in 1921, thanks to the insight of the director of *Cinémagazine* Jean Pascal, he became the magazine's correspondent in Hollywood. This was a role Florey, known as Bob, played until the closing of the magazine in 1935.

In Hollywood, Robert "Bob" Florey worked as a foreign press agent and secretary in Hollywood for Douglas Fairbanks, Mary Pickford and Max Linder. In 1923, he was retained by Rudolph Valentino to act in this capacity when Valentino and his new bride Natacha Rambova traveled to Europe on their honeymoon. Florey acted as front man for the tour, organizing press in advance of the Valentino's arrival in a city and dispensing photographic materials and press releases.

Valentino would fire Florey in 1923, which was revealed by Valentino collector William Self. Self knew Robert Florey and admitted he was the only person who had anything bad to say about Valentino adding, "But this was because Florey was the only person who was personally fired by Valentino."

In 1924, the account of the trip to Europe was published in a publicity generated and fictionalized travel diary allegedly written by Valentino. As some of the confidences Valentino shared with Florey about the French people and women were included in this diary, it is reasonable to assume Florey was fired for sharing those remarks. These remarks instigated a furor in France for Valentino.

In 1927, Florey published a biography on Valentino and in 1948, he published a book titled, *Hollywood, Yesterday and Today* in France. In this book he included a chapter titled, "The Magic Lantern" about his time spent as Valentino's press agent. Florey's accounts include insults about Valentino and portray him in a less than favorable light.

In 1956, Florey reissued his "Magic Lantern" as an eight installment series on Valentino titled, "Inoubliable, Inoublié, Rudolph Valentino-Survit à Sa Légende". (Unforgettable, Unforgotten, Rudolph Valentino Survives his Legend) which he published in French in the fan magazine, *Cinémonde*. This was in commemoration of the thirty year anniversary of Valentino's death. In all of his publications the account remains the same.

He includes studio-generated versions of Valentino's early years which were fictionalized and includes a few myths such as his saying Valentino's coffin was left in a shed awaiting burial in Los Angeles because there was no money to pay for the funeral and burial. This is false and the funeral was paid for in full. This and other points made by Robert Florey must be read with a critical, and informed mind.

Left to Right: Charlie Chaplin, Jean De Limur & Robert Florey

The Unforgettable, Unforgotten, Rudolph Valentino Survives His Legend

by
Robert Florey
Published in
Cinémonde 1156 – 10/4/1956

Reproduced with the permission of the Bibliothèque Nationale de France
Translated from the French
by
Renato Floris

Installment # 1

Robert Florey is today in the USA, a kind of king of TV. He makes more than forty films a year - knew Rudolph Valentino well and as he was, more than thirty years ago, his secretary, his confidant, his friend ... he evokes here the life of the most beloved actor in the world, such as was told to him, one night of confession, on the edge of the Pacific...

"I slept on the benches of Central Park after my luggage was confiscated because I was unable to pay for my room. I slept here and there with seldom enough to eat. In Europe the war was raging and my mother could not send me any subsidy. I learned of Italy's entry into the war one day as I was walking aimlessly on 6th Avenue. I thought about enlisting, but my myopia prevented me from being a soldier. It was then I became a social dancer in nightclubs. I met Bonnie Glass and we organized a number at Maxim's. I then danced with Joan Sawyer, who needed a new partner.

I experienced ups and downs, delusional failures and disenchantment. As I was deeply discouraged by serious troubles which befell me, I agreed to leave for San Francisco with an operetta troupe. After a few weeks, the series of performances was terminated and I danced in a small theater located not far from the Barbary Coast. It was there when I was surprised to learn the United States entered the war.

I went down to Los Angeles without much hope of making it in the movies. I just thought I could work on it. For almost a year I appeared in many films and was even engaged by Universal Studios as an Italian military expert. I tried to attract the attention of the directors and even when I wasn't summoned, I appeared in fancy outfits: riding britches, boots, open collar shirts and a riding crop. I greeted everyone with a smile. Shortly after I left Italy, my mother and sister Maria returned to France. My mother died there at the end of the war and news of her death made me inconsolable. My dearest desire was to succeed here, to become rich and famous and to bring her here so I could take care of her."

At the mention of this death, Rudy again marked a long silence, which was discreetly punctuated by the sound of the sea. Certainly, on that evening, death was in sight.

"I then worked as an extra and played small parts and I did pretty well. Finally, Emmett Flynn secured a bigger role for me in *The Married Virgin*. He changed my name because he thought Guglielmi was almost unpronounceable in English. I chose to be called Rodolfo Valentino. My directors found this name romantic and it was only later I changed it to Rudolph Valentino."

His voice suddenly became more metallic, as if a passion was driving him.

"Today, despite being famous, I believe I do not earn enough money to be able to satisfy all my ambitions. I am only paid a few thousand dollars to shoot each of my films, while they bring in millions. I don't want to stay with the Famous-Players and I'm wondering how I could possibly break my contract. And then, I would like to be able to return to Europe, to see Castellaneta again, to commune there with my mother's soul. I am not happy here."

Again he was speaking quietly in a shadowy voice almost a voice from beyond the grave.

"Why am I getting into so much trouble because I married Natacha? My first marriage only lasted one night, four years ago. Now, I love Natacha but the authorities force her to stay in New York until the legal period between my divorce and my second marriage has passed. And then Professor Winton[1] starts to worry me with his dire predictions.

My mother often told us the soul does not die when our bodies cease to live. She was right and I too believe death is only the beginning of another life. The soul is immortal and I am not afraid of death. Ever since poor Wallace Reid[2] died, I want to greet him every time I pass in front of his dressing room. I want to say to him, 'Hello Wally, we are all thinking of you. We know very well that the body dressed in golf clothes on display in front of the church among the flowers was not you. We know this

---

1 Professor Winton was the clairvoyant frequently consulted by Valentino.

2 *Wallace Reid* (St. Louis, April 15, 1891-Los Angeles, January 18, 1923), was an American actor, director and screenwriter, star of the big screen during the silent era. While on a set in Oregon filming, *The Valley of the Giants* (1919), Reid was injured in a train accident and in order to continue working, he was prescribed morphine to relieve pain. Reid soon became addicted to the drugs but continued to work feverishly during a period in which films were being lengthened from 15-20 minutes to more than an hour, requiring more physical effort. His addiction to morphine worsened and at that time there were no rehabilitation programs. Towards the end of 1922, his health dramatically worsened. After contracting the flu, he fell into a coma without recovering and died shortly after.

because we feel your presence among us, you are still young, cheerful, joking.' So, my dear Bob, when I am no longer of this world, my soul will continue to live. I don't know if I will correspond with my friends but I know I will not disappear without leaving a trace."

It was starting to get cold. The waves billowed in front of us and the Pacific wind gave us chills.

"Let's go home" I say. "It's getting late. Put away your dark ideas. If you want, I'll go with you to Europe next summer. You will see your sister, your brother, the little house where you were born. As far as your salary is concerned, things will turn out well in the end. Do not be too impatient, you have already satisfied one of your ambitions; you are famous. And don't go back to Professor Winton's. You're young, you have the future ahead of you. Let's go for a walk and tomorrow we will camp in the Palm Springs desert."

Rudy stood up and put his hand on my shoulder. He smiled and for a second he looked like my dear friend Mosjouskine as we slowly walked up the pier."[3]

---

3   Ivan Il'ič Mozžuchin, Frenchized as Mosjoukine (Penza, September 26, 1889-Neuilly-sur-Seine, January 18, 1939), was a naturalized French Russian actor and director in the 1920s. In France he achieved great success. His death, which occurred in misery and abandonment in 1939, is shrouded in mystery. It was said that in the squalid room in which he was found dead, there were many letters, still sealed from his female admirers, and great sums of money and valuables amounting to a small fortune. The writer Romain Gary was his biological son.

Installment # 2

Cinémonde 1157 – 10/11/1956

Thirty years ago Rudolph Valentino died: in three days an attack of acute peritonitis prevailed. Crystallizing an unprecedented glory, this brutal death created a myth. Our friend Robert Florey, who was at that time the secretary and friend of Valentino, evokes here the life of the actor-idol, as related to him one evening, in a moment of abandonment.

At the beginning of 1923, Rudolph Valentino asked me once again to accompany him to his palmist. The latter, Professor Winton, had been living in Ocean Park for fifteen years in a shop he rented at 2928 Ocean Front Avenue. Everyone was convinced he could read the future like in a book and most of the actors came to consult him.

He operated between a fairground shooting range where pipes were broken and a souvenir shop. The walls of his narrow consulting room were lined with the hand-prints of his most famous clients. Despite the heavy drapes hung behind the doors, the noises, cries and music of the surrounding popular fair reached the shrine. There the smell of incense struggled against the fumes from a hot dog vendor's frying.

Professor Winton enjoyed a good reputation and the most famous characters in Hollywood swore by him. It was because his predictions often came true. Valentino would visit him at dusk so he wouldn't be recognized in the street. He parked his Cunningham[1] far away by the sidewalk, a block from the shop. We crossed the avenue with rapid steps, fearing being spotted by the last bathers. We would have preferred to have been shadows.

That evening Valentino asked for the long reading; the five dollar one. We had to stay at least for forty-five minutes. Winton told Rudolph he would soon be making a long journey, that he would still have glory days but that his existence would be short.

"It's not the first time you've made this prophecy to me," Valentino told him. "I know my lifeline is short but I trust my star. I am sure in twenty years I will come to consult you again."

It was almost dark when we left and Rudolph brushed Winton off with a laugh. But when we got back into the car, he looked worried.

---

1 Cunningham cars were such luxury vehicles, that by 1922 the company no longer provided a public sales list. The cost was confidentially communicated to the potential customer who requested it. Ironically, the hearse which carried Valentino from the Good Shepherd Church in Beverly Hills to Hollywood Forever Cemetery was built on Cunningham mechanics.

"Let's go have a bowl of clam chowder at the Crystal Pier"[2], he said, "then we'll walk a bit."

Three minutes later we were at the Crystal Pier. Malibu did not exist at that time and many stars resided at Crystal Pier. Sitting on the high stools in front of the outdoor counter of Joe the Greek's wagon, we were served shellfish soup. Joe poured red wine into coffee cups, which he more or less illegally bought from a rabbi. Rudolph was silent.

We then walked to the end of the jetty, which has now disappeared, and sat on a bench. He lit an abduhla[3] and blew out the smoke. We could only hear the sound of the sea. There was a long moment of silence, then Valentino said to me.

"I don't believe in all this nonsense. Anyway, I won't go to this professor's house again."

"Every time you repeat the same thing," I told him, "but you always go to consult him at least once a month. If you don't believe his predictions, why are you still visiting him?"

"The first time he looked at my hand through his big magnifying glass, he told me I was going to be famous. Now he only talks about my imminent death and I'm not even twenty-nine. There is something about all of this which troubles me."

"You'll reach such an old age that in 1960 you will play senior roles and still have to wear makeup to make you look believable." I tell him this to cheer him up.

But he didn't smile and continued as if to himself,

"It will be ten years next December since I landed in Brooklyn. The crossing took two weeks and I arrived on New Year's Eve. I didn't speak English and didn't know anyone. I was nineteen and with $300[4] in my pocket. It was a melancholy day. It was better for me to let time pass by a bit. My mother was French and her father was named Pierre Barbin. She grew up during the siege of Paris and the Commune and saw the "Pruscos"[5] parade on the Champs-Élysées. Later her father took her to Italy where she met Giovanni Guglielmi, then doing his military service in the cavalry[6].

The uniform had its effect and she married the horseman. When he left the army they settled in Castellaneta. It was there I was born on May 6, 1895. My parents made the ideal couple. In 1904, they decided to live in Taranto. For four years I attended

---

2   The Crystal Pier was located in Santa Monica, at the foot of Hollister Avenue and was the favorite place of the beach goers on Crystal Beach in the late 1920s. The pier was also called the Hollister Pier, Bristol Pier and the Nat Goodwin Pier.

3   The actual name of the cigarettes brand was Abdulla, they were made in London with Turkish tobacco and Rudolph Valentino's favorite. He smoked 100 Abdullas a day.

4   When Rudolph arrived in America in December 1913, he was 18 years old and not 19. Also, the $300 he arrived with in 1913, by the current market exchange rate as of June 2021, had a value of $8,145.00.

5   Pruscos was a slang definition to define Prussian occupants during the the siege of Paris, lasting from September 19, 1870 to January 28, 1871. The consequent capture of the city by Prussian forces led to the French defeat in the Franco-Prussian War and the establishment of the German Empire as well as the Paris Commune. It's also not possible that her father brought Gabrielle to Italy after the siege of Paris as he died in Taranto in 1868 before all those events.

6   To better know about the military life of Valentino's father read the book by Aurelio Miccoli. "Valentino e il Professore – Quello che so di Rodolfo Valentino" Scorpione Editore – Taranto 2021.

school in this city. But I preferred to contemplate the extraordinary colors of the Ionian Sea rather than to understand what was being taught in class. I was still very young when my father died. My mother's grief was immense but the bond which attached her to the memory of my father was such, she continued to live and act as if he was still present among us.

In 1908, I entered the College della Sapienza, which was a military preparation school. When I was fifteen I thought of becoming an officer in the royal cavalry; the wonderful uniforms of the Savoy Calvary made all the girls dream. But my mother explained to me how you had to be very rich to achieve such an ambition."

Valentino lit another cigarette and continued.

"My father did not leave us enough money for me to become a cavalry officer. I would be content to try with the Naval Academy where the students did not need to dress so pompously. Unfortunately, I was refused entrance and it was a great humiliation for me. I did not know what to do."

You could barely see the smoke from his cigarette. Only, at times, when he brought it to his mouth and inhaled, a red glow drew his face.

"My mother then advised my entering the Academy of Agriculture and consoled me by saying Italy was full of officers and soldiers, but lacked farmers. Several of my comrades from this school had been to Paris and one of them even stayed in the United States for several years. Listening to them, I started to feel constrained in Italy. It must also be said that I had had enough of these agricultural studies. I asked my mother to let me take a trip to her native country. She told me a great deal about it and I was eager to know France, so she gave me enough money to carry out my plan. I arrived in Paris quite disoriented, spent a few weeks there and as my resources were almost exhausted I returned to Italy; stopping in Monte-Carlo where I left my last liras on the green roulette table of the casino[7].

Throughout 1913, I racked my brains to try and find an exciting job. The only interesting prospect seemed to me to be emigration to the United States where gold was said to be found in the streets. For several months, I kept telling my mother that my future was in New York and begged her to help me get there. 'If you go to America, Rodolfo,' she replied, 'I will never see you again.' But I was stubborn and she finally gave me the amount I needed to pack my trunks. I embarked for the new continent on December 9, 1913, in search of glory, fortune and adventure.

Completely at a loss when I arrived in the big metropolis, I rented a room with a compatriot in the "Little Italy" district and quickly spent my money in the big restaurants and the theaters of Broadway. Because I graduated from the Academy of Agriculture, I found a job in Long Island with a Mr. Cornelius Bliss as a garden designer. But this did not last long and it was then I knew actual misery."

---

7   This statement is without any foundation as in the Montecarlo Casino only adults of age can access with the exhibition of a valid document and, at that time, the majority age in the Montecarlo was 21 years and Rodolfo was only 17.

Installment #3

Cinémonde 1158 – 10/18/1956

Being in the U.S.A. a kind of king of TV – where he makes more than forty films a year - Robert Florey knew Rudolph Valentino well. There, he was, thirty years ago, his secretary, his confidant, his friend ...On the occasion of the thirtieth anniversary of the death of the most beloved actor in the world, Robert Florey was kind enough to evoke his memories for the readers of Cinémonde and relate what the life of the extraordinary idol was like, as he saw it unfold before his eyes.

Just arrived at his house, above Whitley, Rudolph told me he was hungry. He began to devour slices of salami which he accompanied with gulps of bootleg red wine. Then he played his favorite record, "Canadian Capers" and began to dance in the manner of a style which was popularized by Joe Frisco[1]. He seemed happy again and acting quite carefree. Before going to bed he said to me,

"Next summer, we will go to Europe with Natacha."

But three years later; Rudolph Valentino was dead.

A few months ago, as cameraman Paul Ivano and I searched for exterior locations, we learned from the newspapers that Valentino's first home was in the hands of wreckers. We decided to take a detour through Wedgewood Place to see what was left.

The new freeway, linking Los Angeles to North Hollywood, cuts right through the heart of the city and passes under Whitley Heights which is called, "The Land of the Ghosts" now because of the missing artists who once lived there. The new freeway will be linked to Highland and Cahuenga at the bottom of the north slope of the hill[2].

---

1   Joe Frisco (born Louis Wilson Joseph, November 4, 1889 - February 12, 1958) was an American vaudeville artist who first made a name for himself on stage as a jazz dancer, later merging his stammering voice with his dancing and becoming a famous comedian. His dance style was called by some the "Jewish Charleston", and was a choreographed series of shuffling gaits, camel steps or a way of walking also known as "animal ragtime dance" with comic twists.

2   The Hollywood Freeway began construction in 1946, dividing Whitley Heights. This development impacted dozens of significant homes. Rudolph Valentino's residence on Wedgewood was destroyed. Harold Lloyd's home was moved to Iris Circle. After the Topside estate was demolished, the Whitley Heights Civic Association sought to retain the character of the neighborhood. Community involvement led to the inclusion

The initial demolition work took place a few days earlier and only a few sections of the walls, floors, the staircase and the foundations were left. Everything facing Wedgewood Place was missing, so we could look straight into the house Paul and I hadn't had a chance to enter in twenty-eight years.

I could see the rubble from Rudy's entrance hall and bedroom, as well as the staircase leading down to what was the dining room and living room. The house was built on the side of the hill, so that its entrance was level with the street and the other rooms were below.

Wooden planks had been placed across the gaping openings and signs informed passers-by that it was dangerous to enter. Passing under the rope stretched across the stairs, I entered the house. First, I found a piece of colored tile which I picked up and remembered Valentino bought similar tiles while we were in Italy.

At the bottom of what used to be the garden, grass was growing through the cracks in the large pool. Piles of rubble were everywhere and as I walked I crushed fragments of stained glass from the tall Spanish-style windows in the living room. From below, looking towards the top of the hill, I felt like I was in the middle of an abandoned studio set. In two or three days, there would be nothing left. I walked up to the entrance but I was unable to feel the emotion I had expected. This house was very dead. I remained motionless for a moment.

Valentino was proud of this house because he had lived in many more or less comfortable apartments from Main Street to Hollywood Boulevard with the luxury varying according to his means. Now here were only ruins. With Paul Ivano, we then decided to continue our pilgrimage and visit the other places where we knew Valentino. But Paul wanted to go to the cemetery first. We walked down Vine Street and turned left onto Santa Monica Boulevard and a few moments later we arrived at the cemetery which stretches out behind the Paramount at RKO studios.

After slowly walking up the large alley separating the rows of tombs from the flower beds, I stopped by a large, curiously styled building. There, in crypts which fit together like shoe boxes, rest the embalmed who did not want be interred in the earth after their death.

In a book I wrote on Pola Negri in 1926, I noted the following lines:

"Valentino's swift and stormy life was to end in an unforeseen and romantic climax. The whole world sent messages to his deathbed and Pola Negri performed the great scene of the disconsolate. Detained during Rudy's brief illness at the Lasky studios, where she was filming *Hotel Imperial*, she sent her sublime words D'Annunzio style[3] by cables, telephone and radio.

---

of Whitley Heights on the National Registry of Historic Places in 1982. It was added to the Historic Preservation Overlay Zone in 1992.

3   Gabriele D'Annunzio, Prince of Montenevoso (March 12, 1863 – March 1, 1938), was an Italian poet, playwright, journalist and soldier during World War I. He occupied a prominent place in Italian literature from 1889 to 1910 and later a political life from 1914 to 1924. He was often referred to under the epithets, *Il Vate* ("the Poet") or *Il Profeta* ("the Prophet").

She went to New York for the funeral and mourned. She recalled, in her role as widow with supremely aesthetic attitudes, Isadora Duncan when she lost her two children before the war[4]. Common people would have been simpler, but how can we judge exceptional beings whose every deed and gesture will be noted and amplified and who live in a kind of hypnosis on the summits where the crowd have placed them?

For Pola found the one of a kind, the perfect antithesis of Chaplin, the lead young actor among all the young actors and he was divorced from Natacha Rambova. And then did not this idyll masterfully serve the advertising interests of the two stars? Valentino needed a new sparkle and Pola, to reign in the hearts of American "fans" could not do better than to associate with one of their creations. By that, she became an American citizen. But it was written that such a perfect union; a marriage of sovereigns where inclinations, interests and speculations combined perfectly, was too perfect to take place."

A few days before he left for New York, I saw the perfect couple for the last time; Rudy driving an open limo he brought back from Europe. He was dressed in white flannel, wearing a borsalino and a matching tie. Pola was sitting very close to him and their audience of Hollywoodians, accustomed to seeing strange things in the street, watched them pass while engaged in some mouth-to-mouth resuscitation.

A few weeks later when the coffin containing Valentino's body was brought back from New York and taken out off the train and placed on the platform of the old Santa Fe train station, it was no longer a question of world glory to solve but a very down to earth problem. Who was going to pay for the funeral? Valentino didn't have a dollar up front, his house wasn't even fully paid for and he only received a share in the profits of his latest films. And no one seemed to want to pay for the funeral expenses. The coffin was therefore transported to the cemetery of Santa Monica boulevard and temporarily stored, after the religious ceremony, in a shed[5].

---

4   Duncan's life was marred in 1913 by a terrible tragedy. Her children Deirdre and Patrick, aged 7 and 3, were returning by taxi in the company of their nanny, when an engine problem forced the taxi driver to stop and get out of the car to restart it. A trivial distraction. The taxi driver forgot to set the handbrake and the car slipped into the Seine, killing all three passengers.

5   A completely invented story, the body of Rudolph Valentino was never temporarily placed in a shed but was settled in a niche that belonged to the screenwriter June Mathis.

Cinémonde 1160 – 11/1/1956

Robert Florey became the number one director of TV in Hollywood and he knew Rudolph Valentino well more than thirty years ago and was his confidant, his friend ...
For Cinémonde, Robert Florey was kind enough to evoke the life of the most beloved actor in the world, this life which has become legendary in certain dimensions, but which also conceals those moments of tense emotion which generate human pathos ...

Silvano Balboni, an Italian cameraman, owned crypts for perpetuity in the wall of the mausoleum. Two of these three crypts[1], were occupied by his wife, June Mathis the screenwriter and by his mother-in-law. When Balboni decided to return home to Italy, he spontaneously offered the third crypt to Valentino's coffin. So Rudy now rests with June Mathis, who recommended him so highly to Rex Ingram. Without the charitable gesture of Silvano Balboni, only God knows what would have happened to Valentino. This because no one ever thought of paying for his burial, and especially not the ladies in black or white who arrive to be photographed before the marble slab where his name is engraved.

Moreover, these self-promoting enthusiasts hardly knew Valentino during his lifetime: otherwise in the small glass vases arranged on each side of the plate, they would have placed the violets he loved so much.

A few minutes from the cemetery, towards Sunset Boulevard and Wilcox Avenue, a statue has been erected in memory of the actor[2]. It is neither pretty nor tall. Children are playing in the small garden, it is difficult to find it and few tourists visit it. As Paul Ivano and I were looking at the bronze, a bird landed on its head and began to sing. Was this a sign of Rudy's immortality which he promised he would give me?

Again in our car, we turned left onto Sunset Boulevard, which we followed for about 6.5 miles. We climbed to Falcon Lair where Valentino also lived. This house was larger than the one in Wedgewood Place and had no particular style. Valentino's taste in

---

1   Of the three niches purchased by Balboni in the Hollywood Forever Mausoleum, number 1200 was for June Mathis' mother, number 1199, where Valentino was initially buried, for June Mathis and the third one, number 1205, for Balboni himself. Following the sudden death of Mathis, which occurred on July 26, 1927, Valentino's remains were moved, on August 6, 1927, to niche number 1205 where the actor's remains have been lying ever since. Silvano Balboni then sold the niche to the Guglielmi family when, in 1936, he decided to return to his native Italy. The legend of a Valentino's coffin being abandoned in some remote deposit was particularly dear to Robert Florey, who told about it extensively. On October 26, 1934, an article appeared in *Le Journal de Paris,* entitled "HOLLYWOOD, Marche Funèbre" signed by Francis de Croiset, in which Florey declared Valentino's body was left, "curing" in a remote depot near a parking lot.

2   Aspiration, the statue in honor of Valentino, is located in the center of DeLongpre Park which is located in Hollywood in the block between DeLongpre Ave, N. Cheyenne Ave, N. June St and Fountain Ave.

furnishing and decorating was odd. He liked the Renaissance, Byzantine, and Hispaniola-Moorish styles.

A comfortable throne with a high back of 6.5 ft., and covered in crimson velvet, was for him the ideal armchair along with Circassian daggers, the marquetry, the columns, the gilded moldings, the velvet hangings and the Henri II furniture. While in the city he took particular care to dress only in the latest fashion, or even the next one, but he would gladly have worn at home the costumes of the courtiers of Henri III[3], the Venetian doges or even the Sheik's burnooses.

Rudy didn't have time to live in this Falcon Lair home for long and he hadn't even finished the gardens when he died. The house remained empty for a long time and it was then it was said to be haunted. Research proves it was simply termites: these insects are the plague of California and when they start devouring the woodwork of a house at night, the noise of their mandibles is of a such a sound one hears it from far away.

A company of theologians occupied Falcon Lair for a few months, then the house was closed again and finally sold so that it is not known exactly who owns it now. The "Falcon's Lair" is no longer a good real estate deal. Twelve years of America, five of successes, thirteen films of unequal value; what remains today of the career of Rudolph Valentino? Memories and those silent images we show in film clubs and on television.

A few months after Valentino's death, George Ullman informed me he was going to auction off all the properties of his friend, of whom he was the executor. The auctioneer A. H. Weil was first in charge of disposing of Falcon Lair. As soon as the ads were published, a crowd of curious and tourists arrived in Beverly Hills.

The auction began slowly with the first offer only $50,000[4]. Three hours later the auctioneer reached only $115,000. In the end, New York jeweler Jules Howard bid for the house at $145,000. Adjacent land was auctioned for $20,000 to Mr. McCoy, and the two Voisin automobiles plus the three American cars went for $12,000. Valentino's four horses, "Firefly", "Yaqui", "Ramadan" and "Haroun" earned another $3,250.

A few days later, a huge crowd gathered on Highland Avenue outside the door of the Hall of Art Studio where Rudy's personal effects and belongings were to be auctioned. Thousands of people, hoping to take home an inexpensive souvenir of the actor, jostled to try to enter the gallery despite the efforts of several dozen policemen. In the great hall where the sale was to take place, the people were crowded so close together there was no way to move.

---

3   Henry III of Valois (Fontainebleau, September 19, 1551 - Saint-Cloud, August 2, 1589) was king of France from 1574 to 1589. Fourth son of Henry II and Catherine de' Medici, he was the last king of the Capetian dynasty Valois. Henry III possessed grace and royal majesty. Always in search of elegance, he took great care of his appearance. A lover of fashion (in particular of earrings and perfumes), he was the first to wear disturbing images such as that of the skull, albeit on the buttons on the doublet and on the ribbons of his shoes; as he did on the occasion of the death of his favorite, among his many lovers, Maria de Clèves. Henry III's court consisted of a large group of favorites who enjoyed dazzling careers and were called Mignon. These courtiers used to dress like the ruler in decidedly eccentric ways emulating the king's tastes.

4   To understand the value of the 1927 monetary figures, it is necessary to multiply the figures by 16, exactly 15.74, as of June 2021.

The list of Valentino's clothes to be liquidated included, among other things, three red fox hunting jackets, thirty street suits, thirteen gentleman-rider vests, seven light suits, six flannel pants, eight sweaters, sixty pairs of gloves, one hundred and twelve ties, one hundred and twenty-four shirts, one hundred and forty-six pairs of socks, one hundred and ten handkerchiefs, twenty pairs of suspenders, sixty pairs of shoes, twenty-two white jackets, seventeen hats which were almost all of white felt, thirteen canes, six pairs of boots, ten coats, ten tuxedos and suits, ten riding trousers, one hundred and ten hard collars, twelve belts, twenty-eight pairs of garters, seventy flannel vests and boxer shorts.

To all of this many other objects were added: cigarette holders, bracelets, watches, cuff links, chains, rings, pins and more or less precious stones. George Ullman reserved the collection of daggers and sabers and bought most of Rudy's clothes. The poor man had tears in his eyes and I did not know what to say to console him.

I looked at all these effects stacked on tables, thinking how Valentino had purchased many of them with me while we were in London. I recognized the ties from Burlington Arcade, the hats from Locke's, the suits of the Regent Street tailors and there was a Dunhill pipe[5] I gave him. Included in the books being auctioned, were the ones I left at his house, which he had probably never read.

Adolphe Menjou was the first of the actors present to acquire a Spanish dresser and a Spanish screen for which he paid over $1,000. Shawls and rugs, draperies hit the auction block, as well as the Edgewater Club[6] membership card which cost Rudy $500 and was sold for $200. The auctions had started on December 10, and were to last until the 24. The objects which were being liquidated seemed inexhaustible.

The silverware succeeded the "Phoenix", Rudy's boat which was sold for $2,910, whereas it cost him $9,000. His bedroom furniture sold for $875, and the throne he was proud of found a buyer for $300. Natacha's aunt bought a $100 Chinese costume album for $300 and Eleanor Boardman-Vidor spent $9 on a book with Rudy's signature.

Twenty shares of the "El Capitan" movie theater, which Valentino owned, were also sold, as well as his interests in various commercial enterprises. Even Jules Howard, who bought Falcon Lair, spent $1900 on a painting of a half-naked Spanish lady which had adorned Rudy's bedroom. Buyers argued over small items, programs, postcards, party favors and all the other possessions left by the actor. Four months after his death, all which once belonged to him was dispersed. But since many accounts had not been fully paid, George Ullman used the money to settle the debts which were left.

---

5   Florey was not the only one to see an object he donated to Valentino sold at the auction. Douglas Gerrard, a close friend and mentor of Rodolfo, recognized some of the clothes he lent to Valentino and which had never been returned , which took on the role of sacred relics.

6   In the 1920s and 1930s, numerous trendy beach clubs were built along the Santa Monica beach, including the Edgewater, of which Valentino was a member. There was also the Santa Monica Athletic Club, the Beach Club, the Santa Monica Swimming Club, the Deauville, the Wavecrest, the Breakers and the Gables Beach Club, an impressive Tudor-style building. They were all meeting places for Hollywood stars and intelligentsia.

Installment #5

Cinémonde 1161 – 11/18/1956

Robert Florey, who became the No. 1 TV director in Hollywood, got to know Rudolph Valentino well: thirty years ago when he was his confidant, his friend …
For Cinémonde, Robert Florey was kind enough to evoke the life of the most beloved actor in the world and retrace the major stages of his career.

Fox's #1 director Emmett Flynn invited me to watch the boxing matches taking place one night in Vernon, outside the Los Angeles area. Flynn honored me with his friendship and his loyal appreciation. This after I pointed out to him when he was filming a scene representing the Emperor at Elba, how it was wrong to show him reading the Comœdia newspaper and smoking a cigar[1].

At first he was suspicious, because he had unlimited confidence in his props people, and then after hearing my information, he realized I was right. He took the opportunity to call me "professor". Emmett Flynn, a former driver, came to the cinema like so many others in those heroic times and his film *A Connecticut Yankee* placed him in the first rank of directors. A little earlier he entrusted Valentino with his first important role in *The Married Virgin*.

At that time, even if I understood English well, I spoke it with difficulty. I had only been in California for a few weeks, but I was able to ask Emmett what were the reasons which led him to choose Valentino.

"I saw this handsome boy outside the studio door almost every morning," Flynn told me, "and sometimes even on set, playing small roles or in the cafeteria. He had a good demeanor, radiate charm, and greeted me with a warm smile whenever he saw me. He was just the right type for the character of an Italian aristocrat. I couldn't think of using the Vitagraph star Antonio Moreno, because the role wasn't big enough for him.

I summoned Valentino, who was still called Guglielmi, for the next day. He arrived in my office with a carnation in his buttonhole, his pearl gray felt hat on his head and cane in hand, a bracelet circled his wrist. His elegance surprised me and so much so I immediately hired him, without even asking him if he felt capable of playing the part.

---

1 The Emperor was Napoleon, *Comœdia* was a French newspaper published in Paris between 1907 and 1941. As for tobacco and Napoleon, he did not smoke either cigars or pipes, but sometimes limited himself to quickly sniffing a pinch. He never drank liquor and hated the drugs which he often refused to take even on a personal doctor's order.

He looked so sure of himself I had no doubts about his talent.

He didn't act any worse than anyone else. He confused me a little by asking me to let him speak French or Italian in order to improve the character, During filming, I had no idea what he was talking about, but his expressions matched exactly what he was supposed to say. He was sure the studio would hire him on a year-round contract, but it didn't. When the film was finished, he was let go."

And so spoke Emmett Flynn. For him, Valentino was an Italian passer-by, very noble and very handsome, who had enough conscience to interpret only characters whose lines he wanted to understand.

When I arrived in Los Angeles, I met the director Rex Ingram and his wife Alice Terry. Max Linder introduced me to them as he knew everyone. Rex Ingram studied sculpture at Yale University in 1913 and 1914, and began as a young actor for Edison Studios and then for Vitagraph Studios. In 1917, he was one of the first to enlist in the Air Force. After the war, he returned to the studios as a screenwriter and then as a director. He had already made a dozen trivial films when he was commissioned to direct *The Four Horsemen of the Apocalypse*, a film based on the Blasco Ibanez novel. June Mathis wrote the adaptation and was responsible for the editing.

In finding an artist who could play an Argentinian character of French descent, Ingram conducted many screen tests. He was about to choose Antonio Moreno, born in Morocco from Spanish parents and who seemed to appear exclusively in Latin roles. Lou Tellegen was then discussed, but June Mathis recommended Valentino whom she had seen in *A Delicious Little Devil*, *Once To Every Woman*, *The Fog* and *Passion's Playground*.

First they dressed Rudy as a gaucho, then as a French soldier. He was photographed as he mimed certain scenes and the results were conclusive. Rex Ingram was more interested in his lighting and compositions than in acting. He loved atmospheric films and was constantly surrounded by hunchbacks, giants, dwarfs and weird characters. After *The Four Horsemen of the Apocalypse*, he went on to direct a dozen more movies in Hollywood and in Europe. He then converted to Islam. He retired in a small house, north of Hollywood where he died, withdrawn from the world and in his sixties.

I had dinner with him after he finished editing his film, *The Conquering Power*. He was preparing *The Prisoner of Zenda* and *Turn to the Right*. June told me how reluctant Ingram had been to accept Valentino and how he had even almost refused. I asked him why.

"Until then," Ingram told me, "I had only directed commercial films with Carl Laemmle, when Richard Rowland, the boss of the Metro, gave me June Mathis' manuscript. She recommended me to him. This film was no small matter. Rowland warned me the executives of his firm weren't too keen on doing it as they thought audiences were starting to shun war movies.

By insisting on filming it anyway, Rowland was risking his reputation. To put the odds on my side, I only wanted top-notch actors and technicians. I had neither antipathy nor animosity towards Valentino. I met him several times at Universal, but I did not believe he could play the Julio Desnoyers of Ibañez.

During a preliminary conversation I found him obsequious and aggressive and then having watched *A Delicious Little Devil* again, in which he played a flat cap Apache, I thought he was grimacing too much. In my opinion Julio needed to look more powerful, more sober, more French and I was thinking of bringing in a star from Paris. But June Mathis was insistent. She was trying to make me understand that she was pleading Valentino's case as she had pleaded mine to Rowland. Finally, I made some tests. I was only grateful I hired Valentino because this film was very successful, and critics say the actor was the incarnation of Julio Desnoyers. I was happy to work with Valentino again in *The Conquering Power*".

The following week, I spoke about Ingram with Valentino. He told me how appreciative he was that he followed June Mathis' advice, but that it was difficult to work with him and that their temperaments, so different, did not always match.

"He didn't let me do what I wanted," Valentino told me, "he seemed to think more of his lighting effects than of my acting, which sometimes annoyed me."

I knew what that meant, because when Valentino wasn't happy he would get sulky and remain ill-humored all day long.

Rex Ingram was a talented and intelligent director. Valentino was then in the midst of training without much dramatic experience and he was convinced that everything he did should be applauded. He did not like to be corrected especially in front of his co-stars. He could not bear the slightest contradiction and if Ingram was concerned primarily with his framing and his compositions, Rudy was making a great deal about the essential accessories for the character he was playing. He was the actor of long cigarette holders, junk jewelry, half-leather half-suede shoes, canes, scarf ties; a European gentleman as he imagined him.

Robert Florey, who became, in Hollywood, one of the first directors of American TV, knew Rudolph Valentino well. He was, in those times, his confidant and friend.
For the readers of CINÉMONDE he was kind enough to evoke some memories of this time and thus bring to life, out of the distorted image created by sideshow mirrors of his legend, the true profile of the one who was, thirty years ago, the most beloved actor in the world.

If Valentino had lived longer, I believe his career would have ended with the advent of the talkies, as it was with Mosjoukine. And Ivan Mosjoukine was a professional actor, while Valentino was just a character actor.

While touring the United States, going from town to town performing his dance number with Natacha every night, after having broken his contract with Famous Players Lasky, I often had the opportunity to speak with him in the special railway wagon they occupied. I once asked him what his life would have been if, instead of accidentally becoming a screen star, he continued to dance in the nightclubs on Broadway.

"I certainly wouldn't have stayed in the United States," Valentino replied. "During my first years in New York, I had to suffer so much there that I had come to curse that city and wish to leave it. In order to eat, I engaged in all kinds of trades. Sometimes I spent the night in small cinemas which worked non-stop, when I didn't have enough to pay for a room.

Ten cents was enough for me to get in, and a lot of bums did exactly like I did. Most of the time, I would fall asleep because I was so tired it was impossible for me to take an interest in the woes of Charles Ray or Mary Miles Minter. At that time, I would have been really surprised if someone prophesied a future for me, of any kind, in the cinema business.

I secured an engagement in a small club and I was dancing with the lady patrons, when I met a fellow at the bar who was tap dancing and doing a "soft shoe dance". He had just returned from South America where he spent several months, and told me he was thinking of returning. He earned a lot of money and was received very well. According to him, a socialite dancer was more likely to succeed in Rio or Buenos Aires than in New York and there were many lucrative trades which could be practiced there.

Listening to him, I imagined I would be more comfortable in Argentina or Brazil.

But the trips were expensive and I didn't have a dollar in my pocket. For me to find a job would not be a problem, but the problem would be the expensive round trip. Those brave souls who dared to go there illegally had infinite difficulties with the authorities and they had to live in hiding. As the idea of being repatriated to Europe was unbearable to me, I continued to vaguely hope to leave for South America. Then I was engaged in an operetta troupe which was touring to the west coast and California, but I did not yet think to make films. Everything which happened to me afterwards was simply miraculous."

From Tacoma, Valentino telegraphed me to join him on June 9 at the Denver station, where his "Colonial" wagon was going to stop the night before. It was there I found him. I hadn't seen him for two months and he seemed concerned about his break with Famous Players Lasky. He was, however, forbidden to film or appear on theatrical stages until the end of 1925, which forced him to a wait for about thirty months. He was obliged to do his dance numbers in the open air, in halls of private companies or in a circus tent. The highlight of the evening was the "Tango of the Four Horsemen", which he danced with Natacha. Then he chose the most photogenic young girl from the audience, promising her vaguely she would become his onscreen partner.

A few musicians accompanied him on this journey and when the train stopped for a few moments in a small town, many women and girls, alerted by the newspapers, were waiting for Rudolph with their arms laden with flowers. Almost every day, some of them entered "the Colonial", trying to hide there so that they could travel with their idol. Before departure, we had to check all the corners of the car and remove these clandestine ladies. Valentino also had a method of his own to overcome his admirers, a method of charm. He accepted bouquets, signed autographs and distributed his most recent photos, of which he had large stocks.

In Chicago and then in New York, it was delirium. We attended the premiere of *The Young Rajah* - a very poor movie - with June Mathis. The crush of Valentino admirers became so frantic we had to leave the cinema by the fire escape. In front of the Blackstone Hotel in Chicago, we had to fight to clear his way. His "fans" tore buttons from his clothes and tried to steal his tie. The police were powerless against these thousands of people.

At the Ritz-Tower[1] in New York, the cheers of the crowd amassed in the street forced him to wave from the window, like a monarch while the policemen remained below permanently to unblock the traffic jams. Slowly backing into the room, still smiling at the crowd, Valentino said to me:

"Not long before I left for the west coast, I was sleeping in the summer under those Central Park hills you see right across the street. The police chased me away in the early morning and I wandered around this hotel, penniless and hoping to find something to do to earn the ten cents needed for a cup of coffee and a donut for my little breakfast. My clothes were crumpled, I was unshaven. I had an empty stomach. No one

---

1   Surely Florey is referring to the Ritz Carlton Hotel, incorrectly mentioned as the Ritz Tower.

was giving me a look but then the miracle of the cinema happened: these passers-by who ignored me and who would have left me to starve are now massed under my window and cheering me on. They saw me on the screen dressed as an Arab, a bullfighter, a soldier, a Hindu and that was enough for them to wait for me downstairs for hours. Still, I am the same man. How to explain the stupidity of that crowd?"

Before going out and facing his audience, Rudy, who was vain, gave himself a makeover. He was a little ashamed of his boxer's ears and his budding baldness and was dousing his head in hair lotions. He had started to coat the top of his head with a sort of very thick black varnish which stained the pillowcases of the hotels pillows for which they made him pay a high price. As it had become impossible for him to exit the door of the hotel because of the crowds, he would do so through the entrance of the staff: he thus went through the door he had so longed to go through in his difficult years.

The publicists of the studios for which he was filming advertised Valentino in the United States, but as his films had not yet been shown on the European market, the weeklies I received in 1921 did not publish his portraits. Every day, he asked me to take care of his advertising for France and Italy. By September 1923, none of his films had yet been released in his native country. Rudy, who was planning a glorious trip to Europe, realized there was the risk his arrival would go unnoticed. Rome and Paris triumphantly welcomed Douglas Fairbanks, Charlie Chaplin and Mary Pickford. Rudy wished the same success.

I traveled to New York with Douglas Fairbanks and Clarence Ericksen in November 1922, while we were preparing for the *Robin Hood* campaign. I took advantage of my stay in that city to visit Valentino, who lived on sixty-seventh street, number one-west, where he stayed for two months. He told me his films made with Metro would be released in France shortly. He gave me an envelope of photographs and asked me to secure covers for him in *Cinéa, Mon-Ciné* and *Cinémagazine*. Six weeks later I was forwarding from Hollywood press clippings about him.

I kept most of his messages. He almost always wrote to me in French, because he was proud to know this language and if I reproduce extracts from it today, it is because after thirty years my correspondents continue to ask me about him; asking me about his style, about the man he was, about the manner in which he spoke. It will be possible to realize this in reading those excerpts in the following installment - which I have reproduced keeping his original spelling[2] - to demonstrate just how much publicity interested him.

---

2 In the announcement of the publication of the extracts of the letters sent to him by Valentino and written in French, Florey specifies he would keep the original spelling. In reading Valentino's writings, we understand that French was a language he could speak and read but not a language he could write correctly. There are so many spelling and grammatical errors it is useless to count them.

Installment #7

Cinémonde 1163 – 11/22/1956

Robert Florey, who became one of the first American television directors in Hollywood, knew Rudolph Valentino well. He was, in past times, his confidant and his friend ...
He evokes here some memories which bring to life the one who was the most loved actor in the world ... Today he delivers extracts from letters written by Valentino.[1]

(Letter dated December 29, 1922, extracts)

"I have happily just received your nice letter which is the first one I received since your sudden departure for the beautiful Hollywood as you call it."

"I wonder if it's true that you wrote to me or if it's just to make me believe you did... Thank you very much, old boy for the good publicity you give me and I will order Abbe to print for me a set of new photos which I will send to you as soon as they are ready. At the same time I'm going to send you two speeches I gave on a radio show, which almost a million radio fans heard; the first against the bad method of producing films adopted by trusts like Famous Players etc. and another where I explain the mission of the cinema in the future of the world."

"I would like you to translate those two speeches and send them to your overseas magazines. I believe this is good publicity. Tell those two brave boys, Limur and Caracciolo, to write me a note, and tell Jean not to forget to exercise my horses with Caracciolo if they want to. Send me their addresses. I have to stop now since I have to leave for Philadelphia for a radio interview.
Greetings to all my true friends and many wishes from me and my wife too. Yours, always your friend, Rudolph. "

(Letter of May 19, 1923, extracts)

"In my last letter I promised to write you as soon as I have good news to give you and here I am in the process of fulfilling my promise."

---

1   As Florey has already specified in the previous installment, he carried over Valentino's original French writing without making any correction of his many spelling and grammatical errors.

"To begin with, I'll tell you that I decided to go to Europe at the end of this tour, that is to say for sure after the 8th of July. I don't know yet if it is for movies or for a vacation, but I will definitely be leaving on S.S. Aquitania or on the S.S. Olympic, around July 23 or 24."

"You are going to say to yourself, 'I'm happy but what the hell is he doing'...or better... 'this is good news for Rudy but not for me'... I gave the order to Kenneth to book a first class cabin for you to England departing from New York around July 11th or 12th so you can arrange a resounding reception for me in London. Also you will go to Paris to do the same thing and return to England in time to welcome us at the ship's arrival. You will reserve rooms for us and for you at the Ritz in London and at the Ritz in Paris ... You have to keep this absolutely secret until you are on the boat and better still until I am in Europe...Thank you for sending me your book *Filmland* and I am happy with the success it received. We will write a book together on Valentino's life and another, also illustrated, on my return to Italy after ten years ..."

(Letter of May 20, extracts)

"I also want to tell you that while in New York the other day, I posed for new photos of which I chose twenty-eight different poses, and I ordered two hundred glossy reproductions of these and different ones, so you will have enough photos of me to begin with until I get to London and Paris to check in. I also decided that the tenth of July may be a little late for your departure and I changed your passage for the first of July... "

(Letter of May 26, extracts)

"Just a word at full gallop to tell you that you will be leaving for England exactly on July the 3rd by the Cunard S.S. Aquitania. I have reserved for you and paid for... a first class cabin. It is a beautiful luxury boat and I am sure you will be very happy and very comfortable there. Hurry with your passport etc. because we must not wait until the last moment ... "

"Before all, you must understand very well that if you were so stupid to get married this naturally would spoil future plans and then, as a friend, I tell you, frankly, don't get married because you have a good future in front of you and it would be a shame to ruin it as you still have a lot of time to marry. As for the woman, one lost and then one thousand found. Apart from that you will have enough to do not to think about it and we will have a successful time in Europe ... "

A friend passing through New York, informed Valentino that I intended to get married. This was false and Valentino had thus reacted to the announcement of this canard. I answered Rudy to reassure him and told him it was not my intention to marry or plan a wedding before I left, which prompted from him, when I joined him, a long speech on his views on the subject of wedding. He always dreamed of an ideal companion, of an ethereal wife not made to ignite so much desire but as to ennoble it, of a woman offering grace, delicacy, harmony, elegance and uniting material beauty and the ideal beauty of form.

The woman he was looking for was not from this world; he would have wanted her to be exquisite, delicate, virginal, dazzling, angelic, fresh, divine, serene, fascinating, diaphanous, of an extreme sweetness of character and, above all, abstract. However, in love Valentino was disappointed, or perhaps it is more correct to write he was disappointed because his first wife fled from their marital home at dawn the day after their wedding night and his marriage to his second marriage was short lived.

Valentino's premarital adventures, of which he often spoke to us, left him with only bad memories. American women, moviegoers saw him as the ideal lover. They all envied the fate of his lovers whom he carried off in the desert on an Arab horse and the young girls refused to leave the movie theater and used to watch the film three or four times. They even forgot to chew gum or eat their popcorn and wrote him endless letters which he showed us afterwards saying: "You see how I am loved!"

In 1912, while he spent a few weeks in Paris, he met a young music hall dancer. For some reason which he never explained to us, she refused to satisfy his carnal desires and even told him she felt insulted. He was only eighteen years old then, but the bitter impression that rebuff left on him continued to bother him ten years later.

One day when we were in Milan, I was taking notes for the book dedicated to his life, which he was dictating to me.

"The girls in the Parisian reviews are uniformly ugly," he told me. "The pretty girls in the drawings of Fabiano, Heronard, Vincent, Léonnec and Benda only exist in their imagination. The naked women of the Folies-Bergère are awful, too plump and none of them can compare to the New York show girls."

I replied that surely he was exaggerating, and that his eyes were probably in his pocket because in Paris there are as many pretty women as in any city in America. But he did not want to give up and later, when the communications we prepared were published, I had to deny his denunciation of the aesthetics of the women of Paris.

"I tell you I know women and I am paid because I know them. But it's not that simple. Yes, the most beautiful women can be seen at Ziegfeld or on Hollywood Boulevard", he replied with his Italian accent; which became even more pronounced when he was irritated. Perhaps he had not forgotten the little 1912 Parisian.

Changing the conversation, he asked me for a list of the names of all the notable personalities, and especially of the members of the London aristocracy of whom I had taken note, and who he intended to mention in these memories. He took great pride in the fact he was introduced to Sir Gerald Du Maurier[2] one evening when he went to see him perform and he was invited to the artist's dressing room. Another joy for him was to have traveled with Georges Arliss[3] and to have even dined in his company.

---

2   Sir Gerald Du Maurier was one of the best English actors during the first third of the 20th century and due to his illustrious career as an actor-manager he was made a baronet by King George V in 1922. Born in Hampstead, London on March 26, 1873, he was the son of the Anglo-French writer and illustrator George Du Maurier, best known for creating the character of Svengali in his 1894 novel "Trilby", and of Emma Wightwick. Sir Gerald was also the father of the writer Daphne Du Maurier, whose greatest success was the novel "Rebecca - The First Wife".

3   George Arliss, born Augustus George Andrews, (London, April 10, 1868 - London, February 5, 1946), was a traveling companion, with his wife Florence, of Valentino and Natacha and had lunch with them in their private cabin during their 1923 crossing for their return to Europe. Arliss was an actor who had great success in English theaters. In 1901 he embarked for the United States on a tour with the troupe of Mrs. Patrick Campbell. It was his intention to stop in America only for the duration of the tour, but the success he enjoyed made him decide to stay abroad. He began playing great historical figures on the Broadway stage along with his wife, Florence Arliss. Arliss entered the cinema when he was already 53, debuting on the big screen in James Young's "The Devil", a play he had already performed in the theater in 1906. He achieved success and notoriety with his interpretation of "Disraeli", a biographical story about the British Prime Minister Benjamin Disraeli. The performance earned him the Academy Award for the Best Actor in 1930. However, Arliss did not fully understand or completely appreciate the value of the award, ignoring the awards ceremony at the Capitol Theater in Los Angeles, and instead went on a vacation to France. At the ceremony, Darryl F. Zanuck, a representative of Warner Bros, the production company of the film, received the prestigious Oscar statuette in Arliss' name.

Installment #8

Cinémonde 1165 – 12/6/1956

Robert Florey, who became in Hollywood one of the foremost directors of American television knew Rudolph Valentino well, of whom he was, thirty years ago, the confidant and the friend …
By visiting in his home and sharing the same friends, Robert Florey was able to get an exact idea of the real life of the actor which is now distorted by legend.
For the readers of Cinémonde, *he was kind enough to evoke memories of that time, through which the nature of the of the most beloved seducer in the world comes to light.*

Who really was Valentino? How many times have I had to answer this question! It seems to me the best way to reply is to relate certain traits of his behavior.

From 1921 to 1923, the group of close friends who were entertained in his home included Manuel Reachi, Paul Ivano, who was a photographer before becoming a cinematographer, the English actor Douglas Gerrard, Jean de Limur, who was an actor before moving on to direct, Mario Caracciolo a.k.a. Carillo, a former officer in the Italian army and myself. A few stars, such as Chaplin or Max Linder, sometimes came to his house, but rarely. The only person Valentino visited regularly was Nazimova, whose help was invaluable to him.

Most often during this period, Valentino preferred to stay at home. He went out, it seemed, as little as possible. And I don't remember ever seeing him at Max Linder's. He seldom frequented nightclubs, shunned trendy cabarets and we only went on rare occasions to the Ship's Cafè in Venice or the Sunset Inn in Santa Monica. He didn't go to the movie theaters, except for his premieres. Politics, history, geography left him totally indifferent.

He was neither gourmand neither gourmet, and ate frugally. He showed more enthusiasm for rubbing a clove of garlic on a crust of bread than for the prospect of a banquet. Anchovies, tomatoes and oil, sausage and fruit were his best meal. He didn't like complicated dishes and I often accompanied him with Caracciolo to a small Italian grocery stores on Main Street where he bought Greek olives, chestnuts from Lombardy and boxes of antipasto from his country.

I never caught him listening to classical music records. But he was never tired of popular tunes like *Wabash Blues, Saint Louis Blues, Cry Baby Blues, Dapper Dan, Everybody Knows, Avalon, My Man* and of course *The Sheik of Araby.*

117

He hardly read and never opened the new French novels I brought him. On the other hand, he leafed through magazines and sports reviews.

He loved to ride horses, especially in Palm Springs and play medicine ball. He spent an hour each morning training his two German Shepherd police dogs, Sheik and Marquis, which he whipped if they did not obey quickly enough. This was while swearing in Italian because the Italian took over when he was angry.

He was passionate about new models of sport cars and he would have owned at least six, if his income had permitted.

He had bitter memories of his years of misery and in this he thought above all of establishing a fortune. He wanted to save money in order to protect himself from material worries.

"I will never be poor again, he said, I will never be hungry."

And yet he spent everything he earned.

He was sometimes extremely generous, then suddenly becoming stingy with his property. He was surprisingly gullible, to then display a reluctant mistrust the next day.

We never had a serious topic of conversation with him. He mainly engaged us with what was happening in the studio.

One evening, I was waiting for him at his place with Douglas Gerrard and we read about the news of the day; a story of masked gangsters who attacked a bank on the boulevard. The event caused quite a stir and we were all very heated about it. Rudy stormed into the living room and deflated our enthusiasm by shouting:

"Did you hear the news? Rod la Rocque is now cutting his sideburns to a point like I do. He also has a famous toupee!"

It was impossible for him to stay still for long except when it came to costume making tests or painting his portrait.

He laughed at admitting he was bad enough in elementary school and added he owed his education to the life he had led. Apart from the drawings of Natacha, who executed among others the costumes for Nazimova in her production of the *Salome* of Oscar Wilde, and the paintings of Beltran Masses portraying him, Rudy had no attraction for modern art. But his atavism drove him to admire Italian Renaissance and Rococo style works.

In the presence of a true artist like John Barrymore, Valentino displayed an inferiority complex. On the other hand, he felt very comfortable in front of the stars who owed their glory only to the cinematographic miracle.

He was generally even-tempered and laughed readily. Then suddenly, for no apparent reason, he sank into depths of despair from which it was difficult to rescue him. Several times we saw him with tears in his eyes, agitated by obscure forebodings.

"I haven't enjoyed life enough," he told us. "I hate the films I have to make and I would like to join Natacha in New York. I feel lost."

He also complained about his stomach, which made him suffer consistently. He ingested great amounts of baking soda.

Max Linder used to organize infamous dinners to which the greats of Hollywood were invited. He was constantly updating his guest lists. Several times, as he made these lists, I asked him to think of Valentino.

"Your friend Valentino is very nice," he replied, "and very likable, but we have no common subject of conversation. When he dines with me he doesn't say a word unless we start talking about his films. And, said between us, he did not invent the gunpowder[1]."

On the other hand, George Jomier[2] welcomed him willingly. Every week he gathered friends in his "Dovecote" on Hartford Avenue and cooked French dishes for them. It was customary to serve on disparate dishes while using newspapers as a tablecloth. Upon departure, everyone had to sign on the door, as Jomier intended to pass this door on to posterity through the Los Angeles Museum.

One Sunday, Jomier invited us to join Fatty Arbuckle, Thomas H. Ince, Max Linder and Gaston Glass. After the meal, Fatty took some dice from his pocket and offered to play Craps[3]. After an hour, Valentino had lost about fifteen dollars. It wasn't much, but he was furious because he didn't like to lose. Coming down from the "Dovecote" he looked wrathful. He had hardly thanked Jomier nor greeted the other guests.

"I don't like Fatty," he told me, "he always makes tricks and jokes that I don't like. I don't like wasting my money in such a stupid way. If George invites him again, I won't go back to his place ..."

An hour later, he was no longer thinking about it. But his anger returned over a bottle of Flora delle Alpi brought to him by his bootlegger.

"See, if I hadn't gone to lunch, I could pay cash for this bottle without having to draw a check. I hate wasting my money like this."

"But you could have won," I tell him.

"It's the same. I lost $ 15, and with that bottle it's $25 coming out of my pocket today."

However, Valentino was not stingy, his bank account proved it. He was stirring up more bad blood for a few dollars lost like that, than for a larger sum loaned to a friend

---

1   In French it is written: *il n'a pas inventé la poudre*. That is, he did not invent gunpowder, a popular French expression of defining him as a simpleton, a not too intelligent person, a simple-minded one.

2   Georges Francois Armand Jomier, born in Paris on October 14, 1874 and died in Santa Monica on June 12, 1950, was the director of the Berlitz school in Los Angeles. He has been called the, "beloved teacher of French and friend of the cinema people", as he was the French teacher of the stars. Arriving in Hollywood in 1908, at the dawn of cinema, he soon became friends with everyone who mattered and was also a consultant when it came to films about France. Jomier was also a gourmet cook and his dishes were defined as, "Masterpieces of French cuisine". It is said Schenck loved his soups, that Mary Pickford loved his "Poulet en Casserole", while Gary Cooper loved his "Poisson rôti aux herbes". It was said his dishes were so delicious even the saints would surrender their vows. Jomier established the tradition of dinners in his home, which he used to call, "The Dovecote".

3   Craps is a dice game in which players bet on the outcome of their roll, or a series of rolls, of a pair of dice. Players can bet money against each other or against the dealer.

which was never repaid. The extras were well aware of this, those who never turned in vain to this paradoxical patron.

Valentino had just arrived in London when he told me he was negotiating a contract with J.D. Williams, a well-known producer who was with First National Pictures and who was the founder of the Ritz Carlton Pictures Corporation. Talks with Famous Players Lasky were well underway and J. D. Williams was trying to work things out and avoid a lawsuit. Valentino was convinced the court would prove him right and he would no longer have to work for the company he left even while his contract still explicitly attached him to the company.

A compromise was reached. Valentino would return for a time to Famous Players Lasky, be given a nice increase in pay and then would become the star of the Ritz-Carlton Pictures Corporation productions.

During a press conference, which followed the case negotiations, Valentino then delivered the following statement:

"My contract with J. D. Williams, which will take effect when the arrangements for my work with Famous Players Lasky have been settled, will give me the right to choose the directors, screenplays and actors for my next films. It will allow me to produce films which are much more artistic than those produced by ordinary companies. Commercial rigidity is something which too often paralyzes. I will have the privilege of surrounding myself with the best directors, the most skillful screenwriters and the most prestigious cast. From the choice of the story to the editing, I will be fully responsible for all the details of the production. Do not think me presumptuous, but it is to the public I owe my position as a movie star and I am always anxious when my name is inserted in the credits of a film."

"What kinds of movies are you going to shoot now?" A reporter asked him.

Having been caught off guard, Valentino replied it was still too early to talk about that. He insisted he was Latin and that he would choose roles commensurate with his Latin personality.

All of these beautiful words were not part of reality; *Monsieur Beaucaire, A Sainted Devil, Cobra, The Eagle* had no more merits than *Camille* and *Blood and Sand*. What the audience expected from him had nothing to do with art. He understood that, perfectly, since he reappeared in the beloved character of the Sheik.

After his death, the producers attempted to launch several "Latin lovers", obviously inspired by Valentino. But a shadow that has now become a myth cannot be flushed out.

THE END

Rudolph Valentino & That Left Eye

Taranto is an ancient city on the Ionian Sea in the southern Italian region of Apulia. It has been a vital commercial and military port since its founding in the 8th century B.C.E. Founded by Spartan colonists who were exiled sons of unmarried Spartan women, by 500 B.C.E. Taranto was one of the largest cities in the world with a population of 300,000. Taranto boasts many famous citizens, from a 4th century B.C. E. Philosopher Lysis of Tarentum to Hollywood director Quentin Tarantino, whose surname has its origins from the city.

Although much is made of Rudolph Valentino's roots being in the nearby city of Castellaneta, his home from the time he was nine years old in 1904 until he left for America in 1913, was the city of Taranto.

In 1910, Rudolph was fifteen years old and living in the great city by the sea which teemed with temptation. He was enticed and mesmerized by the music halls, the dancing venues and above all the signorine, or the ladies of the brothels. Prostitution in Taranto then was a thriving trade as the numerous brothels catered to thousands of sailors coming and going in the busy port. Laws existed governing the brothels, with the legal age of admittance to a brothel being eighteen. In general the proof of age of a younger man was not checked and the madams at the brothel's doors turned a blind eye.

The teenager Rudolph's dallying in those brothels by the sea would ultimately affect his life profoundly. It is a fact Rudolph Valentino suffered from syphilis which he contracted from prostitutes in Taranto, a fact presented definitively by his own family and by himself as he detailed his predicament in letters which still exist today.

Yet, the very mention of his condition inevitably sparks a firestorm of emotions. It is still an inherently controversial aspect of the life of the much idolized icon Rudolph Valentino and his passionate following is vehemently and deeply divided on the subject. How did this disease affect Rudolph Valentino's life and specifically how did it impact his military involvement in Italy which resulted in his status as "deserter" from the Italian army?

Despite the centuries long history of social stigma associated with the very subject of syphilis, the impact of this disease on so many aspects of Valentino's history now makes the issue impossible to ignore. As illuminated by new revelations, newly found documentation and research, we respectfully ask: Was Rudolph Valentino blind in his left eye? Was he declared a deserter from the Italian army? How were these two misfortunes connected?

Every biography of Valentino relates some account of his teenage escapades in Taranto. However, the most compelling insight into this time in his life was written by

Valentino himself in 1910, at fifteen years of age. He writes his friend Bruno Pozzan on August 29, 1910:

"Not long ago, a 17-year-old cabaret singer was in Taranto and I had a great time with her. Then, while I am courting cabaret singers, I make love with prostitutes, leaving one to take another."

In another letter to Bruno, Rudolph writes,

"I am at home sick now with an illness I caught from some prostitutes."

This second letter is cited from the PhD dissertation of Valentino's great grand niece and Valentino family spokesperson, Jeanine Villalobos. Her revelations on this subject stand as definitive word. She comments how Rudolph, "exhibits very little shame about the illness."

Villalobos sets the disease within the historical context of Italian culture at the time, writing, "contracting a venereal disease was a sign of masculinity." She also refers to Rudolph's being, "symptomatic intermittently throughout his life". She elaborates how the illness was of great concern to his mother and relates how Valentino discussed news about various medications and cures with the family.

With this definitive study from Ms. Villalobos, we are able to state as fact Rudolph Valentino contracted syphilis as a teenager from the prostitutes in Taranto. We can also state as fact this syphilis manifested as ocular syphilis leaving him blind in his left eye.

In a medical paper on the subject titled, "Recognizing Ocular Syphilis" from the website retina.com/articles May, June, 2018, it is explained how ocular syphilis is not an uncommon complication of syphilis and 27% of those who contract the disease will have it affect their eyesight.

It is also a point to be made that although the disease rendered Valentino blind in his left eye, he was often in remission, as Ms. Villalobos wrote, "he was symptomatic intermittently". This made it possible for Valentino to hide this condition however this did not lessen the suffering for him nor his quest to find treatment and a cure.

At the time, syphilis had no cure and would not until 1943 with the advent of penicillin. The best someone could hope for then was to try and keep the disease in remission. Pre-1943, people suffering from syphilis faced a constant monitoring and diverse forms of treatment. The reason Valentino kept this hidden was obvious as even today the social stigma about this disease is prevalent. It is perceived as a disease which was a punishment for sin; the sin of promiscuity. It is not surprising this was not made publicly known until the Villalobos dissertation.

I first learned of this in 2003, while researching my Valentino biography *Affairs Valentino*. I was then conducting interviews with Valentino memorabilia collector William (Bill) Self in his home in Bel Air, California. It was Bill Self who told me Rudolph Valentino's brother Alberto once told him personally, his brother Rudolph contracted syphilis from prostitutes in Taranto as a teenager. That was the extent of Self's revelation.

This subject is still suppressed for many reasons and is something which is not mentioned; not only because of the social shame and stigma but because it is a critical piece of proof of Valentino's sexual orientation. I oppose the censorship of key elements of Valentino's true history by those who portray Valentino as a closeted gay man. Valentino's letters to his friend Bruno Pozzan are valuable historically in this regard. Ms. Villalobos felt Valentino's letters to his friend Bruno, historically so valuable, she cited them in her PhD dissertation.

Valentino as the Sheik

Considering the fact he suffered primarily symptoms of ocular syphilis, Valentino might not have manifested symptoms systemically. But the medications available at the time were toxic and consisted of metal based compounds of arsenic and mercury which were both poisonous. The arsenic compound Salvarsan was the foremost medication used then followed by NeoSalvarsan, which Valentino was taking, according to Ms. Villalobos.

Another treatment which was widely accepted was the theory that sweating and even a fever lessened the outbreaks and the severity of symptoms. Hyperthermic cabinets or sweat boxes were used and perhaps Valentino's almost obsessive physical working out was a form self-treatment to keep the disease in remission. Did his sweating and working up a sweat lessen and suppress the effects of the syphilis?

It sheds new light on the strength of Valentino both physically and psychologically, in realizing that another manifestation, or symptom specifically of ocular syphilis is photophobia; an acute sensitivity to light. One must imagine Valentino on a movie set in those days with the intensely bright kleig lights. Was his "sguardo" his infamous glance with those piercing eyes a result of his effort to endure the pain of photophobia?

This condition made it difficult for him to drive as well and is no doubt the reason for his many car accidents. Valentino had a driver's license from New York, but the state of New York issued the first driver's licenses in 1910, with no requirement for a medical examination of either sight, hearing or reflexes. So absurdly, even a deaf and blind person could obtain a driving license.

Every biography on Valentino addresses the subject of his poor eyesight whether it concerned his driving or whether it was expressed through the accounts of his co-stars and friends. None of this was revealed until it was presented by the Valentino family.

Ms. Villalobos writes,

"...It is likely that Rodolfo's syphilis excluded him from service..."

It is likely the syphilis could have been a cause for exemption from the military as this was the second most common reason for disability in WW1; second only to the influenza epidemic of 1918-1919. According to new documents discovered in local Italian archives by Professor Aurelio Miccoli, we can state as fact that the left eye blindness was the official determining factor in Valentino's military involvement in Italy.

The story of Valentino's conscription history; his being drafted into the Italian army is now documented with Miccoli's discovery of Valentino's official record on file in the State Archive of the Province of Lecce. By 1914, so many Italians had expatriated that their returning to Italy for a military draft became impractical. Every four or five years the government would declare an amnesty for the crime of desertion.

Draft notices were always delivered to the emigrants by the Italian consulates and the Italian American press encouraged emigrants to return to Italy. This was considered the honorable course to take when drafted. This situation presented substantial hardship for the Italians living outside of Italy.

Before leaving for America in December of 1913, Valentino submitted a self-declaration of good health and readiness to be drafted when he turned 19 years of age the following year. He was required to do so in order to secure a passport.

Valentino was drafted on Dec. 30, 1914 at 19 years old, but because he was in the U.S., his date of summons was postponed until Dec. 1, 1915. He was then classified in the first and optimal category deemed ready and able to fight. Because Valentino did not appear for the draft call, he was declared a deserter on December 6, 1915; this being filed with the Military Court of Bari on December 31, 1915.

Between December 1915 and the spring of 1917, Valentino was awarded the status of deserter. At that time 100 people in Valentino's district were also declared deserters.

When the U.S. entered the war in the spring of 1917, Valentino sought to enlist in the U.S. military as this was a way to satisfy the requirement. His mother encouraged him not to join the air force and he was refused because of his poor eyesight.

After being refused in U.S. and Canadian Air Forces, this information was relayed to the Taranto conscription office. They issued a formal notice of exemption for Rodolfo Guglielmi in 1917 but this order was rejected by the governing body. The military court of Bari denied the lower office order. For this reason, Valentino then turned himself in to the Italian Consulate in Los Angeles on May 29, 1918 for his physical exam and he initiated the process of permanent exemption. It was then it was recorded officially he was blind in his left eye.

The issue was still unresolved bureaucratically when Valentino returned to Italy in 1923. An important event took place for him when the Italian government declared an amnesty for deserters in September of 1919. With this he no doubt felt safe to return. But in fact his paper work processing his status was so bogged down in Italian bureaucracy, he would not be fully discharged as a deserter until March of 1925.

In an interview granted by Valentino's sister-in-law Ada a few days after his death in 1926, she addresses the subject of Valentino being a deserter from the Italian military. I cite the article which appeared in the Turin newspaper *La Stampa* on August 27, 1926.

"And here the lady recalls another complaint against Valentino; that of not having returned to Italy for the war and being labeled a deserter. No desertion she says. Rodolfo Guglielmi was, while in America, repeatedly subjected to health examinations by the Italian authorities and exonerated for health reasons."

On Valentino's conscription record there are a few years of fascist insults scrawled on the form dating up until 1938, such as the mocking of his name as: Valentini...Ineligible! Requiem! Alias AKA, King of the artists... etc.

The handsome teenager Rodolfo, without a doubt made an impression on the madams working the doors of Taranto's brothels and had no problem gaining access as a welcome customer. Valentino grew up in a city where the main tourist attractions were those brothels; a city which was founded by the Spartan sons of unmarried women. Men of all kinds used to go to those brothels including military officers, husbands, boys for their first experience and the curious who loitered outside never entering the brothel or investing a penny.

"Come on in! Either give us the business, boys, or get out of the way!", the madams were reported to have called to those loitering. Rodolfo did not loiter and would suffer the ramifications for the rest of this life.

Synopsis in Valentino's File in the State Archive of Lecce

Translated
by
Renato Floris

On May 6, 1895, Rodolfo Pietro Filiberto Raffaello Guglielmi was born in Castellaneta, a city at the time part of the province of Terra d'Otranto with its capital being Lecce. He was better known by his stage name of Rodolfo Valentino; a true icon of silent cinema and undisputed star in Hollywood.

The young Rudy, before embarking on his dazzling artistic career which would result in his reaping laurels in the "Mecca" of U.S. cinema, fulfilled the obligation of a medical examination at the Military District of Taranto and was enrolled in the draft of his class of birth, in the first category, which classified him as being ready and able to be sent to arms.

This document on file summarizes his personal details, some personal, anthropometric and personal data: Guglielmi, Rodolfo, agronomist, 1 meter and 75 cm tall, son of Giovanni and Maria Barbino, obviously capable of reading and writing.

In reality, his mother was Marie Barbin, being of French origin, but the Italianization of foreign names and surnames was not uncommon.

From a wealthy family and after the untimely death of his father, a veterinarian, the young Rodolfo emigrated abroad before the initiation of the military draft of his birth class.

After the outbreak of the war he was called to arms on December 1, 1915, but he did not answer the call, residing in the United States since the end of 1913, according to what is reported in his biographies.

He was therefore declared a deserter on December 6, 1915, like many Italians who emigrated abroad who did not respond to the appeal. His failure to present himself was reported to the Military Court of Bari on December 31, 1915.

He would surrender himself to the Royal Italian Consulate in Los Angeles on May 29, 1918.

Once the war ended, he benefited from the amnesty granted for military crimes on September 2, 1919 and, by February 18, 1925 and by order of the investigating officer of the Military Court of Bari, no criminal proceedings were initiated against him.

In the same year he was ruled exempt by reason of blindness in one eye following a decision by the management of the Military Court of Bari (March 5, 1925). At that time, in fact, he had applied for American citizenship for work reasons, and to obtain this, a document of suitability for military service was required.

But it was prevented by the title of deserter with which he had been stamped in Italy. He therefore preferred to obtain a declaration of physical ineligibility for the service. His personal story through the meager data provided by the matriculation registry and some biographical notation, helps to make sense of the sequence of dates and measures mentioned.

The story of Valentino's desertion deserves a broader reflection, which signals a phenomenon that is anything but marginal in the context of the Great War. The deserters, in many cases, were Italians who emigrated abroad for work before their call to arms. In the registry which reports Valentino's conscription record, more than one hundred young people of his birth class are also declared deserters because they did not comply with military obligations, after having expatriated, some in the United States (especially in New York, but also in Boston, Pittsburg, San José, Chicago), some in Canada (Toronto), some in Argentina (Buenos Aires). Some of them, came from municipalities in the Taranto district, others from municipalities in Basilicata located in the Matera district, which in regards to the draft was headed by the military district of Taranto.

Signed by *Maria Rosaria Tamblé*

Commentary

by

Renato Floris

In Taranto, Valentino spent a sort of sabbatical year consisting of a "reckless" life which could be defined as frequenting entertainment venues where he courted the entertainers and socializing with the officers of the warships which were in the port of the city. He also hoped to refine his limited knowledge of the English language by accompanying the English tourists who came to visit Taranto every fortnight.

Rodolfo, being strongly attracted by female graces, enjoyed the company and the graces of available "signorine" as they used to refer to prostitutes at that time. Rodolfo confessed to his friend Bruno, a former companion at Sapienza, that this life was not the best and he had acquired a venereal disease from frequenting the "signorine". This a disease which, according to confirmation in the doctoral dissertation of the great-granddaughter of Rudolph Valentino, Jeanine Villalobos, was syphilis which would cause total blindness in his left eye.

At the time, syphilis was a disease difficult to cure and also debilitating on a social level. Until recently, to access any function in a public facility one had to show a negative result of the test created in 1906 by August Von Wassermann. Wassermann is credited for having discovered the first biological method to make a precise diagnosis of syphilitic infection.

I believe the commonly proposed explanation of thoracic deficiency as being the reason why Rodolfo was refused admission to the Morosini Naval Academy in Venice is false. This excuse of chest deficiency is implausible because the physical parameters of military readiness were regulated by strict guidelines which took into account the measurements of the supreme head of the Royal Army, King Vittorio Emanuele III. His physical measurements set the standard and his height was 5' and consequently he was not equipped with a mighty chest.

Therefore, I believe the "excuse" of thoracic insufficiency is not supported historically and I believe Valentino was rejected entrance into the naval academy because he had a positive Wassermann test. This was suppressed, as syphilis, at the time, was a infamous disease.

The Rudolph Valentino Love Child Theory

by
Evelyn Zumaya

Rudolph Valentino's Deathbed Whisper

According to the surgeon attending Rudolph Valentino in the days, hours and minutes before he passed away, at some point Rudolph realized he was dying.[1] Dr. Howard Meeker witnessed this realization.

Rudolph's guardians maintained their deathbed vigil as the grieving warriors who would see him through; his godfather, Francesco, "Frank" Mennillo and his trusted manager and closest friend George Ullman. In the waning hours of his life, Rudolph felt no pain and told George Ullman to let the sun light greet him. On that last morning of his life, Rudolph motioned for Frank Mennillo to hear his few final words. He whispered them to Frank Mennillo who would share the message with one person; Rudolph's only brother Alberto.[2]

Frank Mennillo and George Ullman met Alberto when he arrived in New York City after his brother's death[3] and the godfather's first order of business was to pass on Rudolph's message.

What was said? What could have been important enough for Valentino to whisper secretly to Frank? What was Alberto's reaction? Would Alberto's reaction to his brother's deathbed whisper change the course of everyone's lives? Did Alberto's reaction and subsequent action, initiate decades of subterfuge persisting to this very day? I present my case, based on twenty years of research and analysis, that this is exactly what happened.

---

1 Jeanne De Recqueville, *Rudolph Valentino, In English,* translated by Renato Floris, Viale Industria Pubblicazioni, Torino, Italy, 2020, p. 137, Dr. Howard Meeker writes, "Yes, I saw him die bravely, courageously, he was not a coward. His confessor was satisfied with his religious expressions. I, who operated on him and witnessed his final breath, I can only write I was impressed with how brave he was to bear great sufferings, and yet, even at such a tragic moment, remained uncanny. I never understood his strange smile as it to tell us, 'Farewell' ".

2 Baltasar Cué, *The True Rudolph Valentino*, translated by Renato Floris, Viale Industria Pubblicazioni, Torino, Italy, 2019, p. 120, "It has been said that moments before Rudolph died, he whispered some secret words in the ear of his great comrade Frank Mennillo. Mennillo would then, in turn, only whisper them in the ear of Alberto Guglielmi Valentino."

3 "Valentino's Dying Words Told to Brother in Secret", *Daily News,* New York, New York, September 2, 1926

I never set out to prove Rudolph Valentino's nephew Jean was his love child. I set out to disprove the theory. As of this writing, I have been unable to do so. For many years I said nothing about the love child theory publicly and postponed the decision whether to address the subject in my Rudolph Valentino biography, *Affairs Valentino* until I could assess any evidence I discovered. Little did I realize the subject of Rudolph's love child would establish a central element in my research and eventually in my book's narrative.

While researching *Affairs Valentino*, I sought a single piece of evidence which would prove or disprove my theory that the child raised as Rudolph Valentino's nephew, Jean Valentino was his biological love child. In archives in the United States and in Italy, I discovered a trail of documents and missing documents, revealing cryptic clues to events which took place long ago. Not one of those discoveries, to date, disputes the theory.

The first inkling baby Jean could have been Rudolph's love child was suggested to me in 2003 by my literary agent, Sam Fleishman. He mentioned the possibility during our discussion as to the why and when of Rudolph's departure for America. I told him the explanations varied, from his quest for adventure to his family banishing him after deeming him incorrigible. There are accounts of a contentious Guglielmi family meeting where funds were pooled to fund Rudolph's passage and every Valentino biographer purports a variation on one of these themes.

The studio-generated version, tells the story of Valentino arriving in America to seek adventure. This is still the version predominately believed to be true. I found this Rudolph Valentino rags to riches story to be nothing more than Hollywood invention. In polishing the star's public image, studio executives deemed it wise marketing to generate sympathy for a brave and struggling immigrant rather than hint he could have been exiled because something preposterous occurred or hint he arrived with a great deal of money to wealthy, welcoming relatives and sponsors.

My literary agent pursued his theory by asking me when Valentino left Italy and I replied, December 1913. "When was the nephew born?" he asked. At that time I did not know. I responded to his implication the child could have been Valentino's love child and the reason he left Italy with disbelief. Nevertheless, I agreed I would in the least locate Jean's birth certificate and proceed from there. The theory would be easy to disprove if the nephew's birth occurred too long after Valentino's departure. Baby Jean's birth had to be before September 1914, in order for him to have been Valentino's biological child.

When I began my search for Jean's birth certificate in 2003, the internet was not quite as valuable a resource as it is now and most archives were not yet online. Despite, I sought a way to request a copy of Jean's Italian birth certificate which would hopefully still be on file in an archive in Southern Italy. I knew the Mormons then offered access to their international archive of genealogical records and it was through their organization, "GenSearch", I filed my request.

Jean's birthplace of record was the city of Santeramo in Colle and I forwarded the required ten Euro bill to cover the cost for the copy from the city archive. It was almost a month before the envelope from Italy arrived. I phoned my agent before opening the missive because I thought he should know immediately if his theory was feasible.

When I had him on the line, I opened the envelope and read the recorded date of Jean's birth as August 14, 1914. Incredibly, it was biologically possible for him to be Valentino's child. Calculating the period of gestation, Jean would have been conceived sometime in late October or early November. Rudolph Valentino left Italy a month and a half later.

From that moment on, the search for information regarding Jean as Rudolph's possible love child was present in nearly all aspects of my research. Initially, I found the idea too outlandish to be true and felt confident any trail to prove such a thing would have vanished long ago. Yet the idea haunted me and became increasingly impossible to ignore. The serendipitous story seemed at times to be telling itself despite my cynicism.

For example, while researching conditions Valentino endured on his first trans-Atlantic voyage in 1913, I consulted a veteran oceanic traveler and sea-faring historian. He was surprised to learn the date of Valentino's crossing, as he felt it unusual a family would send an eighteen-year-old, alone, on an Atlantic crossing during the winter.

"Then the great ocean liners had no stabilizers," he explained, "and inefficient heating systems."

He thought it would surely have been a rough crossing as winter seas were always turbulent, the weather bitterly cold. If Valentino was simply chasing adventure in New York City, he might have waited a few weeks or even a few months for the arrival of spring, calmer seas and warmer temperatures. What was the rush to have Rudolph so far away? Why did he leave during the auspicious Italian Christmas holiday? Why would he abandon his family then; his sister and brother and his widowed mother when the first Guglielmi grandchild was on the way? This would have been a time of joyous anticipation and Guglielmi family traditions.

It was then impossible to travel casually between New York City and Taranto, Italy. For southern Italians in 1913, New York City was a lifetime away and most people emigrating had little intention of ever returning to the homeland. For Gabrielle Barbin Guglielmi, Rudolph's mother, the probability of never seeing Rudolph again was then her reality.

Was he banished forever by his angry relatives during that infamous family meeting? What happened? The timing and circumstance of Rudolph's December 1913 departure felt desperate to me.

From 2003 until his untimely death in 2016, I was blessed to have had the esteemed Rudolph Valentino and Natacha Rambova scholar, Father Michael Morris, o.p.[4] as my dear friend and mentor in all things Valentino. His guidance and analysis contributed immeasurably to *Affairs Valentino* and from the first time I presented the love child theory to him, he was convinced it was true. He never ceased encouraging me to persevere.[5]

Initially, he suggested I locate Jean's baptismal and marriage records, explaining if he was married in a Catholic church he would be required to produce a baptismal certificate. I took Michael Morris' advice and searched in newspaper archives for announcements of Jean's marriage. If he were married in a Catholic church, I could access the archives of that diocese to find the birth certificate and any other information which might be included. Jean was married twice and although he was well-known as Valentino's nephew at the time of both marriages, my search resulted in a single notice of Jean's first marriage, a civil ceremony in Los Angeles newspaper archives.

As I expanded my search for Jean's records in the U.S., I discovered a first missing document. In NARA[6], I retrieved the "Declarations of Intention", "Petitions for Naturalization", the "Oaths of Allegiance" and the "Certificate of Arrivals" of both Alberto Valentino and his wife Ada; with photos attached. Jean Guglielmi's "Declaration of Intention" was missing and only his "Petition for Naturalization", "Certificate of Arrival" and "Oath of Allegiance" can be found on file with no photograph attached.

At that time, I was unaware the subject of missing documents would soon define my *Affairs Valentino* research; specifically those documents which should have been available for public access concerning Jean Valentino. However, searching for missing documents related to the love child theory was not my primary focus nor my only research frustration in 2003.

I was then immersed in my search for Valentino's probate court case file; the entire record of the settlement of his estate was missing. The search for those records became my priority after I located the children of Valentino's manager, S. George Ullman. They were adamant I reference Valentino's probate court records to document

---

4 Father Michael Morris, o.p., *Madam Valentino, The Many Lives of Natacha Rambova,* Abbeville Press, New York, New York, 1991 and *Beyond Valentino – A Madam Valentino Addendum,* Viale Industria Pubblicazioni, Torino, Italy, 2017.

5 Michael Morris e-mails to me: 9/3/2003 - "If Jean was married in the church in L.A., he would have had to produce a baptismal certificate before the marriage.", 9/4/2003 - "Why should his (Valentino's) new wife (Natacha) want to get involved in the mess Rudy left behind there? Was Jean's mother still living in the village?", "Her (Valentino's sister's) conservative stance could well reflect a country Catholic family's attitude towards sex and morals that would propel them to send Rudy packing when suddenly Jean popped into their lives." Ibid: "There are no photos that I know of showing Natacha and Jean together. But there are photos of Alberto with Natacha and Rudy. If Alberto visited the chateau, why didn't Jean? Or did he?"

6 National Archives and Records Administration, Pacific Region, Laguna Niguel, California.

their father's performance as Valentino's executor. In 1930, Alberto Valentino sued their father for mismanagement of the Valentino estate and although Ullman was exonerated on all charges, the Valentino family continued to state the opposite. George Ullman's children were eager to have the facts be known.

During my search, I was informed by the Los Angeles County Hall of Records that the original case file, " Rudolph Guglielmi, a.k.a. Valentino, Probate Case #83678", was not available for public review due to the case file being missing from its rightful housing.[7] I was eventually able to locate copies of many of those missing records consisting of some one thousand pages which were transcribed when George Ullman filed his appeal of the lower court decision.[8]

Within these one thousand pages, I discovered a curious document; a second page to Valentino's will labeled, "Paragraph Fourth" which I had never seen nor read. The content of this document and its very existence was then not publicly known. As I read this codicil to Valentino's will, I realized why; it was on this document, "Paragraph Fourth", Rudolph Valentino designated Jean as his sole heir.

On Paragraph Fourth, Valentino also designated nothing more than unspectacular weekly allowances for his siblings and granted his executor Ullman complete authority over the Rudolph Valentino Production Company. I could hardly believe what I was reading. Until that moment it was believed, because of Alberto's accounts in interviews over the years, that he and his sister and Natacha's Aunt Teresa Werner were the rightful heirs. I went back and checked all the Valentino biographies I could get my hands on and none of them mentioned Paragraph Fourth.

There it was; the mythical second page of Valentino's will with George Ullman's role clearly defined. He was to produce movies and generate income for Rudolph Valentino's sole heir Jean, who would inherit the estate when he turned twenty-five. The revelation Valentino left his estate to Jean and the realization this fact, which was so clearly outlined on Paragraph Fourth, had been subsequently stolen and hidden from public access, served as a significant contribution to the love child theory. What happened to the original copy of Paragraph Fourth? Why was it still being reported by the Alberto Valentino family that Valentino left his estate to his siblings and Natacha's Aunt Teresa Werner? As I sought more information about this enigmatic document a mystery began to unfold. The story went like this.

Upon his return to Los Angeles after Valentino's death, executor George Ullman retrieved the *Last Will and Testament* of Rudolph Valentino from the star's office safe in Falcon Lair and found Paragraph Fourth missing. Ullman recalled Valentino telling him he left this page as instructions for his use as executor. It was, however, no where to be found. Indeed without this piece of paper in hand, Ullman's authority as executor was

---

7   Certificate of Clerk as issued by the Superior Court of the State of California for the County of Los Angeles, Case No: PO83678, Signed by J. Herrera, Deputy, on May 3, 2004

8   The lower court decision made Ullman financially responsible to reimburse the cash advances to the estate to the very people who spent and benefited from the advances. He was exonerated on all charges on appeal.

vague and compromised. Did he have the authority to continue running Rudolph Valentino Productions? This one question became the primary impetus in Alberto's filing the lawsuit against Ullman in 1930.

Based on the sketchy information in hand, Ullman proceeded to advance estate funds to the three people mentioned on that single page of the will, Alberto Valentino, his sister Maria and Natacha Rambova's aunt Teresa Werner. He drew checks for $10,000 several times for Alberto and advanced, in good faith, over $70,000 total to these three people.

During Alberto's litigation against Ullman in 1930, a carbon copy of Paragraph Fourth was recovered in Valentino's attorney's files and admitted by the court as a legitimate portion of Valentino's will. The abrupt appearance of this document had an immediate and disastrous effect on everyone involved.[9]

With the appearance of Paragraph Fourth, Ullman learned he had been disbursing those advances of estate money to the wrong people while assuming they were Valentino's rightful heirs. As executor he was held legally responsible to reimburse the entire amount to the very people who had just spent the money.

When the copy of the document was admitted to the court, Alberto claimed it was a forgery and demanded the judge summon the secretary and her typewriter to the courtroom to prove his point. Contributing to the mystery surrounding this document naming Jean as Valentino's sole heir, allegations flew in the court room between handyman Lou Mahoney and Alberto as to who removed the original document from Valentino's office safe in the days after his death.

I detailed the legal significance of this document in *Affairs Valentino;* its significance to George Ullman, to Alberto and Jean Valentino and to the history of the settlement of Valentino's estate. Paragraph Fourth's significance to the love child theory would be the mystery of how this document disappeared from Valentino's office safe. Was it removed to prevent the probate court from ever knowing Jean was Valentino's rightful heir? And if so, by whom?

At the time the carbon copy of Paragraph Fourth was admitted into court record as a legitimate portion of Rudolph Valentino's will, it was revealed three people knew the combination to Falcon Lair's office safe: Alberto, Falcon Lair's handyman Lou Mahoney and Valentino. It was a matter of simple deduction to know who walked away with that critical document in hand. At some point during the days following Valentino's death, previous to George Ullman and Alberto's arrival in Los Angeles with Valentino's body, the second page of the will in which Valentino bequeathed his estate to Jean, vanished. With Valentino sealed in his coffin, Alberto on a train heading west with that coffin, it would have been Lou Mahoney who removed Paragraph Fourth from

---

9   Ullman would then learn he was advancing estate funds to the wrongful heirs. He would also learn handyman Lou Mahoney witnessed Paragraph Fourth with his signature and knew about its existence since the day the document was executed. While Alberto claimed the copy of Paragraph Fourth was a forgery and would consequently say nothing about his brother bequeathing his entire estate to Jean.

the Falcon Lair safe. Granted, the handyman signed the document as a witness but what would have been his motivation in tampering with Valentino's will?

Valentino had his attorney execute this will shortly after his separation from Natacha, late in the summer of 1925; a vindictive gesture in which he left her one dollar. Valentino authorized the document with his signature thereby making Jean his sole heir on September 1, 1925. Valentino had this will drawn up while still furious over learning Natacha had an affair. Smarting over their fast and recent separation, he cut her out of his business and his inheritance and left his siblings meager weekly allowances until Jean turned twenty-five.

With the recovery of Paragraph Fourth serving as documentation Valentino bequeathed his estate to Jean and with the knowledge this document was removed in the days following Valentino's death, the love child theory became increasingly difficult to dismiss. Even more so after Michael Morris loaned me his archive of *Madam Valentino* research materials; more revelations would be tucked within the boxes of files.

The Tony Altamirano Contributions

The question remained; why would Valentino change his will when he did and leave everything to Jean? He would have summoned his lawyer Raymond Stewart to execute the will and have it amended with a second page of instructions for George Ullman which would be designated as Paragraph Fourth. This was premeditated, carefully planned and it is not difficult to sense Valentino's resolve.

This was a troubled time for Valentino with his separation from Natacha leaving him distraught and behaving rashly. This was revealed by his house guest that summer of 1925, Spanish painter, Beltran-Masses. Masses discovered Valentino alone in his library one night, sitting with a loaded gun to his head.[10]

Understanding the emotional context of the time frame in which Valentino executed the September 1st will, I believed something else could have occurred to inspire the legal action; something more profound than bitterness over his separation from Natacha. Michael Morris' archive would present a possible explanation.

In the 1980's, while researching *Madam Valentino*, Michael Morris interviewed Leslie Flint; President of the *Valentino Memorial Guild* in London.[11] Leslie Flint told Michael Morris, his friend Tony Altamirano shared a secret with him about Natacha Rambova. Altamirano told Leslie Flint, his close friend Nita Naldi confided in him how Natacha had three abortions while she was married to Valentino.

Flint told Michael Morris how Altamirano said Nita Naldi admitted to him she

---

10 Beltran-Masses finds Valentino with gun to head: *Affairs Valentino*, p. 269 – 270, " Just as he passed the library, he caught a glimpse of the back of the great chair and Rudy's arm holding the revolver to his head."

11 Larry Flint, letterhead from letter to Michael Morris, The Michael Morris Archive, "The Valentino Memorial Guild, Incorporating the Valentino Film Archive and Film Society, (Founded 1926), President: Leslie Flint

personally told Valentino about the abortions; adding she also told him she accompanied Natacha to one of the procedures. When Leslie Flint told this to Michael Morris in 1982, Tony Altamirano was still alive. As a respected friend of many celebrities throughout the 1930's and 1940's, Altamirano was known as a rational and honest man.[12] His story from Nita Naldi was credible enough for Michael Morris to want to include it in his book. Leslie Flint agreed to contact Altamirano and ask for his permission.

When Altamirano learned Flint told this to Michael Morris, he was furious. Altamirano was so upset he wrote Michael demanding he not repeat this confidence shared with him by Nita Naldi in his upcoming book. Despite this, Michael did include the report as a rumor.[13]

If Altamirano's account from Nita Naldi, which Michael Morris found credible, was an accurate one, I wondered when she told Rudolph Valentino. I knew they had a tryst on his yacht after Natacha left Los Angeles in August 1925. This is known from the account of make-up artist Mont Westmore who was on the craft at the time.[14] Is this when Nita Naldi told Valentino about Natacha's abortions? If so then I think it logical to deduce; the news could have been shocking enough to prompt Valentino to eliminate Natacha from his inheritance, cause his suicidal tendencies and inspire the execution of Paragraph Fourth bequeathing everything to little Jean.

Both Michael Morris and I reported Nita Naldi's account of the abortions as a rumor in our respective books. As Naldi's career came to a halt about that same time, her betrayal of her friend Natacha could have been a probable cause for her professional disappearance. It would certainly have been something Valentino confronted Natacha about immediately and she would have reacted accordingly. Did Rudolph Valentino, upon hearing about the abortions, leave everything to his biological son and then plan to kill himself?

Further insight into the love child theory would be inspired by Tony Altamirano as more was shared with Michael Morris by Leslie Flint; this being a print-out of a translation of an interview with Alberto Valentino published in Italian in the American Italian newspaper, L'Italo-Americano on October 1, 1977. Of particular interest is Alberto's response when the interviewer asked him,

"When did Rodolfo know of your son? When he left Italy, naturally your son had

---

12 WorthPoint, item for sale labeled, "Vintage Original Authentic 1948 Ramon Novarro Hand-Signed Christmas Card & Note, "A Prayer of Saint Francis of Assisi, (inscribed from Novarro as),"To Tony Altamirano, Ramon Novarro", Cited from caption, "These items come from the estate of Antonio Altamirano who was a good friend of many film, opera, theater, music and ballet celebrities."

13 The Michael Morris Archive, cited from a letter from Larry Flint to Michael Morris dated January 6th 1982, "...Dear Michael Morris, Thanks for your letter just received, I am sorry that you have had such a stupid and nasty letter from Mr. Altamirano. Some time ago he was very ill and had been attacked by two people in L.A. and suffered head injuries, he is not really altogether at times, I too have had rude letters from him..."

14 Mont Westmore and Valentino's yacht with Nita Naldi: *Affairs Valentino*, p. 268 – 269. Also M. Morris, *Madam Valentino*, "While Mont stood on the bridge with his eyes peeled for treacherous reefs off Catalina, he could hear Nita's melodious voice extolling Rudy's capabilities." Also Westmore's affiliation with Valentino – *The Smithsonian Magazine*, May 2000.

not yet been born."

Alberto replied, "No, of course not! I was not even married yet!" [15]

Later in the interview Alberto drops his bombshell,

"...He (Rudolph) dreamed of having a big family – a big one, he said, with eight or ten children; but he was not fortunate with either of his two wives – so much so that he wished to adopt Gianni (Jean) legally. Naturally, our laws did not permit this to happen so he made him his sole heir." [16]

Alberto's revelation was stunning in regards to the love child hypothesis. He does not say he was opposed to the idea his brother would legally adopt Jean, and explains casually how the adoption was not permitted because Italian laws would not allow Valentino to legally adopt Jean. By law it is required all parental rights be surrendered to allow your child to be adopted. The question arises; were Alberto and Ada prepared to do this? Why would they both not object strenuously to even the idea the "uncle" would try to legally wrest custody from them of their only child?

It is also interesting Alberto calls Jean, "Gianni" and not Jean. Did he not name his child Jean? Why would he have changed the name to the Italian and not the French version? This one point was about to become significant.

And why did Alberto wait until 1977 to admit he knew all along his brother appointed Jean his sole heir? This was a remarkable admission considering the fact that in 1930 Alberto claimed, in a courtroom, Paragraph Fourth never existed. For decades he repeated how the estate was divided between the three heirs while he erroneously impugned George Ullman. This, when Alberto knew all along Jean was the only person entitled to his brother Rudolph's inheritance.

Why did Alberto wait until two years after George Ullman died in 1975, to admit he knew Jean was the sole heir? Why did he not inform executor George Ullman and the probate court of this critical information when he first arrived in Los Angeles after his brother's death?

Alberto continues in the *L'Italo Americano* interview to state emphatically he was not married when his brother left Italy. Alberto and Ada were married on December 19, 1912 and had been married one year by the time Rudolph left for America in December of 1913. If Alberto was telling the truth in 1977, then he admitted Jean was conceived out of wedlock. Or was Alberto struggling to recall the events and dates to coordinate with the story already told so many times over the years? Was the aging Alberto, speaking in his mother tongue, relaxed enough to go off the narrative he himself established after his brother's death and to which he had so steadfastly adhered? Had Alberto Valentino kept that story straight just about long enough?

Alberto's interview in 1977 added considerably to the love child theory. He admits

---

15 Cite original entry in Naples Historical City Archives: Alberto and Ada's marriage dated, December 19, 1912.

16 *L'Italo Americano*, October 1, 1977, titled, "Part I, Translation from "*Italo-Americano*", Oct.1, 1977 – "Interview With the Brother of the Celebrated Actor. With the 'Four Horsemen of the Apocalypse' Valentino Conquers Celebrity, by Argentina Brunetti. Inscription on translation reads: From: Tony Altimoreno, 1/3/1978.

how his brother planned to legally adopt and assume full custody of Jean. Alberto also admits to subterfuge in that he reveals he knew Rudolph named Jean his sole heir when this was in direct opposition to what he had been declaring as truth for decades.

The "Astonishing" Resemblance & Other Factors

In 2003, Michael Morris introduced me to William Self, a retired television producer who lived in the Bel Air neighborhood of Los Angeles. William, "Bill" Self was then the king of Valentino memorabilia and owned it all. It was not just his Valentino collection which made him a critical person for me to interview, he also knew many, if not all, of the key players in Valentino's story who were still alive when he first came to Los Angeles in the early 1950's. He made a point of befriending George Ullman, Alberto and Jean Valentino, Valentino's first wife Jean Acker and his friends Paul Ivano and Robert Florey. Consequently, my interviews with Bill Self in 2003, provided me with a wealth of valuable Valentino information.

Whenever I arrived for an interview, Bill would have a selection of Rudy wares from his collection arranged for me to see. On a few occasions, he would show me his artifacts displayed on the landing of his staircase. It was there one day a framed photograph on the wall caught my eye. I did a double take and leaned in for a closer look.

An 8" x 10" black and white glossy photo appeared to have been taken at a formal dinner. Behind the table posing for the camera; Bill Self in a tuxedo standing next to Rudolph Valentino in a tuxedo? Bill sensed my reaction and said quietly, "Jean. He looked exactly like him." Jean appeared to be about fifty years old at the time with his black hair slicked back, with Rudolph's iconic sloe eyes, arched eyebrows and sinewy hands.

First-hand witnesses commented consistently on Jean's resemblance to Rudolph. Pola Negri was Valentino's love interest in early 1926 when Jean visited Falcon Lair. In her autobiography she remarked about the resemblance when she writes:

"Rudy's brother, Alberto, arrived from Italy accompanied by his wife, Ada, and their seven-year-old son,[17] Jean. Although the father looked nothing like his famous brother, the little boy's resemblance to his uncle was astonishing."[18]

Another first-hand witness to Jean during his 1926 visit to Falcon Lair, was Spanish journalist Baltasar Fernández Cué. Cué was working with Valentino on a book at the time which Valentino was planning to publish as the true story of his life. The book was never completed with Valentino's assistance as he died a few months later. Cué would finish the work and publish it in serial format in a Spanish movie fan magazine,

---

17 Jean was eleven years old in January 1926.
18 *Memoirs of a Star,* by Pola Negri, Doubleday & Company, Inc., Garden City, New York, 1970, p. 275.

Cine Mundial in 1927. In this book, *The True Rudolph Valentino,*[19] Cué writes:

"...despite the pleasure with which he (Valentino) gazed upon his nephew who looked so very much like him..."

It was also in 1977, when Jean Valentino gave a televised interview with Thames Television. A four minute clip of this interview can be viewed on Youtube today. Even though Jean was sixty-three at the time, the resemblance to Rudolph is striking. His eyes and eyebrows, his gestures and mannerisms reveal a likeness. Granted, children have a broad gene pool and often do not resemble their parents. It was in this regard, I made a point of not placing much importance on Jean's resemblance to Valentino. I am, however, still haunted by Bill Self's photograph.

By the spring of 2011, I completed *Affairs Valentino* and made the decision to include the love child theory in the first edition of the book which was published in May of 2011. I presented the theory as a circumstantial case to my jury of readers. By the time I published the book, I uncovered further extraneous evidence which I felt could scarcely be ignored.

1. Bill Self told me he read the letters between Rudolph and his brother Alberto and they were mostly angry letters about money. Why did Alberto feel he had a claim on Rudolph's income? Was Valentino sending money as child support?

2. I also found disparate references to Jean's age. Pola Negri said Jean was seven in 1926, when he was eleven years old. I began to doubt the accuracy of the birth certificate.

3. Why were there no baby pictures of Jean available? Photographs of Alberto and Rudolph as infants and toddlers were available online but not a single picture of Jean as a baby. The first images we see of him are in 1923 when Valentino visited his brother and family in the city of Campobasso when Jean was nine.

4. Valentino biographer Irving Schulman commented on how it was typically the oldest son who was afforded to opportunity to emigrate. Schulman alleges this was something Valentino worried about addressing as he went through customs and processing on Ellis Island.

5. George Ullman did not mention Jean a single time in his 1975 memoir. He certainly mentioned Alberto but for some reason Jean was untouchable.

6. When Rudolph and Natacha traveled to Rome in 1923, she chose to return to France and not accompany him to visit Alberto and family in Campobasso; a few hours drive

---

19 Baltasar Cué, *The True Rudolph Valentino*, Viale Industria Pubblicazioni, Torino, Italy, 2019, p. 123, "Despite how much he (Valentino) and his brother and sister-in-law cared about each other, *despite the pleasure with which he (Valentino) gazed upon his nephew who looked so very much like him...* their attempt to build a home together was a resounding failure."

from Rome. Her reason why is something often discussed and I began to wonder if she knew Jean was Rudolph's love child and chose not to address that part of his past.[20]

My quest for more information regarding the love child theory did not cease with the publication of *Affairs Valentino* in May of 2011. I continued searching in Italian archives and in 2014, I traveled to the city of Valentino's birthplace, Castellaneta. That same year I published a revised *Affairs Valentino – Special Edition* and included the results of the Italian research as a postscript.

I visited not only Castellaneta, but also the neighboring town of Santeramo in Colle where Jean Guglielmi Valentino's birth certificate was filed. I knew in Italy, at the time of Jean's birth, the process of documenting a child's birth involved registering the information with the City Clerk, or "Segretario Comunale", in the presence of two witnesses; most often friends or relatives. It was the duty of the City Clerk to then register this information on a separate document called a "Family Form". In Italian this is called a "Foglio di Famiglia". This document was kept on file in the city of the child's birth for posterity.

During the visit to Castellaneta, I met with Valentino historian Professor Aurelio Miccoli. I was surprised to learn from him how on April 19th, 1914, a few months before the registry of Jean's birth, Alberto Valentino was appointed as the "Segretario Comunale", or City Clerk of the city of Santeramo in Colle. Professor Miccoli added that at that time, Alberto had just turned twenty-two-years-old.

I knew Jean's birth was registered in Santeramo, yet I was surprised to learn Alberto possessed the authority to personally register the birth. In his role as City Clerk, Alberto was in charge of registering all the information of the town's population including births, marriages and deaths. He was also in charge of maintaining the important documents; those Family Forms.

Italian law requires this form stand as a family's composite history and must by law be held on file in every city or town where a family resides. A copy of this document of utmost importance is transferred from town to town as a family or individual relocates. The Family Form was and still is legally required to be on file in any city where one claims residence. This form also designates the "Capofamiglia" or "Head of the Family."

I met with the Santeramo City Clerk and requested to see Jean's birth registry, proof of residency and the Guglielmi Family Form. The pages of the Santeramo ledger, called the "Civil Registry" or "Registro dell'Anagrafe", were yellowed and fragile but Alberto Guglielmi's signature was clearly visible on the registrations of births, death and

---

20 This theory was purported by Michael Morris.

marriages occurring during his brief tenure as Santeramo's City Clerk. There was one exception. The entry dated August 14th, 1914, Jean's birth registry, was signed by the mayor himself and witnessed by two of Alberto's employees in his City Clerk's office. The birth was registered on August 18, 1914, with the address of Alberto and his wife Ada's, Santeramo residence entered as 56 San Eligio Street.

Upon seeing the Guglielmi family's local address, the City Clerk said he would search the files to verify the Guglielmi's residency. He left his office and returned a few minutes later to say he found no record of any residence in Santeramo for Alberto, Ada or Jean Guglielmi. He explained they might have kept a legal residence elsewhere, but decided this discrepancy would certainly be explained on the Guglielmi Family Form.

Another search revealed the Guglielmi Family Form was missing. I returned to examining the one piece of evidence we had found; the registry of Jean's birth. An address was written in pencil in Alberto's handwriting, entered just below Jean's full name and next to the location of his birth with the child's full name and the words, "Resident of Via Nizza 9 in Turin" written below. The Santeramo City Clerk could offer no explanation why the child's address and residency would not be the same as the parents. Was this a second place of birth noted in the registry? Indeed, there was not another similar entry in the ledger.

After locating the San Eligio residence, I had to hope that in 1914, this building's ominous entrance was then not quite as foreboding. Perhaps at that time it was a more livable and charming domicile. In 2014 it was a building with one small barred window and a barred door set inches from the curb. The building appeared to serve as some sort of utility or storage facility.

The next focus of my research would be that cryptic, penciled-in address of the newborn Jean; Via Nizza 9 in Turin.

The only person I could find to speak with at Via Nizza 9 in Turin, was the manager of a hotel next door and he offered nothing in the way of enlightenment as to the history of the building's previous owners or residents. The only information he shared was to say that over the years the building was divided into many apartments.

I then searched for residency records for Alberto, Ada and Jean in the Turin Historical City Archives. I knew on their United States immigration documents, which I retrieved many years prior, all three cited Turin as their last place of residence in Italy. [21] I searched for information about Alberto Guglielmi, Ada "Delmazzone" Guglielmi and Jean Guglielmi. The Turin City Historical Archives house the records of Turin's residents

21 "Petition for Naturalizations" on file in NARA for Alberto, Ada and Jean. "Declaration of Intentions" on file in NARA for Alberto and Ada.

dating back as far as the eighteenth century. The Italian Civil Code requires citizens to file one's residency information in the local Civil Registry.

My initial search revealed only Jean was ever registered as a resident of Turin.[22] I found no evidence Alberto or Ada Guglielmi were ever registered as residents.[23] I also discovered there was no Guglielmi Family Form on file and that Jean's Turin residence was entered as, "Via San Francesco da Paola, 27".

I soon discovered this was the address of a still active and well-known private school, "Istituto San Giuseppe dei Fratelli delle Scuole Cristiane". Jean's Turin Historical City Archives residency record also noted he lived in a "residential community"; this meant he was a boarded student living at the school. His father, Alberto Guglielmi's occupation was registered as "lawyer" and mother's name was noted as "Ada Daimazzini" with her surname circled in pencil and above this written "Del Mazzone". [24]

I then paid a visit to Jean's school, the Istituto San Giuseppe on Via San Franceso da Paola, where incredibly, Jean's school registration card was still on file.[25] The information on his card reported he attended the Istituto San Giuseppe for one school year, 1926-1927. He transferred into the school from the Mamiani School in Rome at twelve years old entering the American equivalency of the sixth or seventh grade. This was not surprising as I knew Alberto returned to New York upon hearing of Rudolph's sudden death in 1926. Jean was registered that year to enter the Mamiani School in Rome yet enrolled in the Istituto San Giuseppe in Turin. Despite his boarding at the school, Jean's home address was entered on his school registration card as Corso Vittorio Emanuele II 115 in Turin.

I then returned to the Turin City Historical Archives to take a second look at Jean's residency registration where I learned he maintained his official residence at the school, Istituto San Giuseppe in Turin until 1935. It was then he changed his official residence to Hollywood, California. On my second visit to the Turin Historical City Archives, I noticed one important detail I previously missed on Jean's residency registration card. It was then I noticed Ada's last name was spelled as Del Mazzone; two words. In my initial search for Ada, I searched her name as one word, Delmazzone.

My immediate search for Del Mazzone was rewarded with the discovery of two women, Ole Del Mazzone, who married a Mr. Imperatrice and her sister Ebe Del Mazzone, who married a Mr. Baldassarri. I found nothing else on their files except the name of their mother, Erminia Filomarino. Initially, I found no record of Ada Del Mazzone and wondered if this could be her family.

I then conducted a search of the mother's family name of Filomarino and discovered she was married to Vittorio "Dalmazzone". The confusion over the spelling of

---

22 "Anagrafe della Citta di Torino", Turin Historical City Archives, Jean Guglielmi.

23 Ibid.

24 Alberto's various occupations: On his marriage record in 1912, "publicist", on NARA records first as "Writer" in 1934, as "Doctor" on Ada's "Declaration of Intention", as "Accountant" in 1940 and "Lawyer" on Jean's school registration in 1926.

25 All Istituto San Giuseppe School Information, on file in school archives.

this unique last name was finally resolved when I located the Del Mazzone Family Form, filed under a misspelling of the father's name, "Dalmazzone". From this document I discovered that Vittorio Del Mazzone was married to Erminia Filomarino.

I also noticed a common date for all four of the Del Mazzone's official registrations in Turin; August 4th, 1914. For this reason, I concluded they were members of one family. According to their Family Form, they arrived in Turin about ten days before registering and all moved to Turin from Sampierdarena, a neighborhood in Genoa.

At that point I still had no proof these four people were related to Ada Del Mazzone Guglielmi. It was then, upon further scrutiny of the faded records, I noticed a faint notation of the Turin address of the Del Mazzone parents Vittorio and Ermina Filomarino; Via Nizza 9, the very same address Alberto penciled in as the residence for the newborn Jean.

Within days of this discovery, I sent a mailing to a list of Del Mazzone and Filomarino families as well as several families with the surname of Imperatrice and Baldassarri. I hoped there might be a distant relative eager to share the family's history. Within a week, I received a call from Mr. Vincenzo Filomarino of Taranto. He confirmed he was a relative of Ada Guglielimi and that I had indeed located her family in Turin and yes, they lived at Via Nizza 9.[26]

Mr. Filomarino's grandfather was the brother of Ada's mother Erminia and Ada's uncle. He said Ada's mother, Erminia was one of fifteen children, including his grandfather. He added that one of the fifteen children was Ernesto, who went to live in America and knew Rudolph Valentino when he lived in New York.[27] He verified Ada was a sister of Ole and Ebe and that there were four other Del Mazzone siblings; sister Ida and brothers Ugo, Emo and Igo. He also related how the Del Mazzone family once lived across the street from the Guglielmi family in Taranto and this was how they knew each other. He forwarded a photograph of Ada as well as a photograph of Jean, taken in 1926, with Rudolph and Alberto on horseback in the yard of the Falcon Lair stables. He also forwarded a copy of Alberto and Ada's hand-written marriage certificate. [28]

Despite the fact Alberto told a reporter in 1977, he and Ada were not married when Rudolph left for America in 1913, the marriage certificate reveals they were indeed married on December 19th, 1912. There was one other curious piece of information included in this document; Alberto married Ada in her home, then in Naples. As she was too ill that day to leave her bed, the city officials, the "Assessore", a justice of the peace and his secretary accompanied Alberto to her sickbed for the marriage.

---

26 All Ada Del Mazzone family information from interviews with Mr. Vincenzo Filomarino.

27 Cite to Port of Entry Documents : Valentino gives his destination/address in New York City on his arrival in 1913 as, "215 Spring Street", the home of Ada's Uncle Ernesto Filomarino, wealthy book merchant and printer.

28 Date of Alberto and Ada marriage also confirmed by Marriage Certificate retrieved as officially certified document from the City Historical Archives of Naples. Noted on Marriage Certificate, Ada received permission to marry at home by "justification" as reason of illness.

I had finally verified the address Alberto posted in Jean's Santeramo birth registry as that of Ada's parents in Turin. But I was once again left with more questions. Why would Alberto include the address of his mother and father-in-law as a place of birth for his son, Jean? Why was Jean a resident of Turin at the time of his birth? And why did Ada's parents move there with two of her sisters from Genoa just a few weeks or days before Jean's birth?

Clearly, by end of July 1914, two families were in motion. The Guglielmi family in Taranto had somehow managed to have their twenty-two-year-old law student appointed as City Clerk in Santeramo and the Del Mazzones of Genoa were moving to Turin and an apartment at Via Nizza 9.

In 1913, Vittorio Del Mazzone and his wife Erminia lived in the rough Sampierdarena neighborhood of Genoa. It is not certain whether Vittorio, his son-in-law, or both men, were employed by the Italian National Railroad. However one fact has been documented; that year, at least two of Vittorio's seven children lived at home; daughter Ebe and daughter Ole.[29] His daughter Ada, married Alberto Guglielmi the previous year.

Over the years prior to moving to Sampierdarena in Genoa, Vittorio Del Mazzone moved his family frequently. The previous year, they lived in Naples and before this, in Taranto. In Taranto, the Del Mazzone family lived across the street from the widow Gabrielle Barbin Guglielmi, her two sons, Alberto and Rodolfo and daughter Maria.[30] And in 1912, when Ada and Alberto were married, Vittorio Del Mazzone and his family were living in Naples. The urgency of Ada and Alberto's wedding might have had something to do with the Del Mazzone parent's impending move in 1913. For by that time, father Vittorio was again preparing to relocate and this time to Sampierdarena in Genoa.

As the Del Mazzones moved from Naples to Genoa, Rudolph Valentino had just completed his schooling in Genoa where he attended the technical school; the Royal School of Agriculture Bernardo Marsano in the neighborhood of Sant'Ilario. He was enrolled in this school in 1910 and boarded there for two years. By 1912, he returned to Taranto. While he was dallying with the women of Taranto, a twenty-five-year-old Ada and her husband, twenty-one-year-old Alberto moved back to Taranto from Naples and the Del Mazzone family moved north to Sampierdarena in Genoa. From that fateful summer of 1913 on, the stories of the Guglielmi and Del Mazzone families forever merged.

29 Anagrafe della Citta di Torino, Del Mazone Family Form and residency registration cards
30 Interview with Mr. Vincenzo Filomarino

Was the Guglielmi family forced to deal with some devastating event which occurred by the end of the summer of 1913 and early fall? I allege this event was so grievous as to prompt the drastic banishment of Rudolph Valentino by his mother Gabrielle in December of that year. What could have prompted such an action and at a time of year when the Atlantic winter seas were rough and families in Italy traditionally celebrate the holidays for two weeks? Why would Rudolph be exiled and alone, so hopelessly far from home at such a young age? Why then? It is widely reported young Rudolph had a reputation for his exploits with the ladies and that this was one explanation for his abrupt departure.

However, in Italy, then and now, such a reputation is something most men admire; overtly or secretly. It is not uncommon. It is the women who bear the weight of the shame of sexual promiscuity; the man is perceived as a sexually gifted hero in the estimation of Italian men. I also believe Gabrielle, a mother who loved her son Rudolph dearly; would never have acted rashly on his behalf, taken a family meeting lightly or made the heart breaking decision to send her dearest offspring impossibly far away without serious provocation and reason to do so. A reputation of Lothario is not considered a serious provocation in Italy. There also exists a distinct element of emergency and a sense of finality in not only the sudden departure of Rudolph in December of 1913, but in the subsequent and documented actions of everyone involved.

I believe a more probable provocation, or "shame", was the common complication resulting from promiscuous behavior. In light of the events which were about to transpire, it is not illogical to deduce Rudolph impregnated one of those "many" women in Taranto. In the staunchly Catholic Italy of 1913, there was no birth control, no abortions and even the merest dalliance could result in a pregnancy. There was also no sex education. Unexpected pregnancies, as the result of a lack of knowledge on the subject of sex, were not an uncommon occurrence. However, they did require that families go to extreme lengths to save the family and the mother's reputation and social status. It was also critical the family do all that was possible to establish the child's registered history and official documentation.

In a culture where women were sharply and ruthlessly defined as either "haloed Madonnas" or "debased prostitutes", an Italian family facing an unexpected pregnancy would go to extremes to prevent the mother from being known as a "fallen woman". There was no integration between the rigid classifications of women as either temptress or Madonna and an unwanted pregnancy was a call for swift action.

Such a complication could have been resolved by marriage. If this had happened, then the story would have ended there. In Rudolph Valentino's case it did not. There was no marriage yet there was a child conceived sometime around mid-October 1913; a child whose birth would be registered as having taken place during the first part of August 1914. I conclude that the timing of Rudolph's banishment was the onset of a plan which was intelligently devised and executed to prevent a family's secret from ever becoming public knowledge; the effort to protect the sanctity of a woman's reputation.

If this were the case, then the question remains; why did Rudolph not marry the woman? I do not believe he would have willfully abandoned a pregnant woman and he would have taken the honorable route in such a situation. Perhaps he could not do so, because she was already married.

At that time there was no possibility of divorce in Italy; couples might live separately but no one divorced. If the woman Rudolph impregnated was married, she would have to pass the child off as her and her husband's own or disown the child by placing it in an orphanage or with other family members. Such a child was often raised as a brother, sister or cousin.

The prevailing cultural attitude in Italy towards this situation at the time was to bestow some sympathies for such a pregnancy upon the husband as the "cornuto" and address all blame for the predicament upon the woman's moral weakness. However, a married woman's lover was silently admired by all for his sexual prowess. The elaborate cover-ups of an unexpected pregnancy as the result of a wife's infidelity, were not set into motion to protect the woman's lover or the betrayed husband. They were enacted to rescue the woman and the child's reputation from the stigma of illegitimacy and promiscuity.

Yet, in examining all of the evidence surrounding the timing and suddenness of Rudolph's winter departure, I found there to be an added element of profound shame. There seems to be an undeniably heavy twist on this particular story which sent two desperate families into action. If this pregnant woman was just one of Rudolph Valentino's flings in Taranto during the summer and fall of 1913, even a married woman, then this story would have ended there. It did not.

With Rudolph ensconced on the other side of the world, in New York City by the beginning of 1914, Mother Gabrielle and the other Guglielmi family members who met at that infamous meeting which decided his fate, apparently continued developing their plan in advance of the baby's arrival that summer. Certain unique events occurred.

On April 19, 1914, Alberto received the implausible appointment by the mayor of Santeramo in Colle and became a City Clerk. For the next few months he held this position; although he either did not officially register his residency in Santeramo or hide proof of this by removing the Guglielmi Family Form from the city archives.

And some time towards the end of that July, Vittorio and Erminia Del Mazzone and their two daughters Ole and Ebe left their Sampierdarena home in Genoa to move to Via Nizza 9 in Turin. By the fourth of August, ten days before Jean's birth was registered in Santeramo, they registered their official information in the Civil Registry in Turin.

Santeramo's twenty-two-year-old City Clerk then registered Jean's information in the ledger of birth records. What prompted him to notate the child was a resident of Turin? Was Santeramo's Mayor aware of the family's predicament and did he suggest Alberto do so? Why was it written in pencil? Did Alberto intend to erase this at some point in the future? Was Ada living with her family in Genoa and then in Turin where she delivered the baby with her mother and sisters? Or was Jean born to one of Ada's sisters?

It was at this point in my investigation, I turned the focus of my attention on Rudolph Valentino's mother Gabrielle's French nationality. For Jean's first name was, as is the tradition in Italy, that of his paternal grandfather. But why was he given the French version of his grandfather's name? Why was he simply not named, "Giovanni"? Italian culture is steeped in such tradition and this was certainly an anomaly.

With Alberto's access to Santeramo's official civil registries and Family Forms, I began to question the very integrity of the records themselves. I even doubted the veracity of the actual date of Jean's birth. Had the French born mother Gabrielle, still mourning the deaths of her husband and her first child, determined Jean's name and even his birth date? Had Alberto acted dutifully upon his mother and the family's instructions? For "Jean's" birth date was registered as the same date, August 14th, as his Aunt Bice's death.

Had Jean, in actuality, been born in Turin and his mother, a Del Mazzone, given birth surrounded by her family who would care for her and the child? And if Ada was Jean's mother, it is worth considering in this analysis the many reports of her grave health problems during those years. Not only was she married while bedridden, but as late as 1936, when she was weighed and her height measured for her "Declaration of Intention", upon her official entry to the United States, at five-feet-six, she weighed a mere one hundred and five pounds. Was she too ill or frail to care for the baby? Was the birth of the child physically devastating for her? In 1926, George Ullman commented on her health when he wrote in his memoir that Ada's "illness" prevented any construction on Falcon Lair from taking place during her visit.

This said, the fact remains; with Alberto employed as Santeramo's City Clerk that summer, mother Gabrielle had ready access to a copy of her grandson's birth registry. With this in hand, she could then have documented the child and perhaps included him legitimately on her passport. I have often been asked why I thought Gabrielle, a devoted mother and woman in her sixties, would travel to France, to Besançon, near the then erupting western front of World War One. Why would she leave her new grandson Jean and son Alberto in Taranto and move so far away and to such a dangerous place? Perhaps this was not the case at all; perhaps she did no such thing.

The currently held explanations for Gabrielle's departure from Taranto in 1915, with her daughter Maria, are vague, contradictory and vary from her seeking health treatments to serving the war wounded. There is also a report she left Taranto to avoid the war. This last explanation is false as she would have been, at that time leaving an area of no military conflict to head to the French city of Besancon and directly towards the war with her daughter.

Besançon was not located in the area of France experiencing the most intense fighting along World War One's western front. It was, however, situated a mere one hundred miles from the fighting along the German and Swiss boarders. The arena of conflict in the First World War in Italy was contained well within the north and northeastern areas of the country. No direct threat was ever posed to the citizens of southern Italy, such as Castellaneta and Taranto.

Gabrielle's departure in 1915, meant she moved to Besançon with her daughter Maria to travel to the region directly abutting the bloody western front along the French and German border. For the outbreak of the First World War occurred when the German army first attacked France through neutral Belgium on August 4th, 1914. Clearly, there had to be an explanation as to why a rational and loving mother would make such a seemingly reckless move.

Many records in the Besançon City Archives were destroyed in a great fire during the war and the staff in the city offices share the same story offering similar apologies for the scant available records as a result of this tragic event. Only one record remains intact concerning Gabrielle Barbin Guglielmi's life there for three years during the war; her death certificate dated January 1918.

It was upon reading this death certificate that I experienced a jolt of understanding as to the "sorrow" which haunted Rudolph Valentino, the tears he shed upon his return to Italy in 1923, and the "something that he dared never speak of." For mother Gabrielle registered herself in Besançon as the widow of "Jean Guglielmi". [31]

When she filed for her residency in Besançon, she did not use her deceased husband's Italian name, "Giovanni". Instead, she registered her husband as "Jean". Had she instructed Alberto to also register Rudolph's baby as "Jean" instead of "Giovanni" as she intended to raise the child in France? For it was within a few months after Jean's birth when Gabrielle did leave Taranto. Did she take with her a copy of the baby's birth registry making it possible for her to have the authority to cross the Italian-French border with a child, with a French name, who was registered on her passport?

On her way to Besançon, did she pass by Via Nizza 9 in Turin, to claim her grandson? Did Gabrielle's death in 1918, result in Jean being brought back to Taranto as a three-year-old where he would be raised as Alberto and Ada's son? And in 1923, did he meet his real father Rudolph for the first time and sit with him for his first known photographs?

---

31 Besançon Historical Archives, Ville de Besançon, (Doubs) , France

The possibility Rudolph Valentino was Jean's father and Ada his mother became a further intriguing prospect for me while reading a letter Rudolph Valentino wrote to his sister-in-law, Ada in November of 1918, ten months after his mother Gabrielle passed away in Besançon, France. The letter was written in a tender and intimate tone with Rudolph speaking candidly with his sister-in-law about lovers, love, women, wives and life in America. Most notably, Rudolph wrote Ada a curious and revealing comment about the then four-year-old, Jean.

In a letter written by Rudolph Valentino to Ada dated November 17th, 1918, [32] I excerpt his Italian, "....Vedevo Jean già diventato grande, con una bella divisa da ufficiale di Cavalleria, realizzando ciò che è sempre stato un sogno per me; poiché se ha il mio carattere deve certamente amare i cavalli e l'uniforme militare."

Rudolph Valentino's words as translated:
".....I envision Jean as having grown, wearing a beautiful Calvary officer's uniform, manifesting something that has always been my own dream; if he truly possesses my own character and grows to be like me, he will certainly love horses and military uniforms...."

Brothers do not typically nurture visions or dream that their brother's sons will develop in their likeness, possessing their "uncles" uniquely, specific mannerisms and physical characteristics. Rudolph Valentino's "dream" for Jean to grow in his image was not a comment made as an observation as to the boy's own predilections at the time or his emulating an "uncle" he had yet to even meet. The letter was written when Jean was of an age when children are focused intently upon their immediate and childlike needs. Rudolph's plaintive passage, phrased as a "dream", is revealingly poignant in its sincerity and longing.

Yet, the single most convincing piece of love child theory evidence would be the cover-up itself. I allege the decades of maintaining this cover-up involved court records being stolen, elaborate plans executed, false narratives purported for decades with all actions fiercely guarded by the Valentino family and supported by the unquestioning devotion of Valentino memorabilia collectors. By bestowing choice items from their vast archive of Rudy relics as reward for allegiance, the Alberto Valentino family wields an effective currency to keep the cover-up and Alberto's false narrative running smoothly.

---

32 Excerpted from passage included in the Kaplan Edizioni, Compendium of Convegno Valentino speeches, p. 78.

1. Why hide that original, and entire probate case file of Valentino's court records if there is nothing to hide?

2. Why was Alberto still claiming *Paragraph Fourth*, designating Jean as sole heir, never existed as late as 1930 and why would he not share this publicly until 1977? Why was he denying the document's existence?

3. Where are the photographs of Jean as a toddler between the ages of one to three years old?

4. If the family has those photos, why not share them?

5. Was it a coincidence the date of Jean's birth was entered into the Santeramo in Colle civil registry as having taken place the same day of the year as his Aunt Bice's death?

6. Why were Alberto and Ada willing to surrender their parental rights to Jean and turn full custody over to Rudolph?

7. What happened to the missing Family Forms in Italian archives?

8. Why was Jean given the French version of his paternal Grandfather's name instead of the Italian, Giovanni?

Regarding Valentino's deathbed words whispered to his godfather Frank Mennillo, it is logical to deduce Valentino told him he left everything to Jean and the will was in his safe. Mennillo passed this on to Alberto Valentino who would have made a call to Falcon Lair's handyman Lou Mahoney. With access to the Falcon Lair safe, Mahoney would then do Alberto the favor which would forever earn him a lifetime position of stature with the Valentino family. He removed that second page of the will, Paragraph Fourth. Despite the subsequent appearance of Paragraph Fourth, the document would disappear a second time when Alberto failed to mention its very existence nor the fact Jean was the sole heir until 1977.

The love child theory provides an explanation for many events which would not have otherwise had any reason to have occurred. Why would Alberto admit his brother planned to legally adopt Jean? In the official registry of Santeramo in Colle, why did Alberto pencil in Jean's residence on the day he was born as some 645 miles away in Turin? Why did Valentino's mother, Gabrielle Barbin, travel to France with her daughter to a major front of fighting in World War One and do so only a few months after the birth of her first grandchild? These questions could be answered individually, but the totality of the evidence and the timeline of events presents a compelling blueprint for the love child theory.

A Modest Proposal About Hypodermic Needles

by
Renato Floris

There are a few questions which have long been in my thoughts and for which I seek precise and definitive answers. They are as follows:

1 -What prompted a loving mother, Gabrielle Guglielmi, to send her beloved son Rodolfo overseas, well aware she would never see him again and why would she do so after covering him with gold?

*This story is reminiscent of something Mussolini said infamously about Gabriele D'Annunzio: "D'Annunzio is like a rotten tooth... which is either pulled out or covered with gold." I would say that where Rodolfo was concerned, the family behaved just like that, even better, as they covered him with gold but also uprooted him by sending him overseas.

2 - What was the reason for the hasty marriage between Alberto Guglielmi and Ada Del Mazzone, a marriage celebrated in her home as she was very ill and bedridden at the time?

3 - What induced Alberto, a person defined as serious and studious, to drop out of law school to quickly secure a city clerk's license and accept a job as a bureaucrat?

4 - What prompted Valentino spokeswoman, Jeanine Villalobos to ask Micheal Morris if, while in Turin, Evelyn Zumaya discovered anything about Ada's hypodermic needles and injections?

*With regard to hypodermic injections, it should be borne in mind that, at the time, syphilis was treated with hypodermic injections of mercury salts. Those who managed to survive until the mid-1940s were then effectively cured with penicillin.

5 - Why, as reported in the dissertation by Jeanine Villalobos, did Rodolfo write a letter to Ada in which he discusses his treatments for syphilis and new treatments which might prove effective. And why, again to his sister-in-law Ada, does he write: "If Jean looks like me"...?

6 - What prompted a person, on a gay culture blog, to confirm not only that Valentino was not gay but also that Jean was the son of Rodolfo Valentino and that Jeanine Villalobos, his personal acquaintance... confirmed to him Jean was in fact Rodolfo's son?

7 - Who was the first woman so loved by Rodolfo that she was defined by Alberto as being a show woman much older than Rodolfo?

8 - Why did Alberto admit publicly Ada had a past as a show woman?

9 - Why did Alberto say, in an interview released in his old age, that when Rodolfo left for America he and Ada were not yet married?

10 - Why was it published first on August 13, 2012 and confirmed on February 2, 2021, on a Genealogical site managed by Leszec Mila, that Ada Del Mazzone, before being a wife

of Alberto Guglielmi, was a partner of Rodolfo Valentino?

11 - Why did Rodolfo want to adopt Jean and why did he name Jean as his sole heir?

12 – Why are there are no photographs of Jean before 1923, when he was already nine years old?

13 - Why was Ada consistently reported to be in bed ill, sickly as reported by Ullman and others at the time in 1926?

With the cold mind of a criminologist, free from prejudice or expectation, I analyzed all these questions, collected what information was available and thought about it a lot. With much forethought, here is the scenario which emerges.

Rodolfo was certainly blessed with a strong, charismatic personality and possessed a real talent for gaining the sympathy of those around him. In his sabbatical year, after being expelled from the Perugia boarding school, he freed himself from commitments and felt an overwhelming need to enjoy a cosmopolitan city, full of entertainment opportunities.

As he himself tells his friend Bruno, his main occupation was to have fun, to go to the port when, every fortnight, English tourists arrived to improve his knowledge of the English language. He would then visit naval officers on the warships at anchor in the port of the city of Taranto. Then Rodolfo, still writing to his friend Bruno, relates how he frequented cabarets where his business was to woo the female artists. One last passion of Rodolfo which he writes about to Bruno will mark him throughout his life; this was the assiduous frequenting of the many brothels in Taranto where he contracted syphilis from prostitutes.

The picture which emerges is this:

Rodolfo courts Ada who was then a cabaret artist in Taranto. She was seven years older than Rodolfo but his charisma exceeded the age limits. He had sex with her and infected her with syphilis. I don't think any woman could have resisted the vital, strong erotic energy unleashed by Rodolfo and was this what happened to Ada?

When the disease manifested in Ada, the honor of her family needed to be saved and Ada's parents fought for a solution to the offense. If Rodolfo had been older he would have been required to marry Ada. So the only possible choice was the eldest brother who too was younger than Ada but only by four years. Ada was bedridden, ill with the syphilis received from Rodolfo when she married Alberto who became the scapegoat for the recklessness of the two lovers.

Alberto, now in charge of a wife, had to abruptly terminate his university studies to quickly find a profitable business, thus obtaining the prefectural (city clerk) license to start a career as a public official. His being forced to give up on his plan to become a lawyer haunted him throughout his life; so much so that on the registration form at the San Giuseppe college in Turin, where Jean was hastily enrolled after the death of Rodolfo, Alberto's profession is indicated as an "avvocato" (lawyer).

Regarding Jean's birth, which, as reported, took place on August 14, 1914, eight months after Rodolfo's arrival in the United States. The dates may vary, they can be "adjusted" according to the need as a birth does not necessarily need to be reported immediately. It is acceptable to just let a little, or not so little, time pass and then, at the moment deemed appropriate, supported by two indulging witnesses the birth is reported. The date could also be that of a father's sister who died at a very young age, just an August 14, many years earlier.

There is very little of Jean's presence in Italy and it is not excluded that grandmother Gabrielle took charge of her grandson and brought him with her and the daughter Maria to Besançon.

For all these reasons Alberto believed himself to be his brother's first legitimate heir and that all the belongings of Rodolfo were his: properties, money, cars, dogs, jewelry and, why not, a bright future as a movie star. The rightful heir, Jean, could patiently wait. Confirming Alberto's unique stance on this is the position of his sister Maria who never demanded treatments similar his, even though she had exactly the same rights as her brother.

I imagine Alberto was greedy for compensation for having been forced to throw his life into such a sacrificial situation. At the time of Valentino's death Alberto lived in Rome and was waiting for some significant state office appointment. This is proven by the fact that he enrolled Jean in the Mamiani high school evident of his intention to stay in Rome. Rodolfo's death caused Alberto's plans for the future to fall like a house of cards. He faced an uneasy future and for this he threw himself, like a vulture, on his brother's remains.

I also wondered what the scenario might have been if Rodolfo hadn't reached the highest position in the Hollywood Olympus. Obviously the hypotheses can be many depending on the social status reached by Valentino. Would Alberto have deigned to cross the ocean to visit a brother in difficulty, a brother who had not been able to provide him with tailor-made clothes in which to be portrayed, albeit a little awkwardly? I really think he would not have visited Rodolfo had he been poor. Alberto himself declared that there was never a great relationship between him and his brother.

When Rodolfo left for the New World he did not go to hug his brother in Reggio Calabria. He went instead to Turin to say goodbye to his "Prima Donna" who should have been in that city. Here a small legitimate doubt arises; Ada's family at the time resided in Sampierdarena, a working-class district of Genoa from where they would later emigrate to Turin from May 2, 1914, to live in a railway workers' apartment in Via Nizza 9. This is the address shown in pencil on the registration page of Jean's birth in Santeramo In Colle in the Province of Bari.

Another consideration spontaneously arises for me personally as an Italian with mother, father and ancestors all being Italian. If I had left forever I would have had a considerable part of the family in tow who would have waved huge white handkerchiefs for the last farewell.

The subdued departure of Rodolfo from a lonely pier seems to me from a

153

screenplay for a B or C film and could it have gone hypothetically like this?

"Hi mom, I'm leaving, I'm going to America and we'll never see each other again, I'll write to you if you like."

"Sure son, write to me and in the meantime, I will update you on the baby who is about to be born, I will send you a few dollars when I can and I recommend that you put your head in order and do not infect other girls. Greet and thank Ernesto and Francesco for me who have promised to do so much to help you. Good-bye forever."

And so it was the odd inquiry by Villalobos about Ada's hypodermic needles which prompted a deeper investigation and I would acknowledge her for that inspiration.

The following is a partial list of the public records missing from their rightful housing in the United States:

1. The original and entire file of the California Supreme Court case of Guglielmi v. Ullman, # 83678, *"In the Supreme Court of the State of California, In the matter of the Estate of Rodolpho (sic) Guglielmi, also known as Rudolph Valentino, deceased. S. George Ullman, Appellant, vs. Alberto Guglielmi, Maria Guglielmi Strada, Bank of America National Trust & Savings Association, a national banking association as administrator of the estate of Rudolpho Guglielmi with the will annexed, Teresa Werner, Ray L. Riley, State Controller, Respondents."*

2. The Harry Baskerville Audit of S. George Ullman's executor accounting of the Valentino estate.

3. All evidence admitted in the case of Guglielmi v. Ullman, including Executor's First Account, Supplemental Executor Accounts and attached Schedules,

4. The original copy of Paragraph Fourth appointing Jean Guglielmi as Rudolph Valentino's sole heir as submitted to the court by Attorney Raymond Stewart

5. The complete "Reporter's Transcripts" of court testimony delivered in Guglielmi v. Ullman including Direct Examination and Cross Examinations.

6. Natacha Rambova and Rudolph Valentino's divorce and property settlement entered as court exhibit.

7. The Cinema Finance loan records and accounting

8. Itemization and accounting of estate assets and Ullman's book keeping ledgers as admitted as court's evidence

9. Falcon Lair Grey Book household ledgers and all original extracts.

10. The original Rudolph Valentino Production Company ledgers including the Pan American Bank loan records, VAB records and all tax assessment records of payments and abatement.

11. The Cosmic Arts by-laws, accounting registers and inventory including Executor's Exhibit #2.

12. The assignation of Cosmic Arts to Rudolph Valentino Productions documents and contracts

13. The original United Artists contracts as filed as court's evidence as "Executor's Exhibit One".

14. Cosmic Arts contracts and book keeping ledgers

15. Executor's Exhibit #4, the letter written by Maria Strada to George Ullman.

16. Jean Guglielmi's, "Declaration of Intention", first page with photograph, which is missing from the National Archives of Registered Aliens.

The following public records were found to be missing from their rightful housing in Italy:

1. Proof of Alberto and Ada's Turin residency from the Turin Historical City archives
2. Guglielmi Family Form or "Foglio di Famiglia" in Turin Historical Archives
3. Guglielmi Family Form missing from Campobasso
4. Guglielmi Family Form missing from Filadelfia
5. Guglielmi Family Form missing from Putignano
6. Guglielmi Family Form missing from Santeramo In Colle
7. Proof of Jean Guglielmi's Santeramo In Colle residency
8. Proof of residency in Santeramo In Colle for Ada and Alberto Guglielmi
9. Proof of Alberto's Guglielmi's residency in Campobasso
10. Proof of residency for Alberto, Ada and Jean Guglielmi in Putignano
11. Proof of Ada Guglielmi's residency in Campobasso

Jean, Rudolph, Ada & Alberto

Jean Valentino visits Falcon Lair in Los Angeles - 1926

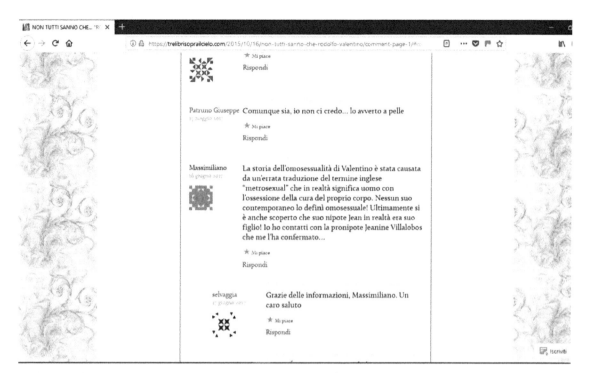

The story of Valentino's homosexuality was caused by an erroneous translation of the English word "metrosexual" which actually means man with the obsession with the care of his own body. No contemporary called him homosexual! Lately is also suspected that his nephew Jean was actually his son! I have contact with his grandniece Jeanine Villalobos who confirmed it to me...

https://trelibrisoprailcielo.com/2015/10/16/non-tutti-sanno-che-rodolfo-valentino/comment-page-1/#comment-7774

Definitive and unexceptionable statement found on a gay culture blog devoted to literary criticism.
Excerpt from blog thread under Fair Use guidelines

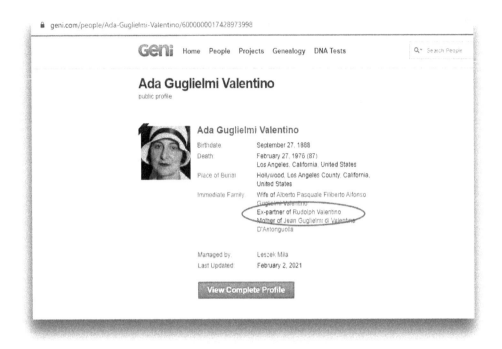

Found online, on a Polish family site. Excerpt from blog thread under Fair Use Guidelines

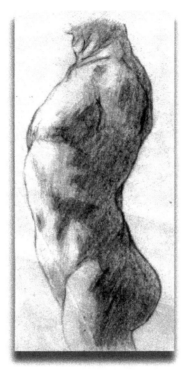

Pencil Sketch of Rudolph Valentino by his
Wife Natacha Rambova

Natacha Rambova -
Rudolph Valentino's Queen

Natacha Rambova

"Her Years As Valentino's Wife"

Why Natacha Rambova's Marriage to the Greatest of Screen Idols
Came to a Tragic End

By HERB HOWE

The New Movie Magazine, December 1929-May 1930

Passing the Vesuvio, an obscure little Italian restaurant in the basement of a brownstone front directly behind the Capitol Theatre in New York, I was stopped by gusts of memory. It was here I often lunched and dined with Rudie Valentino, who with characteristic sentiment remained loyal to the place long after fame offered him its caviar.

Memory-drawn, I turned and went down the few steps to the arched entrance beneath the stairs that led to the floor above. The one window of the place gazed at me lifelessly, shrouded in curtains a little soiled. Faint eddies of dust whirled on the stone pavement in the corner by the door as if they also were seeking entrance. A few folded papers, soggy and stained and dead, lay there. Across the arched opening under the stairs an iron lattice grating had been drawn so that the vestibule to the inner door was dark and hollow like a tomb. The grating was padlocked.

Natacha Rambova &
Rudolph Valentino

It, too, was gone.

In the still dreariness I recalled our last evening there. I had come alone to dine on the good but cheap table d'hote. There were several diners in the place, mostly Italians and their girls. I took a small table by the kitchen door where I could exchange words with the plump signora who emerged steaming from time to time to look over her guests. I had come to know her through Rudie. He always exchanged banter and Italian compliments with her.

The waiter was in the act of placing my plate of minestrone when a hush fell on the room like a stroke of paralysis. The plate of soup remained suspended beneath my nose as though the waiter had turned to bronze, and the spoons and forks of the other diners were similarly transfixed in mid-air. The whole room was stricken by the opening of the outer door.

"*Buona sera,*" called the husky voice of the signora, coming out of the kitchen to greet the arrivals. "*Buona sera, signora, come sta?*" boomed the reply, and then the same voice, "Hello, Herb, come have dinner with us." Rudie had entered, working his usual spell, and with him Natacha, his wife, and Natacha's white-haired aunt, to whom Rudie was so devoted that in his last will he named her affectionately his beneficiary.

I moved to their table and tried to feel at ease among the surrounding waxworks. Rudie never appeared conscious of stares. He enjoyed attention and accepted it with lusty naturalness where other stars are rendered coyly artificial.

The other people in the restaurant recognized the Valentinos, of course, but their eyes—the only mobile parts left them—turned queryingly on me. I spilled my soup with hands that behaved as if in husking mittens. Apparently my identity had to be explained to spare me the inconvenience of developing apoplexy. "If they don't stop staring," I said, my complexion ripening to mauve, "I shall arise and announce I'm the late John Bunny staging a come-back."

Rudie released a hearty guffaw and the diners thawed. The dinner went merrily with Natacha's wit; Rudie had a huge appetite for humor as well as for food.

Natacha Rambova & Rudolph Valentino 1924

That was our last dinner; a vivid memory. Turning from the bleak little ristorante, barred and sealed, its own mausoleum, I vowed to find Natacha at once and lunch and laugh once more.

NATACHA RAMBOVA. The name in letters of stone appear above a shop next to Fifth Avenue on Fifty-second Street. Rich fabrics and pieces of antique jewelry are in the window, beyond which your curious gaze is lost in folds of gauzy green.

I opened the door. In the center of a spacious salon, modernistically spare, with furnishings of silver and burgundy, stood that dominant, regal girl, dressed in black velvet, her small head turbaned in flame with braids of brown hair coiled close to her ears — the girl who in her own words has been called "everything from Messalina to a dopefiend."

I expected to find her restrained. A volume of tragedy has been written since that night we parted over the gay Italian meal. Unmercifully flayed after her separation from Rudie, she went for seclusion to her mother in France. She re-emerged briefly at the time of Rudie's death, then disappeared again. I knew there had been shabby years. People reported seeing her now and then on the Avenue. She was always alone, dressed severely plainly, but her head was held high by that indomitable will of hers. She tried many things; vaudeville, dancing classes, writing, decorating. Finally a small shop, then success and a larger one. All the friends of her opulent hour passed her by long ago; her clientele has been built solely on her art as designer and is strictly Park Avenue, without a stage or screen celebrity.

Even her worst enemy has admitted the genius of Natacha, that unquenchable flame of ambition that sweeps out from her ruthlessly to combat Hollywood and its intrigues implacable instinct, a fighting' spirit of Amazonian fierceness. Yet, for all her electric vitality, I think Natacha's spirit is a little weary. Very young, she has witnessed with shrewd eyes the mockery of the world's spectacle, and from the highest throne of idolatry this age has known, she has experienced its sharp irony.

I recalled the days I spent in her apartment collaborating with Rudie on his life story. Because of some legal technicality pertaining to his divorce from Jean Acker, he. and Natacha were forced to maintain separate apartments for several months after their marriage in Mexico, but of course Rudie spent most of the time in Natacha's.

There was a moment of constraint as Natacha and I set down on the divan. To break it, I referred to the hours spent on his life story. "Now we ought to do your life," I said. "But I guess all your real names have been told." "Yes, and I've been called a lot of names that weren't mine," laughed Natacha. "No, I'm here to tell you right now that I don't give a hang for publicity. God knows there has been too much for me already. I've been called everything from Messalina to a dope-fiend." "Did you feel it much?" "I was tortured. I was tortured to agony," she said. Her eyes met mine in an eloquence of silence. In that minute the interval of years passed by. I felt certain I knew her as I hadn't before.

She turned the poignancy of the revelation with a quick laugh. I always loved the laughter of Natacha. It is clear and gay. And it can shield a multitude of sorrows with its courage. "They even said I have no sense of humor!" Her laugh mounted. "That's equivalent to saying I am dead. Without it, I would have been, long ago."

Those who said it, couldn't have known that her real name is O'Shaughnessy. No more did those who thought to defeat her.

In the Hollywood days, the studio rang with her battles for Rudie, his stories, his salary, his costumes. "Oh, I was a fool," she exclaimed with a rueful smile. "But I was young and optimistic and full of fight. I didn't realize the uselessness. I was butting my head against a wall. They don't care about your ideas or about you. They want to crowd as many pictures into as little time as possible, to collect on you as swiftly as they can. What happens to the star is of no concern."

"I can't think of any position more difficult than that of an idol's wife," I said. "It was hellish," she affirmed. "Rudie hadn't one faint gleam of business sense. He knew he hadn't and relied on me. He was a big, sweet, trusting child who wanted to be loved above all things. And that desire to be liked by everyone left him open to imposition. He would agree to anything to be agreeable. When he realized he had made a mistake, I rushed into them shouting, 'No!' And you know how popular that word is in Hollywood!

This of course gave them a fine weapon against me. Everyone knew Rudie was sweet and agreeable at all times, therefore if anyone suffered it was because of *Mrs. Valentino.* A girl would be presented for a part. Perhaps she was five feet eight and the part called for a kitten. I would say I couldn't see her as the type. The girl was dismissed: 'Mrs. Valentino didn't like you.'

"It was fiendish. Yet I felt I was necessary. Rudie felt I was, you know that. But he had pride, a legitimate man's-pride, and they worked on that. They commenced bringing him clippings which said 'Mrs. Valentino wears the pants,' 'too bad Rudie can't be his own boss,' and so forth and so forth. These rankled. Eventually, if I so much as observed it was a nice day, Rudie, about to agree, would catch himself and say, 'No, it is *not!*' Of course I realized how he felt. He didn't want to be putty even in his wife's hands. We would laugh about the clippings; nevertheless, they made a wedge.

Rudie was frightfully sensitive. He couldn't stand the least criticism. And being an actor—a much finer actor than most people realized, he was pliant. If I shaped some of his convictions, I at least had his interest at heart. Others at the studio—the clipping-bearers, for instance—did not. They imposed on him in every way conceivable. They borrowed money, they took his time, they sold his stuff, and one of his closest 'friends,' I discovered, was speculating in the market with his money. A trusting soul, if there ever was one,

Rudolph Valentino & Natacha Rambova

it was dreadful to open Rudie's eyes to people who appeared so nice to him, who he thought *liked* him.

"I would kill off one crop of sycophants and—so help me!—the next morning there would be another. I never saw anything to equal it. They sprang up over night like toadstools. Only a person who has experienced Hollywood would believe me. They not only wanted to get in his good graces, each wanted to monopolize him utterly. And when they couldn't they said I did!

"Oh, I tell you it was sweet for me." She laughed a little ruefully. "I can't understand now how I ever could have been so foolish as to let it wear me down. It did. You lose perspective.

It's inevitable that you lose it. They force you out of your mind. Perhaps if you could go through it first and then go back . . . but you have to go through it to know. You simply cannot keep your perspective.

Another thing, I didn't want to go to parties. I'm not a particularly sociable mortal. I didn't care for society and didn't go before, and I couldn't see any reason for going after we were in a certain position. That of course did not endear me with people who wanted the Valentinos for show pieces at their affairs. I didn't care if I was unpopular, but it hurt Rudie to be. Deeply ingrained in him was the desire for popularity, to be liked.

I remember the first day he came on to the set, I disliked him. At that time I was very serious, running about in low-heeled shoes and taking squints at my sets and costumes. Rudie was forever telling jokes and forgetting the point of them, and I thought him plain dumb," Natacha laughed. "Then it came over me suddenly one day that he was trying to please, to ingratiate himself with his absurd jokes. Of course I capitulated. 'Oh, the poor child,' I thought. 'He just wants to be liked—he's lonely. . . .' And, well, you know what that sentiment leads to. . . ."

Rudie was lonely. I never knew a lonelier man. He craved affection so. I remember the first time he spoke Natacha's name to me. We had had dinner in his one-room-and-kitchenette apartment in the Formosa. He had engaged a woman to come in and serve for the occasion, and it was wistfully festive. I had done the first stories about him, he was deeply grateful. Hollywood, for him, was a forlorn place until his success was firmly decided. They looked upon him as a dubious Italian with sleek hair who had been a tango dancer in a cabaret, who was pathetically poor and altogether of no consequence in film society. Even after New York recognized him as an artist in "The Four Horsemen," Hollywood sat back in its provincial smugness and had to be shown. Rudie showed me some of his first notices proudly.

While I was waxing sincerely fervent over his prospects, he tentatively ventured the name of Natacha Rambova. Had I heard of her? I hadn't. She was doing some really remarkable sets, he said. He thought her a fine artist. Perhaps my magazine might be interested in some of her drawings to publish. His suggestion was so timorous I gave no importance to it. On another evening, some time later, as we sat until the revealing hours of morning over coffee in a downtown cafe, he told me:

Natacha Rambova

"She is a wonderful girl, very much alone like myself. I go to her house evenings and we talk about things that interest us, things that don't seem to interest many people here; books, new plays, the modern art movement, and of course our work. Our tastes are very similar. It is just a friendship, which I need very much. I don't know where it will lead. I hope it will keep on growing."

Then after their marriage: "There was nothing mad or hysterical about our love. It commenced slowly in friendship, as I told you, and just blossomed naturally. She gives me companionship, sincere and sympathetic companionship—the thing I have always longed for, the thing a man needs above all else to complete himself."

Their separation was one of the many great tragedies that may be laid at the gates of Hollywood, most worldly of places on earth today. For the idol it is a garden of many blandishments, the sireny of which, continually repeated, leads to dizziness if not destruction.

I do not believe Natacha ever departed from the mind of Rudie, nor actually from his heart. He was proud, he had been wounded and was confused, yet over his last will when he was ill his thoughts must have hovered over their associations, for he named, with deep affection, her aunt who was a symbol of them. "It was Hollywood that separated you," I said to Natacha. She only nodded.

Do you think it possible for two people to succeed with marriage there?" I asked, "not just ostensibly I mean, but actually? ... or even with great friendship?" "The only possibility, I think," she said, "would be if they kept entirely out of it all and recognized it for what it's worth. But ah!—that's it. You are young, appearances are deceptive; you don't realize you are losing perspective and being absorbed until you are swallowed up.

"Hollywood is a hot-bed of malice. It seethes and boils in envy. Never a good word is spoken of anyone unless for publicity or to gain some personal end. Sweet words of flattery have vinegar on their breath. Eyes of malevolence watch you and even as you turn you feel the tearing tongues of back biters. People go places out of fear. Fear is on parade: fear of being forgotten if you are not in the procession, fear of being talked about if you stay away and fear of the ravening critical eyes when you are present.

"It's a terrible place. Thank God I'm out of it all!" She spoke with mirthful detachment even of Hollywood, with an amused mockery that embraced herself. "It's like the war," I said. "You can laugh at it all when it's over." "Exactly," she said. "And particularly at your own ridiculous self, taking it so seriously." "And you will never return?" "Well, hardly! I haven't heard from anyone there and never expect to hear. ..."

The telephone rang an interruption. "Who is it?" she asked the assistant. "Some studio. ... I don't get the name. ..." Natacha was aghast. . . . "Can you beat that ! Speaking of the devil and. . . . You brought this on!" She went to the phone. "Believe me or not," said she, returning. "They called to ask me where the 'Beaucaire' costumes are that I designed six years ago. Beat that! How in the world should I know where their costumes are?"

"You'll have to go back, Natacha," I said solemnly. "You'll have to go back and find those costumes for them or they'll add *thief* to your string of names." But Natacha was reduced to muttering astonishment and didn't heed me. "Now what on earth possessed them to call me . . . How did they know where I was . . . My heavens!"

Last year Natacha designed the sets and costumes for the American opera at the Champs Elysees Theater in Paris. They received the marked attention of artists and critics. It was suggested that she should return to the cinema as an art director. "You were ahead of your time before," they said.

"Yes, I'm always ahead of my time and getting kicked out for it," mused Natacha. "Never again!

"No sir, I'm content sitting right here," she said, glancing around her shop. "I am a business woman and I shall continue to be one until. ..." A transient shadow passed over her eyes, a trifle weary, and I knew the vaulting spirit of Natacha had touched futility "until I can go off to live in an adobe shack with some books, at the end of nowhere. ..."

She looked at me now, the amused expression she had maintained through the conversation faded out.

"I am glad Rudie died when he did; while the world still adored him. The death of his popularity would have been a thousand deaths to him. Rudie belonged to the age of romance. He brought it with him; it went with him. I think it was a climax he would have wished. I'm sure of it."

I said, "He died still in that fabulous dream of romance such as few men on earth have had, so the tragedy of awakening was averted. And I believe the last words he would have spoken were those that wrung our hearts in "The Four Horsemen," the words of *Julio* dying in a trench in France: *Je suis content.*

Rudolph Valentino and his wife Natacha Rambova swimming in the Tahquitz Canyon Falls in Palm Springs, California

Who Was Cassio?

By
Evelyn Zumaya

Natacha Rambova's Last & Lost Movie

In 2017, I authored a book on Rudolph Valentino's second wife, Natacha Rambova titled, *Astral Affairs Rambova.* I felt one time frame in her life story was not covered in sufficient historical detail; the immediate days following her separation from Valentino and her subsequent year's involvement in specifically spiritualism. For a period of four years, Natacha Rambova immersed herself in the occult; holding seances and traveling with her personal psychic George Wehner. *Astral Affairs Rambova* is the story and documentation of those years.

As I neared completion of the book, I received an article from an archivist in London which was clipped from *The Exhibitor's Herald and Moving Picture World* and dated August 25, 1928. The article was an advertisement for a movie titled, *Who Am I?* starring Natacha Rambova and an actor, Cassio. There was at that time no mention of this film in Natacha's history or filmography and I could scarcely believe what I was reading. Yet, there it was, an image of Natacha Rambova seated left, facing forward and to her left an actor in mid conversation with the caption reading,

"Right: Star and feminine lead in a feature-length comedy made by the Prince Film Producing Company. Cassio, Italian comedian, heads the cast of *'Who Am I?'* in which he is supported by Natacha Rambova, widow of Valentino, who is shown with Cassio here. The picture is the first of a series being directed by John L. McCutcheon."

A search of "Rambova and Cassio" in newspaper archives revealed a few more mentions in which Cassio was billed as the "The European Charlie Chaplin", "Comedy Star of International Fame" and "A Cousin of Rudolph Valentino. [1] It was alleged he was sponsored in America by an ex-official of the Italian government, Joseph Cassisi. [2] In one article Cassio was referred to as an Italian Cavaliere; a prestigious honor bestowed on

---

1   Ibid.
2   *New York Daily News*, June 26, 1928.

notable Italians by the King of Italy, then King Vittorio Emanuelle III.

These articles advertising the movie, *Who Am I?* shared more thrilling news. Natacha Rambova was scheduled to appear in a second film, a "talkie" titled, *That's Nothing* with Cassio and his Prince Film Producing Company of 1480 Broadway at 42nd Street, New York City [3] Did Natacha Rambova make a talking film? Was there actually a recording of her voice?

My first reaction to news of this film was that I found its timing mystifying. At the time of its release in the summer of 1928, Natacha Rambova was involved in other serious endeavors and seemingly had gone down her many other paths. That summer she granted several interviews to announce her dress shop was such a success she was expanding into the wholesale market. She was also involved with both the Theosophical Society and the Roerich Society and enjoying the early days of her love affair with Svetoslav Roerich. She had not appeared in a movie in three years and her few stage appearances since that time were nothing to write home about. So I wondered, how was she convinced to appear in *Who Am I*? And who was Cassio? Why did this film have no mention in her history or filmography?

I set out to learn all I could about Cassio and began by contacting the Cineteca di Bologna in Italy; a prestigious European film library. I forwarded my request for information and they replied saying they had nothing in their archives regarding Cassio's career in Italy or in Europe. They did find references to him regarding his American films. The most important information I learned from the Cineteca di Bologna was that Cassio's birth name was "Dominic Nicassio".

An online search of ship's manifests revealed a listing of Dominic Nicassio's initial arrival in New York aboard the vessel "Guiseppe Verdi" arriving on August 26, 1922 from Naples. He was then twenty-five years old and his occupation listed as "Artist". He was born in Canneto di Bari and was the son of Gennaro Nicassio and Vita Gaetana Cesarea Guglielmi.

At this point in my Cassio quest, the London archivist forwarded a link to the Sixth-Annual Silent Film Identification Workshop investigating "Mostly-Lost Films", sponsored by the Library of Congress in June of 2017 and held in Culpeper, Virginia at the Packard Campus for Audio Visual Conservation. One of the film historians participating in the event was Dr. Robert J. Kiss who delivered a lecture titled, "Silent Film's Most Forgotten Star? The Lost Italian-American Laughter of Cassio."

I contacted Dr. Kiss and he shared his Cassio research including the images he used in his lecture and a transcript of his speech. The history of Natacha Rambova's last and lost movie began to take shape.

---

3   *The Exhibitor's Herald and Moving Picture World*, August 25, 1928.

Dr. Kiss' lecture focused on the silent genre he refers to as, "...the fly-by-night world of poverty-row, silent comedy films shot in and around New York City during the 1920's." [4] His particular attention was paid to "...East Coast Italian-American poverty row comedies produced between 1923-1929." [5]

According to Dr. Kiss, Dominic Nicassio changed his name to Cassio after getting the idea from the "Cassio Film Company" which was owned and operated by his cousin Trifone Nicassio and his father Vittore.

Cassio began his career in America as a member of a vaudeville act performing as the "DeRosa's". It was there he met his wife, Valentina in 1925. Cassio then collaborated with his cousin Trifone and Uncle Vittore to learn the business of comedy film making. He would soon establish his own business, The Boheme Film Company and partner with Caterina Avella.

Caterina Avella not only acted in Cassio's Boheme Film Company films but wrote the screenplays. The short comedic films produced by Cassio and written by Avella addressed themes specific to the Italian immigrant population such as proficiency in English and Americanization in general.

CASSIO

Comedy Star of International Fame

Current Production

"WHO AM I?"

Supported by

NATACHA RAMBOVA

1547 BROADWAY   NEW YORK CITY

By the beginning of 1928, Cassio changed the name of his company to the Prince Film Productions Company. He announced he was again collaborating with actress and screenplay writer, Caterina Avella on a full feature movie titled, *Who Am I?* which was scheduled to be filmed at the Pathé Manhattan Studios. The bigger news was that *Who Am I?* would feature an appearance by none other than Natacha Rambova.

In Cassio's promotion for this film, he made a few additions to his bio. In advance of his screen appearance with Natacha Rambova, Cassio marketed himself as "Domencio Cassio Guglielmi" and alleged he was "Rudolph Valentino's cousin". His personal promos included the titles of "Cav." short for "Cavaliere" and "U Barese", which is an Italian Province of Puglia slang expression meaning "The man from Bari". [6]

In his lecture, Dr. Kiss points out that although Cassio's mother's surname was Guglielmi, as was Valentino's, and although Cassio came from a city only thirty miles from Valentino's birthplace of Castellaneta, he was unable to find any genealogical

---

4   Transcript of lecture by Dr. Robert James Kiss.
5   Ibid.
6   *Film Daily,* March 2, 1927 and *Motion Pictures*, February 18, 1927.

connection between the two men.

At this point in my research, I contacted the expert researcher Professor Aurelio Miccoli, noted Valentino historian living in Castellaneta, in the Region of Puglia and Valentino's birthplace. While researching his book on Rudolph Valentino's childhood, *The Infancy of the Myth*, he became familiarized with local archives, genealogical resources and was locally renown as a scholar studying the history of Rudolph Valentino's family. Professor Miccoli agreed to investigate any connection between Cassio and Rudolph Valentino's families. Was there a connection which might explain why Natacha Rambova would agree to appear in Cassio's film? Did Rudolph Valentino have a cousin producing Italian-American comedy films in New York in the 1920's?

Professor Miccoli first located Cassio's birth certificate and his parent's marriage certificate in the archive of the city of Adelfia; a city created in 1927 through the unification of two small cities, Canneto and Montrone. Cassio was born in Canneto on November 28, 1897, with his mother being Vita Gaetana Cesarea Guglielmi, his father Gennaro Niccasio and his brother christened Vincenzo.

Professor Miccolo's search for existing family members in the Puglia region was successful. Through his local connections with historians, an interview was arranged between Professsor Miccoli and Cassio's great-nephew, a lawyer and actor Avv. (Italian prefix for lawyer) Gianni Monteleone of Adelphia.

Mr. Gianni Monteleone shared the family's history regarding Cassio with Professor Miccoli. He is the great-nephew of Cassio. His maternal grandfather was Cassio's brother Vincenzo, his great grandmother Vita Gaetana Cesarea Guglielmi who was a cousin of Valentino's father Giovanni Guglielmi. Mr. Monteleone recalled how his mother attributed their artistic interests as a family to their famous relative Rudolph Valentino. "We are all artists!" she told her son.

During Professor Miccoli's interview with Mr. Monteleone, he was invited to photograph a collection of framed images of Cassio's American film career which were prominately displayed in the Monteleone home. There were many family stories shared about their artistic and colorful relative, Cassio; including his chronological history and the mention of his passion and sensibility for beautiful women.

Professor Miccoli had confirmed the familial connection between Cassio and Rudolph Valentino. This presented further questions; did Rudolph Valentino know his cousin Dominic in Italy? Had they met in New York when Cassio was preforming in his vaudeville act as the "DeRosa's"? When did Natacha Rambova first meet Cassio?

From the time lines of both Rudolph Valentino and Cassio's lives, it can be surmised that they could have met in New York after 1923 as they were both living in the city at the time. It is not known whether they were close in Italy before Valentino left for America in 1913. With only a two year age difference between the two cousins, it is possible that as teen-agers they spent time together. With the connection between the two men confirmed, I was intrigued to know more about Rambova's last movie

In Dr. Kiss' speech, he surmises the plot of *Who Am I?* as no copy of the script has been located to date. He pieced the basic plotline together from the scant press coverage and a few surviving images. The story line appears to have been centered around Cassio's character having amnesia and his confusion over whether his wife was a plain woman, played by Camille Renault [7] or Natacha Rambova, "the woman who always wore the pearls."

Perhaps Cassio was inspired to use the subject of amnesia in the film's script by reading the headlines in Italian-American newspapers at the time. In Italy in 1927, the high profile case of Bruneri and Canella was then holding audiences rapt. Emotions about the case ran high with Italian-American populations divided over the gripping drama.

The case involved the story of a man named Canella, a World War One amnesia victim who wandered lost in Northern Italy and an impostor, Bruneri, who came forward to assume Canella's identity. The impostor Bruneri resembled Canella and would actually convince Canella's wife he was her lost husband well enough she would bear three children with him. Even when the court ruled Bruneri a total fraud, Canella's wife was not convinced and left for Brazil with the man she believed to be her husband, the bandit Bruneri. Did the story on all the front pages of Italian-American newspapers at the time inspire Cassio's *Who Am I?*

On July 2, 1928, Cassio began distributing his first full length movie, *Who Am I?* by having it shown in East Coast Italian-American theaters. He appeared confidant with his success in having Natacha Rambova star in his film and made an announcement on August 22, 1928, revealing his new invention which he called, "Moviesound".

"A new talking device will be used by the Prince Film Company for a series of features starring Cassio, Italian-American comedian and cousin of Rudolph Valentino.

It is known as 'Moviesound' and is a brand new patent different from those now on the market. Cassio has completed his first independent picture, *Who Am I?* and will

---

7   Camille Renault was an actress who promoted herself as being French but she was from Kokomo, Indiana.

make *That's Nothing* a talking picture as his second feature-length comedy." [8]

According to Dr. Kiss, in an article published in *Cinemagraphico* published in Rome on October 7, 1928, it was revealed Cassio was not so well known in Europe. As some of his personal promotional claims were questioned, he struggled to secure a broad enough audience for *Who Am I?* With box-office returns meager, Cassio lost money on its release and his Prince Films Production Company went bankrupt. There was also no money to invest in his Moviesound device or in his next film *That's Nothing*, a talkie slated to star Natacha Rambova.

By August of 1929, Cassio was unable to pay the rent at the Lloyd's Film Storage Facility and all twenty reels of his footage were sold at auction. Prince Film Company and Cassio's career as a film producer folded. Cassio returned to the vaudeville circuit but would surface one year later in Dayton, Ohio.

According to the local newspapers in September of 1930, "Cavaliere Cassio" announced he would be opening the Aum European Studios in Dayton on October fifteenth. His studio would offer a broad curriculum; "Dramatic Courses, Taught for Opera, Drama Talkies, Stage and Screen." [9] Cassio's press release promoted himself as Rudolph Valentino's cousin and states he spent the previous two years as the director of the Paramount Conservatory of Art in New York. [10]

Cassio's school of operatic instruction announced that one of his "Italian artist teachers" would be Carla Castellani. Carla Castellani was a well-known soprano then singing in La Scala in Milan and as she would not visit the United States until the fall of 1946 when she made her American debut touring the country singing in *Tosca*," it appears Cassio's Aum European Studios never realized.

According to his great-nephew, Mr. Gianni Monteleone, Cassio then returned to his home town in southern Italy with his wife and young son Gennaro. It was then he organized many dramatic productions and stage shows in Puglia which were well received.

In 1935, a ship's manifest lists Cassio, "Dominic Nicassio" and his wife Valentina and son Gennaro as passengers arriving in New York City. Cassio and his wife would divorce in September of 1939 and he moved to Providence, Rhode Island to find work as an actor.

Dr. Kiss reported that after a stage performance in Providence, Rhode Island on April 19, 1940, Cassio collapsed and died of a heart attack at forty-two years old. Curiously, a United States Census worker recorded a Dominic Nicassio, "actor" as a lodger at 84 Broadway in Providence on April 24, 1940. [12]

---

8   *Exhibtor's Daily Review,* archive.
9   Aum European Studios advertisement, *Dayton Daily News,* Sept. 21, 1930.
10 "Will Have Direction of Aum European Studio Here", *Dayton Daily News* September 28, 1930.
11 "Opera Schedule", *Chicago Tribune*, October 13, 1946 and October 20, 1946.
12 The Sixteenth Census of the United States, 1940.

Perhaps the reason for Natacha Rambova's appearance in Cassio's one full-length movie was found in a small mention in the French publication, *Ciné-Comœdia*. It is reported she made the film because she and Rudolph Valentino promised Cassio they would help him.[13] The article was titled, "A Family Affair" and read:

"Cassio, cousin of Rudolph Valentino, has remained in excellent terms with Natacha Rambova. The wife of the celebrated artist had promised Cassio that she would not to lose sight of him and even, on occasion, offered to help him. This was not a promise in the air, since we learn that Cassio has made two films including one scheduled to be a talkie. Cassio, on the screen, will remain Cassio. This is a wise decision even heroic, because it is certain that Valentino's name has tempted him very often. But this is due to the fact that Valentino's brother, Albert, comes to Hollywood to make sensational debuts in the film titled: Tropic Madness. Albert, himself, will be called Valentino, whose real name, like his brother, was Guglielmi. Let us wish him to have, as we say, backbone, because although it's a wonderful inheritance, it appears heavy to bear."

Dr. Kiss poses the question; if Cassio was a Guglielmi relative why had he not made mention of this earlier when Valentino died in 1926. This could be explained as Cassio had no audience to explain this to at the time. But the question also arises; was Valentino's brother, Alberto Guglielmi, then in Hollywood pursuing his own movie career, in contact with Cassio?

Alberto Guglielmi was then in the throes of aggressively policing his brother's legacy and certainly would have protested the use of his deceased brother's name, if the connection was false. Perhaps Alberto Guglielmi hoped his cousin's Prince Film

---

13 *Ciné-Comœdia,* February 14, 1929. "Affaires de Famille - Cassio, cousin de Rudolph Valentino, était demeuré en excellents termes avec Natacha Rambova. Celle qui fut la femme du célèbre artiste avait promis a Cassio de ne pas le perdre de vue et même, à l'occasion, de l'aider. Ce n'était pas là promesse en l'air, puisque nous apprenons que Cassio doit débuter prochainement dans deux films dont l'un sera parlant. Cassio, à l'écran, restera Cassio. Voilà une résolution sage qui peut- être même héroïque, car il est certain que le nom de Valentino e du le tenter bien souvent. Mais ceci s'explique du fait que le frère de Valentino, Albert, vient de faire, à Hollywood, des débuts sensationnels dans le film intitulé: La Folie des Tropiques. Albert, lui, s'appellera naturellement Valentino, comme son frère, dont le vrai nom, d'ailleurs, était Guglielmi. Souhaitons-lui d'avoir, comme on le dit, les reins solides évidemment un héritage merveilleux, mais combien lourd à porter."

Producing Company would offer him screen roles. After two years attempting to replace his brother Rudolph on screen, Alberto Guglielmi appeared in one movie, *Tropic Madness* which opened in December of 1928. Was there an affiliation between Cassio and Alberto Guglielmi? Perhaps so. For coincidentally, while Cassio was promoting *Who Am I?*, an Alberto Production Company was also producing Italian-American short films.

Could Cassio's reels of footage, sold at auction in 1929, still exist in some archive? Will Natacha Rambova's last screen appearance be found; a movie she made as a favor to her lost love Rudolph's cousin?

The photograph of the cast of *Who Am I?*, which Mr. Monteleone so generously shared for inclusion in this book, reveals a cordial grouping including the cast, the cameraman and director. Natacha Rambova sits demurely bestowing a supportive glance towards Valentino's cousin who cast her in her final screen role as the woman who always wore pearls. Her appearance in this lost film stands as the definitive footnote of her love for Rudolph.

The Frank E. Campbell Archive
The Sarcophagus
The Frank Mallen Composographs

Receipt for the floral delivery displayed around Rudolph
Valentino's bier in Frank E. Campbell's Gold Room

Finding the Sarcophagus of Rudolph Valentino

by
Evelyn Zumaya

The interview had all the elements of a scene right out of an Alfred Hitchcock movie; a Peter Lorre look-alike mortician, tastefully blacked-out mortuary windows and air sickeningly sweet with a mother lode of fresh blooms awaiting the morning's funeral. In search of details about Rudolph Valentino's death, I traveled a long, long way for this interview. Despite the macabre setting and the fact that the gracious mortician was far too welcoming for my comfort, I forged on. Perhaps my uneasiness was due to the chilling realization he was employed by a corporation proudly billing themselves as the, "world's largest death-care provider."

At some point during the interview, I was asked if I'd ever heard of Valentino's second coffin. The mortician explained how it had long been rumored within the funeral business that an outer casket encased Valentino's coffin on the train ride from New York to Los Angeles. I said I knew nothing about an outer casket and asked why such a case would have been used. He went on explaining how in order to transport a corpse across state lines, coffins were required by Federal law to be encased in a sarcophagus or shipping case. Valentino's coffin was encased in just such a shipping case which was custom-made for the journey and believed to still be in existence. Although the mortician claimed he had no idea where the case was located, he promised to make a few phone calls to see what he could find out.

That was the end of our discussion of the shipping case and I proceeded to photograph the Valentino file on record in Campbell's archive which included the lengthy invoice for services rendered, paid in full and a massive scrapbook of newspapers clippings.

For a short while after that interview I had no clue my presence at Campbell's piqued interest in the location of Valentino's shipping case. The imaginations of several morticians were indeed sparked and this inspired a covert operation to locate and capitalize on the missing shipping case. About one month after the interview, I opened an e-mail from "the world's largest death-care provider" to see photographs of a metal coffin loading onto the screen. While the images were downloading, I received a call from the mortician with news this was Valentino's shipping case. Furthermore he'd found the owner and was trying to secure permission for me see the hidden treasure.

I told him I thought the piece should be authenticated by an expert and once again asked him for the owner's contact information. With this he said he would get back to me and hung up. I would have to be content with the thrilling photographs for a while longer. Yet almost immediately, the intrigue surrounding the location of the case and the identity of the owner became so intense I began to wonder if I would ever see it.

The mortician called me several times to update me on the status of my request to see the case. He also asked me what I thought the cash value of such a piece could be.

I told him I didn't have the slightest idea of its monetary value and reminded him I was only interested in its history.

I prepared to move as soon as I was given a go ahead and assumed I would make a quick trip to wherever, snap a few pictures and have my story. Instead, I soon landed squarely in the middle of heady negotiations for the sale of the shipping case and would risk my neck for a just a few moments with Rudy's mythical sarcophagus.

The Rudolph Valentino Sarcophagus - Image

Access to the actual case complicated, as the mortician made his power play to position himself as the only contact with the owner and thereby cash in on any deal the shipping case's owner might make. Granting new meaning to the word cagey, he brainstormed an elaborate but thinly-constructed system of communication to guarantee his role.

He asked me not to call him at work, to only call him through a second contact, to use his cell number and personal e-mail, etc. and I was never given the owner's name. As he began his methodical and territorial watch over the artifact, the welcoming host who greeted me in his office a few months earlier morphed into agent OO undertaker.

He informed me the owner was interested in selling the shipping case and added he'd run into a snag because a few of his mortician cronies heard about the case's impending sale and were scheming for their cut. The mortician was thoroughly dismayed at this turn of events and lamented to me about it. He was so distressed and paranoid at the deteriorating status of his gambit, I could almost hear the sweat beading on his forehead.

Ignoring the cloak and dagger, I called the cell phone of mortician's mystery contact number two and after some doing, I was at long last given an address where I could view the case. I scheduled immediate travel arrangements and boarded a plane for Los Angeles. Within a few hours I landed, rented a car at the airport and was following my usually unreliable MapQuest directions to the designated address.

Interior of the sarcophagus cover with inscription - Image courtesy of Frank E. Campbell, All Rights Reserved

The address was that of a mortuary located deep in some inner city skid row real estate. It was the kind of neighborhood no prudent soul would dare cross without a police escort. Nevertheless, it was easy to imagine a time when the establishment could have been surrounded by a more Mayberry-like backdrop. But on the morning of my appointment the streets were alive and humming with prostitutes pacing for work, homeless campers organizing their life's possessions on the sidewalk, and wild-eyed, ranting desperados preaching to whomever would listen.

Having arrived a few minutes early, I made a quick dash into a nearby McDonalds for a sorely needed cup of coffee. This was no predictable Micky Dee safe zone that sunny morning. After noticing several of the tables were burned char black in an apparently substantial blaze and that the disheveled, armed guard posted in front of the counter was swaying and half conscious, I made what I hoped would be a subtle retreat to my rental car. I failed miserably only to be followed through the parking lot by a squirrley-eyed teenager. At this point I made the executive decision to spend the remaining few minutes before my private viewing of Rudolph Valentino's long lost shipping case sipping my coffee in the safety of the rental car driving around the block.

Meanwhile inside the mortuary, the bronze and copper casket was being dragged out of its warehouse storage for the first time in seventy-seven years. Like a great vessel run aground, the case was so cumbersome it took three mortuary workers to heft the unwieldy bark onto a mortuary gurney. They had their orders to have the neglected relic on display in one of their private chapels by nine o'clock sharp. Just before the hour they wheeled the shipping case into the small sanctuary, lifted off the heavy cover and propped it against the wall.

It was up to the floor mortician that morning to oversee the arrangements in each of the mortuary chapels and it was during his inspection of the shipping case installation he noticed an inscription on the casket's tarnished lid. After retrieving a can of brass polish from his office he began to wipe away the years of neglect. The inscription read, "Rudolfo Gugliemi, Rudolph Valentino, Born May 6, 1895, Died August 23, 1926." The mortician found the inscription curious because his name also happened to be Rudolph.

Mortician Rudy had just finished his brass polishing when I arrived. He escorted me into the side chapel off the lobby where the gurney was positioned in front of several rows of church pews. After months of anticipation, I paused to appreciate the point blank impact of the moment. The e-mailed photographs did this masterpiece no justice.

Inscription on cover with Guglielmi mispelled

The case was in extraordinary condition and appeared to have been hand made. The delicate beads of solder were so expertly placed I was sure some jeweler in 1926 must have labored an eternity in its execution. In his best professional whisper, mortician Rudy left the chapel telling me to take my time. He didn't seem sure why I was there and probably wondered why I would come so far to sit in a church pew paying my respects to an empty casket.

I was there to document the objet d'art and as soon as he departed I got down to work. The case was mine to investigate and inspect from all angles so I set up my tripod and took a quick twenty or thirty photographs. I brushed my hand along its dusty interior and examined the detailed tooling of the handles. Scratch marks from the transport of Valentino's interior coffin were still evident. The mortician had polished the cover of the case to a brilliant shine and I noticed Guglielmi was misspelled.

Staring into the long metal box it was hard not to visualize its cargo of long ago. It was in this case Rudolph Valentino's lifeless body jostled along the rails on his last ride home to California. I felt no subtle twinge at that thought and at the evidence before me of the brutal honesty of Valentino's death. After weeks of negotiating access to view the shipping case, I was suddenly gripped by the desire to pack up my briefcase and camera and get as far away as I could from the grisly find.

I stopped by Mortician Rudy's office on my way out to shake his hand and thank him for his time. Before I left I decided to have a stab at it and asked him directly if he could give me the owner's name. Apparently he had not been briefed on the subterfuge preventing me from knowing the identity of the case's owner. For with no hesitation he jotted down the man's name and phone number. I thanked him again, dashed back to the rental car, and headed off to the airport and home.

When I placed the call to the case's owner, he granted me a stilted interview but was slightly confused as to how I got his number, assuming I was an interested buyer. I finally had the story and photographs but it would be a bit longer before I could make any graceful exit from the thorny subject of the shipping case. I realized my error in telling the mortician at Campbell's that I had spoken with the shipping case's owner, when he became immediately paranoid I would compromise his deal. I assured him I would not reveal the owner's name to anyone out of courtesy for his arranging my viewing of the case.

Within a few days I made another trip to Los Angeles for an interview with Valentino memorabilia collector, Bill Self. Like the naive child of the Valentino world I was at that time, I told him excitedly about my find and how I had seen the case. I showed him the photographs, did not tell him I knew who the owner was and left to fly home to San Francisco.

Like any other artifact pertaining to Rudolph Valentino, from the moment the case was discovered its cash value increased with each passing day. The day after my visit with Bill Self, the mortician called me to say he had spoken with Self and learned he was also interested in buying the case.

Self then sent me an e-mail informing me he had just spoken with the mortician at Campbell's and added he had already seen the shipping case that day, was in contact with the owner and about to refuse the mortician's offer to buy it for $15,000. I called Self and asked him how he learned the identity of the owner. He told me he recognized the case from a photograph of Valentino's coffin being offloaded and knew the mortuary was one belonging to the Cunningham family. Incredibly, they were still in business and still had possession of the shipping case. Bill Self had his hands on that case within five minutes of my leaving his home that day.

Of course the mortician suspected I betrayed him by telling Self the owner's name which I had not, but his hopes for the ready cash fell through. Although Bill Self told me the price of the shipping case was too steep for him, in hindsight I believe at that point Self already had that case in his collection. I asked Self a few times if he knew what ever happened to the shipping case but he never gave me an answer.

According to Campbell's records, the case originally cost nine hundred dollars. This would be about $9000 today. Two other charges were added to the original cost of the shipping case; a mechanic was paid fifteen dollars to solder the base to a brace in the train car and an engraver was paid twenty-five dollars to misspell Rudy's name on the cover.

The unexpected appearance of this artifact confirms there are still treasures to be found and new stories to be told about Rudolph Valentino. I lament I told Self about the shipping case because as is the case with almost every other Rudolph Valentino artifact, this museum piece has vanished into a secret archive of some private collector, never to be seen by Valentino's public again.

I never heard from the mortician at Campbell's again and I think he waited a bit too long to close a deal on the shipping case. He and I underestimated Bill Self's ability to find the owner and arrive with the cash in hand.

The Frank E. Campbells' scrapbook documenting the news coverage during Valentino's repose in the Gold Room

Pola Negri Verges on Collapse—Three

POLA NEGRI COLLAPSES AT BIER OF SCREEN SHEIK. The reputed fiancee of Rudolph Valentino, near to the point of breakdown, is shown in the doorway, on the arm of George Ullman, Valentino's friend and manager, who forced the crowds to get the actress to her motor.

Body of Valentino Lies in State in New York

Unending Stream Again Passes Valentino's Bier

Crowd Is Orderly and Reverent After Riots of Tuesday in Which 100 Were Hurt; Visitors Genuflect, Bless Themselves.

NEW YORK, Aug. 25.—(I. N. S.)—An unending stream of people, formed into a line six deep for blocks, today passed into Campbell's funeral church on Broadway, where the body of Rudolph Valentino lies in state, and paid tribute to the famous motion picture star. Fully 10,000 were in the surging crush of humanity. They passed the casket at the rate of eighty a minute.

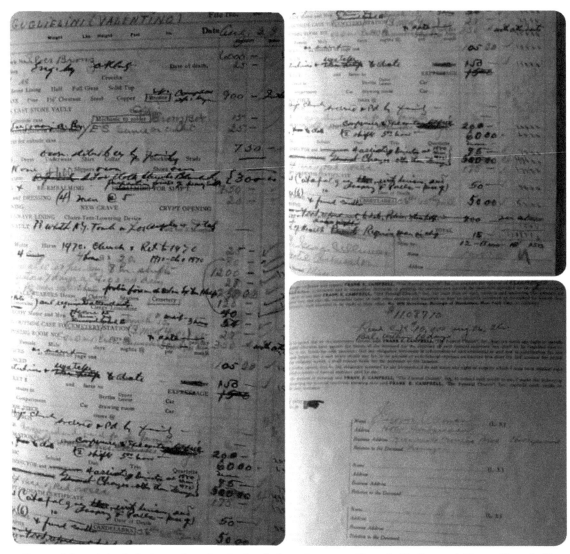

Some of the original photographs taken in the darkened room at Campbell's Funeral Home. Campbell's scans of these records follow.

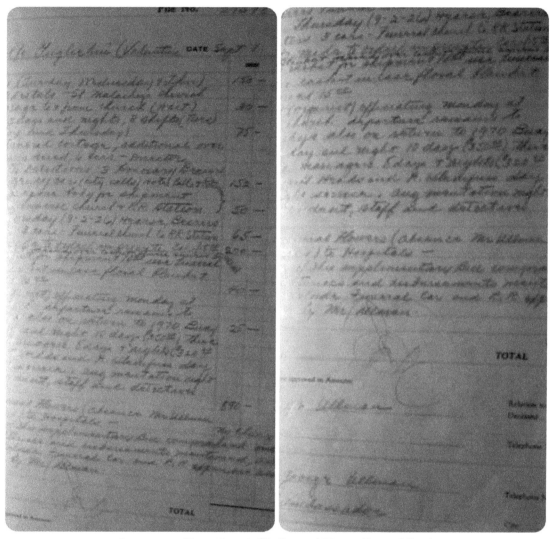

Invoices on file in Campbell's Funeral Home. (Scans follow)

I hereby authorize and request **FRANK E. CAMPBELL**, "The Funeral Church", Inc., to conduct the funeral of _Rudolfo_
Guglielmi deceased, and in connection therewith to perform the services and furnish the materials specified on the pages attached
hereto. I agree to pay said **FRANK E. CAMPBELL**, "The Funeral Church," Inc., for each item of such services and materials the amount set
opposite such item, and also the reasonable value of such other services and materials as may be properly rendered or furnished by him in connection therewith; such payment to be made at their office, **No. 1970 Broadway, Borough of Manhattan, New York City,** as follows:

$11,087.10

Recd Ck $10,000 Aug. 26, 26.
Bal. within 10 days.

It is agreed that by the acceptance thereof, said **FRANK E. CAMPBELL**, "The Funeral Church", Inc., does not waive any right or remedy
which he would otherwise have against the Estate of the deceased for the recovery of such funeral expenses, nor shall he be required first to
have recourse to the Estate for such payment; that my obligation hereunder is independent of and additional to and not in substitution for the
liability of said Estate; that if said estate should pay for or on account of such funeral expenses an amount less than the full amount for which
I have hereby obligated myself, I shall remain liable for the payment of the balance.

It is further agreed, that by the obligation assumed by me hereunder, I do not waive any right or remedy which I may have against said
Estate for reimbursement of funeral expenses paid by me.

For the purpose of inducing said **FRANK E. CAMPBELL**, "The Funeral Church", Inc., to extend such credit to me, I make the following
statement concerning my financial condition, knowing that said **FRANK E. CAMPBELL**, "The Funeral Church", Inc., extends such credit in
reliance upon such statement:

Contracting party
must fill this in ☞

Name _S. George Ullman_ (L. S.)
Address _Hotel Ambassador_
Business Address _7000 Santa Monica Blvd (Hollywood)_
Relation to the Deceased _Manager_

Name _____ (L. S.)
Address _____
Business Address _____
Relation to the Deceased _____

Name _____ (L. S.)
Address _____

_This initial contract between Frank E. Campbell and S. George Ullman reveals Ullman paid a
deposit check of $10,000.00 personally, with the balance due in ten days. The total cost of
Valentino's Funeral being $11,087. Image courtesy of Frank E. Campbell – All Rights
Reserved._

Name GUGLIELINI VALENTINO   File No. **27598**

FUNERAL DIRECTOR

FUNERAL SERVICE AT *St Mali*   Day *MON.*   Date *AUG. 30* at *11 A*

Officiating Clergyman—REV.   MASONIC   EL

Do we Order Clergyman YES—NO   Ordered By

INTER   CREMATE *Woodlawn Rec. Vault*   City   S

On *Monday*   Date *Aug 30 after Service*   M

EXPRESS—BAGGAGE VIA   Railroad   at
S/S Line on

Funeral Director to meet family at Bureau of Information   Minutes Be
Train Time

SPECIAL INSTRUCTIONS

Clothing will be delivered to 1970 by family on *all dressed*   at

Clothing to be called for by us at   on   at

Casket to be delivered   Day   Date   at

Casket to remain closed thruout service

Candelabra   Chairs to be delivered   at

We are to
Family will Notify out of Town Undertaker

Will arrange time body will go in church later

NEW YORK, N. Y.

The office of _____ Cemetery is hereby authorized to open up

indicated on dia

on

Time of arrival at Cemetery _____ M.—Evergreen Lining _____ Lowering Device _____ Tent

From Campbell's ledger - Image Courtesy of Frank E. Campbell, All Rights Reserved

Rudolfo Guglielmi (Valentino DATE Sept 1 19 26

	AMOUNT		
Gold Room (Tuesday, Wednesday & Thur) Bronze Pedestals — St Malachy's church	150 —	150 0	
truck cartage to & from church (wait) Watchers 3 days and nights, 3 shifts (Tues)	30 —	30 0	
Wednesday and Thursday)	75 —	75 0	
Livery — Funeral cortege, additional over first bill rendered, 6 cars — Director, Flowers, City Detectives, 3 Honorary Bearers also emergency cars (city calls) Hotel Calls & Return	152 —	152 0	
Service to prepare body for shipment Page Bearers Funeral church & R.R. Station	50 —	50 0	
Livery Thursday (9-2-26) Hearse, Bearers — Directors 3 cars — Funeral church to RR Station	65 —	65 0	
Supports, Media to order in private Car (15°° ... Getting outfit for shipment 70°° use Funeral ... Lead box casket in case floral Blanket is not used 15°°	200 —	200 0	
	40 —	40 0	
Mr Hall (organist) officiating monday at funeral church departure remains to t Malachys also on return to 1970 Bway	25 —	25 0	
Mr Hull day and night 10 day (350°°) Three resident Managers 8 days & nights (320°° department Heads and H. Klukfuns day and night service, augmentation night superintendent, staff and detectives 220°°)	890 —	890 0	
special funeral Flowers (absence Mr Ullman instructions) to Hospitals —	no charge		
the items of this supplementary Bill comprised only services, materials and disbursements mentioned, and do not include Funeral car and R.R. expenses assumed personally by Mr Ullman.			
TOTAL			

Specifications & charges relating to the transport of Valentino's coffin from New York to California. S. George Ullman's signature partially obscured. Image Courtesy of Frank E. Campbell, All Rights Reserved

192

Campbell's itemized invoice for services rendered - Image Courtesy of Frank E. Campbell, All Rights Reserved

Frank Mallen's Composographs

An authoritative account of the New York tabloid's exploitation of Rudolph Valentino's illness, death and funeral can be found in *Sauce For the Gander*[1], published in 1954 by Frank Mallen. Mallen was employed as the picture editor for the most popular tabloid in New York when Valentino died in August of 1926; *The New York Evening Graphic,* known as *"The Graphic".* The paper was relatively short-lived and published by Bernarr MacFadden. Frank Mallen's first-hand account of the tabloid's involvement in Valentino's final hours, the rioting which took place outside Campbell's Funeral Church and his funeral contributes to an accurate telling of this tragic tale.

According to Mallen, the *Graphic* initially believed the report Valentino was admitted to the Polyclinic Hospital to be a movie studio publicity stunt; perhaps orchestrated to promote Valentino's blockbuster new movie *The Son of the Sheik.* When *Graphic* staff discovered Valentino was undergoing surgery, they began their sensationalizing of Valentino's illness. Headlines blared the unthinkable; had he been poisoned, shot by a jealous woman, her husband or lover?

During the first days of Valentino's hospitalization, one tabloid published an edition with a headline reading, "Valentino Dead!" However, beneath this in small letters it read, "Broadway Hears. Doctors Deny." This issue sold in record numbers and launched the media hysteria over Valentino's illness and death. Sensing the potential for a bonanza in sales, the race was on among the tabloid reporters to be the first to grab the next breaking news and the first to snap up the banner photo for their papers coverage.

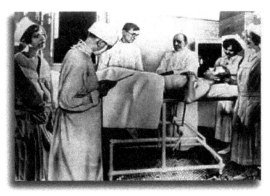

The New York Evening Graphic cosmopograph depicting Rudolph Valentino about to go into surgery

The *Graphic* was known for the creation of composographs; collages depicting locations where a camera could not possibly go, i.e., death beds, police raids, hangings and Valentino being prepped for surgery. In *Sauce for the Gander,* Mallen argues the paper did not create these fake images to fool the public but to enhance a story with illustration. In the case of the full page image of Valentino headed for the operating room, Mallen explains how this composite was the result of a collage using ten photographs and the *Graphic's* staff

---

1 *Sauce for the Gander* by Frank Mallen, Baldwin Books, White Plains, New York, 1954.

posing as nurses and doctors.

According to Frank Mallen, throughout Valentino's illness the tabloids were preparing for his possible death. Meanwhile, the *New York Evening Graphic's* publisher Bernarr MacFadden was selling papers as fast as they flew off the presses. Mallen writes how those presses ran all night long. When news of Valentino's death broke, Mallen says he called Frank E. Campbell of the Campbell's Funeral Church. He claims he told Campbell about Valentino's death when he asked if they had already picked up Valentino's body from the Polyclinic Hospital.

Frank Campbell broke into sobs saying, "It just can't be! No!" It was not minutes later when Campbell struck a deal with the *Graphic's* picture editor, Frank Mallen. Frank Campbell was aggressive publicizing his establishment and maintained a full-time press agent on the payroll; the infamous Harry Klemfuss.

Campbell assured Mallen he would certainly be picking up Valentino's body and then told Mallen to come immediately to the funeral home and bring his photographer. When Mallen arrived, he found the Gold Room where Valentino would lie in repose, already being

Composograph of Rudolph Valentino in the Gold Room at Frank E. Campbell's Funeral Home

arranged for photographs. As Valentino's body had not yet arrived, another coffin with another corpse was positioned into place. With Harry Klemfuss overseeing the proceedings, the photographs were taken and Mallen and his photographer raced back to their offices at the *Graphic* to paste a cut out of Valentino's head onto the hapless corpse they had just photographed at Campbell's. Before Valentino's body ever left the Polyclinic Hospital, the first editions of the *Graphic* hit the streets with a photograph of Valentino already in the Gold Room on the front page.

This inspired the other New York tabloid reporters to descend on Campbell's demanding to know why they gave this scoop to the *Graphic*, Harry Klemfuss said they had no idea how that image of Valentino in his coffin occurred; "Chicanery by the *Graphic*", he claimed! Klemfuss then permitted the reporters to enter the establishment and search the place for themselves to convince them Valentino was not in the Gold Room. After his tour, Klemfuss escorted the reporters to a nearby speakeasy for drinks, paid for by Frank E. Campbell.

From the moment that first image of Valentino in his coffin appeared on the *Graphic* cover, the paper held the lead in coverage. Mallen writes how the reporters from competing tabloids followed his every move hoping he would lead them to the latest scoop. He refers to these other reporters as the "opposition men".

The acting managing editor at the *Graphic*, Weyrauch was horrified and felt this image of Valentino in his coffin was so tasteless it would destroy the paper. When he realized the paper's presses were running all night to meet the demand for Valentino issues, the sound of the coin hitting the coffers outweighed his outrage.

Frank Mallen alleges Frank Campbell made another deal with Valentino's last employer, United Artists' Joe Schenck assuring him the funeral home would keep the news forthcoming to promote Valentino last movie *The Son of the Sheik*.

Pola Negri on the arms of George Ullman and his wife Beatrice

As Valentino's body reposed in Frank E. Campbell's Gold Room, the crowds outside in the street grew to the tens of thousands demanding to pay their final respects to their idol. The hysteria of the crowd was advanced by Frank Mallen at the *Graphic* as well as the other newspapers who were following the *Graphic's* lead in a heated competition for sales. Fake news reports were published, alleging Valentino was drugged or committed suicide. The tabloids published sensational stories advancing the rivalry between Valentino's lovers, Pola Negri and the woman he was with the night he fell ill, Marian Benda.

Valentino's manager, George Ullman is traditionally blamed by many for generating the hysteria in the crowd. Frank Mallen's history of the *Evening Graphic*, refutes this and reveals the tabloids and Frank Campbell's press genius, Harry Klemfuss instigated the frenzy. Frank Mallen includes George Ullman's statement about the mob hysteria surrounding Campbells:

" 'I knew it would have been Valentino's wish that the public – his public – be allowed to see him in death. But I had no idea that the public would act as they did. When I came to the chapel through the surging crowds, it struck me that the way many people were acting was a disgrace. Many women and girls were laughing and giggling. They even giggled as they entered the room where Valentino lay. Some of the men, you would think, were going to a picnic or a three-ringed circus. It was a shock to me. I couldn't do anything else but stop it.' "[2]

According to Mallen, Frank Campbell was plying reporters with not only stories and photo opportunities but with bootleg booze. Campbell's set up ad hoc bars, or "legetions" as Mallen calls them which were designated pop-up speakeasies for reporters.

One such bar was set up in Campbell's basement and this within view of undertakers doing their embalming. The bar itself was set atop coffins. While Valentino rested in a shaky peace upstairs, reporters were drinking illegal liquor in the basement all courtesy of Campbell's. Harry Klemfuss set up other Campbell's free bars in two hotels strategically placed and then a fancier bar for the, "cane carrying type reporters"

---

2 *Sauce for the Gander*, p. 81

in the Hotel Marie Antoinette. Mallen recalls this was a successful venture for all until Campbell received the first bill from his bootleggers.

The riot which took place outside Campbell's Funeral Church was catastrophic with hundreds, including mounted police and their horses injured. Mallen quotes a competitor at the tabloid the *Mirror,* "opposition man" Eddie Doherty, who wrote about the riot:

"Three policemen went through the windows carried by the crowd's impetus, powerless to stem the flood. One was bleeding from a cut on his temple. He stared dizzily. He lifted his club and brought it down. The sidewalk was strewn with glass slivers, with straw hats, with broken umbrellas, with torn pieces of clothing, with odd shoes and rubbers. There went a girl in her stocking feet, weeping hysterically, soaked to the skin, her new hat a ruin. She was crying, 'I must see him!" There was an old woman, holding a shattered umbrella in one hand, a spotty shopping bag in the other and she was crying, 'We will get in. You cannot keep us out!' There were the police charging the crowd, the iron hoofs going click-clack on the wet cement and women screamed and laughed and ran out of the way and then ran back again. The horses had gone into the mob and the mob absorbed them. The policemen use their fists, grab hats, hurl them away, whirl the horses around. Women faint. Women scream. Women fight to get in."[3]

In 1927, Valentino's second wife Natacha Rambova published a book about her life with the star. In this volume, she included a section she titled, "Revelations" which were the transcripts of séances conducted in the weeks after Valentino's death. In these séances Rambova alleged she heard messages from the recently deceased Rudolph Valentino. With the assistance of her personal medium, George Wehner, the messages from Valentino on the astral plane were channeled and transcribed.[4]

The Graphic's composograph illustration for Natacha Rambova's, "Revelations" depicting Valentino with Enrico Caruso on the astral plane.

Natacha presented her manuscript to her friend Bernarr MacFadden and he seized the opportunity and published the "Revelations" in serial format in the *New York Evening Graphic.* Again, picture editor Frank Mallen created the illustrations as composographs. The covers of the *Graphic* portrayed Valentino in heaven with Enrico Caruso and speaking in the great beyond with the founder of theosophy, Helena Blavatsky.

The *Graphic's* composographs by Frank Mallen hold an iconic place in Rudolph

---

3   Ibid., p. 79
4   Rambova's "Revelations" are published in their entirety in *Astral Affairs Rambova.*

Valentino's legacy. Frank Mallen's account reveals how the furor and hysteria was created and exploited by the tabloids and how Valentino's manager George Ullman was not involved in the tabloid's tactics at the time. The Mallen history also reveals the extent of Frank E. Campbell's influence over the tabloids and complicity with the tabloids.

The Deceased Man Who is So Troubling New York

Published in the Turin newspaper, *La Stampa*, Turin, August 27, 1926

Ada – Photo Courtesy of Vincenzo Filomarino, All Rights Reserved

*The Story of Rudolph Valentino as Related by his Sister-in-law
Translated by Renato Floris*

Through a fortunate happenstance, we found ourselves engaging in a conversation with a close relative of Rudolph Valentino, the film star who just passed away with news of his passing filling newspapers around the world. A brother of the famous actor, Alberto Guglielmi, ex-major in the army, who left the military service to devote himself to the film business in his brother's career, was in Paris for professional reasons. His wife was in Turin on her way to meet her husband in France, when news of the death of her relative was broadcast. Immediately, Mr. Guglielmi joined his wife in our city and then left for America. The lady, on the other hand, is still in Turin and residing in an elegant hotel. We spoke with her, the sister-in-law of Rodolfo Valentino; a young, very distinguished gentle lady.

She greeted us with gestures of exquisite kindness. The pain is too recent and acute when she begins to speak of the deceased and her eyes fill with tears and her voice trembles.

"Dead at thirty-one, imagine! And we left him, my husband and I only a month ago when he was so full of life and hope! We said goodbye in New York on July 24th. Rodolfo came from Los Angeles with us to accompany us and to attend the premiere of his film in New York. This was to take place on the 26th, two days later. Who could have thought such a catastrophe could occur? Once in Italy, we received the first sad telegram from his secretary. Rodolfo, returning to his room one evening, passed out while pressing his hands to his stomach. A lightning attack of appendicitis. Then came the operation, the complications, the peritonitis and the end!"

199

Little by little the lady is reassured and she shows us a large photograph of Rudolph Valentino, in the costume of his latest character; dressed in a sumptuous oriental costume and a large turban with his face austere, exhausted. At the bottom of the photograph; a dedication by Rudolph, in round, clear handwriting, as that of a man of position.

Mrs. Guglielmi, despite her bitter condolences, does not hesitate to speak with a journalist. During this week, local and overseas newspapers have published many inaccurate accounts of the deceased; some of which are ridiculously false. She therefore welcomes this possibility to put things back in their precise order as a pleasant occasion and also as a duty. Regarding the life of her brother-in-law, she relates in broad terms, how she, in over a decade since she entered the family, knew and loved him like a brother.

Rodolfo Valentino, or better Rodolfo Guglielmi, was born in 1895 in Castellaneta (Bari) to a very good family. His father, a veterinarian in Castellaneta, was in charge of the conduct and management of the slaughterhouse. The mother was French, daughter of engineer Barbin, who came from France to build the Bari-Castellaneta railway line. Rudolph's father was also a captain in the army and lived in Rome, where he completed a special course in hygiene and bacteriology. It was there his first-child, Alberto, a few years older than Rodolfo, was born. The family moved to Taranto when Rodolfo was 8 years old; three years later his father died. The widow enrolled the boy in boarding school in Perugia and then in the esteemed Nervi School of Agronomy.

When he was about seventeen or eighteen years old, Rodolfo left school with his diploma. But the idea of being an agronomist didn't please him. As he was, as a child, of a lively and restless temperament, as a man the adventurous temperament manifested in him. He still had no precise ideas in mind, but he wanted to do something special, something great. He wanted to see the world. Italy, he said, was too small for him.

His mother wanted to please him and gave him permission and money to enable him to visit America. Mind you, young Rodolfo was to visit America, but not stay there. It was, according to the agreements made by the family, a kind of round trip. Conversely, the young man, who left in 1914, never returned. He liked America and American people and felt at home. He wrote explaining he was fine, and did not plan to return. He disobeyed, in a certain way, the will of his family, but, on the other hand he took care not to give the family sorrow or trouble and never resorted to them for help.

Rudolph began by working as an agronomist. Using his diploma, he designed gardens, took care of flowers and plantations and earned what he needed to live. But he was in the countryside and he didn't like the countryside. He aspired to the bustling and multifaceted life of the city, of the great cities of the New World. He then wandered from one metropolis to another, curious to see and to know, eager for the new, with a confused desire and presentiment of glory and wealth. And in the meantime, to "get by" in those foreign and sometimes hostile environments, he became a tango teacher because he knew how to dance very well. He also found humble jobs, but always approached them with honesty and with nobility of understanding.

He wanted glory and fortune and his persistence resulted in his being rewarded. The one and then the other came quickly to greet him and threw open the doors for him. This was in Los Angeles, the metropolis of American and world cinema. The young man began, like everyone else, by being an extra and by interpreting the first little characters with the nom de guerre of Rudolph Valentino. Gradually, he climbed all the steps of his career. In the "Four Horsemen of the Apocalypse", he was cast in the first role of great importance. It was the baptism of celebrity. A new movie star had arisen to shed its light around the world.

"If you think," comments the lady, "that he started to act in 1919, his was a very rapid career. But it was deserved, he earned it. You have no idea how difficult it is to establish yourself in the artistic field of cinema, especially in America and especially for foreigners. My brother-in-law succeeded, both for his artistic aptitudes and for the qualities of a tenacious, tireless worker. His was not a walk of roses, not even lately. He had the passion for the cinema in his blood, one would have said he was born for this career and he burdened himself with the rigors of rehearsing and filming in the studios like no other. Perhaps it was that passion which relieved him of fatigue. Rudolph Valentino was, believe me, an example of will and work."

"Indeed," continues our kind conversationalist, "in this regard I must make an observation. Many have judged Rudolph Valentino as effeminate. Nothing, is more grossly wrong. It was enough to exchange a few words with him, it was enough to see him to be convinced otherwise. He was, yes, very thorough, to the point of scruple, in his personal grooming and dress. But his was a proud, male character. He was full of energy and will. I don't know how many men have his moral and physical strength. Moral strength has shown it throughout his life, in having set himself a goal of greatness which, at the cost of efforts and sacrifices, he was able to reach. His physical strength showed in his tirelessness to work; he demonstrated it, for example, in his exercises as a skilled horseman and consummate car driver. He made rides which would be exhausting for another. He drove the twelve-hour drive from Los Angeles to San Francisco at the wheel of his car and was soon ready for his return."

Prodigal and Generous

As we know, the American newspapers report the news, determined to arouse amazement, that Valentino left only a half a million in personal wealth. Mrs Guglielmi, on the other hand, is not surprised by this circumstance.

"He was," she says, "of great expense and greater generosity. He spent a lot, but he gave even more, to the left and to the right, without counting it and without thinking about it. He had no sense of the value of money at all, as another practical aspect of life which escaped him. He was happy if he saw the happiness around him and he did his best to surround himself with that happiness, for himself and for others."

"Are you referring to", I ask, "his famous request for American citizenship?"

"My brother-in-law demonstrated, certainly, a sense of gratitude towards the country which hosted him and fulfilled all his aspirations. But there was also a practical reason in him. You need to know those environments to understand them. American citizenship grants certain rights which one who reaches a certain social height cannot do without. These rights which, moreover, if they are to the advantage of the individual, reverberate also with advantage among the Italian community, precisely because as a more respected individual, one assumes a *socially* higher position.

I am sure Rodolfo took that step both for himself and for his compatriots, as has happened and happens to other Italians. The accusations about him were made in error. This is demonstrated by the fact that he did not become an American citizen when he was nobody and he needed to ingratiate himself with people and environments; he took that step only when he was, inevitably, almost forced to do so."

And here the lady recalls another complaint against Valentino; that of not having returned to Italy for the war and being labeled a deserter. No desertion she says. Rodolfo Guglielmi was, while in America, repeatedly subjected to health examinations by the Italian authorities and exonerated for health reasons.

Divorced After Six Hours

"Our Rodolfo", concludes the lady, "has, in all respects held his Italian name high in America, always and everywhere. How do you explain the frenetic success of Rodolfo Valentino in the American public and especially in the female audience? They must have endorsed him because of his great undeniable artistic gifts, his physical qualities, of his race. There are undoubtedly some distinguished actors and handsome young people in American cinema.

Rodolfo imposed himself more, perhaps, by the exotic, which gave him the appearance or manner of the Latin race, whose characteristics were so deeply imprinted in him. The enthusiasm of the American crowds, however, must be commensurate with the great passion which thrives over there for the cinema, a passion of which we, in Italy, have no idea. Here, our audiences, in comparison with America, represents ice cold or in the least lukewarm water compared to fire. This is another reason why Rudolph Valentino was idolized there."

And here we touch on the romantic relationships of the famous actor; and however delicate, as scrupulous interviewers we do not feel like giving up, the kind lady, however briefly, also responds to our curiosity on this subject.

"Rudolph Valentino was not in love and in marriage, he was an unlucky man with two marriages, two divorces. The first divorce occurred only six hours after the marriage was celebrated; the second after two years. It is useless to speak of the first; the second union was, for those two years, very happy. The spouses loved each other tenderly; it seemed that the idyll was to last forever. And instead, suddenly, it ruptured."

If we understand the thought of our conversationalist, the divorce was a clash of race, a different way of approaching and interpreting marriage and the inherent obligations. Although he was Americanized, Rudolph Valentino remained in his conception of love, an Italian; sentimental and passionate. Instead, we know the American woman is more positive and practical; she puts her independence before everything and is capable of sacrificing anything for it. The contrast which led to the separation of the spouses must probably have arisen around the way of interpreting a wife's independence. Rudolph was genuinely saddened.

The sentimental and good side of his character is shown in this circumstance. He could no longer see himself in the house which had been the nest of his happiness and felt overwhelmed by melancholy, deciding to change his home. The brother and sister-in-law traveled to Los Angeles, where they stayed about six months, at his invitation. This was to keep him company, to amuse him, to help him set up his new home which was a magnificent villa in a suburb of Los Angeles, Hollywood, and a picturesque location, from which it is named, "Falcon Lair". "

Therefore the knowledge of the sentimental relationships of the great idol of the female public holds a surprise for us. He was, indeed loved, idolized and even pursued by millions of women. Although in effect, in love this was not his reality and in the sense that, perhaps, in the midst of so many offers of love, he was unable to find true love, the feminine soul mate he so longed for.

He conceived and asked for love in the Italian way; the American women answered him, but in English. In this there was not so much understanding and he remained dissatisfied, disappointed. Oh, the mysteries of the human psyche!

And now, let's confess. Before Rodolfo Valentino, the actor, everyone bowed, recognizing him as one of the most correct, most communicative, most intelligent artists. But besides the light of that glory there was a shadow; next to the artist, the man. It seemed the man was too lucky, too caressed and arriving too soon. Perhaps there is an attitude of envy and wickedness in us as we stand in front of all those who reach such heights. But not anymore. Now we have met Rodolfo Valentino, as an artist and a man. We have seen him in his light and in his shadow, we have seen him work, struggle, suffer like us, the commonality of all mortals. And we have repented, we have reconciled with him. We appreciate the man as well as the artist.

UBALDO LEVA.

The Life, Tastes and Mysteries of Rudolph Valentino

Published in *La Stampa*, Turin, August 27, 1926,
as an unsigned correspondence from Paris.

A stay in Paris -Montmartre! -The travel gramophone and the car -The wonderful dressing gowns!

Paris,the night of the 26th.

Evocative re-enactments of Rudolph Valentino are made by *Paris-Midi* about the last visit the actor made to Paris for the presentation of his film, *The Eagle*.

Seeing Valentino then was not easy, by God, because everyone wanted to reach him, especially his female admirers; who formed a legion with all asking him for a signed photograph. With the utmost good grace Valentino received them all. He put his name on every photograph and granted a loving word to the hopeful who were all moved to have such a wonderful memory in their life; a photograph with the smile of Rudolph Valentino dedicated to them alone.

The representative of the Parisian newspaper saw Valentino as he was preparing to leave in his luxury car. As motoring was one of Valentino's great pleasures, he was proud to say he could completely disassemble his car and reassemble it without the need of a mechanic. The engine held no secrets for him. Animals also had a great place in his life and Valentino happily spoke about the fourteen dogs he purchased in Nice and with whom he played with like a little boy.

When he was in Paris, Valentino spent his nights in Montmartre dancing, because he loved to dance; first the tango and then the waltz. Returning home at dawn, he slept for two hours and then dressed to attend to his work and walks. He was never tired and his personal secretary said that in Paris he had seen him but two hours in five days. This was while he was dressing and also giving business orders.

Valentino owned a collection of dressing gowns in brilliant tones; from velvety, warm reds to purples and all vivid colors demonstrating exquisite good taste. While Rudolph Valentino was grooming himself, an elegant travel gramophone played danceable tunes. His favorite record at that time was a tango titled, "Ahi, Va el Dulce!" Valentino always carried that gramophone with him on all of his travels. His usual and graceful mood made him loved by everyone in his entourage.

The Parisian journalist remembers asking him what he thought of current Parisian fashion and Valentino replied:

"Oh! Women are always very elegant. But I hate short hair because I find it not very feminine."

If he had publicly expressed this opinion, how many female hair cuts could have been spared!

The love with which so many strangers surrounded him was manifested in numerous letters, of which he showed the reporter the multicolored heap.

"And I answer them all! This pleases them so much!"

Valentino simply and kindly accepted his popularity which was due to his looks and charm and the cinema showcased in a special way, making him the idol of many young girls.

The *Paris-Midi* journalist concludes,

"Poor Rodolfo, mourned by so many adoring eyes, whose heart held its own mystery, a mystery so well defended as many onlookers tried in vain to know it. As they fought to see him on his deathbed, I thought with sad emotion of the sweetness of that young man full of grace, who used to say, when he was tired from so many visits and after writing so many letters,

"I don't want to make them sorry."

Revelations on the Beautiful Valentino as a Boarder at Sant'Ilario

Published in *Nuova Stampa Sera*, Turin, December 8th and 9th, 1950

The first class report card of the agricultural student Rodolfo Guglielmi - confidences of the shepherd who taught him to govern beasts - The love escapades of the future star of *Blood and Sand*

S. ILARIO ALTO, December,

Here, on this green hill which steeply abuts the sea of Nervi; here, among farms and greenhouses of tropical flowers, Rudolph Valentino's first love was born. The tall, romantic cypresses, dense all around, saw his passion and hold this memory. At that time there was no concern for a movie's director or the script in the heart of handsome Rudy. He was not yet an actor. He relied entirely on the impulses of his seventeen years.

He who was to become the Great Lover par excellence, the idol of all women, the embodiment of the most universal expression of love, then pined away like an ordinary collegiate. It was his first love, experienced almost as a disease, like a rising fever. It was the one love, "*that is never forgotten*". But that kind of love is also the one which almost never results in marriage. In fact, Rodolfo was destined to seek his fortune in America and his beloved would become the good wife of a railway worker in another distant country. Thus ended his first love.

A Real Naughty Boy

Rodolfo Valentino was a boarded student of this State Practical School of Agriculture "B. Marsano", from November 7, 1910 to October 20, 1912, the year in which he obtained the license as, "Rural Agent". This title enabled him to work as a farmer and manage small and medium-sized farms.

The "Marsano" is a clean and welcoming school, dominated by the wide and wooded slope of the hill serving as an observation post. It is surrounded by orchards and gardens which are not only a decorative element but also the experimental territory for students' practices.

Rodolfo arrived alone. He wrote quickly on the application for admission: Rodolfo Guglielmi of the late Giovanni, veterinary doctor, and Gabriella Barbin, born in Castellaneta (Lecce) (at that time Castellaneta was in the Lecce province) on May 6, 1895. And we can still read today in the 1912 school register under number 190 of matriculation, a note of the school secretary, "The tuition is paid by the mother".

As for the diligence of boarder Rodolfo Guglielmi, the prospectus of the final scrutiny is clear; a 9 in agriculture, 9 in economics and book-keeping, 7 in chemistry, 9 in land surveying, 8 1/2 in Italian, 9 in English, 8 in geography and **merceology**, 9 in Spanish and 8 in practical agricultural work. Despite this first-class report card, the future Rudolph Valentino did not work so hard and was considered rather a daredevil.

Of the current professors and employees of the Agricultural School, including the director Dr. Leonardi and the secretary Mr. Pellegrini, no one met the exceptional student in person because the staff of that time are no longer there. They are all new now. The only living witness of that period, the seventy-eight-year-old Luigi Marsano, who was for about half a century the shepard and the country guard of the institute; he confirms Rodolfo Guglielmi was really a naughty, ardent and generous character. He recalls he was cheerful and in love, he was mischievous and tender. Marsano recalls he was also amused in his study by his lively wit.

Luigi Marsano lives almost behind the school now, in a rustic house. The state awarded him a pension of three thousand lire a month. But he, fortunately, has humor and with his honest face, in which the eyes hide behind a slit in the eyelids, he is cheerful, maintains an iron constitution and still goes barefoot at his age to water the vegetables and mow the hay.

Luigi Marsano was employed by the school as shepard and was custodian of the stable. But he too was teaching courses. The country guard Luigi Marsano taught students how to govern animals, how to milk goats and cows and many other things indispensable to the life of the countryside. He therefore had under him, for two years, Rodolfo Guglielmi. The young man immediately bonded with Luigi for his sturdy constitution and frankness and they became very good friends.

Once Rodolfo ran away from the Institute and hid in the stable to exchange love signals with his girlfriend, who lived in a small house opposite the stable. However, his absence was noticed by the Director who gave the order to Luigi to find Rodolfo and inflict the punishment he deserved. Luigi tracked Rodolfo down but instead hid him in safety. He told the Director he hadn't even been able to find the boy.

Luigi Marsano is as sparkling as a good old wine and his cordial spirit released from his roughness is unexpected. He is not shut off from life, but sociable by instinct. That's why Valentino was devoted to him and trusted him.

"How was this Guglielmi, Luigino?"

"He had beautiful teeth, gianchi comm'u leite", he replies more in dialect than in Italian, "as white as milk". Besides, he was strong. So many times he wanted to fight me in the Roman style. And it took a while before I let him "let go", yes before *I made him sit still!*

These are the things which appear most often in Luigi's speech, the beautiful and very white teeth and the bold strength. He lights up with happiness at the memory. Then it occurs to him that he was also a joker and sometimes spiteful.

One day Luigi said Rodolfo chased all the piglets from the stable to give them freedom in a wild race across the fields, ignoring that the beasts of that age suffer. In fact they all died. A real cataclysm would have happened if the Director of the school had known. But Luigi obtained a certificate from the veterinarian certifying the pigs died of a disease.

But a Heart of Gold

"And what was he like at school, did he study?"

"Eh," Marsano says quickly, winking, "he didn't waste much time with books but he was talented, he was ingenious, he was intelligent. One morning a professor calls him and says, 'You, Guglielmi don't study and I'll miss you". And then Rodolfo stood up and replied: "Dear professor, I know more when I sleep than you when you are awake!" He said precisely these words and I remember them as if it were said now."

Then Luigi pauses for a moment and says, shaking his head, that Guglielmi was very active with the girls. He (watched, pursued) them all and escaped from the dormitory by sliding down the pipes. His comrades sometimes wanted to isolate him, stay away from him. But they needed him too much because he was the only one who passed the completed homework on to everyone.

"He was a naughty boy," Luigi concludes, "but with a heart of gold. He would give the world. And he had courage. One time there was a cow in love which was stomping up and down like mad, and it was frightening. And well, Guglielmi without even thinking about it, rushes to take hold of the beast and guide it into the stable. On my return he says to me, "See, Luigino? when there is a danger we must not waste time ".

And Marsano does not suspect that with this rudimentary language, a mixture of Italian and Genoese dialect, he is painting the portrait and the character of the future star of *Blood and Sand* and of *The Son of the Sheik*.

Nostalgia for S. Ilario

At the end of October 1912, after two years of affectionate friendship, Rodolfo and Luigi parted ways. The following year Guglielmi was preparing to leave for America where after some misery during his early years, he was also employed himself as a gardener showing his diploma as a "rural agent" obtained at this Agricultural School.

"Goodbye, Luigino!" he shouted from afar the day he left the Institute, "I will not forget you."

And in fact, on a splendid sunny morning in 1922,[1] when his very name was sending shivers of emotion all over the world, Rodolfo Valentino stopped with an enormous American car just a few steps from Luigi Marsano's house. He was traveling with his girlfriend Natacha Rambova.[2] He had visited Paris where the welcome was triumphant and now he was going to visit his family before leaving for New York. But his heart longed for the scent of the gardens of S. Ilario and the smile of his dear friend Luigi Marsano.

"I told you I wouldn't forget," he said hugging Luigi. And Rodolfo turned his almond eyes around to focus on the sea, which was as sweet and calm as a lake. Rodolfo was emotional as he spoke about so many past things with his old teacher. Then he rose saying Natacha was waiting for him.

"Let's go have a coffee, Luigino. The Director no longer has anything to say!"

But Luigino was dressed in rags befitting the countryside and did not feel like going with the splendid young gentleman to the places where people would have flocked to see him. He replied how you respond to a friend you meet at the market or on the train,

"Thanks, maybe another time."

Then Rodolfo slipped a five-hundred bill into Luigi's pocket.[3]

"You'll drink it yourself ", he said and left.

Four years later, Valentino died suddenly and, according to some, mysteriously. Luigi was amazed and even today he laments,

"If he had lived," he sighs, "he was so good ..."

Until 1932, Marsano kept the black woolen collegiate cape which Rodolfo gave him as a souvenir when he left the Agricultural School. Luigi defended the cape from all the assaults of collectors. Even a lady who came from America with the intention of buying it. But in the end, an Italian, who almost every day climbed up to see Luigi and who had also offered him a kiss, won the game.

"I couldn't take it anymore," says Luigino with irritation, "and she managed to snatch it from me in 1932 for five hundred liras, Well, it was in bad shape anyway! I still have his memory inside me and around me, in these gardens where I still seem to see him."

Ermanno D'Ercole

---

1 This took place in 1923
2 Natacha was his wife then
3 Value as of 2021 - $7,500.00

St. Ilario School when Rudolph Valentino was enrolled

Valentino, jokingly photographed in the didactic fields of the "Royal Practical School of Agriculture Marsano", in Genoa Sant'Ilario, named after the philanthropist Bernardo Marsano. Valentino attended school there between 1910 and 1912. In this pose he seems to be praying to heaven to help him win the heart of Felicita Sessarego, the cook's daughter or, perhaps much more prosaically, praying for the rain to stop falling.

A New Episode in the Life of the Great Actor is Unveiled

Rudolph Valentino's first love lives in Rome and has been married for half a century

She was born in Genoa and is now the wife of a Turin employee. She met the young man while he was studying agriculture in San Ilario Ligure.

"When we get married, we'll have a little house here."But he had no luck. The departure for America and the desperate letters to his beloved. In 1922(3) the already famous artist returned to Italy and looked for her.

(PHOTO) Felicita Sessarego with her husband in her home in Rome
(From our correspondent)

Genoa, March 9.

The first great love of Rodolfo Valentino, perhaps the only girl really loved by the famous actor when he was very young and still unknown, is Mrs. Felicita Sessarego, married for half a century to a Turin employee, Dr. Ernesto Giudice, who at that time lived in Turin in Via Belvedere, and now resides in Rome.

The protagonist of Rodolfo's first idyll is a Genoese and met the future actor when Valentino, just eighteen, attended an agricultural course at the "Marsano" school in S. Ilario, on the hills of Genoa. Felicita Sessarego was born on November 20, 1890 and is the eldest of the three daughters of the spouses Fortunato[1] and Caterina Marsano.

Both father and mother worked at the school which bore their name, the former as a coachman, the latter as a cook. And their home was not far from the school building. The young Felicita, by general admission, was the most beautiful of the three sisters: tall, dark, with a thin waist and a face which inspired serenity and confidence. Rodolfo Guglielmi, this is the real name of Rodolfo Valentino, immediately fell in love with Felicita.

"You will see, Miss Fely," he said, "that sooner or later I will marry you."

The one who was to become one of the most famous film actors in the world, had come to Sant'Ilario in 1911 at the age of 15, accompanied by his mother who was dressed in mourning for the death of her husband.

---

1   The correct family name of the father was Sessarego and not as was written in La Stampa.

"I am rather worried especially about Rudolph's character," the lady said to the secretary of the agricultural school, "but I hope that here he will be well and his mind will be set straight."

Sant'Ilario Ligure worked a kind of miracle and the undisciplined pupil became the first in the class. It is difficult to imagine the "Son of the Sheik" as a conscientious pupil, loyal to his duty. Yet in the two years of his stay in Sant'Ilario, he was always the best and concluded his studies with these grades: agriculture 9, economy 9, chemistry and agricultural industry 7, surveying 9, Italian language 8, English language 9, geography and mineralogy 8, conduct 6 and a half. The only dark spot in so many splendid grades, the "conduct" and in this field Rudolph Valentino did not shine.

Until the beginning of the last war, on the shelves of the agricultural school of Sant'Ilario it was possible to find some class assignments done by Valentino; the war and the "looting" by the "inconsolable widows" have now left the place empty.

Many still, however, remember the love of the student in agriculture for the beautiful Felicita and the long waits in the square by the boy who was so in love and all in the hope of seeing the girl of his dreams pass by. He was sincerely in love and always talked about marriage.

"When we are married," he said to the girl, "we will have a house built here!" and then he pointed to the top of a square on the hill, surrounded by climbing agave, olive trees and cypresses, and the sea of Nervi.

The man who was to become Felicita's husband was already living in Genoa; a young and handsome employee of the State Railways, the 21-year-old Piedmontese Ernesto Giudice. He had been transferred from Turin to Genoa to being able to be close to his mother, Mrs. Enrica Scagno, a primary school teacher in Sant'Ilario.

"Rodolfo I remember him well," the Felicita says now, "he was the most beautiful of all the boys who attended school. He worked in the experimental fields and sometimes I met him in the evening but he came to see me under the windows of the house and asked me to play the guitar or the mandolin for him. 'Miss Fely,' he told me, 'do you know that I am in love with you?' Then I ran away for fear that my mother would hear such words."

"Well, I can now say it easily," continues Mrs. Sessarego, "I liked that boy. I thought he must be very good and intelligent and that he would certainly be lucky. But I wasn't in love with him. Once he tried to stop me in the street near my house and the school sharecropper surprised him and slapped him. Two years went by and Rodolfo Guglielmi, having left the school of S. Ilario, left as emigrant for the United States. Before leaving he came again under the windows of my house, called to me and blew me a kiss on the tips of his fingers. He was crying, poor thing; and I too was very moved. Then for some time I didn't know anything about him. Suddenly his correspondence began to arrive. They were cards, postcards, love letters," continues Felicita Sessarego, "but by now I was in love with Ernesto and we had already set the wedding date. So I never replied to those letters. The last one I remember came in early April 1914."

In that letter he said, 'I know you don't think about me anymore, but I can't forget you.' On April 22 of the year I married Ernesto."

From that moment the lives of Felicita Sessarego and Rodolfo Valentino took two very different paths. Felicita, married to Ernesto Giudice, remained for some time in S. Ilario, then moved to Rome to live in beautiful house on the outskirts where she still lives, in Viale Camillo Furio.

Her marriage was enhanced by the birth of a daughter, Lucia Clara, who became an excellent pianist and also interpreted, among other things, two films, "Mater Dolorosa" and "The White Angel". Rudolph Valentino, in the United States, had the eventful, famous, adventurous and tragic life which is known. However, the "beautiful" of the screen never forgot Felicita Sessarego, and when he returned to Italy in 1923, he came to Genoa and went to the old school to ask about his first love.

"Felicita is married," the acquaintances told him.

"Too bad," murmured the actor, "I really wanted to see her again."

A few more years passed, but Felicità never knew much about Rodolfo's career. It was only in August 1926 that some friends from Genoa wrote to her to ask if she still had any letters from Rodolfo Guglielmi.

"I didn't even know who he was anymore," confesses Felicita, a little ashamed of having ignored such a famous film actor for so long, "then I asked the reason for that strange request. They told me that Rudolph Valentino, my ancient lover, died on August 23 of that year in New York."

Felicita Sessarego now has only one regret; that of never having seen one of Rodolfo's films.

C.M.

Felicita Sessarego nel 1912

Rudolph Valentino's *My Private Diary*

An Analysis

by
Renato Floris

Introduction

I open this analysis by sharing a comment from the author of *Madam Valentino*, Michael Morris. This was an observation he shared with Evelyn Zumaya in an email dated April 22, 2003. His sentiment has always inspired our work. Morris shares a simple yet exhaustive way to denounce the extent to which the image of Valentino has become flexible and adaptable to various sociological-cultural needs. He writes:

"Film Scholarship is right now...and so much of Hollywood history is being appropriated by special interest groups. Please so keep the notion of 'Virtual Valentino'. This is my theory in nutshell. Once mere humans get caught up in the apotheosis of Hollywood stardom, they appeal to a vast crowd which connects to them in different ways. Like the image of Christ or the Virgin Mary...seen in various aspects by different peoples (white, blond-haired and blue eyed to Anglo-Saxons while Our Lady of Guadalupe is a dark-skinned Aztec to Mexicans, etc). I know this is also true of Valentino. He is a Latin Lover to the Italians and Spaniards, has animal magnetism to millions of females, and is a closeted gay man leading a double-life to countless gays who are doing the same thing.

The word is APPROPRIATION.

All gods and goddesses undergo this process. But the historical man or woman beneath the image, removed from Mt. Olympus, ought to be the subject of the historian. Everyone else is a myth-maker...the fans, the cult followers, the 'faithful' who keep the fire burning (often in spite of the de-mythologizing historian!)"

A substantial contribution to this "Virtual Valentino" was created, in large part, by the press offices of the motion picture studios. Their primary mission was to make interesting, even intriguing and desirable the image of the star they were promoting. We have to remember that the image of the star, of the myth, had to be dreamed of and very often, the image created had little to do with the living, real person. This creation of the image was the first and foremost sales tool used by film production studios.

In the world of cinema fiction, reality has no place and everything must be made up and presented in the most captivating way possible. The world of entertainment is a world of appearances, dreams and shared lies.

It is with reason the term "hypocritical", is derived from the Greek term ὑποκριτής (ipokrites) whose original meaning is "actor" or "simulator". Hence, as actors deceive by definition, even their private life must be narrated in a mendacious but suggestive and intriguing way. The narrations produced by the "studios" were, more than truthful portraits of the narrated character, evocative frescoes of words whose sole purpose was to make the narrated character fascinating, attractive and desirable. In the early days of cinematography, the favored propaganda tools were the many cinema magazines which contained both information relating to upcoming films and gossipy insights into the lives of the stars.

The primary rule of the politics of the studios was explained by Jeanne de Recqueville who commented on this in a televised interview in the 1970s. She recalled how while writing her biography of Valentino, she interviewed the president of Paramount Studios. She asked him for a photo of Rudolph but "Mr. Paramount" said he had none and added, "You know, for us the stars are like tubes of toothpaste. When the toothpaste has been all squeezed out, the tube becomes useless and is thrown away!"

That gentleman did not realize there was still some toothpaste left in the tube known as Rudolph Valentino and, I would add, there is still a lot of it today.

At the time, however, the most powerful tool was to let the stars speak themselves, to have them tell about their life and their travels abroad, especially in an era when most traveling was the prerogative of the wealthy. The reading audience was spread over a broad geographic territory yet, in a certain way, culturally isolated as was most of the United States of the twenties. This was an era in which the knowledge of the "foreigner" was almost nil and they were often viewed with distrust. This despite Americans, excluding the few surviving natives, being children and grandchildren of "foreigners".

The Travel Diary Format

There are several examples of travel diaries written "personally" by the star of the moment, such as those of Charlie Chaplin. Chaplin's first travel diary titled, "My Trip Abroad" was published in 1922 and told of his return to his homeland in 1921 after seven years of intense work in Hollywood. Chaplin's second travelogue titled, "A Comedian Sees the World", was written following his promotional trip to Europe and Asia which began on February 13, 1931 and ended on June 16, 1932. The story was published in five installments in the popular magazine, *The Woman's Home Companion* from September 1933 to January 1934.

Robert Florey, who was employed for a brief while as secretary and press officer for Valentino's European market, sheds light on how Valentino might have had the idea to write his own travel diary in the December 15, 1922 issue of the French cinema magazine *Cinéa.* Florey tells us this came about one evening while dining at Rudolph

Valentino's, with Chaplin as a guest. There was a discussion of the publication of Charlie's, "My Trip Abroad" which was soon to be published in book form. Perhaps it was that very evening, while having dinner with friends, when Valentino first had the idea that he too should recount his journey to mythical Europe.

Travel literature is known for its ability to combine narration and description, for the comparisons of the reality of the narrator to that of the reader, for verification between the "literary" memories of the narrator and the objective reality of the places narrated. Add to this, the possibility of using infinite allegorical metaphorical nuances and, above all, a familial tone of language, similar to that of a grandfather telling his grandchildren the memories of his youth.

The title of Valentino's travel diary, in its first serialized publication in the American magazine *Movie Weekly*, was "*Rudolph Valentino's Own Story Of His Trip Abroad, by Rudolph Valentino*", appearing in seven installments from February 23 to August 16, 1924. It was also published in the British magazine *Pictures and Picturegoer* in sixteen installments from July 1924 to October 1925 with the title, used only for the first episode, "*My Own Story of my Trip Abroad by Rudolph Valentino*". From the second installment, the titled was changed to "*My Trip Abroad by Rudolph Valentino*".

Valentino's *My Private Diary* was based on this travel diary narrative and written in a travel diary format. *My Private Diary* reads as a journal with daily entries and it is these I will scrutinize.

To categorize *My Private Diary* in this respect, we can say it is closest to the eighteenth-century, "grand tourist's diaries",[1] with the difference being that overly personal opinions are generally banned from the "grand tourist's" narration. The "grand tourist diary" genre, descriptions of places and things, prevails in an objective and accurate style which lends itself to the non-critical and faithful mirror of reality. This does not occur in, *My Private Diary* where we find undiplomatic comments often inserted in regards to everything not American or Anglo-Saxon.

We see initially in the title a not so subliminal suggestion implying you are being presented with something intimate, reserved and personal. This, even if in its first draft there was nothing "private" about it and it was simply a collection of travel memories of Rudolph Valentino with his wife Natacha Rambova's European travels during the second half of 1923.

My task is to understand *My Private Diary's* authenticity and determine to which category it belongs as it was published in 1929.

---

1 The Grand Tour was a long journey in continental Europe undertaken by the rich European aristocracy starting from the 17th century and destined to perfect their knowledge with departure and arrival in the same city. It had an undefined duration and usually had Italy as its destination. The success of Thomas Coryat's 1611 book *Coryat's Crudities* is often regarded as the beginning of the Grand Tour craze. While the expression *Grand Tour* seems to have appeared in Richard Lassels' guide *The Voyage of Italy, Or A Complete Journey Through Italy*, published in 1670. Johann Wolfgang von Goethe also made his Grand Tour in Italy from 1786 to 1788 of which he wrote in his famous *Italienische Reise (Italian trip)*.

The publications of the travel diary narratives in 1924 were the culmination of several notable literary efforts by Valentino. The year 1923, was important from a literary point of view for him and began with the publication of, "An Open Letter from Valentino - To the American Public" in the January 1923 issue of *Photoplay*. At the end of the open letter, the publication of the story of "An Immigrant Boy Who Became the Idol of America" or "My Life Story" is announced which was scheduled to be published in the February, March and April issues.

The publication of "My Life Story" presents the question; who really wrote or rather, painted the fresco of words which comprised, "My Life Story"? My answer, without a shadow of a doubt, is that the author was journalist Herb Howe, as he himself relates how he worked on the narrative in an interview with Natacha Rambova. He refers to this in an article published in *The New Movie Magazine*, December 1929 - May 1930. His confession reads:

"I remembered the days I spent in his apartment collaborating with Rudie on his life story. Due to some legal technicalities related to his divorce from Jean Acker, he and Natacha were forced to keep separate residences for several months, after their wedding in Mexico, but obviously Rudie spent most of the time with Natacha.

There was a tense moment when Natacha and I sat down on the sofa. To say this, I referred to the hours spent on her life story. 'Now we should tell the story of your life', I told her. "

The first installment of "My Life Story", published in the February 1923 issue of *Photoplay,* is a quick glimpse into Valentino's childhood, enriched by tasty skits and familiar scenarios which I would describe as being some of the most amusing in the constellation of tales about Valentino.

In this installment we find some inconsistencies such as when Valentino tells of battles with his little sister Maria and says he climbed a lime tree and used the fruits as bullets to hit his playful enemy. In Italy and in Europe there were certainly no lime trees at the time of Valentino's childhood.

It should be noted that in the first installment there is another error related to some Shakespearean verses; "Sighing like a furnace with a woeful ballad to his mistress' eyebrow" is quoted as being part of a monologue of the tragedy *Richard III* while they are part of the monologue, "The Seven Ages of Man", beginning with the famous line: *"All the world's a stage..."* from Shakespeare's comedy *As You Like It*- Act II, Scene VII.

The second installment of "My Life Story", published in the March 1923 issue of *Photoplay,* relates how Valentino emigrated to the United States in search of his own space far away from Italy which, according to him, was too small and oppressive. This installment tells of his arrival in New York and his moments of solitude, of poverty if not real misery and ends with the story of his traveling, thanks to "fortuitous occasions", to the west coast.

The third and final installment, published in the April 1923 issue of *Photoplay*, tells of Valentino's arrival in Hollywood and his rise to stardom, before ending with his plans for the future. The narrative stops there, before the Mineralava tour and on the verge of Valentino's marriage to Natacha Rambova, celebrated at Crown Point in Indiana on March 14, 1923 with Michael A. Romano acting as Rudolph's witness.

In June of 1923, Valentino expands his literary effort with a book of poems *Day Dreams* and on July 24, 1923, Valentino, Natacha and their entourage left the shores of the United States to sail for Europe.

It is essential to point out a clarification regarding the autobiography, "My Life Story" which came to us directly from Rudolph Valentino himself through the Spanish journalist Baltasar Fernández Cué. Cué tells us in, *El Verdadero Rodolfo Valentino, The True Rudolph Valentino*,

"One day he called his secretary and told her to give me the only copy he had of the story of his life, published years before in one of the most important film magazines in the United States. Miss Margaret Neff gave it to me accompanied by other similar documents; this while Rudolph recommended them to me as if they were precious jewels or some ancient parchments[2] which could not be replaced in any way. He made a huge qualification about the quality of the content of one of these documents; he wanted to be sure to emphasize to me that this was a story reputed to be his autobiography titled, "My Life Story".

Michael Romano's *My Private Diary*

In 1929, a friend of Rudolph Valentino and witness to his Crown Point wedding, Michael A. Romano would organize his own publication of the diary titled, *My Private Diary* which would incorporate both the travel diary and "My Life Story" narratives. Romano was an assistant attorney for the state of Illinois, who, with other important personalities of the Italian community in Chicago, founded the "Rudolph Valentino Memorial Club of America". Romano defined the club's purpose as follows, as written in the articles of association: *"To perpetuate the memory of Rudolph Valentino, this giant of the cinema, whose artistic endeavors gave genuine joy and edification to the masses"*. Romano set out to re-publish Valentino's travel memories in the form of a private diary; no longer as magazine installments but as a book.

The book *My Private Diary* begins with an introduction written by Romano who, in addition to a rhetorical telling of Valentino's life as a poor Italian emigrant, elevates Valentino by relating how he aspired to the creation of high works of art and not the production of vile consumer products. Romano tells of a young man who arrived in the

---

2 Valentino's statement certainly referred to the fragility of the copies of *Movie Weekly*, the cheapest of the widely circulated magazines. The paper used to print *Movie Weekly* was very thin and of very poor quality. The cost of a copy of *Movie Weekly* was ten cents when the price a copy of *Photoplay* was $0.25.

United States as "an immigrant boy, nameless, penniless, unknown" who "by his indomitable will and courage surmounted all obstacles and attained that pinnacle upon which only the truly strong can pose".

It is my firm opinion Romano wanted to boost morale in the Italian community in the United States, a community in need of hope, with a shining example as if to say: "Courage, you too use your indomitable will and courage and surmount all obstacles and attain that pinnacle upon which only the truly strong can pose, and just as Valentino you can triumph. "

A dominant motif is Romano's exaltation of all that is American and how all things American are superior to all that is not American. Romano closes his introduction with a quotation from William Shakespeare's sonnet seventy-three on the value of memories of a dear and important person who passed away:

> *This thou perceiv'st, which makes thy love more strong,*
> *To love that well which thou must leave ere long.*

The credentials are thereby all in place for the reader to presume the diary was written by Valentino himself and during his trip to Europe. For me there are many points to be made as evidence this is not an original product, but a patched-together editing of Valentino's memories, despite it being filled with accounts of his travel, personal and historical events. The first evidence of this non-originality which caught my eye, was the difference in the length of the texts between the article, "My Trip Abroad" and *My Private Diary*.

It should be noted that *My Private Diary* is a reworking of what was published, five years earlier, both in *Movie Weekly* and in *Pictures and Picturegoer*, with references to *"My Life Story"* as well, but with substantial additions; one hundred and forty to be exact. Three years after Valentino's death, these new entries we find in *My Private Diary* range from a single word to several pages of text. For example, the entire entry of September 9, 1923, is not included in "My Trip Abroad". How could Valentino have added text to Romano's 1929 publication?

In conducting my research for answers, I based my work on the text of *My Private Diary*, on the text of "My Trip Abroad", published in *Pictures and Picturegoer*, and on the translation into Italian of *My Private Diary* by Paolo Orlandelli, published by Lindau, in Turin in 2004.

Regarding Dates

The disparity in dates and travel arrangements also are a clue to the work's non-originality and is such that the Italian translator of the diary, Orlandelli made the allegation Valentino did not care about the dates, claiming he lived in his own dimension. He thus gives us the impression Valentino was really a wide-eyed dreamer.

We find in many sources how Valentino was extremely attentive to his business and knew perfectly well both the dates and the destinations of his travels.

The real problem is revealed how those who physically compiled the diary, probably based on scattered notes, did not bother to go and fact check. These magazines were conceived for rapid consumption, a sort of fast read for cinema enthusiasts, which once read, would be thrown into waste paper baskets[3].

In a letter dated May 19, 1923 sent to his then secretary Robert Florey, almost at the end of the Mineralava tour, Valentino communicates his decisions and writes:

"To begin with, I will tell you that I have decided to go to Europe at the end of this tour, which is to say for sure after the 8th of July. I don't know yet if it will be for a film or for a vacation, but I will definitely leave with the Aquitania or with the Olympic around July 23rd or 24th."

At the bottom of the letter, he adds,

"We will write together a book on the life of Valentino and another, also illustrated, on my return to Italy after ten years ... "

Florey went on to publish extracts from that letter and other letters in the French magazine *Cinémonde,* in his memory of Valentino published thirty years after his death in eight episodes titled, "Inoublable, Inoublié – Rudolph Valentino Survit a Sà Légende", between October 4 and December 6, 1956. This excerpt clearly demonstrates Valentino was well-aware of the dates of his travels. We also learn from this letter how for Valentino, writing a book about his life was an unfulfilled desire.

He tried a second time to hypothesize his "true" story and worked with the Spanish journalist Baltasar Fernández Cué, drafting his biography to be completed upon returning from the promotional tour for the film *The Son of the Sheik.* Unfortunately Valentino returned to Los Angeles in a coffin and Baltasar Fernández Cué wrote "*El Verdadero Rodolfo Valentino*" as a ten installment serialization published in the Spanish language magazine *Cinemundial,* from May 1927 to January 1928.

Baltasar Fernández Cué had to rely on the material Valentino entrusted to him before leaving for New York, on his own direct experience with Valentino and, unfortunately, on what was previously published on his life.

---

3   Film magazines were very cheap, consider that the price of the February 1924 issue of "Movie Weekly", a special double issue for the release of the first installation of "Rudolph Valentino Own Story of his Trip Abroad", was $ 0.15 equal to the current $ 2.35 while normal numbers cost was $ 0.10 equal to $ 1.57 in 2021. For comparison, the cost of the February 1924 issue of "Photoplay" was $ 0.25 equal to $ 3.92 in the spring of 2021. "Movie Weekly" was the cheapest magazine and some said it used paper so thin that it was compared to that of cigarettes. For this reason, finding undamaged copies of "Movie Weekly" is practically impossible. There are collectors who, for years, have been unhappily chasing the few copies that didn't end up in a paper baskets.

"MY DREAM is coming true!" Within a few lines after these opening words of *My Private Diary*, we find the first serious inconsistencies regarding the actual facts. In the diary it is written:

"Ten years ago I came to America poor, friendless, unknown and penniless, and then...No one even met me when I landed at the pier. No one even knew I was coming...and so on."

Then, it is added:

"I think, though, as I sit here so deeply thinking back that the lowest ebb of my life came on that Christmas eve only one day after my arrival in New York. The abyss of loneliness. I ate a solitary dinner in a small cafe, and the very food tasted bitter with my unshed tears."

These statements are proven to be pure invention, as Rudolph Valentino arrived in New York, after a comfortable first-class trip in which he was registered as Rodolfo dei Marchesi Guglielmi. He arrived with a letter of credit sewn into the linings of his clothes allowing him to collect his share of a paternal inheritance or $4,000.00 corresponding to an exchange rate of $109,121.29 in the spring of 2021.

Upon his arrival he was met by his family friend Francesco Mennillo who welcomed him and took Rudolph to his tailor to have a suit made for him appropriate for the New York of those times. That same day, as evidenced by a witness to the event, Valentino went to 215 Spring Street in New York to join Ernesto Filomarino, his sponsor and uncle of his sister-in-law, Ada Del Mazzone. I interviewed a grandnephew of Ernesto Filomarino, who lives in Taranto, who confirmed Rodolfo was welcomed by his great-uncle and that he spent Christmas 1913 with him and his family.

To all this we must add how Valentino declared to Robert Florey that in Christmas 1913 he had in his pocket, "only", the sum of $300.00 which is equal to the current $8,184.10. To allege Valentino was a poor man on arrival is in the least risky and as the Italian translator of the diary claims:

"Rodolfo appears to have received his share of his paternal inheritance, about $4,000, in liquidation. But already during the crossing he had spent and lost a considerable part of that sum gambling "

A researcher citing a source as it "*appears*" is merely perpetuating suppositions. Valentino did not travel with the sum of four thousand dollars in cash but with a letter of credit and, obviously, a portion was in cash for the expenses to be incurred during the voyage and the first days in New York. There, at a bank he could collect the money which was transferred and drawn from the account of the Credito Italiano family bank. Out of this same account Valentino also received a sort of pocket money, sent by his mother Gabrielle, of $5.00 dollars a week, equal to $135.15 in May 2021.

Regarding the allegation Valentino spent the voyage gambling, it has been shown this could not have occurred as he was not an addicted player and there is ample evidence of this. The legend that a seventeen-year-old Valentino had already lost all his last money at the Casino of Monte Carlo during his return to Italy from Paris is also not credible. In European casinos even access to the casinos by minors has always been prohibited. At that time, minors under 21 were not granted access even to the building and the age had to be proven by showing a legally recognized document. Valentino, at that time, was seventeen-years old.

The text in *My Private Diary* devoted to Valentino's arrival in New York is rhetorical, a marketing of Valentino targeting actual poor immigrants who seeking fortune, sailed the Atlantic in the midst of a thousand difficulties and under desperate conditions, to escape misery and reach the mythical America.

Implausible Statements Attributed to Valentino in *My Private Diary*

In the introduction, Valentino promises Natacha to take her to see where he, as a boy, played "Hop Scotch" or the game of the "Campana". (Note that in Italy the game of "Campana" has always been considered a game for females and, especially in the late nineteenth and early twentieth centuries it is unlikely a male would play it.)

Orlandelli changes the name of the game by translating it as, "I was playing Leapfrog", which sounds more virile than,"Campana".

The most unlikely affirmation attributed to Valentino is that he intended to take Natacha to visit the burial site of his parents which would seem to be in Castellaneta. This would have been impossible as it is not known where Dr. Giovanni rests in peace while his mother is not buried next to her husband as she died in France in Besançon, in the civic hospital on January 10, 1919. She was buried in the Cimetière des Chaprais, interred by her daughter Maria and her Tranchart cousins residing in San Vit, near Besançon.

It is also attributed to Valentino, that in speaking about his mother Gabrielle, whom he describes as a gallant, little figure, he says she learned the lessons of courage and fortitude by enduring the terrors and privations of the siege of Paris. How would Valentino state something so historically incorrect about his own mother?

Two important clarifications are to be made on this point. The first relates to the possible presence of Gabrielle Barbin at the siege of Paris, which took place between September 19, 1870 and January 28, 1871 and the fleeting republican proclamation of the Commune of Paris between March 18, and May 29, 1871. After confirmation from a French researcher regarding Gabrielle's presence in France at the time, she was not in Paris but in the place of the origin of her father in Coucy-Le-Château-Auffrique in Aisne in the Picardy region. Gabrielle was not in Paris during that turbulent historical period.

The second clarification to be made about this statement attributed to Valentino is related to the profession of his grandfather. His mother Gabrielle's father, Pierre Philibert Barbin[4] was not Parisian and not a medical scholar but a civil engineer

---

4 Pierre Philibert Barbin was born on April 2, 1818 and died on November 18, 1868 in Taranto, when

specializing in railway iron bridges. As a result of his professional ability, he was invited to Puglia to design and pursue the realization of the bridges which span the ravines.

Towards the end of the diary, we are to believe Valentino comes to his senses and reveals his grandfather Pierre Philibert becomes, as if by a miracle, no longer a doctor but the engineer who built the railway bridges over the ravines. Perhaps the copy editors of the diary should have shared common and more reliable information.

However, the miracle did not happen for Orlandelli as he confirms Valentino's grandfather was a French doctor. He also claims Valentino was born in the province of Taranto when that province had not yet been created and, at the time, was called the Province of the Terra d'Otranto with Lecce as its capital. The province of Taranto was created in 1923, however it was called the Ionian Province and then became, definitively, the Province of Taranto only in 1951. We know as fact Gabrielle in 1890 married Dr. Giovanni Guglielmi, civic veterinarian and director of the municipal slaughterhouse of Castellaneta in the then province of the Terra d'Otranto with Lecce as its capital.

Existing documents prove Valentino's father Giovanni was never a cavalry officer and was called to the compulsory military service, in the infantry, on February 5, 1874. He was discharged on September 11, 1875. After graduating in veterinary medicine in Naples, he embarked on a military career as a complementary veterinary officer which he abandoned on August 30, 1878[5].

Another statement attributed Valentino in the diary is a reference he makes about his relationship with his sister Maria:

"There had once been four of us children in my father's house; but it was with Maria that I conspired and connived."

Giovanni and Gabrielle's children were four, but the diary's "Rodolfo" forgot to mention there was little choice to be made between which sister to play with. The eldest, Grazia Bice born on June 1, 1890 died on August 14, 1891, four years before Rodolfo's own birth. Are these inaccuracies to be believed as just more from the distracted dreamer Rudolph Valentino?

A Jumble of Inaccurate Dates

In addressing the inconsistencies or discrepancies between the dates Valentino is alleged to have reported in the diary and the verified and documented dates I cite the following.

Valentino, at one point is said to have written he arrived, for the first time, in New York on December 23, 1913, while the immigration records show he arrived on

---

Gabrielle was twelve years old. On the death of her father, Gabrielle, her sister Leonie and her mother, Marie-Rose Willien, returned to Picardy to the Barbin family and there are traces of Gabrielle's presence there in 1872 when she was sixteen years old. Then following a great economic depression in that area, Valentino's grandmother Marie-Rose Willien returned to Taranto with her daughters.

5   About Giovanni Guglielmi in the army is possible to know more reading the book by Aurelio Miccoli. "Valentino e il professore QUELLO CHE SO DI VALENTINO" - Scorpione Editore – Taranto 2020

December 22, a minor inaccuracy.

The one date not included in the diary is the date of departure of Rudolph and Natacha in 1923, which is traditionally held to be July 23, when I found it was actual July 24th. The date of departure was well known for some time by Valentino who, on June 2, 1923, sent a letter to a Mr. Barony in which he communicated he will leave for Europe on July 24. Another confirmation of this date comes with the publication, appearing in some U.S. newspapers on July 23, of the announcement that the following day the Valentinos would set sail for Europe. A sort of call to gather flappers to run to the dock and greet their idol.

The dates regarding the trip from Croydon, London airport to the Le Bourget airport in Paris, are mostly wrong. The diary cites the date of that departure as August 1st while the verified date is August 15th. How could Valentino be so in the clouds he would not manage to recall any of the following dates correctly?

August 9, 1923 is stated as the date of the departure for Deauville, when the actual and verified date is August 24, 1923.

October 11, 1923 is stated as the date of the arrival in Plymouth from Cherbourg for a return to London, when the actual and verified date is October 27, 1923.

While the diary reports the date of October 15 as the date given for the departure from Southampton for New York and the name of the ship as the S.S. Belgenland, the accurate date is November 3, 1923 and the name of the ship was S.S. Aquitania.

October 21, 1923 is reported in the diary as the date of arrival in New York when it was November 9, 1923.

This is but a sampling of inaccurate dates in the diary and I reject the hypothesis that Valentino was so much in the clouds he did not know the dates of the voyages or the name of the ships which brought him back to the United States. If this were the case, he would still be wandering around on the docks of Southampton in search of his ship!

The Stages of the Journey

Valentino's trip to Europe took place in stages; London and its surroundings, Paris and Normandy, a visit to the Natacha's parents in Juan Les Pins and after that Italy with significant destinations in Milan, some between Milan and Rome, then Campobasso, on to Castellaneta and Taranto, then a return to Rome via Naples.

Then, in an impressive leap, the Valentinos arrive in Nice. They then journey by car on to Cherbourg where again they risked their lives due to the stormy sea. Then, with a little delay on the schedule they finally regained the shores of Great Britain on October 27. After a week in London for a quick farewell to the beloved city, on November 3rd, they embark on the *S.S. Aquitania* to return to New York where they land on the 9th of that month.

London

The journey begins in London, a city Rudolph loves very much. For London and England our star demonstrates a deep love. The Valentino's presence in London, from the point of view of *My Private Diary*, is formal and, I dare to say, boring as it reads as an excerpt from a high society magazine with lists of illustrious names designed to add luster to luster. I can say this part of the narrative resembles the Grand Tourist's style.

Paris

As soon as Valentino arrived at Le Bourget, Romano's diary copy editors have him launch into an apotheosis of England. I am amazed he did not launch into a praise of France and the French since he had ancestry from France. Instead he affirms how certainly in his blood runs the memory of a past ancestor who lived in England and adds:

"We know one another of old, London and I".

Valentino here touches on psychology and says that a feeling of, "throw back" flows in his veins, or a "deja vu", thanks to some British ancestor. On this point Orlandelli defines the term "throw back" as "phylogenetic regression". Instead of translating, "throwback" as a "return to the past", he adds "phylogenetic regression", which complicates the matter because the terminology "phylogenetic regression" can be used in the context of biological inheritance, cognitive psychology and psychoanalysis. It would have been better to simply write, "return to the past" or more poetically, "deja vu".

In France, the *Private Diary*, "Valentino" literally goes wild with considerations which are nothing short of derogatory concerning all that is French. Everything is of low quality, the dancers of the Folies Bergère are for him plump without charm, the food is poor and the people, especially in Deauville are of an impossible boorishness.

These statements by Valentino gave rise to heavy reactions from the defensive French press and in particular in the film magazine *Cinémagazine* on May 16, 1924, as written by one outraged journalist, André Tinchant. A voice rose in defense of Valentino, that of director René Clair who sent *Cinémagazine* a letter clarifying all the misconceptions which provoked Tinchant's reaction. The defense was published in the May 30 issue of that year.[6]

---

6   Both the article by Tinchant and the letter by René Clair are included from page 240

After a visit to the Natacha's parents in Juan Les Pins, Valentino, Natacha and Aunt Tessie leave France to cross the nearby border with Italy. Before leaving the Côte d'Azur, Valentino indulges in more negative comments about his mother's homeland. Valentino is amazed how some people can go to the Côte d'Azur during the winter period as, in that season, the cold and humid reign, leaving room for a few days of shy sun. He specifies that, in that period, the Riviera is exactly the opposite of what it should be.

Then they enter Italy from France, crossing the border between Menton and Ventimiglia, at the barrier of Ponte San Luigi. There Rudolph apparently engaged in an unpleasant exchange with a carabiniere in charge of passport control whom he defined as "*a yokel carabiniere*". This seems, from what we know about Valentino, a sentence out of place for a celebrity looking for approval.

In Milan, the Valentinos met with Maria, Valentino's sister who was there working as a salesgirl at the "La Rinascente" department store. Maria then becomes a new travel companion.

In Bologna, the diary informs us the Valentinos, Aunt Teresa and Maria went to the grand hotel Vaglione, a further typo because in Bologna there is no such hotel and never has been. The luxury and traditional hotel in Bologna was the Baglioni hotel, in Via dell'Indipendenza, a hotel which is now called Majestic. Orlandelli corrects, by default, the misspelled Vaglione to Baglioni without giving note of his correction.

We then read about an invitation to visit the castle of Vincigliata which is said to be located fifteen miles from Bologna and owned by a certain Baron Cassinni, or Baron Alberto Fassini, to correctly say the name.

Baron Fassini was the owner of the castle, but the Vincigliata castle is not located near Bologna but near Fiesole in the province of Florence almost sixty-eight miles from Bologna. Then, in the diary narrative, as if almost by magic, the castle of Vincigliata is transported to the vicinity of Florence. Here too Orlandelli corrects the original text of the diary and changes the name from Cassinni to Fassini.

Baron Fassini, in addition to several other ancestral residences, also owned the fortress Sangallo in Nettuno. This was a fortress in which Valentino was a guest of the baron and which excited the actor's imagination so much that he, in a letter sent on March 15, 1924, communicated to the Baron he wanted to make a film about Duke Cesare Borgia known as the "Prince Valentino". He asks the Baron to grant him the opportunity to shoot some scenes in the very fortress where, at the beginning of the sixteenth century, Prince Valentino had one of his fortresses.

In the diary narrative it is said that in the seabed facing this fortress San Gallo there are, submerged in the waters, the remains of a Roman villa. It is claimed the ruins remain visible when there is low tide. In reality the tides of the Tyrrhenian Sea, on the Roman coast, have tides which rarely exceed twenty inches and therefore no ruins can emerge from the waves.[7]

On September 7, still according to the calendar of the diary, the Valentinos arrived in Rome where they stayed at the Grand Hotel Excelsior on Via Veneto. That same evening Valentino tells of a dinner in the hotel with Baron Fassini and an unidentified Count Cine, who would have been the secretary of the U.C.I. (the Italian Cinematographic Union). Count Cine would also have accompanied the Valentinos to attend filming that took place in Villa Borghese. Here lies a question to which, unfortunately, I cannot answer. Who was Count Cine? A definitive answer is given by Orlandelli who changed the name to Count Cini. If as the translator, he refers to Vittorio Cini the error is macroscopic because Vittorio Cini became Count of Monselice on May 16, 1940. The Count Cini had various business interests and preeminent political roles but never had interests in the world of film production.

Regarding this trip to Rome, the narrative in *My Private Diary* differs substantially from the account which was published in the February 1925 issue of *Pictures & Picturegoer* magazine. In the *Pictures & Picturegoer* installment, we jump from September 8th to September 10th and there is no trace of annotations relating to any events on September 9th.

In *My Private Diary*, we find that entry for September 8, initiated a long and intense piece relating to Rome and, in particular, to the Colosseum, described as a decidedly macabre place. The piece describes Valentino's nocturnal visit to the Colosseum in the company of Baron Fassini. However this visit was preceded by a dinner with the Baron which was followed by a tour of what is referred to as the, "*Circa Monza*" "Where the automobile races were held", followed by a walk in St. Peter's Square to then approach, in the middle of the night, the mythical Colosseum.

I was struck by this "*Circa Monza*" mention because the only circus in the area is the *Circus Maximus*, a large stadium where chariot races were held. But the fact that the copy editors wrote "where car racing was done", denotes no historical knowledge and a linguistic confusion between the Circus Maximus and the Monza motor racing circuit, near Milan, which is more than 370 miles north of Rome. Perhaps the hasty copy editor was deceived by the date September 9, 1923, the day on which the third Italian Grand Prix and the first European Grand Prix were held in Monza.

I think these scrambled dates occurred both for the lack of knowledge of Italian geography and history and for a hasty edition without any verification due to the technical times for sending the magazine to print.

The "philologist" Orlandelli corrects Circa Monza to, "Circus Maximus and where

---

7   In fact the remains of a grandiose imperial villa, called Villa of Nero are located in Anzio and not in Nettuno. But the ruins of this villa are not submerged by the waves and are situated on the northern promenade of the city, adjacent to the old lighthouse. The ruins extend for hundreds of meters overhanging the sea and today are part of the archaeological park of the localities for the "otia" (leisure) of the Roman emperors. There are also, about ten miles south of Nettuno, the ruins of a submerged Roman villa, in the locality of Torre Astura, the villa, also known as Cicero Villa was part of a complex of villas to the delight of various emperors and notables of ancient Rome.

the wagon races were held" while in the original text of the diary it is clearly written, "we went to Circa Monza, where the automobile races were held". The "where the automobile races were held", however is not the same as referring to "wagons" or Roman chariots. The lack of notation here on this is truly regrettable.

The diary entry for September 8 ends with the following sentence,

"There are new thoroughfares, wider streets almost everywhere and there has been a general demolition of the old-time slums. This is conjunction with the general modernized sanitation, which has caused Rome to be one of the most sanitary and healthiest cities in Europe."

Here is a rare and positive consideration regarding something that is not American! We then find the most conspicuous addition in the book version of the narrative. This addition includes, a "learned" discussion on Rome and some of its historical events, which in the book occur on September 9; something which does not exist at all in the magazine installments.

This addition is in regards to the plundering of Rome and the Colosseum. This is set within a mass of cliches and historical platitudes, such as the Latin motto "Quod non fecerunt barbari fecerunt Barberini" which translates as, "What the barbarians did not do was done by the Barberini." In the original text of *My Private Diary* this Latin sentence is translated, "What the Barbiere (the barbers) did not do to Rome, the Barberini did." The phrase refers to sadly several infamous episodes in the history of Rome. I cite but a few.

In 1625, Pope Urban VIII, a Barberini, had the bronze beams of the Pantheon removed and melted, to build the canopy for the Saint Peter's Basilica and cannons for Castel Sant'Angelo.

The origin of the saying cited in the diary was also ascribed to the construction of Palazzo Barberini with materials taken from the Colosseum. At the time the pope was the absolute king of Rome and could dispose of the antiques as he pleased, both for his own use and as a concession to friendly families. The ancient monuments became, for a long time, quarries of building material for many noble and cardinal residences and the Colosseum was the antiquity which paid the highest price.

Regarding the so-called sacking of Rome, the narrator of *My Private Diary*, mentions the barbarian peoples of the Goths, Visigoths and Huns as invaders of the Eternal City. Note that Attila, king of the Huns, never managed to get even close to Rome and did not sack it. Of all the barbarians mentioned by the pseudo Valentino in the diary, only the Visigoths deserve a citation.

Then, perhaps, thanks to the information on many tourist brochures, the pseudo Valentino pauses for a long time and rattles off a sort of lecture on the Colosseum described as a gloomy and disturbing monument, full of gruesome narratives. At a certain point a literary quote is also triggered:

"Right below the Coliseum there is a tremendous drop called, fitly, the Place of the Suicides, because the fact that so many of these fatalities occurred there. The protagonist in D'Annunzio,"Triumph of Death" fell to his death over this 1,200 foot drop. It is vertiginous, hence, I suppose the physical part of the fascination."

Therefore, according to the author of *My Private Diary*, under or in the vicinity of the Colosseum there would be a place called the Place of Suicides, it would be a sort of ravine over 1200 feet deep and a usual place for Roman suicides. This is included with the quotation from the novel, *The Triumph of Death* by Gabriele D'Annunzio, in which he tells the story of two lovers, Giorgio Aurispa and Ippolita Sanzio, who end their lives embraced, in a murder suicide, with a jump from a high cliff in Abruzzo, near Ortona Mare in the province of Chieti, 145 miles away from the nonexistent ravine at the Colosseum.

The Colosseum was a well-known place of suicides but those anxious for death did not throw themselves into a non-existent deep ravine but climbed up to the top of the building and then, from there, leaped down with a jump of about 160 feet.

Perhaps the editor of the diary wanted to make, at all costs, a cultured quotation given that D'Annunzio and his novel, full of references to the philosophy of Friedrich Nietzsche, was very fashionable in those years. But if the copy editors had actually read *The Triumph of Death* they would have been careful to accurately cite that infamous quote.

Meanwhile, Orlandelli was careful not to literally translate what is written in the diary, namely, "The protagonist in Dannuzio's "Triumph of Death", fell to his death over this 1,200-foot drop," and instead writes, "The protagonist of "The Triumph of Death" by D'Annunzio dies after a fall of 1299 feet..." without indicating where those feet were.

The Colosseum is located on flat land at the eastern edge of the archaeological complex of the Imperial Forums. There is not even a shadow of horrendous chasms. I think that the historical confusion relating to the horror of suicides was due to a cursory knowledge of an ancient and suggestive Roman myth[8].

To these inaccurate and confusing statements, the editors add the name of Freud and touch on psychoanalysis with scattered citations. All this approximate cultural condiment was certainly created for, as they say in France, "Epatér les bourgeois", that is "to amaze the naive" and create the conviction, in the readers, of finding themselves in the presence of a scholar with a solid knowledge of classical culture.

---

8   An hypothesis, which sincerely would surprise me if true, is that the writer was referring to the myth of the Lacus Curtius. An interesting archaeological find discovered in 1903, precisely in the Imperial Forums, not far from the Colosseum, of which Titus Livius also reported, telling that it was what remained of a deep chasm opened in the center of the Forum. Several attempts were made with baskets of soil to fill it, but in vain. According to the Augurs, the chasm would be filled only by throwing the most precious thing of the Roman people into it. Then the young knight Marcus Curtius, believing that the most precious thing of the Roman people was the courage of his warriors, fully armed, mounted his horse, galloped into the abyss and sacrificed himself and the horse in honor of the Manes by throwing himself into the terrifying chasm, "and a crowd of men and women threw fruit and votive offerings after him", then the precipice closed.

Orlandelli tells us how the Guglielmi family was originally from Rome and they emigrated to Martina Franca, in Puglia, in the first half of the 19th century due to a duel in which a member of the Roman powerful Colonna family was killed by a Guglielmi. He claims it was then, following a massacre by brigands in Martina Franca, they moved to Castellaneta around 1850[9].

These are imaginative statements as Giovanni Guglielmi was born in Martina Franca and he was the one who moved to Castellaneta having won the public contest for the position of municipal veterinarian and director of the Civic Slaughterhouse.

In the diary Valentino tells us he dined at Palazzo Tittoni, one of the historical residences of Baron Fassini. It is surprising there is no reference made to the fact that Palazzo Tittoni is located in Via Rasella 155 not far from Via Rasella 131 where on April 5, 1892, Alberto Guglielmi, the elder brother of Valentino, was born.

Again with regards to Rome, Valentino commits some mistakes which are unforgivable for an Italian. For example:

I believe he would never refer to Via "del Babbuino" as Via "Babuina", or Via "del Quirinale" as Via "Quirinale", Via "Agostino Depretis" as Via "Agnostine Depretis" while Via "dei Condotti" becomes Via "Condotti". It is almost pleonastic to reiterate that the benevolent Italian translator corrects all toponymic errors without notation to the original.

Further in the text we find Valentino making more mistakes when the Apulian city of "Carosino" becomes "Carisine" and "Taranto" becomes "Tarento"; in the eyes of a foreigner these differences may seem insignificant but not to those of a native speaker of Italian.

After his stay in the Eternal City, Valentino wanted to visit his brother Alberto in Campobasso especially to meet his nephew Jean, born on August 14, 1914, eight months after his departure for New York. Here too Orlandelli makes a good impression with his note number 45, where he tells of Jean, as "Giovanni", son of Alberto and Ada who lived in Los Angeles and was an architect by profession. Alberto's son was baptized Jean and not Giovanni and in Los Angeles he worked as an audio engineer in the cinematographic field. In many episodes of the *Twilight Zone* series the credits to Jean Valentino are visible.

We must give Valentino a bad mark in geography in the diary because the name of the city is Campobasso and not Campo Basso, and the city was not located in the "province" of the Abruzzi but was the capital of the province of Campobasso, at the time part of the then Abruzzi and Molise region.

Then our diary guide explains the role of brother Alberto, at the time Chief

---

9 With regard to the events relating both to the duel with a Colonna and to the origin of Rudolph Valentino's nobility, it is possible to find exhaustive answers in the chapter XI of Aurelio Miccoli's book. *Valentino e il professore. Quello che so di Valentino.,* Scorpio Publishers, Taranto, 2020.

Secretary of the Municipality of Campobasso, a position he occupied from 1921 to 1924, by saying his role was equivalent to that of an "American lieutenant governor". At that time the municipal secretary was appointed by the municipal council, who chose him from among those qualified to practice by virtue of a license obtained following civil exams. Alberto obtained his license from the prefecture of Reggio Calabria.

His functions were, above all, those of checking the regularity and legality of the resolutions of the municipal council as well as taking care of the minutes of the municipal councils and the regular collection and registration of all Registry office documents. That of municipal secretary was and still is, a consultative and bureaucratic position and certainly not elective and could not be considered a sort of governor at the provincial level.

Then Valentino tells us that his brother, thanks to the great quality of the services provided in the public administration, was awarded the title of Knight of the Kingdom. The appointment as Knight of the Kingdom, especially at that time, was a fairly common tradition as all public employees, once they reached a certain level, received this as a sort of bonus rather than a coveted title.

About Castellaneta

After the visit to Campobasso, Rodolfo, with his sister Maria and Natacha's aunt leave for Castellaneta. As soon as they arrive, Valentino shows his aunt the house where he was born defining it as, "a square, flat-roofed farmhouse built of heavy white stone-the house where I was born". Here too Valentino seems to have forgotten what the building where he was born looked like and makes a blunder. The house where he was born was not a farmhouse but a residential building with a flat roof, which is quite common in homes in southern Italy.

Later he relates how he was sent to Perugia, to the Collegio della Sapienza, an institution, still existing, owned by the O.N.A.O.S.I. (National Opera for Italian Health Orphans Assistance). This school is dedicated to the orphans of Italian doctors and veterinarians, but Valentino does not say he was expelled from that school without having finished the established courses[10].

Then he is merciless in criticizing his homeland and complains in a local hotel there is no bathroom in the entire building. He is amazed when the concierge tells him they don't need it because around the corner there is a Turkish bath.

This fact, whether it is true or fictional, inspires a hymn of praise for America where, even in small towns, hotels have a bathroom. Then Valentino complains that the most elementary aspects of body care are unknown there. He says they don't wash,

---

10 On the ENPAM website (National Social Security Assistance Body for Doctors) it is reported that Valentino was expelled from school because with a small knife or with the point of a compass he injured one of his companions who mocked him for his ears. He was certainly not one who accepted the provocations of bullies, on the contrary he defended himself very well.

exercise, breathe fresh air or follow a good diet. These are nothing but racist statements as if the Castellanetani were all filthy, weak, asphyxiated and eaters of crap. Then he notes that the environment of Castellaneta does not show any changes since he, then nine years old, left the town to go to Taranto. He confirms that the boredom of that town was what prompted him to leave.

The diary narrative then reveals how Valentino's desire to emigrate to the United States arose. He tells us that the small town in which he was born gave peace, serenity and well-being but added that those were things he did not crave and therefore he strongly desired to emigrate to the United States. All well and good except for a small detail. When he left Italy he had not lived in Castellaneta for nine years. Yet despite the family having lived in the city of Taranto since he was nine he writes, "my mother being wise, knew that I should certainly get away from the inert, demoralizing influence of that small town"[11].

This is followed by the narration of his trip to America, the whys and how. What is narrated, regarding his arrival in the Big Apple, is now well known. However, as previously mentioned, the facts reveal a different story. Thanks to an interview given by another emigrant to the United States, the Piedmontese Mr. William Bianchino and to whom I cite directly so he can better give you an idea of how things really went:

"When Valentino came to this country from Taranto, Italy, he came directly to our office because my boss, Mr. Filomarino was a good friend of Valentino's mother".

Regarding the money available to Valentino then, Mr. Bianchino tells us how Rudolph, with his activity as a dancer earned $75 dollars a week, equal to the current $2,062.00 plus a weekly remittance from mother Gabrielle of $5.00 dollars, equal to $137.00 today. That would have been an income of $8,798.00 a month, for an eighteen year old Rudolph, which does not support the theory of his much vaunted misery.

A little further on the diary, Valentino tells us how when he arrived in the United States he had only $400.00, (a value of $11,00.00 dollars as of this writing). Although he tells Robert Florey, who reports in, "Inoubliable, Inoublié", Valentino had in his pocket $300 (or $8,250.00 by today's exchange rates).

There are many subsequent historical inaccuracies in the accounts of Italian history and it would be daunting to correct them all. Suffice to say a few of the more notable are:

The diary Valentino manifests some shortcomings in his knowledge of Italian history in the entry dated, Naples, September 27, where he talks about the castle of

---

11 That is another impressive mistake of those who wrote the diary because Taranto was an important port that welcomed a large part of the Italian navy fleet. Taranto was a living city and Valentino himself tells us, in a letter written to Bruno Pozzan, a former friend of the Sapienza, that he delighted, every fortnight, to go and practice English with the British tourists who visited the city and not only entertained the conversation with strangers but also with the naval officers on the warships in the port of the city, with the attendance of the "café chantant" where he ruthlessly courted the ladies entertainers. He also states how he frequented the numerous brothels where he did somersaults with prostitutes from whom he got syphilis, a disease that was difficult to cure at the time and which accompanied him until his death. Taranto was all but an inert and monotonous city with a demoralizing influence.

Arechi, near Salerno. He says, "One of the points of interest was a huge castle which dates back to 1000 or 1050 and was occupied by Theodoric, the Byzantine Emperor".

The castle was much older than what Valentino reported and was never occupied by Theodoric between 1000 and 1050 of the current era, because Theodoric was king of Italy from 493 to 526 and resided in Ravenna.

We find another historical inaccuracy when Valentino speaks of his time in Salerno, of a treasure buried in a river bed to hide it from invaders. Surely he refers to the treasure of Alaric, the king of the Visigoths who was buried with his horse and the entire booty where the rivers Crati and Busento joined. And it is there that, according to legend, the greatest lost treasure in the history of humanity has been buried from 410 AD until today. The problem is that this location is not in the vicinity of Salerno, but about 162 miles away, further south. Are we to believe this was this another "stroll" by Valentino?

At one point Valentino explains to us that Cesare Borgia also went to Capua when he was politically vulnerable, and from there he escaped to Spain. Things went very differently in fact and Cesare Borgia, also known as "Prince Valentino" was the protagonist of one of the worst events in the history of Europe. Before leaving Capua, Borgia sacked the city and killed 5,000 people. Valentino relates very little in the diary when it comes to the sacking and massacre of Capua [12].

In relating the events of his return to Rome, Valentino narrates how visiting Castel Sant'Angelo he was able to see the secret treasures, golden coins and jewelry of some popes and, in particular, those of Cesare Borgia and Pope Paul III Farnese. However, it should be remembered that in Castel Sant'Angelo there is no treasure which belonged to Duke Cesare Borgia. When Valentino visited Castel Sant'Angelo there were no golden coins [13].

Valentino also tells us that Napoleon III was imprisoned for a short time in Sant'Angelo Castle. In this regard it is worth remembering Napoleon III, who first was President of the French Republic and then second emperor of France, lived in Rome in

---

12 The sack of Capua, committed by Cesare Borgia, also known as the Duke "Valentino", son and henchman of Pope Alexander VI Borgia, following a cowardly betrayal was perpetrated on July 24, 1501. Still, today it represents one of the most dramatic and villainous pages in the history of Italy and Europe, taking into account the presence of the army of Luis XII, of the brutish soldiers of Cesare Borgia and of the interests of Ferdinand the Catholic. It was the ruthless Duke Valentino who gave the coup de grace to Capua, the Queen city of Volturno region, the massacre was unprecedented with so a great damage to the defenseless population, which resulted in some 5000 victims. Cesare Borgia did not flee after the Capua massacre but committed even worse actions and ended up in disgrace. He was completely sacked by Pope Julius II and died of syphilis in the night between the eleventh and the twelfth of March 1507.

13 Speaking of treasures, the pseudo Valentino refers to the Treasure Room. The first news of a gold reserve preserved in the fortress dates back to the end of the fifteenth century. Later it was Sixtus V Peretti (1585-1590) who placed the Treasury there in 1586, kept together with numerous precious objects, such as the Miter adorned with gems and the Papal Tiaras of the pontiffs, closed in iron chests.

The room was closed by two doors whose keys were kept one by the Pope's Secret Treasurer, the other by the Cardinal Dean. The 'treasure' was placed in the large chests, still in the center of the room, accessible by opening six locks, whose keys were entrusted to different people.

exile, at Ruspoli Palace, from 1823 until 1831. The Napoleon Valentino was referring to was a cousin who was imprisoned in Castel Sant'Angelo; Napoleon III's cousin Peter Bonaparte.

Back Home

Another important entry in the *Pictures & Picture Goers* version of the narrative, is the following sentence:

"Home again. In New York again, soon to be at work again! I feel like a schoolboy, like throwing my cap (if I wore one) into the air and shouting "Hurrah! Hurrah! The day after we steamed into harbor, sighting the Statue of Liberty. THE END"

In Michael Romano's book, *My Private Diary*, there is an added word which ends the book in a surprising way. This is a word in Hebrew, *SELAH*! The closure of the book version is as follows:

"What more triumphant conclusion could I have for my return trip to my old home! What greater news could I write back of my after-all victorious return? What higher note of triumph is there on which to conclude these pages of my own diary? SELAH! "

The presence of this term, as a sort of exotic Amen or hurrah, seems to me somewhat off topic in relation to Valentino. The Jewish culture was very far from his formation, nowhere are there indications of such a profound knowledge of the Tehillim. Selah is present only in the Book of Psalms[14].

I would be interested if someone could show me unequivocally that Rudolph Valentino knew well and used the term Selah!

However, this rally cry was not sufficient because the editor of the book then inserts a poem by Henry Van Dyke, "*AMERICA FOR ME*" which basically advises to go wherever you like, wander around the ruins of the old world but nothing is more beautiful after long journeys, to go home, "where the air is full of sunlight and the flag is full of stars."

---

14 To better understand the meaning of Selah, I cite Dante Lattes, an expert on the Torah who cites in the introduction of his translation of the Book of Pslams, with the Hebrew and Italian text opposite as published on Torah.it. "A musical term repeated numerous times both in the middle and at the end of many Psalms and also in the oration of the prophet Chavaqquq, is the word sélah. It is mostly interpreted as an elevation of the voice, and usually occurs either at the end of a verse or at the end of the song, but sometimes also in the middle of a verse...The term sélah was also understood by the ancients in the sense of always, forever (nézach, séla, vaéd)."

One of the first things which meets the eye of the reader of *My Private Diary*, is the ridicule and demeanor of everything that is not "American". The considerations, in addition to those mentioned above, especially towards hotels are belittling and I would say offensive. While of the Milanese hotels the diary says:

"Of course, when one comes more or less directly from America, the land of efficiency and expertness and service, one is apt to find everything slow. People, service, events themselves, take on the aspect of snails."

"The suites are pathetic and summarily furnished ..."

I share as a consideration that such statements could be considered a bit exaggerated for a self-styled ex-sleeper on the benches of Central Park who at the time wanted to market his movies in Europe.

Additionally, I share a consideration about the Italian translation of *My Private Diary* by Paolo Orlandelli. I was continually noticing how he altered the original text of *My Private Diary* without a notation of his changes. This is, for me as a translator, something I find unacceptable.

Note that editing and correcting errors without citing the original is a practice which has nothing to do with the intellectual honesty which must always guide an honest translator. Translating is not only the mechanical transposition of a text from one language to another but also the highlighting of the historical context of the original text without making corrections which are not contained in footnotes. "Adjusting" a text to one's liking is a practice to be avoided as it is misleading.

The translation of a text from one language to another must enable the reader to understand the broad context in which the original contents were created. In the Italian translation Orlandelli does not create historical context and, above all, does not include the historically important introduction of Michael A. Romano. In addition, the translator must report all the contents as they are in the original work without adjusting or modifying but, in the case of inconsistencies, insert explanatory notes. Giving the reader a text which is not the faithful translation of the original is a nefarious operation.

The first and predominant impression of Orlandelli's translation is his assumption Rudolph Valentino was a greedy, promiscuous, insatiable homosexual. This a premise which has no basis in documented fact. The misnomer of Valentino as homosexual is the result of dubious red-light district biographies written to market to the homosexual community.

Paolo Orlandelli deems it critical to relate and is so certain Valentino was homosexual, within some notes he gives bizarre and unverified information about Valentino's sexual relationships, never are confirmed by any evidence. According to Orlandelli, all the visitors to "Casa Valentino" had tumultuous sexual relations with Valentino.

He fantasizes about Valentino as an avid predator of men and a great frequenter of an x-rated club for Hollywood homosexuals of the 1920's he refers to as the Torch Club. In my research, I have never found any reference historically to that Torch Club.

I found but one organization called Torch Club which is an organization intended for boys and girls aged 9 to 12. When such prurient claims are made, it is intellectually dishonest to fail to provide evidence. When in doubt as to such a claim being true and not merely author's fantasies, it makes a better impression to remain silent.

It is lamentable Orlandelli chose to exploit his translation of My Private Diary by seizing this as an opportunity to restate and publicize the glut of fiction which so clouds and tarnishes the historically accurate and documented legacy of Rudolph Valentino.

In this analysis of Michael Romano's *My Private Diary*, I relied on these publications:

"My Private Diary, By Rudolph Valentino with an Introduction by Michael A. Romano", E-book, "*PICKLE PARTNERS PUBLISHING*", 2016.

"My Life Story by Rudolph Valentino", *Photoplay*, February, March, April 1923.

"My Own Story of My Trip Abroad by Rudolph Valentino", *Pictures and Picturegoer* from July 1924 to October 1925.

"RODOLFO VALENTINO – Il mio diario privato", translation to Italian by Paolo Orlandelli, Lindau Edizioni, July 2004.

"Rudolph Valentino Francophobic"

by
André Tinchant
Published in *Cinémagazine,* May 16, 1924

Regarding, "My Trip Abroad", published in *Movie Weekly* from 2/16/1924 to 8/6/1924

I was just a little indignant, I laughed a lot and I would be remiss if I did not share both my indignation and my hilarity, because by giving you the reasons why, I will enable you to judge for yourselves the mentality of the artist we are talking about a lot and that he himself speaks and writes about...perhaps too much.

I have had the opportunity to meet most of the foreign artists, American and non-American, who came to France, both for pleasure and for work. There is no one who has not told me they felt pleasure in living among us and how they aspired to stay in Paris or to return; there is no one who has not given me the most flattering praise of our country and of us French!

Whether their names are Rimsky, Mosjoukine, Lissenko, Pearl White, Fanny Wàrd, Douglas Fairbanks, Charlie Chaplin, Griffith or Mary Pickford, they all expressed unanimously towards us, a feeling of gratitude for the welcome which has always been reserved for them.

There is, however, a discordant note in this concert of praise. A note which comes to us from Rudolph Valentino and I discovered by reading *Movie Weekly*, an American magazine, publishing in weekly episodes, the memories of his trip to Europe. It is good for those who know Valentino's life - and for those who do not know him, at least in broad terms, despite the many fabulous interviews published by his press officer – to read in this comic book, the most recent farce, these memories which are much more a confession of faith than a travelogue.

Packed with hymns to nature, tranquility, family life...it is perhaps amusing to see the handsome young premier, with a rather turbulent past, including the latest scandals (marriage, divorce and then to remarry ignoring the terms of the law) whose popularity dramatically expired in America, assuming the guise of a naïve and incurable romantic, to regain the public's favor?

However, I would not have thought to point out how much "Tartufe" there is in this "diary", had I not also found some enlightening lines, written during his stay in

Deauville, Paris and on the Cote d'Azur.

Of course I am aware Valentino and his wife were very disappointed when they arrived in Paris. In London, where much publicity was generated throughout the press by Robert Florey and Maurice Rosett: before the couple even disembarked, the reception was enthusiastic. I have personally seen the number of letters, invitations and flower baskets which arrived at the Carlton every day. All London knew "Rudy" had arrived; the echoes and sentimental stories, which were wisely inserted in the newspapers and magazines, created a current of a great and amiable acceptance. The welcome was very warm.

It was not exactly the same in Paris, where we obviously know very well how to be enthusiastic, but where we have a greater sense of proportion and we know how to give each person the welcome which corresponds to their personality. Valentino and his wife were received here, very kindly but in silence. The hotel where they were staying was not stormed; they didn't have to send the police along the route of their car. In short, they went almost unnoticed.

The lack of information, the season - it was mid-August - and also the lack of people interested in Valentino, of whom only two films were known and not the best ones, caused this lack of enthusiasm. This is all in all understandable. But for this, undoubtedly, the handsome Rudy accuses us.

It wasn't enough for him to be greeted with great kindness and welcomed by some of our colleagues, he needed the big crowd. A big crowd which was not here and this is certainly the reason why he adorns his "diary" with phrases like these:

"Deauville - We thought we would find the most attractive women in the casino, the best dressed men, but we only met uninteresting people. Literally, not a single elegant woman; just tourists (?) talking and laughing aloud. The Casino cuisine is as bad as the people ..."

"Paris - The French theater does not exist. The beautiful women, which we see on the cover of Parisian magazines, do not exist. The chorus girls of the music halls are far below what I imagined. They can't compare to what we have in America, and I was surprised to find that most of them are fat, I who I imagined the French as slender as sylphs. We went to the Folies-Bergère, it was literally 'putrescent' (sic). The show, the soubrettes, the whole thing, everything is terribly disappointing. From my landing in Cherbourg, I realized how much American things are superior to those found in Europe: chorus girls (insists), women, theater, food (!!) ..."

"Juan les Pins - I don't understand the perversion of people who come to the Cote d'Azur in winter. It's cold on the Riviera, the climate is humid with only a few days of sunshine from time to time. The south of France is not at all what most people imagine..."

Mr. Valentino is not of the greatest importance. His statements tend, however, to create an opinion in America which is not very favorable to us. And, if it is funny to note the bad faith of their author, who judges the theaters of Paris on what he saw there in

August, and the climate of the Cote d'Azur on a stay during the height of summer, it is painful to be "damaged" by a man who enjoyed and accepted our hospitality and our gullibility in welcoming his countless press releases.

ANDRÉ TINCHANT

"Let a friend of Rudolph Valentino add a few words to the article you are dedicating to him in your issue of May the 16th, under the title 'Rudolph Valentino Francophobe'.

I only know of the article published in *Movie Weekly* as the extract you provide. For this reason I can not judge it. But I have the honor of knowing Rudolph Valentino and I can say during their stay in France, Mr. and Mrs. Valentino only demonstrated sincere and very friendly feelings for France.

If Rudolph Valentino severely judges the public of Deauville and those of the Folies Bergère , don't you think, as he did, that this public hardly represents France but more just foreigners in France, which is not the same thing.

I was in Deauville with Rudolph Valentino. If he was disappointed, it was because he found there very few French and so many unbearable foreigners. I must admit on that point, I did not contradict him.

On the other hand, during his walks in the Normandy countryside and on many other occasions, he never ceased to rave about the beauty of our country. All of this would have been nothing but of small importance if the title of your article were not aimed to divulge about one of the few sincere friends of France in America, a false opinion. While so many other American stars, passing through Paris, overwhelm us with compliments and empty promises as they do in all countries, Rudolph Valentino is the only one, I think, who has not spoken much but who has begun to do something for the French people.

He is the only one to have brought a Frenchman, his friend André Daven, with him to New York, to have encouraged him into the studios' world while doing nothing to neglect his success. He is the only one, to my knowledge, who tried to have a French film produced in America.

This is a very recent matter and I know well about this subject. Yet knowing the hostility towards France, of the Anglo-German world of the Hollywood studios and, moreover, of one of our supposed friends, we can only feel true gratitude toward Rudolph Valentino. Finally, he does not announce, like so many others, large work projects in France. He is the only one to really think about it. It is possible in the future he will allow me to give you details on this point.

I would add for his latest film, *Monsieur Beaucaire*, Rudolph Valentino hired, in addition to André Daven, a French girl, Ms. Paulette Duval, and he commissioned the costumes for the movie to a French artist. Don't you think all these facts are more significant than words whose interpretation generate only misunderstandings?

I'm very sorry *Cinémagazine*, so well known in the film world, contributes to giving Rudolph Valentino a fictitious character which is not his. That is why I would be very grateful if you would publish this letter while awaiting the clarifications Rudolph Valentino will not fail to present to you himself.

With thanks, please accept... René Clair"

Cover of the first edition of My Private Diary by Rudolph Valentino
with an introduction by Michael A. Romano, published by Occult
Publishing Company - Chicago Il. 1929

THE SKETCH

Registered as a Newspaper for Transmission in the United Kingdom and to Canada and Newfoundland by Magazine Post.

No. 1593 — Vol. CXXIII.   WEDNESDAY, AUGUST 8, 1923.   ONE SHILLING.

RODOLPH VALENTINO COMES TO TOWN : THE FAMOUS FILM STAR AND HIS WIFE, NATACHA RAMBOVA, ON BOARD THE "AQUITANIA."

Nearly everyone in England must have seen Rodolph Valentino, the famous film star, on the screen. He played the leading rôle in "The Four Horsemen of the Apocalypse," "Blood and Sand," "The Sheik," and other important pictures, and is one of the most popular of all screen stars. He has, however, been actually seen in the flesh by few Londoners, so special interest attaches to the visit which he and his wife are now paying to this country. Mrs. Valentino is Art Director to Nazimova, and is professionally known as Natacha Rambova.

Photograph by L.N.A.

The André Daven Hoax

André Daven in later years as a producer and director

Left to Right: André Daven, Kabar, Rudolph Valentino & René Clair,
Paris, 1923

The André Daven Hoax

How did a relatively unknown Frenchman, André Daven, who appeared in a minor role in one of Rudolph Valentino's films in 1924, come to be known as Valentino's greatest love? In this essay I address André Daven's documented relationship with Valentino. I will present proof for the cause of Daven's abrupt departure from New York City in June of 1924 and the severing of his professional sponsorship by Natacha Rambova and Rudolph Valentino.

I will analyze and refute the dominate misconceptions about this subject including the premise André Daven was Rudolph Valentino's greatest love, the premise he alone discovered Josephine Baker and brought her to Paris and the claim he attended Valentino's New York funeral as a pallbearer.

André Daven's role in Valentino's history began with his discovery by Valentino and his wife Natacha Rambova in the summer of 1923. The Valentino's were honeymooning in Paris and at the time and Daven was working as a free-lance journalist and assistant to Jacques Hébertot, director of the Champs-Élysées Theater .

There are several versions as to how André Daven met the Valentinos. One version has the Valentinos meeting Daven when he interviewed them during their visit to Paris in 1923. While another version is purported by the French journalist, Michel Duran, who wrote in *"Marianne: Grand Hebdomadaire Litteraire Illustre", The Great Illustrated Literary Weekly*, published on August 3, 1933, how André Daven met Mr. and Mrs. Valentino in an upscale bar called the Clown Footit. This bar was located on the Rue Montaigne close to the Hotel Plaza Athénée where the Valentino's stayed when in Paris.

It was in bars such as the Clown Footit where Daven and other Parisian journalists cultivated their well-to-do contacts. Whether for an article they could sell by the inch to a newspaper or magazine or for social prestige, the competition among reporters vying for position was fierce. Conversely, celebrities visiting Paris exploited the eager reporters by sauntering into these bars for a few cocktails with a guarantee of valuable press.

By all accounts, André Daven is described as having been a handsome, dark-skinned young man of slight build who resembled Rudolph Valentino. At the time he was twenty-three years old and living with his girlfriend Yvonne Legeay who was eight years older than André. By all accounts, he is reported to have perfected the demeanor of a prince with a wardrobe demonstrating a fastidious personal taste. It is not surprising Natacha and Rudolph Valentino would be charmed and comment immediately upon Daven's potential career in the movies.

To place his discovery by the Valentinos into a broader perspective, it must be noted Daven was not the only French citizen Rudolph Valentino gave a nod to professionally on the trip to France in 1923. Valentino's desire to establish a collaboration with French cinema was recognized by the French press. According to the Valentino's friend, French director René Clair, Rudy extended his famous hand not only to André Daven but to other actors he also agreed to cast in *Monsieur Beaucaire.*[1]

It was not unusual for the Valentinos to sponsor a new discovery. Natacha discovered the designer Adrian, the actress Myrna Loy and Rudolph would have his business manager S. George Ullman negotiate a contract with Metro Pictures for his *Monsieur Beaucaire* co-star Doris Kenyon[2]. There is ample evidence of the Valentino's entrepreneurial interest in cinema as an art form and their influence as talent scouts and mentors.

At the time of the Valentino's visit to France in 1923, the Champs-Élysées Theater was under the direction of Jacques Hébertot. The theater was founded by Swedish millionaire Rolf De Maré in 1919, who established the venue to profile his partner, the famed actor and dancer Jean Börlin.

By the fall of 1920, Jacques Hébertot assumed directorial management and under his direction the theater came to be known for ambitious cultural productions including ballet performances, art exhibitions and stage productions. Jacques Hébertot would greet Rudolph and Natacha on their arrival in Paris, act as their host and promote them as visiting artists of merit. André Daven was then working as Hébertot's assistant and this is how he was discovered and found himself, upon the Valentino's invitation, arriving in New York City on the ocean liner *Aquitania* the following year.

It is logical to presume he came to America hoping to become a movie star like Rudolph Valentino. Manhattan awaited and he surely envisioned all the luxuries of Valentino's wild success for himself; a glamorous lifestyle of the rich and famous. As Jeanne DeRecqueville observed in her Valentino biography[3], André Daven was granted an auspicious beginning in the American movie industry when Rudolph Valentino and Natacha Rambova agreed to act as his sponsors and mentors. However, the reality of Daven's lifestyle in New York was something less than he imagined.

In one of André Daven's letters written to his girlfriend Yvonne Legeay, he relates how Rudolph and Natacha were paying him sixty dollars a week for his appearance in

1   "He (Rudolph Valentino) is the only one, to my knowledge, who tried to have a French film produced in America. This is a very recent matter and I know well about this subject. Yet knowing the hostility towards France, of the anglo-german world of the Hollywood studios and, moreover, of one of our supposed friends, we can only feel, toward Rudolph Valentino, true gratitude. Finally, he does not announce, like so many others, large work projects in France. He is the only one to really think about it. It is possible that in the future he will allow me to give you details on this point. I would add that for his latest film, Monsieur Beaucaire, Rudolph Valentino hired, in addition to André Daven, a French girl, Ms. Paulette Duval, and he commissioned the costumes for the movie to a French artist."

2   *The S. George Ullman Memoir,* p. 37.

3   Jeanne DeRecqueville, Rudolph Valentino in English, Viale Industria Pubblicazioni

Monsieur Beaucaire and an extra fifty dollars a week for clerical work generated by advertising. One hundred and ten dollars a week, even with the rate of exchange, was not a millionaire's ransom in New York City at the time.

To put Daven's salary into perspective, Valentino paid his staff in his home Falcon Lair in Los Angeles, thirty to fifty dollars a week with his handyman Lou Mahoney being paid forty dollars a week.[4] He paid his Los Angeles secretary and clerical assistant Raymond Fager sixty dollars a week and his New York secretary Estelle Dick, forty dollars a week. André Daven was paid a staff's salary with only slightly more financial prestige than the secretary or the handyman.

It is well-documented André Daven had expensive tastes in clothing and was accustomed to frequenting the swankiest bars and nightclubs in Paris to hob nob with the elite. Consequently, he needed to secure additional funding for a comparable New York City lifestyle to supplement his one hundred and ten dollar a week paycheck from Valentino and Rambova.

This fund-raising effort on Daven's behalf brings us to the reason he left New York. As Parisian journalist Michel Duren wrote, "Daven came back to France quite abruptly".[5] It was then Daven lost the Valentino's sponsorship when he sailed from New York City in June of 1924. This departure date is confirmed by Daven's own statement in 1926 upon his return to New York, when he stated upon entry his last departure from New York was June of 1924.

In addressing the false narrative about Valentino and Daven's relationship, the documentation reveals Daven left "abruptly", but not after a lover's quarrel and not because he was offended having so few scenes in *Monsieur Beaucaire*. The rumors alleging Natacha Rambova was concerned Daven would upstage her husband have no basis is fact.

In light of what actually took place, this appears to be the explanation Daven gave to the press and to those who asked why he left New York so suddenly. I first presented Daven's true reason for leaving New York in a speech I delivered on the inviation of the University of Turin in 2009.[6] I cited the 1975 memoir of Valentino's trusted business manager and close friend, George Ullman[7] where he writes:

"In Paris, the Valentino's were interviewed by a reporter, who in general resembled Rudy. They were so enthused over their discovery that they persuaded this young man to accompany them to New York (at their expense of course) and had him as a guest in their Park Avenue apartment. Rudy actually insisted that André Daven be given a small part in the Monsieur Beaucaire picture, but without any training or ability, his screen debut didn't develop.

---

4   *The California Court of Appeals case of S. George Ullman as cited from the court ordered Baskerville audit of the Falcon Lair expenses under the heading of "Salaries, February 1926"*

5   Article by Michel Duran as Published in *"Marianne : Grand Hebdomadaire Littéraire Illustré."* (The Great Illustrated Literary Weekly.) on Aug, 3, 1933

6   *Evel;yn* Zumaya speech delivered at the Convegno Valentino

7   *The S. George Ullman Memoir,* p. 24.

But what did develop was that Daven ran up large bills for dental work and purchases and even borrowed five hundred dollars from one of our friends. All of this came to light after André suddenly decided to return to Paris with no more than a perfunctory farewell to Rudy and Natacha. Later I sent him a statement of his indebtedness to Rudy, but his reply, written in French, was to the effect that Rudy had interrupted his newspaper career and that he held them responsible for time lost! This is just one other example of the manner in which Rudy and Natacha spent money on a whim."

I cited this source in my speech in Turin as a direct quote from the man who was there when Daven left, who paid Valentino's bills and administrated his professional life at the time, S. George Ullman. Ullman revealed the details only in 1975, when as an elderly gentleman he wrote a memoir of his life and times with Rudolph Valentino. In learning more specifics about Daven's departure recently, I believe this was something Valentino did not want to make public.

George Ullman portrays André Daven as not a great love but Valentino's understudy who borrowed money from his friends without his benefactor's knowledge and executed a restoration of his teeth with the Valentino's dentist and left New York City "abruptly". There are additional points made in the Daven false narrative: the hunting trip, Josephine Baker and the pallbearer.

The false narrative also asserts Valentino and Daven were lovers because they went on a hunting trip together. I challenge this innuendo by saying a choice of sporting activity and enjoying said activity with a friend can not be cited as evidence of one's sexual orientation. A hunting trip is only proof Valentino and his minimally paid understudy, André, hunted down and killed some unlucky and innocent creatures, butchered them and took their trophies home.

Yet this scenario of killing innocent animals for sport has been exploited in the false narrative as being a romantic, x-rated romp by two closeted homosexuals. As no proof is presented other than innuendo, I state a hunting trip is not proof of homosexuality.

It is further purported André Daven discovered the iconic jazz performer Josephine Baker and that he is responsible for her success in bringing jazz to Paris. It is claimed Daven discovered Baker in a Harlem nightclub during his 1924 stay in New York City and he then took her and a troupe of thirty other African-American performers from New York to Paris at his own expense when he returned so "abruptly" that June of 1924. This is false.

If Daven did return to Paris in June of 1924 with thirty other people, he would have had to support them all for about a year and a half because Baker's show did not open until October 2nd of 1925. Furthermore, according to the site of the Museum of

Harlem in Montmartre, it happened in a different way.

Caroline Dudley Reagan, an American entrepreneur, discovered Josephine Baker in Harlem as well as the thirty member dance troupe. She brought them to Paris in 1925 and spent the summer organizing the dance troupe and their move to France. André Daven's involvement in the Josephine Baker story is as follows.

Jacques Hébertot left his position with the theater Champs-Élysées in January of 1925 and owner Rolf De Maré appointed André Daven as artistic director with De Maré retaining the title of Director of the Champs-Élysées Theater. The theater was then converted to a music hall/vaudeville venue and soon experienced financial duress. When Caroline Dudley Reagan proposed to André Daven, she organize an act comprised entirely of black performers, he agreed it could be a profitable venture. Upon his approval, she returned to New York City where she set to work producing the show which would launch the career of Josephine Baker.

André Daven did not pay to bring thirty dancers from New York as he was then in Paris when this show was being organized by Caroline Reagan. There is no mention of Daven in either the official history of Jacques Hébertot or of the theater, yet we find even Daven telling the press he was the director for several years forward. In an article posted on the website, plaisirs du jazz.fr., the following is explained.

"Caroline Dudley spent the summer of 1925 in New York, organizing the dance troupe and details of the show, to be produced under the scenographic authority of Louis Douglas, African-American dancer and choreographer who performed regularly in Paris since 1903.

But their collaboration faced problems when Rolf De Maré and André Daven (artistic director of the Theater Champs-Élysées) attended rehearsals of the dance troupe, which arrived on September 22, just four days before the preview and ten days before the premiere. They felt the show was not "black" enough for the Parisian public - not Parisian enough, in short.

On the one hand, the star of the show, Maud De Forest, exhibited no taste and below the standard they expected for the French show. She was too fat compared to feminine standards of the Parisian music hall, less a dancer than a singer, and which was worst she was a singer of the blues: these properties, which correspond to a niche in vogue in New York since 1920, have no appeal in Paris.

Daven found the collective female choreographies of the Harlem dance troupe too prudish, that is to say too "American", but also neither sufficiently "French" (remember the Parisian music hall emphasizes eroticism) or sufficiently "black" (French colonial curiosity for black female bodies having essentially been based upon their nudity, showing this as their sensuality)."

Josephine Baker and the thirty dancers arrived in Paris close to the scheduled premiere and when Daven previewed the show, he panicked. It was not what he expected. He recruited Jacques Charles, a director from the Moulin Rouge who rushed to the Champs-Elysee theater to see what could be done. Jacques Charles recollects rescuing Daven.

" 'You saved our lives,' said Daven. Yet I am still waiting for a simple letter of thanks. Theater directors quickly become oblivious when they stop being worried. As for Josephine Baker, she could have sent me her photograph in the costume which she did not want to wear and which she has been wearing ever since!"[8]

In regards to the allegation Daven was a love sick and grieving pallbearer at Valentino's funeral in August of 1926, we know the following. In examining Daven's port of entry and departure documents, we find he was not in America during the summer of 1926.

Daven was not a pallbearer and the gentleman falsely identified as Daven is Michael Romano, assistant state attorney of Illinois. Romano stands between Douglas Fairbanks and Rudolph Valentino's godfather, Frank Mennillo.[9] Michael Romano was a friend of Valentino's and organized the memorial for him in Chicago.

While researching Daven's comings and goings during the summer of 1926, it is evident that six months earlier around the end of January 1926, Daven launched a new career path by exploiting the Hollywood connections he made through the Valentinos. By 1926, Daven appears as a French press agent for stars such as the Talmadge sisters and Gloria Swanson.

It is also alleged Daven was grief-stricken in New York at Valentino's funeral. He was then in Paris and embroiled in a complicated breakup with his girlfriend Yvonne Legeay. In January of 1926 their break up resulted in a lengthy lawsuit which was covered in the news and which involved another great deal of money needing to be paid.

Considering the circumstances of how Daven left Valentino's sponsorship, the details of his lawsuit with Yvonne Legeay are insightful. He left New York and his benefactors holding a debt which he incurred in 1924 and by 1926 he was being sued by a French furniture designer at the Maison Martine in Paris; the owner of this establishment being Natacha Rambova's favorite designer Paul Poiret.

Daven returned to New York City for just two weeks the beginning of February 1926 and at that time Valentino was not in New York City. He arrived from Europe with his brother Alberto and his family on the *Leviathan* which stopped in Le Havre, France on its way to New York and by February 2, Valentino and family were on a westbound train headed home to California.

Daven garnered some press upon his arrival with the small, nationally syndicated piece with photo reading:[10]

"Best Dressed – André Daven, Hailed as the best dressed man in Europe, André Daven, director of the Theatre Des Champs-Élysées, Paris, is visiting America as the guest of Gloria Swanson and her husband, the Marquis de la Falais."

If André Daven was the great love of Valentino, would Valentino not have known

---

8 *Candide* on June 16, 1932
9 *The New York Daily News*, August 30, 1926 and same publication on August 31st
10 *The Corsicana,* February 1, 1926.

he was arriving in New York at the time and met with him? Would they not have traveled together? Would Valentino not have seen him in Le Havre? I found nothing to say the two men ever met again after June of 1924 and based on the discoveries to date, I believe they did not.

By the time Daven arrives in New York as the guest of his new client Gloria Swanson, life was complicating for him as his lawsuit with Yvonne Legeay and the Maison Martine was being widely covered by the Parisian press, such as in *Le Petit Parisian* and *Candide.* Titles of the coverage being sentiments such as "When Love Dies or The Danger of Not Knowing How to Hate" and "The Liquidation of Love." This coverage reveals the following about André Daven.

André Daven and Yvonne Legeay lived together as lovers and shared an apartment in Paris. They began dating sometime around 1922 and ended their engagement in January of 1926. They had no children, but according to court reports they shared a dog and also the financial management of their household.

Yvonne would claim in court that when she met André, he was broke and working as a gigolo and that it was she who financed their home and supported him. Upon the dissolution of their household, Yvonne moved into a new apartment on the Rue Magellan and André refused to allow her take their commonly owned furniture. Somewhat remorseful, he agreed to pay one year of her rent and agreed to assist her in furnishing her new apartment. They were off to Poiret's Maison Martine where they placed an order for 45,000 francs worth of furniture.

By the time the bill came due in the summer of 1926, André had just returned from a trek to Africa where he was bitten by a tse tse fly which infected him with a debilitating sleeping sickness. He slept for most of the summer of 1926 and would contract pneumonia which further complicated his recovery. Meanwhile, Yvonne phoned Daven's office in Paris and his secretary agreed to write a note to the furniture designers assuring them André would soon be awake and pay the 44,860 Franc invoice.

When he did wake up, he was livid with the news and said he had no intention of paying for the huge order. He and Yvonne fought and both retained lawyers to set in for the long haul which it turned out to be; André's lawyer arguing he had only given Yvonne advice in her selections and Yvonne saying he bought it all for her.

Daven also argued he gave Yvonne a ring worth 120,000 francs and she argued she never saw such a ring. So it went for six years until 1932, with Daven determined not to pay for Yvonne's furniture. The case ground its way through all eight levels of jurisdiction in Paris with the court finally ordering both Yvonne and André to pay Paul Poiret's House of design 44, 860 francs.

Meanwhile, Daven had fallen in love with Daniela Parola; another beautiful performer at the Champs-Élysées Theater. By the time he was embroiled in court with Yvonne and waking up from his tsetse fly slumber, he was already in bed with Daniela Parola and obviously very much in love with the young beauty because they would marry on June 21, 1927 with Rolf De Maré as their best man.

André and Daniela would live together the rest of their long lives. Interestingly, Daniela Parola, as reported in *Le Gaulois* on May 14, 1926, appeared as a supportive performer in a show titled, "The Paris Review", starring Yvonne Legeay.

While it is alleged Daven was in New York acting as Rudolph Valentino's pallbearer, he was actually in Paris, sleeping through the tsetse fly bite, embroiled in a lawsuit with his ex-girfriend Yvonne Legeay and while beginning his love affair with Daniela Parola.

Prior to the creation of the false narrative, or hoax, about Valentino and Daven, Daven receives little mention in the histories of Jacques Hébertot, the Theater des Champs-Élysées or in Josephine Baker's life story. In Hébertot's official history, he is granted the title of Director during his tenure with the theater, but during Daven's alleged tenure, the director is cited as Rolf De Maré. Daven has no mention.

It is key in this argument to point out the homophobic basis of the false Valentino/Daven narrative. This is evident in the mention that Valentino and Daven had homosexual associates as this is presented as proof they were gay. It is homophobic to perpetuate a gay by association premise and thereby presume someone is gay because they have homosexual associates, family and or friends. This implies, if not states that one's sexual identity is contagious. This is the basis for the false narrative Valentino and Daven were lovers. This zeal to claim the insinuation as fact perpetuates antiquated and negative homosexual stereotypes. Why did this happen? Jeanne DeRecqueville addressed this:

"Hébertot was formal: Rudy was not gay.

Robert Florey shares his opinion, he wrote it to me.

Homosexual claims about Valentino are a relatively recent insinuation. It came about because it has been discovered that the subject of someone's homosexuality in general is selling very well and when this is claimed about Valentino it sells better than any other."

The documentation of the true relationship between Valentino and Daven was discovered by Valerie Verneuille, who contacted me regarding her translation of the Robert Florey piece, *The Magic Lantern*. Madam Verneuille discovered an item for sale in the catalog of the auction house in Paris, Drouot Richelieu Appraisals, dated March 31, 2006. For sale was a letter written by Rudolph Valentino to Jacques Hébertot, one in a lot of Hébertot's personal letters. The letter was transcribed in part within the description section of the auction catalog and stated the letter was written by Valentino in New York on July 4, 1924.

"He (Rudolph Valentino) thanks him (Hébertot) '*for the always loyal and generous way with which you defended me against the quite nasty slanders that Ciné-Magazine and Comœdia made toward me'*. Then he, Valentino talks at length about their friend André Daven whom he took under his wing in New York, '*... it seems that I think it is my duty, knowing the sincere affection you have for the boy, to let you know the very dishonest way that he has thanked me for all that I did for him and tried to do* *for him'*.......Valentino gave him numerous clothes, paid for his voyage, paid him a salary, set him up in a good hotel, got him '*hired by Paramount to play the role of my brother in Beaucaire', etc.* Then he advised him, he got him a job as ' publicity man' for Paramount in Paris, he paid for his return and an advance.......He learns now that he borrowed and tried to borrow money from many friends to whom he had introduced him: '*... he owes me nearly 35,000 francs, which I consider lost. What hurts me most is not the money, but the ingratitude and hypocrisy with which he has acted toward me'.....etc.* "

The calculated exchange to today's market value (2020) of the amount Daven owed Valentino would be $17,419.26 U.S. dollars.

In conclusion, based on the documentation available, we find Daven was no great love when Valentino paid him a twenty dollar bill more than his handyman, not a great love when Daven took advantage of Valentino's generosity by incurring a debt for him of 35,000 francs. The self promotion by Daven after Valentino's death was also recorded as in the Michel Duran article. Daven went on to utilize his Hollywood and Valentino contacts, securing work as a French producer for American and German companies.

André Daven's good looks opened doors for him but he demonstrated a cavalier attitude in incurring debt on friends who trusted him. After over twenty years researching Valentino's history, that Valentino and Daven were not lovers and both men, according to all the existing first hand testimony and documentation, lived their lives as heterosexuals.

Who was the greatest love of Valentino? Natacha Rambova and for André Daven this was obviously his beloved wife Daniela Parola.

DROUOT
ESTIMATIONS

AUTOGRAPHES
PHOTOGRAPHIES
LIVRES ANCIENS ET MODERNES

VENTE A PARIS

DROUOT RICHELIEU - SALLE 11
VENDREDI 31 MARS 2006

à 14 heures

47   **Rudolph VALENTINO** (1895-1926) acteur. L. A. S. et L. S. «Rudy», Cunard RMS «Aquitania» 3 novembre 1923 et New York 4 juillet 1924, à Jacques HEBERTOT ; 4 pages in-8, et 3 pages et demie in fol. à son en-tête.

                                                                       400 / 500

3 novembre 1923, à bord de l'Aquitania, qui l'emmène à New York, «très loin de la jolie France» et «de deux des meilleurs ami que j'ai jamais eu, toi et André (Daven)» ; il le prie de récupérer ses complets que son hôtel de Londres va envoyer à Paris : «De cette façon j'aurai tout mon garderobe complet pour le numéro de Monsieur»... New York 4 juillet 1924. Il le remercie «de la façon toujours loyale et généreuse avec laquelle tu as pris ma défence contre les plusiers calomnies assez méchantes que Ciné-Magazine et Comœdia a fait passer sur moi». Puis il parle longuement de leur ami André DAVEN, qu'il avait pris sous son aile à New York, «parce que j'estime que c'est mon devoir, sachant l'affection sincère que tu as pour ce garçon, de te faire connaître la façon très deshonnaite avec laquelle il m'a remercié de tout ce que j'ai fait et esseyez de faire pour lui»... Valentino lui a offert de nombreux habits, payé ses frais de voyage, lui a versé un salaire, l'a installé dans un bon hôtel, l'a «fait engager par la Paramount pour jouer le rôle de mon frère dans Beaucaire», etc. Puis il l'a recommandé, lui a obtenu un poste de «publicityman» à la Paramount de Paris, lui a payé son retour et une avance... Il apprend maintenant qu'il a emprunté ou essayé d'emprunter de l'argent à plusieurs amis auxquels il l'avait présenté : «il me dois a peu près 35 000 francs, que du reste je considère perdu. Ce qui me fait beaucoup de mal ce n'est pas l'argent, mais l'ingratitude et l'hypocrisie avec laquelle il c'est conduie envers moi»... etc.

Letter written by Rudolph Valentino to Jacques Hébertot
relating the behavior of Andre Daven and the debt incurred

Daniela Parola & André Daven

Words of Clarification

by
Evelyn Zumaya

Although the focus of *Affairs Valentino* is not Rudolph Valentino's sexual orientation, I learned during my research it is the center of attention of many people's interest in the silent film icon. Whenever I mentioned Rudolph Valentino, I was inevitably asked, "Wasn't he gay?" Initially, I had no definitive answer and held to the prevailing belief he might have been gay or bisexual. I set out in search of an authoritative answer to this question and assumed the trail would be ice cold. To my surprise this was not the case.

From the onset, I knew two particular books on Valentino, *Valentino, A Dream of Desire* by David Bret and *Valentino, An Intimate and Shocking Expose* by Chaw Mank and Brad Steiger were the primary sources for the belief Valentino lived his life as a closeted homosexual. However, after fact-checking these publications I found them to be highly-fictionalized and inaccurate accounts of Valentino's life. I then broadened my research and learned there were other authors who have perpetuated antiquated stereotypes, unfounded rumors and made many false claims about Valentino. Consequently, in regards to Valentino's sexual orientation, his legacy is a textbook case of fan fiction and innuendo disguised as fact.

Unlike other celebrities whose stories have been fictionalized after their deaths, the chronology of the fictitious portrayal of Valentino reveals this all began during his brief lifetime. Why and how Valentino came to be the victim of such flagrant disregard for the truth is the subject of this article. As I worked my way through a surplus of published material, I resolved to present the facts as they presented themselves and not be swayed by any interest group or agenda. This complex story spans eight decades and began the moment Rudolph Valentino's first blockbuster hit, *The Sheik*, flickered onto movie screens across America in the fall of 1921.

The Outrage

The public response to *The Sheik* is so well documented it scarcely merits repetition. Suffice to say, reaction to Valentino's overt on-screen displays of passion and a misogynist story line ran the gamut of emotion from obsession to outrage. As the first, dark-skinned foreigner to be cast as screen hero instead of villain, Valentino inspired a loyal fan base as well as an organized opposition from parents, clergy and conservative organizations such as the Daughters of the American Revolution, the

Veterans of Foreign Wars, the Boy Scouts, the United Presbyterian Church, the Catholic Knights of Columbus and the General Federation of Women's Clubs.

As a national preoccupation with *The Sheik* intensified, blame for the hysteria was placed squarely upon the film's lead actor. An anti-Valentino movement gained momentum with the Catholic Church contributing to the furor by declaring his films an immoral influence on youth and listing two of his movies, *The Four Horsemen of the Apocalypse* and *The Sheik* on the church's weekly list of movies deemed inappropriate for church members' viewing. Anti-Valentino angst made its way to the halls of the U.S. Congress on June 29, 1922, when Senator Henry L. Meyers delivered his argument for censorship of the movies by specifically naming Rudolph Valentino and *The Sheik* as being the most offensive to his sensibilities and the greatest threat to young people.

The same year *The Sheik* premiered in Hollywood, Congress fueled the uproar by passing a discriminatory immigration bill, The Emergency Quota Act; a controversial law limiting the number of Italian immigrants. With an influx of Italian immigrants straining urban infrastructures and an already difficult job market, anti-Italian sentiment ran high. Racist temperance organizations portrayed Italians as excessive drinkers and fundamentalist Protestants labeled them "agents of the Pope". On the sets of his films, Italian immigrant Rudolph Valentino did not escape this xenophobia as he was often referred to as a "wop" and a "dago".

His predicament was further exacerbated by the cultural disparity between his homeland of Italy where men commonly wore colored shirts and jewelry as a sign of style and success and America in 1921 where it was not acceptable for men to look too fashionable. In keeping with his heritage, Valentino demonstrated his success by wearing chain bracelets, a wrist watch, colored shirts and ties. However, the predominately white, Anglo-Saxon male establishment at the time adamantly held that beauty in America had but one gender and that was feminine.

This presented Valentino's critics with fodder to deter his influence over young people. What more effective way, they reasoned, to discourage emulating the Sheik than to associate him with every demeaning stereotype they could devise. They asserted Valentino paid too much attention to his well-appreciated beauty and was therefore held responsible for an "unmanly" trend in young men's fashions. The implication was made that one's sexuality is defined by their clothes and fastidiousness. This became a key component of the anti-Valentino movement. He was mocked as a "dandy", a "pansy", "less than manly" "weak-willed" and "effeminate"; code words for homosexuality at the time. As Valentino rose to fame, headlines reading, "Valentino, Movie Hero of the Vaselined Haired!" and "Valentino, Model for Effeminate Lads is Here!" incensed his fans and established the groundwork for decades of innuendo.

Although Valentino was infuriated by these inferences, the seeds planted by his xenophobic and homophobic opposition would eventually bear fruit. Oddly, the belief Valentino lived his life as a closeted homosexual is most often purported today by homosexuals who are unwittingly carrying the ball for a bigoted enemy who would have targeted them for persecution years ago. By failing to recognize the history of prejudice and ignorance behind the original assertion Valentino was gay, they have picked up right where Valentino's most narrow-minded and intolerant critics left off.

In the lexicon of "code words" for homosexuals there was one phrase which had a disastrous impact upon Valentino personally. He went to his early grave anguishing over this particular epithet and many in his inner circle blamed his sudden demise upon this phrase. The moniker still haunts his legacy as in his listing in Entertainment Weekly's, *The 100 Greatest Stars of All Time,* he is still referred to as a "pink powder puff".

The Pink Powder Puff Legacy

On Sunday, August 15, 1926 Rudolph Valentino slept off the effects of anesthesia in a room on the eighth floor of New York's Polyclinic Hospital. Earlier that evening emergency surgery was performed on the movie star to repair a perforated ulcer. An hour after this operation Valentino was strapped to a vertical bed board; his body slumping forward in leather shoulder harnesses to allow proper drainage from tubing surgically sutured into his abdomen. Two nurses staved off the advancing infection in their famous patient's body by salting his wound with saline flushes through this surgical tubing.

Standing at Valentino's vertical bedside was a concerned George Ullman, his manager and closest friend. As soon as George noticed his friend, "Rudy" rallying from the ether, he motioned the nurses aside and leaned forward. It was then that the man who'd inspired irrational love and devotion around the world (as well as hatred) opened his eyes and mumbled into consciousness by uttering,

"Well, George, did I behave like a pink powder puff or like a man?"

As much torment as he endured over this particular epithet, Valentino was never called a pink powder puff. The phrase came to be associated with him after an anonymously written editorial appeared in *The Chicago Tribune* a few weeks before his death. The article blamed his influence upon the appearance of pink powder vending machines in men's bathrooms and read in part,

"Why didn't someone quietly drown Rudolph Guglielmo, alias Valentino, years ago?....Better a rule by masculine women than by effeminate men!"

Valentino challenged the author of the editorial by inviting him to tie on a pair of boxing gloves and settle it in the boxing ring. No one accepted his challenge; an excerpt of Valentino's published challenge read,

" ...(I will) demonstrate to you that the wrist under a slave bracelet may snap a real fist into your sagging jaw and that I may teach you to respect a man even though he happens to prefer to keep his face clean.."

George Ullman was convinced to his own dying day in 1975 that his friend Rudy might have had more strength to fend off the septic infection which took his life had it not been for his anguish over this epithet. Shortly after Valentino's death, George Ullman wrote of his friend "Rudy's" frustration at being unable to avenge the editorial.

"I want it understood that the vehemence with which I denounce the anonymous writer of this cowardly attack upon my friend is not based so much upon what the article contained as upon the deep hurt it gave Rudy, embittering as it did his last days of his life and, in my opinion, hastening his death."

"He (Valentino) would repeat (the phrase Pink Powder Puff) seemingly in agony of soul, as if fearful that, in the minds of some who did not know him, the thought of effeminacy might stick."

Dismantling the Myths

Valentino's employers in the motion picture industry contributed to the confusion over Valentino's true identity by issuing stock, sanitized press releases for publication in fan magazines. If Valentino's opposition assaulted his truth with accusations of his "less than manly" influence upon young men, his employers also portrayed him as someone he was not; a tee-totaling boy scout.

When a few events in Valentino's life did make headlines, especially when they involved his love life, even the slickest public relations departments in Hollywood were powerless to prevent the rush to print all the dirt. In the eyes of his fans and his enemies, Valentino had become one with his erotic screen characters, especially *The Sheik*, and this made him particularly vulnerable to unchecked commentary about his sexual behavior.

This speculation has never waned in intensity or sensationalism and salacious copy about Valentino has clicked off the presses without pause. Silent film historian Kevin Brownlow once wrote, *"Rudolph Valentino has been subjected to more slander and innuendo than virtually any other motion picture star."* As I waded deeper into my investigation to ascertain the truth about Valentino's sexual orientation, I agreed.

Nearly all of the slander and innuendo to which Brownlow refers, no matter how cleverly contrived and presented, has always been and still is a rehash and embellishment of a few basic misconceptions about Valentino. Akin to a child's game of whispering a secret from one ear to the next, each time these misconceptions were repeated, the outcome became more outrageous. Understanding the origins of these misconceptions requires deciphering fact from fiction concerning a few key events in Valentino's life.

Before Valentino made a name for himself in the movies, he married actress Jean Acker. A few hours after their marriage, bride Jean Acker jilted her bridegroom and avoided his attempts to consummate the marriage. After pleading with her to be his wife in every sense of the word, a frustrated Rudolph Valentino confronted his wife and hit her in the face. Their marriage is a favorite Hollywood history trivia question as it is alleged to have lasted only one night. In fact they were married for over one year.

While Valentino awaited his divorce from Jean Acker, he turned his attentions on art director, Natacha Rambova. Despite the fact he was still a married man, Valentino and his mistress Natacha make public appearances together and lived "in sin" in a tiny bungalow on Sunset Boulevard. During Jean Acker and Valentino's divorce proceedings, she swore under oath how she and "The Sheik" never consummated their marriage. In response, Valentino presented several letters he'd written to Jean as evidence she refused to consummate the marriage.

It was not until after Valentino's death that a file was discovered in his attorney's office revealing Jean Acker's claim; a medical condition prevented her from having sexual intercourse. Today it is alleged she was an outspoken lesbian. Although I found no public statement to verify this, Jean Acker lived the remainder of her life with a female partner, Chloe Carter.

Whether Valentino's first wife was a lesbian or not, provides no definitive proof he was also gay. However, publications alleging his homosexuality tout this "gay by association" theory. I allege; although Valentino admittedly did not consummate his first marriage, he did not "catch" homosexuality from Jean Acker.

This "gay by association" theory is today a predominant argument for Valentino's alleged homosexuality. This is bolstered by the fact that Valentino, his first wife Jean Acker and his second wife Natacha Rambova were all affiliated with actress and producer, Alla Nazimova. It is alleged Nazimova was a lesbian and consequently it is widely assumed all of her friends and associates were also gay by association. It is believed today Nazimova was a lesbian lover of not only Valentino's first wife, Jean Acker, but also of his second wife, Natacha Rambova.

As of this writing, the sole piece of evidence presented as proof of a lesbian relationship between Alla Nazimova and Natacha Rambova is a single photograph of the two women wearing Chinese pajamas. Chinese pajamas do not a lesbian make. They were vogue at the time, worn in public and even Valentino and his manager George Ullman were photographed wearing the popular Chinese pajamas.

Another common misconception regarding Valentino's sexual orientation came into existence shortly after Valentino and Jean Acker's divorce was granted. This involved Valentino's second wedding night. His divorce decree from Jean Acker stipulated a one year waiting period before he was free to remarry. Valentino and Natacha Rambova attempted to circumvent this requirement by driving across the

Mexican border to wed. In the company of close friends they were married in Mexicali, Mexico only a few months after Valentino's divorce from Jean Acker was handed down.

The newlyweds left Mexicali and drove north to Palm Springs, California to spend their wedding night. They were unaware that in order to circumvent the law they should have consummated their marriage in Mexico. By returning to California to spend his wedding night, in the eyes of the law Valentino demonstrated a willful intent to break the terms of his California divorce from Jean Acker and had committed bigamy.

As soon as Valentino returned to Los Angeles, he was arrested, thrown in jail and charged with bigamy. His Mexican marriage to Natacha Rambova was absolved and he faced a potential sentence of ten years in a state penitentiary and a possible fine of five thousand dollars if convicted. During his preliminary hearing on the bigamy charges, several of his friends who'd attended his Mexican wedding took the witness stand on his behalf. Hoping to assist their friend avoid a lengthy prison sentence, they all held to the same story; Mr. and Mrs. Valentino had not consummated their marriage on their wedding night in Palm Springs because the bride was too ill and slept alone.

The fact Rudolph Valentino and Natacha Rambova had been living together before their Mexican marriage and consummating for months was never brought to the court's attention. Only the circumstances of their wedding night were of concern to the court. The bigamy charges against Valentino were dismissed after the testimony of one key witness; a Cahuilla Indian. The Indian passed by the house in question on that Palm Springs' wedding night and testified he spoke with Valentino while he dozed on the front porch. Neither Valentino's friends nor his attorney informed this critical passerby that his brief conversation had not been with Valentino but with one of Valentino's friends. While the Cahuilla Indian made his mistaken identification on the porch, the newlyweds slept together as they had been for months.

The court dismissed the bigamy charges citing a lack of evidence and ordered Valentino and Rambova to wait the remainder of the year until his divorce from Jean Acker was final before remarrying. Years later, one of the witnesses who came to Valentino's defense implied to an interviewer how the story of Natacha Rambova's wedding night illness was fabricated to ensure Valentino avoided jail time and a sure end to his career.

However, over time the events of Valentino's Palm Springs wedding night became more foundational material for the theory that both Valentino and Natacha Rambova were gay. It is alleged today he spent that wedding night sleeping with the other men in his wedding party and Natacha Rambova slept with Alla Nazimova. After finding no documentation to support these claims and after reviewing the court proceedings of Valentino's bigamy hearing, I believe no evidence exists to justify categorizing Jean Acker and Natacha Rambova as "Valentino's lesbian wives" or "Valentino's gay wives."

Natacha Rambova's unpopularity provoked nearly as much innuendo and stereotyping as did her husband's popularity. An onslaught of code words portrayed Rambova as a "bachelor" woman who loved dogs more than children and inferred her husband bowed to her controlling will. In the early 1980's, Rambova's biographer, Michael Morris, wrote his authoritative *Madam Valentino, The Many Lives of Natacha Rambova*. Morris interviewed many of the main characters in Rambova's life and learned nothing from them which verified the claims she was gay. Commenting on this to me, Morris wrote:

"I think the fact love soured between Valentino and Rambova made Natacha very appealing to lesbians because she was so beautiful, dominating, and self-possessed. If she could walk away from the world's greatest male lover, then, it is automatically assumed that she must have preferred women. What people don't bother to investigate was that her lovers both before and after Rudy were all strikingly handsome, debonair, European men. Rudy was just one among many."

My *Affairs Valentino* research discovered first-hand accounts revealing Rudolph Valentino and Natacha Rambova's marriage was not platonic and not arranged, but a passionate, volatile union. Their marriage was witnessed by members of their inner circle and their divorce after five years of marriage was bitter, painful and raw with emotion. Their final separation occurred after Valentino discovered Natacha in an afternoon tryst with a married man. Shortly after her infidelity, Natacha left Hollywood. It is alleged it was then one of her close friends, actress Nita Naldi informed Valentino his wife Natacha aborted three of his children. Whether this was true or not, it was no secret Rudolph Valentino wanted children and a wife to stay at home and mother them.

In the 1920's men with no children were as vulnerable to the same innuendo as were women with no children. For this reason the assertion Valentino was gay thrives not only by his alleged unconsummated marriages and alleged gay wives, but in some measure by his apparent failure to produce children.

Pulp Fiction

In 1925, a collateral campaign to impugn Valentino originated in Rome. It was then Valentino applied for American citizenship and in response, Italian Dictator, Benito Mussolini banned Valentino's movies in Italy and confiscated all films, fan magazines and periodicals bearing his name. The dictator then released a paperback book about the native son titled, *Rodolfo Valentino, A Passionate Expose Against the Renegade of Our Country*, which alleged Valentino was a "miserable renegade, an indignant citizen revoking his origins" and an "atrocious offense to all Italians". In regards to his anti-Valentino campaign, Mussolini's staunch ally would be the Vatican where the publication, *L' Osservatore Romano* denounced Rudolph Valentino as a

267

symbol of wanton worldliness commenting, *"..his popularity is regarded as a sign of the decadence of the times."*

When Rudolph Valentino died on August 23, 1926, the Vatican responded to the news by issuing another statement declaring the movie star's life less than exemplary. Despite the tens of thousands of fans rioting for three days outside Campbell's Funeral Home to gain access to Valentino's casket, the Catholic Church denied him a funeral at St. Patrick's Cathedral in New York.

It was at this time a Vatican reporter for *The Chicago Daily News*, Hiram Kelly Moderwell was living in Rome. When Hiram K. Moderwell heard the news of Valentino's demise, he traveled from Rome to the village of the movie star's birth, Castellaneta where he allegedly conducted several interviews. With the Sheik dead and gone, Hiram Moderwell sensed an angle.

Vatican reporter Hiram Moderwell claimed he located several citizens who related lurid and allegedly unreported tales of Valentino's childhood. These stories involved his being molested by a childhood nurse, exposing himself in church and being beaten by a cruel father. At the same time Moderwell left his Vatican post to dispatch reports of Valentino's childhood sexual misadventures to his Chicago office, he was extolling the virtues of Valentino nemesis, Benito Mussolini. Moderwell writes;

"They call him Mussolini, dictator. To the unpatriotic, to the anti-social and anti-civilized, to the lawless, to the Bolsheviks, he is dictator. To Italy, full of sterling human worth, to Italy, in my judgment, Mussolini is liberator."

If Hiram Moderwell, the pro-fascist, Catholic reporter set out in search of his version of Valentino's childhood with the intention of diminishing the truth of Valentino's legacy, he would ultimately be successful.

With the publication of his allegations regarding Valentino's childhood, other authors sensed the financial reward in writing sexually explicit material involving Valentino. These authors realized that dead men don't protest and by writing Rudolph Valentino into any sexual scenario guaranteed brisk sales. This realization inspired inventive new episodes of Valentino's alleged "sexual displays in public" and "sexual confusion" to be expounded upon by authors focused on profiting on Rudolph Valentino's "secret sex life." Somehow years after the fact, a string of authors were about to claim they were privy to a covert and previously unknown life of Valentino.

The Faux Diaries

During the early 1930's, the fake diary format became the favored literary device granting credibility to these sexually titillating, fan-fictional works about Rudolph Valentino. These peeks into the pages of his alleged private diaries presented sufficient voyeuristic intrusion to generate book sales. The authors of these diaries played upon the public's confusion over whether these books were actually authentic diaries. For during his lifetime, Rudolph Valentino did issue a few publicity articles written in a diary format for fan magazines.

However, nothing of a sexual nature was ever included in his ghost-written diaries. But as the fan magazines in which these original and authorized articles were published quickly became unavailable to the public, it was easy for dishonest authors to tweak the enticing format. The resulting fictional diaries of Valentino became little more than pornography and are often referred to today as "Valentino's unpublished diaries." None of them were credible, unpublished or Valentino's.

The most notorious writer to profit from this diary format was Samuel Roth. Five years after Valentino's death he published his *Intimate Journal of Rudolph Valentino*. Known for his literary pirating practices, Samuel Roth published primarily adult reading material. Other titles released around the same time as his *Intimate Journal of Rudolph Valentino* were *Padlocks and Girdles of Chastity*, *Sacred Prostitution and Marriage by Capture*, *Venus in Furs*, *Self-Amusement and its Specters* and *The Secret Places of the Human Body*. In 1936, the FBI and The U.S. Post Office raided Roth's warehouse and discovered three thousand pirated books. He was arrested for his criminal literary practices and served a sentence of three years in a federal penitentiary in Lewisburg, Pennsylvania.

Roth wrote his *Intimate Journal of Rudolph Valentino* in the first person and formatted the text as Valentino's daily entries such as,

"The thoughts which seethe through my mind tonight are of so violent and horrible a nature that I will not trust names even to this secret journal of mine..."

"I was completely exhausted and raging mad. For three hours I had made frantic love to the stubborn wench, and for three hours she had resisted me...."

"Savagely, I picked her up in my arms and kissed her and carried her into her bedroom. I am disgusted with myself. I did not know that man could be so fickle. When I am away from her, I long for her and want her, and when I am with her, I loathe her slimy body."

Roth's diary would serve as inspiration for a subsequent variation on the theme of Valentino's alleged sexual escapades. Some thirty years after Samuel Roth's effort, another diary attributed to Valentino appeared as an anonymous article in the French language magazine, *La Presse's*, February 27, 1961 issue. This article would be the first publication in which Valentino was portrayed as being homosexual. The anonymous author of this faux diary portrayed Valentino engaging in homosexual love affairs with two noted Parisian men, Jacques Hébertot and André Daven. In the *La Press* article, the anonymous author explicitly detailed Valentino making passionate love outside the opera with a gay lover, "like two tigers."

"Nous nous sommes aimes comme deux tigres."

The scant biographical information in this piece demonstrates the author's lack of interest in scholarly intention or knowledge of the specifics of Valentino's life. Typical of the article's many factual errors is one scenario in which Valentino pauses in the streets of in Paris on June 14, 1923 to admire his name in lights advertising his latest film, *Monsieur Beaucaire*. *Monsieur Beaucaire* would not open in movie theaters until the following year.

In Jeanne DeRecqueville's biography, *Rudolph Valentino*, published in 1978, she debunks the *La Presse* diary. Her biography of Valentino has never been translated from French and for this reason DeRecqueville has received little acclaim in the U.S. for her authoritative research on the subject of Valentino's alleged homosexuality.[1] While writing her biography, she corresponded with several of Valentino's personal acquaintances, including Robert Florey and René Clair and included their comments on the subject in her book. All of these individuals claimed Valentino was not gay and that authors purporting this theory were simply trying to cash in on his sex appeal.

DeRecqueville also challenged the *La Presse* article's anonymous author to produce a single page of the alleged diary which was claimed to have been handwritten by Valentino. She reprinted a letter in Valentino's handwriting in her biography for use as comparison by a hand writing expert willing to make a professional authentication. Her challenge was never met. Despite the *La Presse* article's lack of authenticity and historical inaccuracy, its fictional episodes were absorbed into Valentino's legacy to subsequently be presented as fact.

Mr. Mank

Four years after the publication of the *La Presse* article, a man named Chaw Mank seized the format of the anonymous diary as inspiration for his book, *Valentino, The Intimate and Shocking Expose*. With the publication of this book in 1965, Chaw Mank became the leading expert on Valentino's alleged gay life. Chaw Mank claims to have had a personal relationship with Valentino some forty-five years prior to writing his book. As an obsessive celebrity hound and autograph seeker, Chaw Mank had similar "personal relationships" with over forty celebrities and their business managers.

When Mank died in 1985, his home at 226 E. Mill Street in Staunton, Illinois was filled to the rafters with stacks of boxes and crates of papers accumulated during his years of celebrity pursuit. He claimed personal relationships with dozens of stars and boasted he wrote 25,000 letters a year to these celebrities. Writing at that feverish rate, he was posting nearly seventy letters a day.

During the 1920's, Chaw Mank was publisher and sole employee of his bi-monthly *Movie Fans Newsletter* and he organized fan clubs for some fifty celebrities. He regularly mailed those stars questionnaires along with requests for one of their personal Christmas cards to reprint in his newsletter. Most of Mank's celebrities, including Rudolph Valentino, did respond to his fan club questionnaires and sent along friendly letters and photographs for use in his publication.

---

1   The book has since been translated into English by Renato Floris and is available online as *"Rudolph Valentino – In English"* by Jeanne DeRecqueville.

Mank's claim these celebrities ever divulged anything of a graphically sexual nature to him is questionable. With his ability to relay whatever they divulged to him to his fan clubs via his newsletter, he would have been the last person they would have confided in. Nevertheless, Mank asserts Rudolph Valentino did just that.

Chaw Mank was a man of diverse interests and one of his other fields of endeavor was the hand-stitching of the many celebrity autographed patches of cloth he collected into his celebrity quilts. He was also an avid collector of country music star autographs and wrote a few country western songs including *"I Don't want a Bracelet of Diamonds, I just want Elvis."*

In 1965, Chaw Mank collaborated with author and self-proclaimed authority on unidentified flying objects and alien abductions, Brad Steiger to write their book on Valentino's alleged gay life, *The Intimate and Shocking Expose of Rudolph Valentino*. A few other titles attributed to Mank's co-author Brad Steiger are *Flying Saucer Invasion-Target Earth, Flying Saucers Are Hostile, Strangers From the Skies,* and *The Flying Saucer Menace.*

Brad Steiger also touted his expertise in the field of demonic possession and his "*S-Files*" reveal his belief he has been contacted by a race of extra-terrestrials who live in underground bases buried under the sea. He writes how these "non-terrans" often introduce themselves to him in human form after his lectures and he professes to have worked with these aliens developing a smokeless, non-pollutant, no-knock fuel made from tap water. He also reported on his many clandestine exchanges in seedy bars with "moon maidens" who never became inebriated no matter how much alcohol they drink. But in 1965, Brad Steiger's interest in writing about Rudolph Valentino was based upon one more down-to-earth fact; he believed his father-in-law was Valentino's illegitimate son.

In suburban Illinois in the early sixties, Brad Steiger met and collaborated with Chaw Mank and escalated the rhetoric of the fictional *La Presse* article's diary of Valentino's alleged secret sex life by adding their own fictional dialogue. However, Mank and Steiger guaranteed sales of their publication in expanding their portrait of Valentino by making him bisexual.

 Their sensational novel is laden with X-rated reference and is, in their own words, the "shocking expose of the fiery love god, Rudolph Valentino." They portrayed their subject as a sexually confused man who fumbled helplessly through one homosexual and heterosexual situation after another while spending his days living a life of debauchery in the gay bath houses of Hollywood.

They state in the first pages of their book how they "supplemented" Hiram Moderwell's childhood stories of Valentino and then write a lengthy and graphic narrative of precisely how that childhood nurse sexually molested Valentino. Their Valentino as a child is "cruel" and a "bully" and before Mank and Steiger age him past infancy, they bombard their readers with repeated references to his penis. I found the predominate mention of Valentino's childhood genitalia in Mank and Steiger's book offensive and nowhere more so than in the telling of the tale of Valentino's pedophile nanny. The authors revel in their references to his "tiny member" and "the little fellow", "tool of pleasure", "member" and "glandular proof of his impending manhood."

While writing their "Expose," Mank and Steiger were so invested in obscenity that in the one hundred and ninety two pages of this book there are some eighty sexual scenarios. The book's sexual content is such that today it is archived in the rare manuscripts department in Cornell University's Kroch Library, under "Human Sexuality."

Some of the author's graphic and contrived escapades involve pages of intimate fictional dialogue and appear to have been copied directly from the *La Presse* article. But in Mank and Steiger's version they portray Valentino resorting to homosexual activity only after "failing" to satisfy a woman. They write how after one humiliating failure he shed tears of "embarrassment "and then "sprayed vomit in disgust" whereas the woman then calls him a "god-damned queer." Mank and Steiger write just enough biographical information about Valentino to justify categorizing their book a biography.

Steiger and Mank expound at length upon Valentino's "silly" interviews before his death in response to the pink powder puff incident. They ridicule his interest in boxing by implying he only feigned interest in the sport and befriended Jack Dempsey as a "pathetic attempt to prove his manliness." Today Brad Steiger claims he had "no ax to grind" with Valentino but the book's cover screams, "Was he Sheik or Sham?" and the titillating dialogue he and Mank composed is disparaging, contrived and homophobic. For example:

"Would you like me to give you a rubdown, dear?" Bob asked Valentino as the two of them lay taking a breather at the pool's edge. There it was; the overt proposition. Valentino's stomach fluttered and he unconsciously clenched and unclenched his fists. "Very well, "he said."

Since Chaw Mank did correspond with Valentino decades earlier, he and Steiger had possession of authentic material they could exploit. Valentino could never have imagined Chaw Mank would later splice his gracious comments forwarded for use in *The Movie Fans Newsletter* into X-rated narrative in order to imply he was casually commenting upon the text. For example, after Valentino writes,

"I should say more humbly that I hope that I see beauty when and where beauty is to be found...Just because it is a sunset I do not always find it beautiful., etc."

Mank and Steiger segue this text from Valentino into another graphic scenario of aversion to women and a homosexual rendezvous in Paris. Following another passage attributed to Valentino which reads,

"I like the Madonna in women. The most serene women in Italy are the Madonna type...serene faces, calm, soft eyes, overlying something deeper and stronger."

Mank and Steiger conclude,

"Rudolfo's early experiments with physical love bewildered him and caused him to be an unsatisfactory lover of either sex."

Even though the authors include a poignant quote from Valentino in which he laments he is "misunderstood," they proceed to contribute to the situation. If Chaw Mank were, as he alleges," the first real fan of Rudolph Valentino", he is guilty of horrendous betrayal.

He and Steiger crawl over Valentino's person with discussions of his genitalia, his pubic hair and whether he was able to have an erection. They repeat and elaborate upon the misconceptions about his "unconsummated marriages" and the familiar refrain of "lesbian wives" is repeated. They portray Valentino as so emotionally frail he trembles in fear in Natacha Rambova's presence.

As with other fictional biographies on Valentino, factual problems in this publication abound. Mank and Steiger write one scene of Valentino as he is weeping in his dressing room on the set of his film, *The Young Rajah* during the summer of 1922. He is grief-stricken after hearing the news his ex-girlfriend has just shot and killed her ex-husband Jack DeSaulles in New York City. The problem with this story is that by the summer of 1922, Jack DeSaulles had been dead for six years and was murdered in 1916.

In the foreword of Mank and Steiger's *Shocking Expose*, the following quote is found.

"One never knows when a harmless bit of exaggeration may someday return to require the substantiation of an outright lie."

The irony of this statement would be felt by Brad Steiger when I located him and asked him a few questions regarding his work on Valentino. When asked to substantiate some of his apparent "exaggerations," he said the book was based upon "Chaw Mank's own memories." One of Mank's memories, he claimed, was that Valentino's marriage to Natacha Rambova was a platonic one of convenience and as" Valentino's two wives were lesbians, and Nazimova, who had a great influence upon their lives was an outspoken lesbian, these apparent facts strongly suggest that the marriage was arranged."

Hearing this distillation of eighty years of innuendo, I asked him how he could make such assumptions. He told me he and Mank assumed Valentino was gay or bisexual because Valentino's first wife Jean Acker was a lesbian. He continued by explaining they formed this belief because Valentino and Jean Acker divorced, "on grounds of non-consummation when he wished to marry Ms. Rambova...which seems suggestive and supportive of the allegations of homosexuality."

I then asked how this logic could possibly follow and told Steiger I was only interested in primary source references and factual documentation. He reiterated he had no documentation or first-hand accounts other than Mank's memories. I pressed him to offer a single one of Mank's sources, names, dates anything to support the scenarios in their book which were covered in detail. Steiger had none to offer. His only explanation was to maintain Mank relied upon hearsay accounts as, "he did have extensive contacts among the Hollywood gay community at the time." Some time after speaking with Steiger, I interviewed an elderly gentleman who personally knew many of Valentino's closest friends and family members including Robert Florey, Paul Ivano, his first wife Jean Acker, his brother Alberto and nephew Jean among others. I asked him what they thought of Mank and Steiger's premise Valentino was gay. He assured me they were all frustrated with the development. They'd lived their daily lives in Valentino's presence and knew a stridently different man than Mank and Steiger portrayed. He said they all lamented, "Poor Rudy!" and found the book "disgusting".

There are a few authors of publications such as Mank and Steiger's *Shocking Expose* who have not escaped criticism unscathed. After author Sheldon Saltman's book, "Evel Kneivel on Tour" was published in 1977, Evel was so incensed by the author's claims he attacked Saltman with a baseball bat. Knievel went to prison and Saltman's failure to source his slanderous accusations with documentation left him wounded in a hospital bed.

Shortly before Rudolph Valentino died in 1926, he leveled a furious response to the author of the pink powder puff editorial in *The Chicago Tribune*. If the author of the piece had come forward no doubt some blood would have been shed. And if Valentino had lived long enough to read Mank and Steiger's book, they might have suffered the same fate as Sheldon Saltman.

But by the time Mank and Steiger wrote their book, their subject had been dead for forty years and they did not fear Rudolph Valentino's wrath. In fact in 1977, the same year Evel Knievel went to prison for assaulting the author of a scurrilous book written about him, Mank and Steiger signed a movie deal for theirs. The Ken Russell production of the film, *Valentino,* starring Rudolph Nureyev and Michelle Phillips was loosely based upon their *Shocking Expose*.

After all there was money to be made and despite all of Valentino's aging friends and loved one's protests, his role as the great, great lover evolved to include every sexual orientation. By 1977, the implication of "Pink Powder Puffery" evolved into the open statement, "Valentino was gay." While Mank and Steiger's book is today believed by some to be a credible reference, I found many of its references to be offensive, denigrating and homophobic. One such reference was Mank's referral to the attendees at a gay memorial service for Valentino as "the assembled deviates."

In 1998, the temptation to capitalize on Mank and Steiger's book was apparently too great for author David Bret. Perhaps he believed, incorrectly, that only a few copies of the book remained in the hands of Valentino collectors or on the musty shelves of used book stores. He laid claim to Mank's Valentino fiction and released his own update. In the opening of David Bret's book he ponders, 'if Chaw Mank is anything to go by..." but then proceeds to neglect his own caveat. He infused Mank's innuendo and fantasies about Valentino with his own brand of literary overkill.

In the lexicon of fictional celebrity biographies marketed as being non-fictional, David Bret's biography of Rudolph Valentino, *A Dream of Desire*, is a virtuoso performance. This book reads as if the author condensed every morsel of false innuendo ever written about Rudolph Valentino into one tome. His factual errors are so numerous it would be impossible to itemize them all here. Suffice to say, I itemized one hundred and eight references to be factually incorrect.

Bret's apparent rush to churn out his book resulted in a dizzying array of typos which could have been avoided with minimal editing. A photograph of Valentino's sister-in-law is mistakenly labeled his sister and Natacha Rambova's pet lion cub's name is Zela on one page when a few pages later it is Zeta. One of Bret's most notable errors is a photograph labeled, "Above, Valentino and his second wife Natacha Rambova and his lover André Daven in Paris in 1924." In fact this "lover" of Valentino's is not Daven but Valentino's brother, Alberto. Additionally, Bret's chronological order of events in Valentino's life is so randomly presented that on a few occasions he contradicts himself.

Bret holds Chaw Mank to be the definitive word on Valentino by quoting him repeatedly and implying they shared a personal correspondence during the writing of his book. This is unlikely as Chaw Mank died in 1985, thirteen years earlier. Bret uses line by line parallels from Mank's book such as, Chaw Mank's, "Bob, the husky young escort" becomes Bret's, "Rob, the hunky young escort." Bret's inclusion of specific scenarios and his listing of "The Unpublished Diaries of Rudolph Valentino," in his twelve item bibliography reveals one of his prime sources was the fictitious and anonymously written *La Presse* article.

By relying on third and fourth hand hearsay information and innuendo which he presents as fact, Bret claims an intimate knowledge of Valentino's sleeping arrangements and portrays his subject as sado-masochistic and sexually insatiable. Bret also asserts that every single one of Valentino's male friends and acquaintances, business or personal, totaling some thirty five men, were all his gay lovers. Bret's list of Valentino's gay lovers includes everyone from his manager, George Ullman to his handyman Lou Mahoney to movie censorship czar, Will Hayes.

David Bret presents no proof for any of these affairs and I was able to disprove many of them with a few clicks of the mouse on The International Movie Data Base website. For example on two occasions, from 1918 to 1920, Bret casts Gary Cooper in the role of Valentino's lover. The problem with this story is that Gary Cooper did not arrive in Los Angeles until late in 1924 and his first feature film appearance was not until 1926, the year Valentino died. During the time frame Bret reports that Gary Cooper was engaging in homosexual affairs with Valentino in Hollywood he was working as a political cartoonist for *The Independent Record*, Helena, Montana's daily newspaper.

Bret writes at length regarding two of Valentino's acquaintances as having been his "great loves." It is not documented this was the case regarding Rudolph Valentino's friendships with Jacques Hébertot and André Daven. Jacques Hébertot, the director of Le Theatre des Champs-Élysées was a personal friend of both Valentino and Natacha Rambova. When they visited Paris he hosted dinners in their honor and introduced them to the literary and artistic French elite.

For the good part of his book Bret quotes Hébertot as his source of information on Valentino's alleged gay Parisian life. Yet three-quarters of the way into his book, Bret admits his source was not Hébertot but someone claiming to have had a one night stand with Hébertot in 1945, a Roger Normand. According to Bret, Roger Normand was a "singer-dancer-actor" who succumbed to Hébertot's charms and had a one night stand with him some forty years earlier. Bret alleges it was then Hébertot told him, Valentino was gay.

Valentino biographer Jeanne DeRecqueville had access to a correspondence between Rudolph Valentino and Jacques Hébertot and refutes any claim these two men were anything but cordial friends. Ironically, the letter Jeanne DeRecqueville included in her biography as a handwriting challenge to the anonymous author of the *La Presse* article happened to be a letter from Valentino written to Jacques Hébertot. After reading this letter I can say it is nothing more than a polite exchange of casual news and travel arrangements.

According to Bret, the second of Valentino's alleged gay Parisian lovers was André Daven, Jacques Hébertot's assistant and a newspaper reporter. I learned through my research Daven was Natacha Rambova's "discovery" and she, not Valentino, invited him to come to New York City to appear in Valentino's movie, *Monsieur Beaucaire.* Both Rudolph Valentino and his wife Natacha Rambova were charitable to many of their friends and protégées. As benefactress, Natacha Rambova's discoveries included not only André Daven but actress Myrna Loy and fashion designer, Adrian.

In the case of André Daven, David Bret misrepresents the Valentino's admirable generosity by claiming their interest in these people was sexual. According to new documents recovered, Monsieur Daven came to New York at Natacha Rambova's invitation, lived in New York at the Valentino's expense where he borrowed huge sums of money from their friends which he never repaid. He also charged on credit an enormous bill for a complete overhaul of his teeth with the Valentino's dentist.[2] Since they knew nothing about his dental reconstruction until the day the bill arrived, they were livid at the unwelcome news. Bret writes Daven's abrupt departure from New York was due to a lover's spat with Valentino. The actual reason for the bad blood

---

2   The total of Daven's debt to Valentino was 35,000 French Francs as $29,400.00 U.S. dollars in 1924, which by today's exchange rate would be $449,000.00. As reference, a letter written to Hébertot by Valentino on July 4 1924, which was sold at auction in which Valentino writes: '... *he owes me nearly 35,000 francs, which I consider lost. What hurts me most is not the money, but the ingratitude and hypocrisy with which he (Daven) has acted toward me'.....etc. "*

upon Daven's departure was not a lover's quarrel as Bret states but an effort on Daven's behalf to avoid Valentino's demand for payment in full for his costly dental work.

Author Jeanne DeRecqueville writes regarding the correspondence between André Daven and his girlfriend in Paris which was written during the time he visited New York. DeRecqueville quotes Daven's letters in which he complains about his fifty dollars a week salary earned working as a secretary and the small room and used typewriter the Valentino's provided for him.

Nevertheless, today on The Internet Movie Database, André Daven has a single byline as quoted from David Bret's book, "The greatest love of Rudolph Valentino." This byline is cited from David Bret's erroneously labeled photograph of Valentino's brother. It would be the fact that Daven and Valentino went fishing together which would be held by Bret as definitive proof they were lovers. I hold that fishing trips, Chinese pajamas and the sexual orientation of your friends does not determine one's sexual preference. The existing documentation reveals André Daven was a passing character in Valentino's life and someone who left Valentino's life in 1924, on bad terms and owing his a great deal of money.

Bret's most prurient claim involves one of Valentino's poems titled, "You." Valentino wrote and dedicated this love poem for his wife Natacha and published it in 1923 along with others in a small book of poetry he titled, *Daydreams*. Bret informs his readers Valentino formatted this poem in his book in the shape of his own penis. According to Bret, Valentino's format of this "phallic" poem was "deliberate" and this prank "incensed the Hay's office." I have a copy of this rare book and unless Will Hay's was somehow offended by and Valentino's penis actually resembled a four inch by three and a half inch square block of text, J'accuse, Mr. Bret.

A Dream of Desire's bibliography consists of twelve books and various "unpublished" works with no information as to where a reader might access these sources. These unpublished works include, "Rudolph Valentino's unpublished diaries 1923-1926".[3] One curious mention in his bibliography is Michael Morris', *Madam Valentino*. Curiously because Bret neglects to include Morris' conclusive research on one long-held misconception concerning Valentino and the murder of Ramon Novarro. This originated in 1975, when Kenneth Anger authored the first of his *Hollywood Babylon* books; grim picture books exploiting the seamier and sensational side of Hollywood celebrity.

---

3 When pressed to produce this unpublished diary, Bret cited, *"Il mio diario privato"* by Rodolfo Orlandelli, which is an Italian translation of the widely distributed *"My Private Diary"*, a ghost-written publicity piece published first as serialized in the magazine *Movie Weekly* with the title, *"My Trip Abroad "* then as a book in 1929, with the title, *"My Private Diary"*. In his bibliography, Bret also cites, as irrefutable proof of Rudolph Valentino's homosexuality, the "unpublished" series of articles written in 1956 by Robert Florey, published in the magazine *Cinemonde* in eight episodes with the title *"Inoubliable, inoublié, Rudolph Valentino survit à sa légende "* .. We obtained copies of those 1956 articles and after having carefully read them we did not find any "evident" proof of his claim.

Kenneth Anger reports how actor Ramon Novarro choked to death on a dildo created as a replica of Valentino's penis. He alleged said dildo was given to Novarro by Valentino. This scenario has been savored by many for decades as a source of ghoulish titillation but according to those processing the crime scene and the murderers themselves, it never happened. While writing *Madam Valentino*, Michael Morris interviewed United States District Judge James M. Ideman, the Assistant District Attorney prosecuting Novarro's murderers. Ideman wrote,

"With reference to the claim that Mr. Novarro was choked to death by means of an 'Art Deco dildo,' I can tell you that did not happen...I certainly never made any statement to the effect that such an instrument was used. I did not even know of its existence."

No such dildo was listed on the corner's report of the murder scene and C. Robert Dambacher of the coroner's office wrote Michael Morris saying anyone purporting this theory was in his opinion, *"sick and sensationalizing on the actor's death."*

In André Soares' biography of Novarro, *Beyond Paradise*, he recounts the events of the night Novarro was murdered. He wrote his narrative after conducting personal interviews with Novarros' convicted killers. One of the two brothers convicted of the crime, Paul Ferguson, told Soares from his prison cell that no such dildo was ever seen or used in the murder. Soares writes,

"For him (Novarro) to be chiefly remembered today as a perverted, elderly homosexual killed by a sex toy that never existed is an injustice to both the complex individual and to the accomplished and historically important actor that was Roman Novarro."

It is also an injustice to Valentino to be remembered for having any role in Novarro's death. Furthermore, Novarro claimed the two actors barely knew each other. Even with Anger's lies authoritatively exposed, David Bret repeated this morbid version of Novarro's death in slavish detail while including Michael Morris' book in his bibliography.

It seems unthinkable a book so sensational, fictional, poorly researched and lackadaisically written as *Dream of Desire* could ever have much impact on Valentino's reputation. But the book's appearance during the birth of social media, gave rise to gay Valentino web sites with both Valentino and Natacha Rambova being absorbed into many gay listings. David Bret was received as a reputable author and researcher and appeared as an expert on Valentino touting Chaw Mank and his own fiction as fact in an E! television documentary on Valentino.

Apparently David Bret did not single out Rudolph Valentino as the sole recipient of his brand of fictional biography; he has written many celebrity biographies in the same format. Nevertheless, Bret's work on Valentino inspired the following quote to appear in another book, *Images in the Dark* by Raymond Murray. Valentino's byline in this publication reveals more evidence of the history of innuendo being passed off as fact.

"Several (but not all) biographies conclude that Valentino was a bisexual. He wrote in his private journals of one sexual encounter with a man, and although he married twice, both of them were arranged by actress Alla Nazimova, including his second wife, lesbian set designer Natacha Rambova."

Based on the evidence I discovered, none of this has been proven true. Yet the author, Raymond Murray, the owner of a chain of video stores in Philadelphia compiled his *Images in the Dark* as, "a handy queer video guide". In the preface to his listings of gay movie stars he writes,

"I tried to confirm a person's sexual orientation through direct contact with them or their agent. Some asked not to be included....In other cases, I was simply wrong in assuming they were gay...Some of the stars that made the final cut were included not because of first-(or second) hand knowledge of their sexual orientation but through gossip (sorry, but true), common knowledge or references made on them in other books and magazines. I can dream, can't I?"

Raymond Murray's dream listing of Valentino in his "gossip based" video guide then became the sole source and reference for Rudolph Valentino's induction into The Gay Hall of Fame.

In 2003, the author of *Dark Lover*, by Emily Leider, held to basically the same position as that of Steiger and Mank by alleging Valentino was bisexual. Leider was more ambiguous on the subject and skirted the issue by saying, "bi-sexuality is always an option." She obliquely referred to the fictional anecdotes from the *La Presse* article and David Bret's biography by inferring proof of Valentino's bisexual orientation could be evident in that fishing trip he made with André Daven. She avoids directly asserting Natacha Rambova was a lesbian by saying that she "may have experimented with bi-sexuality" and offers no further support for this supposition than the adage that women wearing Chinese pajamas might be lesbians. I contend clothing does not determine one's sexual orientation.

A Voice From the Grave

I felt I exhausted my search for credible documentation supporting Valentino's alleged homosexuality. Nevertheless, I persevered in my quest for evidence in order to make an authoritative statement regarding Valentino's sexual orientation. I turned to Rudolph Valentino's best friend and business manager, George Ullman.

I was determined to see if Ullman left any archives and after a lengthy search, fraught with many obstacles, I located his two surviving children. During my initial interview, they presented me with the only existing copy of their father's unpublished memoir. Shortly before his death in 1975, Ullman wrote this candid account of life behind-the-scenes with Rudolph Valentino.

As I read through the stack of yellowing pages, I realized many of the dynamic elements of Valentino's life story which Ullman addressed had never come to light in any publication on Valentino I'd read to date. Ullman's memoir painted a portrait of Valentino quite opposite of the one known today. After vetting Ullman's work, I found it to be credible in addition to revealing.

According to George Ullman's children, at the time of their father's death he was unaware of the assertions being made Valentino was gay. As an eighty-two year old man he died still anguishing over the pink powder puff incident some fifty years prior. Consequently, in his memoir he did not directly address the issue of Valentino's alleged homosexuality. It was through Ullman's many anecdotes that new first-hand information revealed an answer to the question," Was Valentino gay or bisexual"? Valentino's heterosexuality was remarkably unambiguous.

The commercial literary efforts of Samuel Roth, Hiram Moderwell, Chaw Mank, Brad Steiger and David Bret were dismantled by George Ullman's credible, first hand accounts. According to Ullman, Rudolph Valentino and Natacha Rambova shared the same bed for years, first as lovers and later as spouses. He debunked the "platonic arrangement" theory by relating anecdotes referencing their sleeping arrangements and with accounts of their "making up" after their many fights. While touring together on the Mineralava Tour in 1923, Ullman's sleeping berth on the train adjoined the Valentino's private quarters. Unlike the authors who claimed a critical vantage point to Valentino's sleeping arrangements years after the fact, Ullman was there and had one.

It would be one of Valentino's most successful on-screen attributes, his lack of self-consciousness in displays of love, which would be further first-hand evidence of Valentino's heterosexual behavior. Off screen, in the company of George Ullman, he acted much the same. He kissed his wife and girlfriends with little modesty and a great deal of passion. His lack of discretion where women were concerned was also evident in his open love affair with movie star Pola Negri. She spent many nights sleeping with Valentino in his master bedroom in the months prior to this death. After his death, her lingerie and negligees were found in his dresser and closet.

Ullman relates accounts of Valentino's simultaneous love affairs with showgirls and co-stars.[4] Although a bounty of credible evidence exists confirming his love affairs with women, I found none confirming he had an affair with a man.

Contrary to Mank and Steiger's claim Valentino's interest in boxing during the final weeks of his life was "make-believe" because he "could not face his wife in the boudoir," this was not the case. Valentino owned a box of eight seats at the American

---

4 Also cite *The True Rudolph Valentino*, by Baltasar Cué, translated by Renato Floris, Viale Industria Pubblicazioni, Torino, 2019, p. 102, "Rudolph was again fully living the bachelor life and the public often witnessed the accompaniment of a lady actress he might be dating. But the women who would truly gain his attention were, of course, the ones the public did not see. There was one woman one day and another the next, countless women who disputed the honor of being intimate with him. Whether in Hollywood or in the surrounding area; in his house or in the ladies' homes or his friend's homes, in hotel rooms, in cabarets, in his yacht of such sad history; here these affairs took place to fill him with joy."

Legion Arena in Los Angeles for the last three years of his life. He and Ullman could be found there every Friday night when they were in town. It was hard to miss their presence as they were well-known for yelling top volume at the action in the ring. Valentino was not only a devotee of the sport of boxing, close friends with Jack Dempsey, but sparred regularly with Ullman, who once boxed professionally. Valentino's interest and involvement in the sport was genuine.

Ullman also revealed details of some of Valentino's brushes with the law while he was intoxicated and in the company of women. As Valentino's manager it was Ullman's job to keep these incidents out of the papers. On a few occasions when Ullman was unsuccessful in his efforts, Valentino's citations by the police for speeding and driving under the influence of alcohol while carousing in the company of a female companion were reported by the press.

And contrary to the allegation made by Chaw Mank that Valentino frequented gay bathhouses, Valentino's household financial ledgers reveal he frequented speakeasies and burlesque clubs. Valentino had his choice of the club's dancers as his evening companion. He once pondered the physical appearance of American women v. French women and argued the most attractive women in the world could be found on Hollywood Boulevard and in the Ziegfeld Follies.

Yet, George Ullman's influence over Valentino's business affairs made him a controversial figure in the movie star's life story. I did not realize this until my initial announcement of my discovery of Ullman's lost memoir. The news this document presented information regarding Valentino's sexual orientation was greeted by a range of passionate response.

In addition to genuine interest and enthusiasm as expressed by many film scholars and fans on Valentino's web sites, I came under withering attack by a group of gay Valentino activists. Granted, I'd formed my opinion about Valentino's sexual orientation based upon my months of research and the evidence in hand, but I was not asking anyone else to do so. I was presenting the facts as they lined up before me and sharing my newly-found evidence.

With fundamentalist zeal these activists cited the undocumented, industrial grade innuendo which I was all too familiar with; "What about Valentino's friendships with.." followed by a list of his possibly gay friends and lavish praise for authors Chaw Mank and David Bret. I was disheartened to learn these apparent experts on Valentino failed to recognize the intolerance, bigotry and homophobia which was the very foundation of the original assertion Valentino was gay. I felt strongly that anyone perpetuating this belief today is part of the problem. I was also disheartened with the apparent lack of drive to correct the obvious flaws in these intellectually dishonest works on Valentino.

I began wondering if Valentino might represent a line in the sand where the postmortem outing of historical figures based solely upon innuendo, hearsay and wishful thinking is concerned. When I began my investigation into this aspect of

Valentino's life, I presumed nothing and accepted no unsubstantiated claim as fact. I came to my own conclusion Valentino was heterosexual based upon the lack of evidence presented by the authors claiming he was gay, based on the evidence Valentino was sexually attracted to women and based on the testimony of those who lived in Valentino's presence and knew his truth.

To those who continue to cling to the legacy of unsubstantiated misconceptions and innuendo written about Valentino, I remind them Rudolph Valentino was not a fictional character and should not be treated as one. When I passed along the key elements of my research to The Gay Hall of Fame Tyneside, I was surprised and impressed when I opened my e-mail one morning to find the following notice from the site's administrator, David Hall.

".... with specific reference to the "Hall of Fame" page, I state that it has never been the intent to "out" any person, living or dead, who is not already credited by history or directly by themselves, as being of homosexual / bisexual orientation. In the case of Rudolph Valentino, I greatly appreciate the research work you have carried out, in particular the interview with the author and acknowledgment that he had not a single fact to back up the claims in their book and value the fact that you have kindly informed me of such. Bottom line, I do care about historical accuracy and consequently the name Rudolph Valentino has been removed from the Hall of Fame page and again may I thank you for your words of clarification - sincerely appreciated."

The Brad Steiger Interview

The following is my e-mail exchange with Brad Steiger verbatim (as preserved on e-mail servers) in which I question his sources for his collaboration with Chaw Mank titled, *The Intimate and Shocking Expose*. My responses to Brad Steiger are in italics with my opening email reading:

Dear Mr. Steiger;

I was happy to find your web address and am researching Valentino. I know you co-wrote a book on him and am wondering if you could tell me what documents/sources you used. I also heard Mr. Mank had a scrapbook of Valentino's. Does Mr. Mank have the book or does he have an estate that would still have this? I am also trying to locate some interviews that an H. Moderwell conducted and I heard you used in your text? Can you enlighten me on any of this?

Thank-you,
E. Zumaya

⇨   Brad Steiger's response:

Sorry, my friend, I cannot enlighten you very much about a book that I wrote nearly forty years ago. Chaw Mank died sometime in the early 1970s. I have moved eleven times since 1966, so I no longer have any file on Valentino.

Best wishes,
Brad

Dear Mr. Steiger,

I thank-you for your prompt reply. I am sorry to hear you have no file from your work with Mr. Mank. As you may be aware your book on Valentino has over the years been plagiarized and consequently is the prime source of the theory Valentino was gay. Since there is no direct reference in your work as to the origins of the homosexual scenarios you wrote about, one is left wondering where they came from.

I am writing two books on Valentino and have interviewed many experts on him as well as a gentleman who knew most of the characters in Valentino's life. In no way have I found any documented evidence to claim he was gay. In my work I will painstakingly investigate this urban legend. I am offering you the opportunity to respond to what will be an analysis of your work's impact over the years. Although you have no written file, you might recall what evidence Mr. Mank had for these stories. I am a careful researcher and welcome your response.

Thank-you in advance for your consideration in this matter,
Evelyn Zumaya

⇨ Steiger's response:

I cannot account for any plagiarized versions of the initial work, and I was not aware that this was the case. The motion picture based on the book bears little resemblance to the actual text. It seems well established that Valentino's two wives were lesbians, and Nazimova, who had a great influence on his life, was an outspoken lesbian. These apparent facts strongly suggest that his marriages were arranged, as was often the case in those days when gays were afraid to come out of the closet. Many of the individuals with whom I spoke who claimed first or secondhand familiarity with accounts of Valentino's homosexuality confirmed this, and I know many individuals with whom Mank had relationships also affirmed that Valentino was gay. Although Mank was unmarried, I doubt very much that he himself was gay, but he did have extensive contacts among the Hollywood gay community at the time.

By the same token, I also included interviews with women who claimed to have had romances, sexual affairs, or who "made out" with Valentino. My position was that Valentino may quite likely have been bisexual. In subsequent interviews at the time of the book's release, I made the point that I doubted that Valentino was exclusively gay in his sexual orientation. Indeed, my wife's father is an alleged son of Valentino. His mother swore to her dying day that Valentino was the father of her illegitimate son and none of the family members doubt her account. I took pains to portray Valentino as an apostle of love and beauty, essentially an innocent exploited by others, who would much rather have been growing oranges in California. In my opinion, he was one of the very first of the screen stars to have had a character created for him by the studios, who then exaggerated whatever sexual magnetism he may have possessed into a larger than life personna that no human could maintain for long under the scrutiny of an adoring, but easily scornful, public.

Dear Brad:

It is not well-established that Natacha Rambova or Alla Nazimova were lesbians. There is actually much documentation Rambova was heterosexual. There is no evidence presented other than she was a friend of Nazimova to claim she was a lesbian. If Valentino's marriage to Rambova was "arranged" why would they have run off to Mexico? And why would his studio have banished her to the East to protect his screen image? Paramount was angered by the marriage. Who would have arranged this romantic disaster other than their own impetuousness? What first or second hand accounts of Valentino's homosexuality are you specifically referring to? When not a single man has come forward in nearly eighty years to claim he was a lover of his.

Yes, there is an abundance of evidence he was heterosexual, but since there was and still is...nothing more than hearsay and second and third hand information as to the possibility he was bisexual, why was that information credible enough to have been reported as fact by you?

Who are these people who claim to have had first or second hand information that Valentino was gay? Most curious. In reality until your book was published this was never an issue. Afterwards these ideas gained immense importance in the gay community and now are assumed to have been fact. Surely you must realize that hearsay is not admitted in a court of law, why here? His heterosexual experiences were witnessed and many woman came forward and kissed and told in great detail. This subject caused Valentino distress during his brief life and it is sad it has found any importance because in actuality it has none. You are correct he may have been happier growing oranges, but the continued implications that he and his wife were gay must certainly still be adding to his unhappiness..somewhere. Don't you think? It is just not right that someone's sexual preference, whether they are gay or straight..is manipulated and/or defined based on hearsay and speculation.

Evelyn Zumaya

⇨   Dear Evelyn:

I was primarily referring to Jean Acker, his first wife. That marriage was annulled on grounds of nonconsummation when he wished to marry Ms. Rambova. Surely that seems a little suggestive and supportive of the allegations of homosexuality. I'm afraid after all these years it is going to boil down to which accounts one believes. I simply cannot believe that there were no allegations of Valentino being gay before our book was published in 1966. What about Hollywood Babylon? And such accounts were in wide circulation among people in Hollywood and New York publishing circles. Believe me, I certainly had no axe to grind regarding Valentino's sexual preference, and Mank, who worshipped the man, surely did not.

I have now written 154 books, and Valentino was waaaaaay at the beginning of my career.   Outside of a couple other biographies, 99.5% of my books are in the metaphysical field.   See www.bradandsherry.com What I am curious to learn is where on Earth you found TWO publishers interested in doing books on Valentino? Outside of film buffs, most young people today believe that he was a character of romantic fiction, like Romeo.   It is difficult to imagine a wide audience for two books on Valentino. But good for you if you have actually found two publishers willing to invest in such projects.

And now I must return to my present deadline, another collaboration with my wife, which, regrettably, is somewhat late arriving on the desk of our editor.

With all best wishes,
Brad

Dear Brad,

I was hoping you would mention the names or circumstances of the individuals who claim gay relationships with Valentino. The identities of Valentino's women are widely known, yes.

Referring to the fact that Valentino's first marriage was not consummated. Why would that make him gay? If Jean Acker was a lesbian, that would not mean Valentino was gay. Hollywood Babylon was published in 1975 and several books that claim he was gay rely solely or heavily on your book. We have methodically researched every book written about him since his death, and indeed your book is the first we have found to even hint or mention homosexuality. If you know a previous book I would love to know about it. I did not believe you and Mank had an "axe to grind," as I personally don't believe there anything wrong with homosexuality. I am merely inquiring as to the specifics of Mank's accounts.

If these accounts were in wide circulation in Hollywood and the publishing world, why is there not a single specific name, date, place or circumstance that can be substantiated? I will assume since there weren't any specifics, there is no real tangible credibility to them?

From what I am hearing from you, there are no names, dates, records or documentation on Mank's claims that Valentino was gay/bi-sexual?

Thank-you for your time in your responding.
Evelyn Zumaya

The Letter to Bruno

Bruno Pozzan was one of Rodolfo Valentino's closest friends. They met and became friends as they were both children of deceased medical professionals; Valentino's father having been a veterinarian. Bruno and Rodolfo attended the Collegio della Sapienza located in the ancient fourteenth-century Sapienza building in the city of Perugia in the region of Umbria. The boarding school complex was created in 1360 by Cardinal Niccolò Capocci with study facilities welcoming Italian and foreign students of theology and law from the University of Perugia.

In 1902, the college was first rented and then purchased in 1936 by the O.N.A.O.S.I. (National Organization for Italian Healthcare Orphans), to welcome orphaned children of both doctors and veterinarians. This school, with the same purpose, still exists today.

Rodolfo's friend Bruno was born in the city of Carmignano di Brenta in the province of Padua, and he and Rodolfo enjoyed a significant correspondence which has recently been dispersed within the Valentino memorabilia collector's market.

The collection consisted of five autographed letters signed "Rodolfo" sent from Taranto between January 27, 1910 and February 11, 1911. Four of the letters survived with the original Valentino autographed envelopes. The collection also contained an autographed postcard sent from Sant'Ilaro Ligure (Valentino's agricultural school) in Nervi, in the suburb of Genoa, postmarked July 17, 1912. Two photographs of Valentino also survived with one inscribed in Italian on the back: "To my dear Bruno... as an imperishable bond of our fraternal friendship. Rodolfo Guglielmi, Taranto, January 27, 1910", and with the annotation, allegedly in Bruno's handwriting, reading: "Perugia, January 28, 1910 at 5:30 P.M."

These letters were once a part of the William Self Valentino collection. Upon his death, the letters were auctioned off to collectors who have sold the various letters individually on an open market thereby losing forever any ability to reference the valuable "Letters to Bruno" for historical purposes.

It is a great tragedy these informative and fascinating artifacts are sold by collectors for a profit; revealing they do not recognize their historical value. The single letter presented here stands as testimony and evidence of the content of those letters to Bruno which are now lost forever. We thank the owner of this letter, Ms. Sky Lesko, for sharing the letter, allowing for a translation and in this, perserving it for posterity.

The following images are protected by copyright and the exclusive property of Sky Lesko and may not be reproduced without her permission.

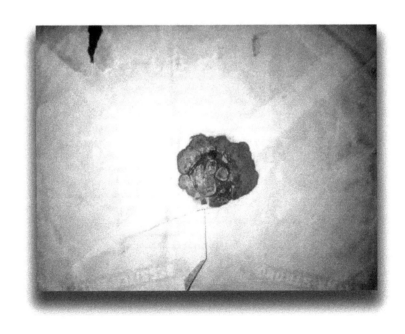

Taranto 29 ...

Carissimo Brino,

... ti ho fatto sempre chiamando,
perché sono stato a bordo della R...
Benedetto Brin ... a ...
... Della Rocca (il figlio del
nostro professore di Costruzioni)
che ho conosciuto a Taranto un
paio di mesi fa, al ...
... a Taranto, e con loro
rimasto con lui a colazione.

Sai che ora la squadra che viene
di addestrarsi sta a Taranto, poi
domani mercoledì 30, partirà per
Venezia, e verso l'11 saranno tutte
le squadre con la venuta del R... a
Taranto ...

ho avuto 3 pacchetti di sigarette estere
che gli sono stati regalati dal Re
del Montenegro. Fortunatamente cati...
di sopra a Piano Barletta, sono
stati circondati e qui non ve ne
è stato nessuna. Quindi mi a causa
ho scritto proprio adesso che sono le
6½ nel ritornare da bordo. Se vedesti
come sono gentili gli ufficiali
di Marina. Poi sono stato presentato
al Comandante in 2° del Pisa, il quale
è una persona gentilissima.
Riguardo alla mia vita non faccio
nulla e continuo a annoi... e mi annoio
ed è per quello che ti ho cercato gli
indirizzi dei giornali; perché voglio
darmi al giornalismo.

Translation of the Letter to Bruno

Translation
by Renato Floris

Taranto 29, August 1910

Dear Bruno,

I couldn't write to you this morning because I was aboard the R.N. (the Royal Ship) "Benedetto Brin", to meet up with the Sub-Lieutenant Della Rocca, the son of our business mathematics professor whom I met in Taranto a couple of months ago at the "Marconi" cabaret variety club and so I stayed with him for lunch.

You know that now the naval squadron that comes from Antivari is in Taranto, tomorrow Wednesday 30, they will leave for Venice, and around the 11th there will be all three squadrons with the coming of the king to Taranto. From Mr. Della Rocca I got three packs of foreign cigarettes that were given to him by King Nicholas of Montenegro. Fortunately, cases of cholera in Trani and Barletta have been limited and there have been none. So no worries. I wrote right now that it is 5:15 (PM) on the way back from the ship. If you saw how kind the Navy officers are. Then I was introduced to the Commander in 2nd of Brin who is a very kind person.

As for my life, I don't do anything and I consume money and I'm bored and that's why I ask you for the addresses of the newspapers because I want to give myself to journalism. Could you ask your relatives in Padua for the addresses of some other newspapers, but not local. You would do me a great pleasure.

Not long ago, a 17-year-old cabaret singer was in Taranto and I had a great time with her. Then, while I am courting cabaret singers, I make love with prostitutes, leaving one to take another.

Give my compliments to Manlio for the race he has won and I wish for him that in the next race he will take not the 6th prize but the 1st. Do you know if Sinigaglia is still in Castelfidardo? If you go to Venice in a few days you will see the naval squadron. If you want a presentation note for Mr. Della Rocca, tell me and I will send it to you. He is holed up now on the squadron's flagship Benedetto Brin, since a boiler exploded aboard the previous flagship Regina Margherita, a few knots from Taranto, and 7 sailors died. So the admiral (of the squadron) who was there before will pass tomorrow or tonight on the Benedetto Brin.

Hi! And a kiss from yours,

Rodolfo.
P.S. Write to me soon and send me the addresses.

The Masked Model

It is reported in most Valentino biographies, his exodus from New York City in 1917 was via a road show which disbanded somewhere across the country for lack of funds. Yet in researching this show's 1917 tour, we find it was a successful production. It was through various newspaper coverage of the day, we discovered the following.

Max Steiner, famed American composer and conductor was once the musical director for the road show "The Masked Model" which traveled the U.S. via "the northern route" in the spring of 1917. Rudolph Valentino was a cast member in the show and this is how he left New York City for the west coast. In his autobiography, Max Steiner recollected how Valentino was fired after a disagreement with the show's director and cast members secretly provided Valentino with food and a place to sleep until the show reached San Francisco.

The show left New York City in early April 1917 and played a two week engagement in Pittsburgh. During this time the cast and the show itself went through many changes in preparation for the trip west. Valentino was billed as "Mons. Rudolph", (Monsieur Rudolph) and he was hired as a ball room dancer. He performed in three numbers, with the audience favorite being a fox trot from "Johnny Get Your Gun". His dancing partner in "The Masked Model" was Edith Mason, a seventeen-year old protegee who was then so popular she was challenging the reputation of Valentino's previous dance partner in New York, Joan Sawyer.

Edith Mason received far more praise for her physical beauty than her dance moves and at seventeen she had already earned a respectable reputation. In every performance, she danced her famous ball room steps with Monsieur Rudolph.

"The Masked Model" would play in Omaha, Lincoln, Iowa City, Denver, Salt Lake City, Reno and San Francisco. After their engagement in San Francisco, they would perform down the California coast to Los Angeles. "The Masked Model" show traveled on a special train with a troupe of sixty-five with the entire tour taking about one month to reach San Francisco.

Reviews across the country can still be found online in newspaper archives, and they were predominately positive. It is obvious the show did not experience financial problems as it is often reported to be the case in Valentino biographies. There can be found only small mentions of fewer ticket receipts after the show reached Los Angeles. Each review of performances across the country reports on the full house and successful ticket sales.

"The Masked Model" cast included many well-known personalities at the time including vaudevillian performer Lew Hern. And at some point during the show, a new performer was added to the bill; Joseph Lertaro. Joseph Lertaro is a cast member of interest as he was Italian by birth and appeared to resemble Valentino. He was twenty-four years old, wore his hair slicked back and exuded old world charm. According to his reviews he could dance and sing.

Joseph Lertaro reportedly was an accomplished singer and often compared to Caruso with reviews praising his voice and his "pleasant" stage presence. Some local papers carried lengthy interviews with the Masked Model's star, Joseph Lertaro and he was very much a star of the show.

Lertaro's father in New York was known as "The Marshmallow King" and consequently in some reviews Joseph Lertaro is referred to as "The Marshmallow Prince". He also claims he was asked to perform with the New York Opera company but he refused the offer.

Rudolph Valentino could not sing like his countryman Lertaro. The two recordings Valentino made are the only record of his voice, but no matter how endearing they are, he knew he had no career in singing and reportedly wanted all copies of the recordings destroyed.

Playbills and reviews continue to include Mons. Rudolph in "The Masked Model" until Reno, Nevada. If he was with the show until Reno, he did not need much help from fellow cast members if he was fired there because San Francisco is only a few hours away. Was he still listed in the cast because the programs were already printed? Did the news reports reference previous notices? Did he actually perform in Reno? It is also noteworthy in reading all of the articles, that Edith Mason seems to have disappeared before San Francisco also.

"The Marshmallow Prince" did not disappear and was front and center when "The Masked Model" played in San Francisco. His role in the show would launch his career which was a successful one. After the road tour, Lertaro went on to appear in many Broadway shows and once starred with Mae West in her, "Mae West and Company".

The stage ballroom dancing was not over for Valentino and he appears in the show "Nobody Home" in Oakland after his stint in "The Masked Model", again billed as "Monsieur Rudolph".

Perhaps Max Steiner had a memory to draw upon and perhaps there was a dispute between Valentino and the show's director. But according to the show's announcements and the general press still in existence today, Valentino does not appear to have been left his position with the show in disgrace.

The show did not go broke but toured all the way to San Francisco and beyond as it headed south to Los Angeles. "Mons. Rudolph" and his dancing partner, Edith Mason appear in the Reno show the end of May prior to the San Francisco show. Valentino did not perform in the San Francisco show but he and Edith Mason appear to have rejoined the show in Sacramento and Fresno from June 12-June 19th.

The curious timing of these appearances meant Valentino was performing in two shows as he is also listed in the cast of "Nobody Home" on June 11th. Granted "Nobody Home" played in Oakland and "The Masked Model" in Sacramento which is located exactly 68 miles away. It could have been possible.

But this disputes the claim by Steiner that Valentino was fired and left in disgrace. In fact we find the opposite as he is advertised for his performance in, "Nobody Home" by citing his "starring" role in "The Masked Model". Although Joseph Lertora was clearly the star of "The Masked Model", Valentino was billed as being the star in some of the promotional advertisements for "Nobody Home". "Nobody Home" was billed as an, "enormous success" and he appears in the cast until early October.

After their appearance in Sacramento and in Fresno, Valentino and Edith Mason disappear from "The Masked Model" cast and he apparently works only in "Nobody Home". We know he joined the cast of "The Passing Show" subsequently and this was how he came to Los Angeles. One other factor could have contributed to the end of Valentino's reputable and prestigious vaudeville stage career about this time.

We learn from the personal account of Douglas Gerrard as related in *The True Rudolph Valentino* by Baltasar Cue, how Valentino arrived in Los Angeles in late fall of 1917 and was suffering from a dubious reputation for having been involved with the DeSaulles divorce and John DeSaulles murder. We also read how Thomas Meigham lectured Valentino about his tarnished reputation and Alla Nazimova openly called him a "pimp". I believe this came about because his reputation worsened after August 3rd.

On August 3, 1917, as Valentino was starring in the, "enormous successful", "Nobody Home", Blanca DeSaulles murdered her husband. I contend that previous to August 3rd, he enjoyed success as a revue dancer as his reputation was not so sullied. His being involved in a divorce in New York was scarcely material to ruin a reputation; but murder sure was.

He was not fired from "The Masked Model" but took on another role in another show; a show billing him as a feature act. He was already well known on the vaudeville musical variety circuit and previous to August 3rd, there is nothing but more work for him and acknowledgment. He was not unemployed but over-employed.

However, on August 3rd, the DeSaulles murder made national headlines and life for Mons. Rudolph became more treacherous. Monsieur Rudolph's professional reputation took a heavy hit when Blanca DeSaulles fired that gun and perhaps it was more for that reason he leaves the cast of "Nobody Home" to head south from San Francisco.

Edith Mason vanishes after the Sacramento and Fresno shows and no trace of her later life and career can be found. There is an opera star named Edith Mason who dominates the search but this is not the seventeen-year old who danced her way across the country with Rudolph Valentino.

"The Masked Model" did not fail financially and I think Rudolph found more employment and left the show in a smart career move. No doubt he was ready to leave the competition with Joseph Lertaro behind for a more starring role in "Nobody Home" and perhaps for the opportunity to dance with Miss Jane Urban!

Jane Urban was hugely popular at the time, a powerful force in the Bay Area's theater scene and the director of the Orpheum Theater. For Valentino to accept a position as her dancing partner then was a savvy career move and he would have benefited professionally. Although he appeared on stage with the impressive Ms. Urban, his rise to even more fame did not occur then.

It is reasonable to add to the reasons why he left San Francisco when he did; the reality his reputation was savaged when Blanca DeSaulles shot and killed her husband. Did he become a pariah? Did Jane Urban want nothing to do with him? The young vaudeville variety dancer, seeking to reinvent himself headed to Los Angeles to seek fame and fortune in the motion picture industry.

The sources for this article include but are not exclusive to:

Goodlins Weekly, May 12, 1917
Los Angeles Herald, June 22, 1917
Lincoln Star, April 19, 1917
Los Angeles Herald, June 25, 1917
San Francisco Examiner, May 27, 1917
Nebraska State Journal, April 29, 1917
Ogden, Utah Standard, May 11, 1917
San Francisco Examiner, May 20, 1917, Ibid, May 27
Lincoln, Nebraska Star, April 19, 1917
American Musical Theater Chronicle by Gerald Bordman
Moving Picture World, July-August, 21_1918
New York Public Library
Pittsburgh Press, April 2, 1917

The Cast of The Masked Model with Valentino Star Billing as "Monsieur Rudolph"

The Cardinal's Mistress

While in Rome with his wife, Natacha Rambova in 1923, Valentino visited UCI, The Unione Cinematografica Italiana. At the time, the movie Quo Vadid was being filmed on the sets on the production studio's lot. Many photos were taken of Valentino on the set with the German actor Emil Jannings, Jannings wife, Natacha Rambova and the Italian producer Arturo Ambrosio. At the time, Arturo Ambrosio was the leading Italian film producer and he was eager to produce a film starring Rudolph Valentino which would be filmed in Rome at UCI.

This film titled, *L'Amante del Cardinale: Claudia Particella, Romanzo Storico* (*The Cardinal's Mistress*) was written in 1910 by the man who would become dictator of Italy, twelve years later, Benito Mussolini. In his early career Mussolini worked as a journalist and editor and it was then he wrote this novel which was published as a serial book in the Trento newspaper *Il Popolo*. It was released in installments from January 20, 1910 to May 11, 1910.

In 1923, Ambrosio promoted this film to Valentino and even went so far as to claim later Valentino came to Rome to specially discuss production of this film. Ambrosio attempted to secure funding for the project and failed. The project was also blocked because by then Mussolini did not want these early novels he wrote to be promoted in any way.

Valentino sent a request to Mussolini to meet with him during his visit and the dictator refused saying he was too busy. Perhaps this was to discuss *The Cardinal's Mistress*, but Mussolini was already withdrawing his approval for the Valentino movie; claiming, "he found it incompatible with his new image and function."

An interesting side note to Ambrosio's projected film for Valentino: one of the screenplay writers was Leone Roberto Roberti, the father of the Great Italian director Sergio Leone the father of the film genre we call the Spaghetti western.

By the end of November 1923, it was still mentioned in the press how Valentino planned to make a movie in his Italian homeland in February of 1924. The termination of this project came about with Mussolini's opposition and Ambrosio's failure to secure funding.

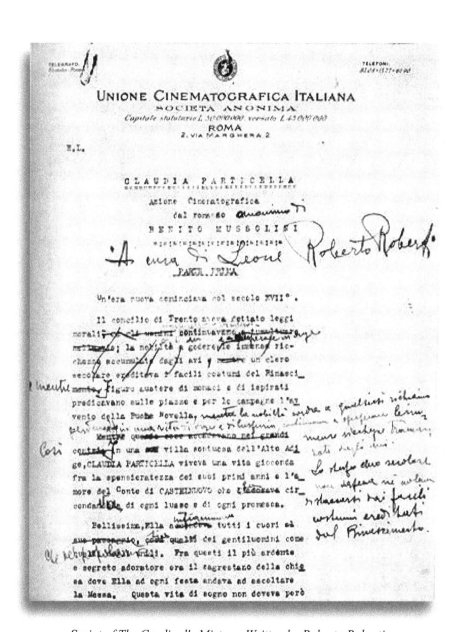

Script of The Cardinal's Mistress Written by Roberto Roberti

The Plot of *The Sainted Devil*

Translated from the Italian by Renato Floris

In Italian the film was titled, Notte Nuziale

The story takes place in the early 1800s and is set in a rich Argentine fazenda owned by the Marquis Baldassare di Castro. It tells of the young son of the Marquis, Alonzo, the male protagonist, with whom Carlotta, the daughter of the unfaithful superintendent of the property, is madly in love with. Alonzo, as per tradition, will have to marry Juliet, a girl of the Spanish nobility promised to him by her father and Carlotta, who is mad with jealousy, meditates a severe revenge.

Juliet finally arrives in Argentina and the wedding is planned, while meanwhile the superintendent, Carlotta's father, plans a robbery with the complicity of a vile bandit called El Tigre. Taking advantage of the confusion and exhaustion after the celebration of the wedding of Alonzo and Juliet, Carlotta tries to seduce the bandit El Tigre, promising him that she will be his if he kills both Juliet and Alonzo.

The violent robbery is set for the wedding night and, after the celebrations and when all the guests have left and the inhabitants of the fazenda go to sleep. After midnight the signal to attack is given, Alonzo's father is killed as well as his mother and elderly grandmother. El Tigre then goes in search of Alonzo to kill him but Alonzo, having heard the screams, runs down the stairs where he was found by the El Tigre who then stabs him.

Alonzo, believed to be dead, was abandoned on the stairs and meanwhile El Tigre, at the sight of the beautiful Juliet, kidnaps her and does not kill her, reserving her beauty for his sexual pleasure. El Tigre then, taking Juliet with him, leaves the fazenda to which he sets on fire.

The following morning Casimiro, son of the farmer and Alonzo's milk brother, having recovered from the terrible night, goes in search of Alonzo and discovers that he is still alive and that the wound is not serious. Alonzo is treated and shortly after is able to plan with Casimiro the hunt for bandits and the rescue of Juliet. Carlotta, seeing that Juliet had not been killed, goes to the El Tigre's hiding place, steals both Juliet's engagement ring and the wedding veil and so dressed she goes to try to seduce El Tigre.

Meanwhile Alonzo and Casimiro arrive at the bandits' hideout whose tracks they had followed. Alonzo immediately encounters Carlotta's father, the infidel superintendent and with a stab, kills him. He then tries to find the El Tigre and his accomplices who had already gone away after having divided the loot.

Alonzo catches a glimpse of Carlotta, however, dressed like Juliet embracing El Tigre and believes that the ugly creature is his new bride Juliet. El Tigre, realizing that he has been discovered by Alonzo, takes his portion of the booty with him and with Carlotta he escapes to take refuge in Bolivia. Meanwhile the poor Juliet is rescued by Estrella, another victim who had been enslaved by El Tigre for his personal sordid pleasure and Juliet managed to escape with her with neither El Tigre and Alonzo realizing their escape.

Alonzo and Casimiro remain confused and unable to punish the guilty ones and save Juliet who Alonzo thought fled with her new lover El Tigre. Alonzo, however, does not give up, appoints a new superintendent for his fazenda and with Casimiro goes hunting for El Tigre, he wants his revenge.

He traverses all the most infamous places in Argentina until he arrives in a sordid place in Buenos Aires which informers told him was a place frequented by El Tigre. Alonzo, upon his arrival in the tavern, runs into Estrella who worked there as a waitress. For Estrella it was love at first sight when she met Alonzo's sad gaze.

Alonzo leaves the place, planning to send Casimiro there the following day. As Alonzo leaves, El Tigre soon discovers the slave Estrella and threatens her with death if she doesn't tell him where Juliet is hiding. Juliet had taken refuge in a convent of nuns and was close to making her vows as the canonical novitiate year had almost passed.

Estrella went to the convent to tell Juliet that El Tigre was looking for her and Juliet replied that she would also gladly die since Alonzo, with whom she was madly in love, was dead, just as her father died in Spain. The following evening Casimiro goes to the inn and the innkeeper tells him that a customer has paid his debt with a ring and asks him if, according to him, that ring is of value. Casimiro immediately recognizes the ring, it is the engagement ring, an ancient family jewel, which Alonzo had given to Juliet. When the innkeeper tells him that this customer will come back that same night, Casimiro runs to call Alonzo who arrives and kills El Tigre who was by now drunk, while Carlotta laughs at him by telling him that Juliet was dead.

Casimiro runs to call Alonzo who arrives and kills El Tigre, while Carlotta laughs at him by telling him that Juliet was dead. Estrella on hearing this realized that the man with whom she too had fallen madly in love was Juliet's husband, but she kept silent out of respect for her friend. Finally Juliet, a few days before the pronouncement of the vows, was able to reunite with the groom and return with him to the fazenda.

Alonzo, after a police investigation was completely exonerated from any judicial consequences. Estrella became Juliet's silent lady-in-waiting. Carlotta ended her days rotting in jail. So they were finally able to live happily ever after.

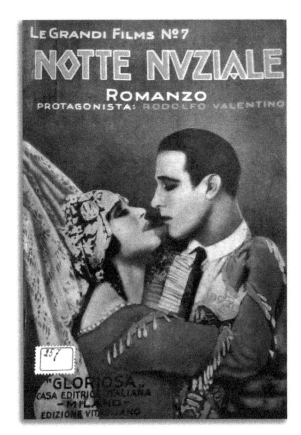

Italian Version of The Sainted Devil

When a Con Man Duped Royalty, Movie Stars and All of New York

The Story of "Dr. Sterling Wyman"

Shortly before silent film icon Rudolph Valentino died in New York's Polyclinic Hospital on August 23, 1926, a Dr. Sterling Wyman introduced himself to Valentino's manager George Ullman. His assertion he was acting on behalf of the funeral home handling Valentino's funeral arrangements, Frank E. Campbell's Funeral Chapel, was believed as truth.

When Campbell's opened its doors to allow the public viewing of Valentino's body, tens of thousands of fanatical mourners rioted in the streets. Ullman took full advantage of Dr. Wyman's eager assistance. The doctor's chivalrous demeanor was also appreciated by Valentino's lover at the time of his death, movie star Pola Negri.

When she arrived in New York to attend Valentino's funeral, Wyman presented her with a ready arm to lean upon while he solicitously dispensed aspirin and smelling salts. In his high-profile position as personal assistant to both Negri and Ullman, Wyman boasted to the press he once authored a prestigious publication titled,"Wyman on Medical Jurisprudence."

When arrangements were made to return Valentino's body to California with a small entourage, including Pola Negri, Wyman assumed he would accompany her on the funeral train. But a few hours before the train was scheduled to leave New York, a reporter suggested to Ullman he should look into Wyman's background. The reporter recalled Wyman was involved in an incident at the White House some years earlier. This prompted Ullman to dispatch another reporter to investigate Wyman's credentials and quickly deny the doctor passage on Valentino's funeral train. By the time the train reached El Paso, Texas, Ullman received a telegram with startling information regarding the doctor's past.

He learned Wyman held no medical credentials and was once a patient in a hospital for the criminally insane. Upon reading this, Ullman issued a statement saying Wyman no longer had authority to act on his or Pola Negri's behalf as the man was clearly 'laboring under some derangement."

A further investigation revealed Wyman previously presented himself in full military uniform to the visiting Princess Fatima of Afghanistan and escorted her to the White House under the alias of Lieutenant Commander Stanley Wyman. Two Secret Service men on duty at the event discovered his true identity and he was arrested and consequently sentenced to eighteen months in a penitentiary.

Dr. Sterling Wyman's birth name was Ethan Allan Weinberg and at various times he posed as a medical doctor, an attorney, a uniformed police officer and an array of diplomatic officials including the United States Consul to Monaco, a special representative to the Republic of Salvador, the Consul General for Romania and Lieutenant Royal Saint Cyr. He assumed his alias of Dr. Wyman while working in a "diploma factory" in Washington, D.C., where he purchased his medical degree for twenty-five dollars.

After his public exposure in the wake of Valentino's death, Weinberg did not retire from his nefarious career. In April of 1928, he inveigled his way through police lines, again in full uniform, to greet the "Bremen Flyers" when they arrived in New York City. Undetected, he escorted the first aviators to make the westward crossing of the Atlantic to their connecting train under the alias of Captain Stanley Wyman.

Ethan Allen Weinberg's bizarre life ended a few years later when he bled to death on the floor of a seedy hotel in New York City. He was employed as the establishment's night clerk when thieves burst into the hotel lobby in the wee hours of the morning. In the course of the armed robbery, Weinberg was shot in the chest and died on the spot.

Today, documentation of his few days as a trusted member of Valentino's inner circle still exists within the archives of Frank E. Campbell's Funeral Chapel. The signature "Dr. Wyman" can be found scrawled on the original invoice of Valentino's funeral and an unflattering mug shot of the arch impostor appears in a crumbling ledger. With quotation marks around his prestigious title, the photograph's caption, "Dr." Sterling C. Wyman, stands for perpetuity as oddly prophetic.

For Further Reading
The Viale Industria Pubblicazioni Library

All books are available on Amazon and other online book selling venues

In English:
Affairs Valentino - Special Edition
by Evelyn Zumaya

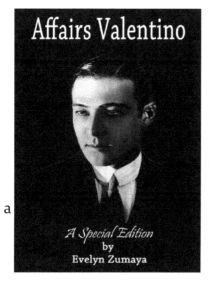

a

Evelyn Zumaya's discovery of unpublished court documents and a lost memoir written by Rudolph Valentino's close friend and business manager George Ullman became the basis for her ground-breaking book, *Affairs Valentino*. *Affairs Valentino* challenges the currently held version of the silent film icon's personality, professional life and business affairs. Rich with new anecdotes and never-before-revealed details of Valentino's personal finances and his relationships with family, colleagues, friends and lovers, *Affairs Valentino* is dramatically different story of Valentino's life than the one that has been repeated for decades. *Affairs Valentino* stands as the ultimate and documented true story of Rudolph Valentino.

First Edition (out of print)

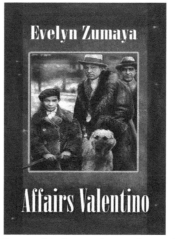

Second Edition (out of print), 2013

307

The S. George Ullman Memoir

by S. George Ullman

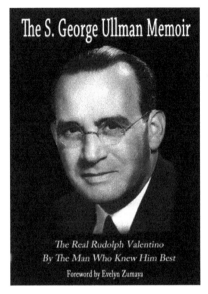

In the days following the sudden death of Rudolph Valentino in 1926, his business manager and closest friend, George Ullman published a book titled, *Valentino As I Knew Him.* Before his own death in 1975, Ullman wrote a second memoir about his life "behind-the-scenes" with Rudy. This memoir is a treasure trove of new anecdotes and information about the movie star's personal and business affairs. Lamentably, Ullman was, and still is, targeted by a few detractors who have aggressively misrepresented his story for decades. It was only after the recent discovery of Ullman's 1975 memoir, that an investigation was conducted into these allegations and documents uncovered which at last revealed the detailed truth about this iconic pioneer in celebrity management. This first publication of *The S. George Ullman Memoir* is accompanied by the entire transcript of Ullman's 1926, *Valentino As I Knew Him.*

Beyond Valentino - The Madam Valentino Addendum
by Michael Morris with Evelyn Zumaya

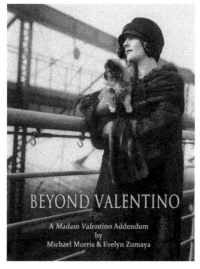

In 1991, Michael Morris published his iconic biography of Natacha Rambova, *Madam Valentino*. He subsequently continued his research, gaining worldwide recognition as the leading Rambova scholar. As his Rambova collection grew, he made the decision to open his archive and share ancillary material he did not include in *Madam Valentino*. With the collaboration of co-author, Evelyn Zumaya, the *Madam Valentino Addendum* was realized.

In this, his "final tribute to Rambova", Michael Morris showcases Rambova's written works, her Egyptological scholarship and her study of myth, symbolism and comparative religion. He has included her essay, "Arriba España", excerpts from her unpublished manuscripts and the story of the discovery of a cache of never-before-published photographs and artifacts. Rambova's contemporaries, as well as her intimate circle of associates are profiled, creating an informed and visual glimpse into her later life as well as her esoteric pursuits. This addendum also includes the enlightening contributions of several renowned scholars, who through their respective fields of expertise delve deeper into the life and times of Natacha Rambova.

The Affairs Valentino Companion Guide

by Evelyn Zumaya

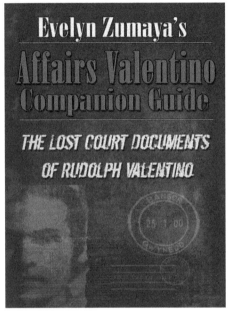

The case file of Rudolph Valentino's probate court records has been missing from its lawful location in the Los Angeles County Hall of Records for decades. With no access to these documents, those endeavoring to tell the tale of the lengthy settlement of the movie star's estate have relied upon surmise and speculation unsupported by facts and figures. As a result, this aspect of Rudolph Valentino's life story has remained a fractionalized, meager and inaccurate account. This would change when Valentino biographer, Evelyn Zumaya conducted a search for the missing archive.

Zumaya discovered the entire original case file had been stolen. After a lengthy investigation, she located more than one thousand hand-copied pages of this missing file. As the first Valentino biographer to access these records, Zumaya based her book *Affairs Valentino* upon this discovery. The wealth of new information divulged in these court records inspired ground-breaking directions in her research, culminating in her creation of the most accurate and documented account of Valentino's business and personal affairs.

In this *Companion Guide*, Zumaya shares the Valentino documents which are most relevant in documenting her work.

Astral Affairs Rambova

by Evelyn Zumaya

In August of 1925, silent film icon Rudolph Valentino and his second wife Natacha Rambova separated. In the weeks following their highly-publicized separation, Natacha Rambova sought refuge in spiritualism and the occult. She attended séances, studied theosophy and made the acquaintance of a deep-trance medium and psychic, George Wehner. Although George Wehner would become Rambova's constant companion until 1930, he has been, to date, a mere footnote in Rambova's life story. *Astral Affairs Rambova* broadens the context of this time in Rambova's life and delves into her relationship with Wehner.

George Wehner would infamously prophesize Rudolph Valentino's death in a séance held with Rambova and her family in their chateau on the French Riviera. This prophesy would take place only a few days before Valentino died and the psychic would write an account of this séance in detail some years later. *Astral Affairs Rambova* is based upon his account and on Wehner's own autobiography, *A Curious Life,* published in 1929, in which he reveals his relationship with Rambova and her family.

The True Rudolph Valentino

by Baltasar Fernandez Cue

Translated by Renato Floris

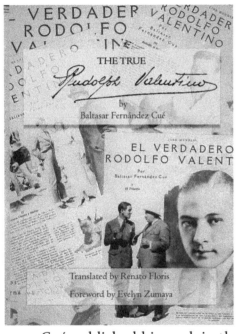

In the months before silent film icon Rudolph Valentino's death, he began a collaboration with Spanish journalist, Baltasar Fernández Cué. That collaboration was this book. Valentino lamented the glut of fictionalization about his life story and asked Cué to assist him in writing his true autobiography.

During the spring of 1926, Baltasar Fernández Cué became a familiar member of Valentino's entourage as he was granted extraordinary access to the star's private life and professional activities. Before Valentino left on his fateful trip to New York City, he gave Cué various personal letters and documents for reference and assured him he would return within three weeks to write his autobiography. Valentino would die soon after in New York City.

Cué published his work in the Spanish language fan magazine *Cine-Mundial* as a ten installment series, from May 1927 to February of 1928. Renato Floris' translation presents this historically valuable book for the first time to an English-speaking audience.

The Infancy of the Myth

by Aurelio Miccoli

Silent film star, Rudolph Valentino, spent the first nine years of his life in Castellaneta, a small city in southeastern Italy. This is the story of his Castellaneta years, a detailed, authoritative account of his essential familial, cultural, historical and even geographical influences. Author and native of Castellaneta, Aurelio Miccoli reveals "Rodolfo", as a curious yet difficult boy and daydreamer. His narrative is rich with the presence of the actual characters and places of Valentino's childhood days. With Miccoli's first hand familiarity with Castellaneta and his lifetime researching all available archives and locales, he has created a highly detailed, factual depiction of flora, fauna, streets and local history, all illustrated with full color photographs. *The Infancy of the Myth* is a scholarly study, an entertaining tale and a pictorial journey portraying the earliest events and influences of a little boy who became one of the world's most idolized screen icons.

Daydreams *by Rudolph Valentino*

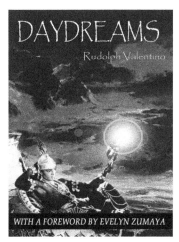

When silent film icon Rudolph Valentino penned this book of poetry in 1923, he was waging a one man strike against his studio demanding higher quality production standards for his films. While he struggled to find a solution to this employment impasse, he delved into spiritualism and wrote his *Daydreams* poems. Shortly after Valentino's sudden death in 1926, his ex-wife, Natacha Rambova claimed her husband was adept at receiving messages from the astral plane via automatic writing. She also alleged he did not write the *Daydreams* poems, but instead transcribed them while in a trance, channeling them from his own spirit guides and deceased poets. The mystery of the true authorship of Valentino's fascinating "psychic" poems remains unsolved and continues to be the subject of discussion for Valentino's many ardent admirers.

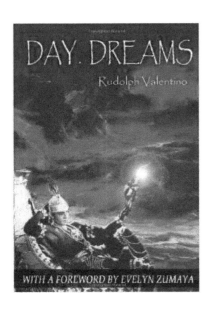

First Edition (out of print) published by PVG Publishing, 2010

In Italian:

L'Affare Valentino *di Evelyn Zumaya*

La prima biografia in italiano di Rodolfo Valentino. Le Stelle e i Divi di Hollywood sono ben conosciuti anche per gli scandali che riescono a generare e la Stella del cinema muto Rodolfo Valentino non si discosta da questa tradizione. La Zumaya ha investito ben 15 anni in accurate ricerche sia sulla vita di Valentino sia all'interno della ristretta cerchia di chi gli era vicino, in modo particolare sul ruolo avuto dal suo caro amico ed amministratore-agente, George Ullman. L'innovativo lavoro svolto dalla Zumaya ridisegna drasticamente la storia di Valentino e rivela segreti esplosivi. Il lavoro della Zumaya è al 100% basato su fatti reali ed è supportato dalla scoperta di circa 400 pagine di documenti mai visti prima, relativi sia alla vita finanziaria sia alla vita personale di Valentino. Il fulcro di questo nuovo archivio è l'ancora non pubblicato diario di George Ullman, in cui egli racconta dei suoi rapporti con Valentino. L'archivio è completato da altri interessanti documenti, mai visti prima. Grazie a tutte queste nuove informazioni la Zumaya ha, finalmente, ricostruito il vero ritratto di Rodolfo Valentino ovvero dell'Uomo oltre al Mito.

L'Infancia del Mito- Il Bambino Rodolfo Valentino

di Aurelio Miccoli

Il Mito del cinema muto Rodolfo Valentino, trascorse i primi nove anni della propria vita nella cittadina pugliese di Castellaneta. Qui si narra la storia dei suoi anni castellanetani; un dettagliato e autorevole racconto di quanto la sua famiglia, la cultura del periodo, gli eventi storici e l'ambiente lo abbiano influenzato. L'autore di questo libro è un concittadino di Valentino essendo anche lui nato e cresciuto a Castellaneta, Aurelio Miccoli, e ci svela un "Rodolfo" bambino curioso anche se non semplice e un gran sognatore ad occhi aperti. Questo splendido e accurato racconto è arricchito dalla presenza di personaggi reali che hanno affollato l'infanzia di Valentino. Grazie alla sua familiarità con Castellaneta e la sua approfondita ricerca in tutti gli archivi locali disponibili, Aurelio Miccoli ha descritto un ambiente molto dettagliato riguardo alla storia locale, alle strade, alla fauna, la flora e la cultura dell'epoca; il tutto supportato da coloratissime immagini. "L'infanzia del Mito" è uno studio accademico, nonché un racconto divertente dei primi eventi e delle influenze su di un ragazzino che è diventato una delle icone dello schermo più idolatrate del mondo.

Rudolph Valentino – In English

by
Jeanne De Recqueville

Translated by Renato Floris

Until this publication, Jeanne De Recqueville's 1978, *Rudolph Valentino* has only been available in French and copies of her book are scarce. Ms. De Recqueville was a Valentino activist in France for some twenty years; appearing as a Valentino authority on television and in documentaries in her role as the President and founder of "The Association of the Friends of Rudolph Valentino."

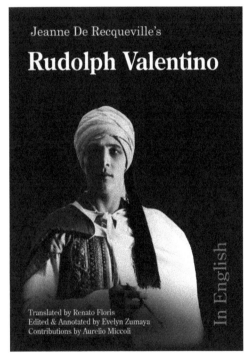

Ms. De Recqueville interviewed many of the people who knew Valentino in France including Jacques Hébertot, René Clair, Yvonne Legeay and Robert Florey. She also corresponded with Dr. Howard Meeker, the surgeon who operated on Rudolph Valentino and attended to him throughout his final illness. The book is in full color with additional essays on Andre Daven, Robert Florey's, *The Magic Lantern*, "The Letter to Bruno" and Aurelio Miccoli's definitive work on Valentino's nobility.

Bibliography

Books:

Allen, Frederick Lewis. *Only Yesterday, An Informal History of the 1920's*, Harper & Row Publishers. 1931.

Alovisio, Silvio and Giulia Carluccio, with Preface by David Robinson. *Rodolfo Valentino, Cinema, Cultura, Società tra Italia é Stati Uniti Negli Anni Venti*, Kaplan Edizioni, 2010, Turin.

Andreyev, Alexandre, *The Myth of the Masters Revived, The Occult Lives of Nikolai and Elena Roerich*, Koninklijke Brill, Leiden and Boston, Netherlands, 2014.

Anger, Kenneth. *Hollywood Babylon II*. Dutton, Inc., 1984.

Balio, Tino. *United Artists, The Company that Changed the Film Industry*, University of Wisconsin Press, 1987.

Basinger, Jeanine. *Silent Stars*, Alfred A. Knopf, 1999.

Beach, Rex. *The Crimson Gardenia and Other Tales of Adventure*, A.L. Burt Company, 1911.

Beckman, Scott, *William Dudley Pelley: A Life in Right-Wing Extremism and the Occult*, Syracuse University Press, 2005

Belletti, Valeria. *Adventures of a Hollywood Secretary, Her Private Letters from Inside the Studios of the 1920's*, University of California, 2006.

Ben-Allah. *Rudolph Valentino, His Romantic Life and Death*, Gem Publishing Co., 1926.

Bent, Silas. *Ballyhoo*. New York: Boni and Liveright, 1927.

Berstein, Matthew. *Walter Wanger, Hollywood Independent*, University of California Press, 1994.

Boller, Paul F. Jr. and Davis, Ronald L., *Hollywood Anecdotes*, Ballantine Books, 1987.

Bonadio, Felice.P., *Giannini, Banker of America*, University of California Press, 1994.

Botham, Noel and Donnelly, Peter. *Valentino, The Love-God*, Ace Books, 1976.

Bothmer, Bernard V., *Egypt 1950, My First Visit*, Edited by Emma Swan Hall, (Oxbow Books, 2003).

Broenniman, Eleanor Ray, *Mystic India Through Art*, Index to the Messenger, 1913-1927, Vassar, 1899

Brownlow, Kevin and Kobal, John. *Hollywood, The Pioneer,* Alfred A. Knopf, 1979.

Brownlow, Kevin. *The Parade's Gone By,* University of California Press, 1968. *Behind the Mask of Innocence,* University of California Press, 1992. With Bengtson, John, *Silent Traces, Discovering Early Hollywood Through the Films of Charlie Chaplin,* Santa Monica Press, 2006.

Chaplin, Charles. *My Autobiography,* Simon and Schuster, Inc., 1964.

Card, James. *Seductive Cinema: The Art of Silent Film,* Alfred A. Knopf, Inc., 1995.

Chin, Gabriel, editor. *Seabury Investigation Report,* Vol.3., New York Corruption Investigation Commissions-1894-1994, William S. Hein Co., 1997.

Cott, Jonathan, Is*is and Osiris, Exploring the Goddess Myth,* (Doubleday, 1994).

Covina, Gina. *The Ouija Book,* Simon & Schuster, 1970.

Crandell, Stephen, Mary Mellon – *The Woman Who Decided to Save the History of the World's Soul,* The Huffington Post, 11, 26, 2014

Cué, Baltasar Fernandez. *The True Rudolph Valentino,* translated into English by Renato Floris, Viale Industria Pubblicazioni, Turin, 2019.

De Recqueville, Jeanne. *Rudolph Valentino,* Editions France-Empire, 1978.

De Recqueville, Jeanne. *Rudolph Valentino – In English,* translated into English by Renato Floris. Viale Industria Pubblicazioni. Turin 2020

Drayer, Ruth A.,*Nicholas and Helena Roerich: The Spiritual Journey of Two Great Artist*s, Quest Books, Revised Edition, 2005. cite p. 283.

Earley, Mary Dawn. *Stars of the Twenties, Observed by James Abbe,* Viking Press, 1975.

Edited by Keylin, Arleen. *Hollywood Album 2,* Arno Press, 1979.

Edited by Sklar, Robert. *The Plastic Age,* Doubleday Canada, Limited, 1970.

Edwards, John. *One Last Time,* Berkeley Books, 1998.

Ellenberger, Allen R., *Ramon Novarro,* McFarland & Company Inc. Publishers, 1999.

Ellenberger, Allan R., *The Valentino Mystique: The Death and Afterlife of the Silent Film Idol,*

McFarland. 2005.

Encyclopedia of Women in the United States, Scholastic Inc, 1996. Produced by Shelia Keenan.

Eyman, Scott. *Mary Pickford, America's Sweetheart,* Donald I. Fine, Inc, 1990.

Feretti, Fred. *Café des Artistes: An Insider's Look at the Famed Restaurant and its Cuisine,* Lebhar-Friedman Books, 2000.

Finch, Christopher and Rosenkrantz, Linda. *Gone Hollywood,* Doubleday & Company, Inc., 1979.

Finler, Joel W., *Silent Cinema,* B. T. Batsford Ltd., 1997.

Florey, Robert. *Hollywood d'Hier et d'Aujourd'hui,* Editions Prisma, Paris, 1948.

Florey, Robert. *La Lanterne Magique,* La Cinematheque Suiss, Lausanne, 1966.

Franklin, Joe. *Classics of the Silent Screen, A Pictorial Treasury,* Bramhall House, MCMLIX, Research Assistant William K. Everson by arrangement with Citadel Press.

French, Philip. *The Movie Moguls,* Henry Regnery Company, 1969. Published in England by Weidenfeld and Nicolson.

Fuller, Loie. *Fifteen Years of a Dancer's Life with Some Account of Her Distinguished Friends.* New York: Restoration Editors, 2015. Originally published in 1913 by Herbert Jenkins Limited. Arundel Place, Haymarket, London S.W., with an introduction by Anatole France.

Gardner, Gerald. *The Censorship Papers,* Dodd, Mead & Company, 1987.

Glyn, Elinor. *Beyond the Rocks,* The Macaulay Company, 1906.

Golden, Eve. *Vamp, The Rise and Fall of Theda Bara,* Emprise Publishing, 1996.

Gordon, Ruth. *Myself Among Others,* Atheneum, 1971.

Guglielmi Morone, Chicca. *Rodolfo Valentino, Una Mitologia Per Immagini,* Libreria Petrini, Turin, 1995.

Harned, Robert L. *Sally Phipps, Silent Film Star.* Published by Robert L. Harned. Brooklyn, New York. June 2015.

Hull, E. M., *The Sheik,* Small, Maynard & Co., 1921.

Hulse, *The Blood n' Thunder Guide to Collecting Pulps,* Murania Press. 2009

Jarvis, Everett G., *Final Curtain,* Carol Publishing Group, 1992.

Kanin, Garson. *Hollywood,* Viking Press, 1967.

Kidwell, Claudia Brush and Steele, Valerie. *Men and Women, Dressing The Part,* Smithsonian Institution Press, 1989.

Kobal, John. *People Will Talk,* Knopf, 1985.
Lambert, Gavin. *Nazimova,* Alfred A Knopf, Inc. 1997.

Larrain, Luz. *Blanca Elena: Memoria Indiscreta De La Quinta Vergara,* Editoral Sudamericana. 1993.

Lawton, Richard. *A World of Movies,* Crown Publishers, 1974.

Lawton, Richard. *Grand Illusions,* Charles Scribner's Sons, 1973.

Leff, Leonard J. and Simmons, Jerold L., *Dame in the Kimono,* Grove Weidenfeld, 1990.

Leider, Emily. *Dark Lover,* Farrar-Strauss, 2003.

Lockwood, Charles. *Dream Palaces, Hollywood at Home,* The Viking Press, 1981.

Loos, Anita. *Cast of Thousands,* Grosset and Dunlap, 1977.

Lynd, Robert S. and Lynd, Helen Merrell. *Middletown, A Study in American Culture,* Harcourt Brace Jovanovich. 1957.

MacKenzie, Norman A., *The Magic of Rudolph Valentino,* The Research Publishing Company, 1974.

Mallen, Frank. *Sauce for the Gander,* Baldwin Books, New York, 1954.

Mannassa, Colleen and Tasha Dobbin-Bennett. *The Natacha Rambova Archive, Yale University.* Gottinger Miszellen, 234., 2012.

Marinacci, Barbara. *They Came From Italy, the stories of famous Italian-Americans,* Dodd, Mead & Company, 1967.

McQuire, William. *Bollingen, An Adventure in Collecting the Past.* Princeton University Press, 1982.

Mercer, Jane. *Great Lovers of the Movies,* Crescent Books, 1975.

Miccoli, Aurelio. *The Infancy of the Myth,* translated into English by Angelo Perrone, Viale Industria Pubblicazioni, 2014. Turin.

Miccoli, Aurelio. *Valentino e il professore - QUELLO CHE SO DI VALENTINO,* Scorpione Editrice – 2021. Taranto

Milbourne, Christopher. *Houdini: The Untold Story,* Thomas Y. Crowell Company, 1969.

Miredi, Antonio. *Rodolfo Valentino, Sogni ad Occhi Aperti,* Libreria Petrini, Turin, 1995.

Mitchell, J.A., *Amos Judd,* Charles Scribner's Sons, 1895.

Mitgang, Herbert. *Once Upon a Time in New York,* Simon and Schuster, 2000.

Moore, Colleen. *Silent Star,* Doubleday & Co., Inc., Garden City, New York, 1968.

Morris, Michael and Evelyn Zumaya. *Beyond Valentino - The Madam Valentino Addendum.* Turin: Viale Industria Pubblicazioni, 2017.

Morris, Michael. *Madam Valentino, The Many Lives of Natacha Rambova,* Abbeville Press, 1991.

Morton, H.V. *A Traveler in Southern Italy,* Dodd, Mead & Company, 1969.

Murray, Raymond. *Images in the Dark, An Encyclopedia of Gay and Lesbian Film and Video,* Plume, 1996.

Negri, Pola. *Memoirs of a Star,* Doubleday & Company, Inc., 1970.

Norman, Dorothy. *The Hero: Myth/Image/Symbol,* The World Publishing Company, 1969.

Oakes, Maud, *The Two Crosses of Todos Santos,* Introduction by Paul Radin, Bollingen Series XXVII, Princeton University Press, 1951.

Oakes, Maud, *The Stone Speaks, The Memoir of a Personal Transformation,* Chiron Publications, 1987.

Oberfirst, Robert. *Rudolph Valentino, The Man Behind the Myth,* The Citadel Press, 1962.

Parker, Tyler, A.S., *The Three Faces of Film,* Barnes and Co., 1960 and 1967.

Peary, Danny. *Close-ups,* Workman Publishing, 1978.

Pelley, William Dudley. *Why I Believe The Dead Are Alive!* Noblesville, Indiana: Fellowship Press, 1972.

Piankoff, Alexandre, T*he Shrines of Tut-Ankh-Amon, (*Bollingen Foundation, 1955).

Prophet, Mark L. and Elizabeth Clare Prophet, T*he Masters and Their Retreats,* Summit University Press., p. 248.

Quirk, Lawrence J., *The Great War Films,* Citadel Press, 1994.

Rogers, W.G., *Wise Men Fish Here, The Story of Frances Steloff and The Gotham Book Mart,* Harcourt, Brace and World, Inc., 1965.

Rambova, Natacha. *Rudolph Valentino: A Wife's Memories of an* Icon, 1921 PVG Publishing, from original content 1926, 2009.

Ramsaye, Terry. *A Million and One Nights, A History of the Motion Picture Through 1925,* paperback Touchstone, 1986 and hardcover, 1926.

Roth, Samuel. *The Intimate Journal of Rudolph Valentino,* W. Faro. 1931.

Roerich, Nicholas, *Altai-Himalaya, A Travel Diary,* roerich.org.

Roerich, Svetoslav, *Art and Life,* International Center of the Roerichs, Moscow, 2004.

Scagnetti, Jack. *The Intimate Life of Rudolph Valentino,* Jonathan David Publishers, Inc. 1975.

Selected and Edited by Behlmer, Rudy. *Memo From: David O. Selznick,* Grove Press, Inc.

Schildgen, Rachel A., *More Than A Dream: Rediscovering the Life and Films of Vilma Banky,* 1921 PVG Publishing, 2010.

Schulman, Irving. *Valentino,* Simon & Schuster, Inc., 1965.

Schulman, Irving, personal notes and loose manuscript pages of: *The Tragedy of Valentino, An Opera Bouffe in Five Acts, The Square Trap, The Short End of the Stick* and *Your Hands Entrap My Quivering Heart.* Accessed in the USC Rare Books Library, Los Angeles, California. Circa 1965.

Shipman, Nell. *The Silent Screen and My Talking Heart,* Hemingway Western Studies Series, Boise State University, Boise, Idaho, @1987 by Barry Shipman.

Sklar, Robert. *Movie-Made America,* Random House, 1975.

Soares, Andre. *Beyond Paradise,* St. Martin's Press, 2002.

Solomon, Aubre. *Twentieth Century Fox, A Corporate and Financial History,* The Scarecrow Press, Inc., 2002.

Sova, Dawn B., *Forbidden Films,* Checkmark Books, 2001.

Steiger, Brad, Mank, Chaw. *Valentino, An Intimate and Shocking Expose,* MacFadden Bartell, 1966.

St. John, Adela Rogers. *Love, Laughter and Tears, My Hollywood Story,* Doubleday & Company, Inc., 1978.

Stuart, Ray. *Immortals of the Screen,* Bonanza Books, MCMLXV.

Swanson, Gloria. *Swanson on Swanson,* Random House, Inc., 1980.

Tajiri, Vincent. *Valentino, The True Life Story,* A Bantam Book, 1977.

Tarkington, Booth. *Monsieur Beaucaire,* Doubleday, Page & Co. 1900. Paramount commemorative edition published by Grosset & Dunlap.

Taves, Brian, *Talbot Mundy, Philosopher of Adventure, A Critical Biography,* McFarland & Company, Inc., 2006.

The Editors of American Heritage/Bonanza Books. *The American Heritage History of the 1920's & 1930's,* Crown Publishers, 1987.

The Editors of Entertainment Weekly. *The 100 Greatest Stars of All Time,* Entertainment Weekly Books, 1997.

The Editors of Time-Life Books. *This Fabulous Century, 1920-1930, Volume III,* New York. 1969.

The Readers of Reminisce magazine. From Flappers to Flivvers. Reiman Publications.

Ullman, George, *The S. George Ullman Memoir, The Real Rudolph Valentino by the Man Who knew Him Best,* Foreword by Evelyn Zumaya, 2014. Turin.

Ullman, George. Valentino As I Knew Him . New York: Macy-Masius Publishers, 1926

Ullman, George. *The S. George Ullman Memoir, The Real Rudolph Valentino by the Man Who Knew Him Best.* Foreword by Evelyn Zumaya. Turin, Viale Industria Pubblicazioni, 2014.

Valentino, Rodolfo. *IL MIO DIARIO PRIVATO* translated into Italian by Paolo Orlandelli. Lindau- 1st edition July 2004 - Turin

Valentino, Rudolph. *Day Dreams.* MacFadden Publications, Inc., 1923.

Valentino, Rudolph. *My Private Diary.* Occult Publishing Company. 1929.

Valerio, Anthony. *Valentino and The Great Italians.* Guernica, 199

Vaughan, Heather A., *Natacha Rambova, Dress Designer* (1928 – 1931), *Dress, The Annual Journal of the Costume Society of America,* Volume 33, 2006

Viera, Mark, Sin in Soft Focus: Pre-Code Hollywood, Harry N. Abrams, Inc. Publishers, 2003.

Walker, Alexander. Rudolph Valentino. Penguin Books, 1976.

Wehner, George and with an Introduction by Talbot Mundy, *A Curious Life*, 1929, Horace Liveright, New York, 1929.

Zierold, Norman. The Moguls. Coward-McCann, Inc., 1969.

Zumaya, Evelyn, *Affairs Valentino, Special Edition,* (Viale Industria Pubblicazioni, 2015).

Zumaya, Evelyn, *Astral Affairs Rambova,* Viale Industria Pubblicazioni, 2018.
Zumaya, Evelyn and Michael Morris, o.p., *Beyond Valentino,* Viale Industria Pubblicazioni, 2017.

Zumaya, Evelyn. Affairs Valentino, Companion Guide, The Lost Court Documents of Rudolph Valentino, Viale Industria Pubblicazioni, Turin, 2014.

Archives:

Archivio Barone Fassini – Roma

Archivio di Stato Città di Campobasso, Ufficio Anagrafe

Archivio di Stato di Lecce

BnF - Bibliothèque Nationale de France, Paris

Besançon, France Archives, Ville de Besançon (Doubs), Le Fonctionnaire Municipal Délégué.

Bibliomediateca Mario Gromo del Museo Nazionale del Cinema – Turin

Cinémathèque Française, collections iconographiques - Paris

Cineteca Di Bologna Archive, Bologna, Italy

Find a Grave Memorial.

Frank Mennillo Archives

Gallica, National Library of France, Digital Library. Bibliotèque nationale de France. @gallica.bnf.fr

George Ullman Archives

Hastings Law Library, San Francisco, California

Historical City Archives of Turin

Irving Schulman Personal Archives & Special Collections @ University of Southern California.

Istituto San Giuseppe, Turin

Lantern Archives

La Stampa - Turin- Historical Archive Since 1867

Los Angeles County Records Center-Archives Limited Civil-Marriage Records 1925-1940.

Los Angeles County Sheriff's Department-Records Division-Case #481-480 Garnishment 1947.

Los Angeles Public Library- History and Genealogy Departments

Margaret Herrick Library

Michael Morris Archives

Motion Picture Magazine Archives

Naples Historical City Archives

NARA, U.S. National Archives and Records Administration, Laguna Nigel, California and Riverside, California

New York City Historical Society

New York City Police Museum Archives

New York Public Library

The Chicago Tribune

The New York Daily News

The New York Times

The New York Public Library, Archives and Manuscripts Division

The Los Angeles County Hall of Records

The Los Angeles Times

Palm Springs Historical Society Archives

Picture Play Magazine
Proquest Historical Newspapers

Putignano City Archives, Comune Di Putignano

San Francisco Hastings Law Library

Santeramo en Colle, Italy- City Historical Archives

Simon Fraser University, Library SFU Digital Collections.

Stanford's Green Library Microfiche Archives

U.S. District Court, Central Division Los Angeles

Utah Museum of Fine Arts

University of Wyoming, American Heritage Center

Periodicals (*included but not exclusive to*):

American Weekly, May 22, 1949, "Genevieve's Daughter"

Business School Review Elects - New Editorial Board Choose Officers for Magazine for 1923-1924 - Citation for Edgar Broenniman, *The Harvard Crimson*, October 1, 1923

Cinémagazine, May 16, 1924 – André Tinchant – "Rudolph Valentino Francophobe"

Cinémagazine, May 30, 1924 – A Propos de Rudolph Valentino (lettre de M. René Clair)

Cinémonde, October 4, 1956 to December 6, 1956 – Robert Florey *"Inoubliable, inoublié, RUDOLPH VALENTINO survit à sa légende."*

Cinemundial, May 1927 – February 1928 – Baltasar Fernández Cué, "El Verdadero Rodolfo Valentino"

Classic, December 1923 – Rudolph Valentino, "When I come Back, A Promise"

Exhibitor's Herald Morning Picture World, July-September 1928

Exhibitor's Review and Motion Pictures Today, Friday, February 28, 1930

Exhibitor's Trade Review, August 1925

Fate Magazine, March 1956, "Valentino...and His Unseen Guides", by Robert Gladwell

Huff, Theodore. "The Career of Rudolph Valentino", Films in Review, Volume III # 4, April 1952

La Rampe, Paris, 1915-1937

Life, November 14, 1938

Literary Digest, August 20, 1927

Literary Digest, September 11, 1926

Literary Digest, January 14, 1922

Madden, Elsie, "Are They Making Valentino A Saint?" article contained within Schulman archives and dated 8/1928

Photoplay Magazine, March 1922 - Valentino, Rudolph, "Woman and Love"

Photoplay Magazine January 1923 "An Open Letter from Rudolph Valentino - To the American Public".

Photoplay Magazine February, March, April 1923 "My Life Story" by Rudolph Valentino

Photoplay Magazine, January 1924 . "Natacha Valentino inspired Paul Poiret"

Photoplay Magazine, February, 1926 - Quirk, James R, "Speaking of Pictures"

Photoplay Magazine, May 1926 - Herzog, Dorothy, "Syncopated Heart"

Photoplay Magazine, June 1926 - "We Suggest New Coiffures for the Stars"

Photoplay Magazine, August 1926 - "Turbans: Why not roll your own?"

Photoplay Magazine, February 1927 - Smith, Frederick James, "Does Rudy Speak From the Beyond?"

Pictures and Picturegoer – July 1924 – October 1925 – Rudolph Valentino "My Own Story of My Trip Abroad"

San Francisco Chronicle, August 3rd, 1987 - "Early Hollywood Star Pola Negri Dies"

The Autograph Collector, October 1992 "The Chaw Mank Estate, The Inside Story"

The Bookman, January 8, 1923

The New York Times, October 27th, 1991 - Koszarski, Richard, "The Un-Sheiking of Rudolph Valentino"

The New York Times, November 14, 1982, Bender, Thomas, With Love and Money, Review of William McQuire's, *Bollingen, An Adventure in Collecting the Past*"

Time Magazine, January 11, 1926 - "Foreign News"

Time Magazine, August 30, 1926 - "National Affairs Section"

True Mystic Science Magazine, November 1938 issue, son of Leslie Grant Scott and R.T.M. Scott, R.T.M, Scott Junior was the magazine's editor in November of 1938

E-books & Online references:

ebook - *"My Private Diary by Rudolph Valentino With an Introduction by Michael A. Romano"* - *Pickle Partners Publishing 2016*

Dante Lattes, I*ntroduction of his translation of the Book of Psalms,* http://www.archivio-torah.it

Stepno, Bob, *The Evening Graphic's Tabloid Reality,* www.stepno.com/unc/graphic/

The Theosophical World View, Theosophical Society of Canada, Accessed on September 9, 2018, https://www.theosophical.ca/about-us1

Acknowledgments

We wish to thank everyone who has supported our work over the years and contributed in so many valuable ways. The Ullman family, the Mennillo family and the Filomarino family who have all brought so much new insight into the Valentino history.

In particular we wish to thank Louisa Antoinette Marie Filomarino, granddaughter of Ernesto, and Vincenzo Filomarino, grandnephew of Ernesto, for their contribution of photographs, archival material and family memories.

Thank-you to Kathy Barilly and Alexia Vanhee at the Biblioteque Nationale de France – Paris, for their effective and flawless support in the search for, "Inoubliable, Inoublié - Rudolph Valentino survit a sa légende" by Robert Florey.

Thank-you to Bertrand Karael, curator at the Iconotheque of the Cinémathèque Française - Paris, for the certification of the image relating to Rolf de Maré, Rudolph Valentino and René Clair in Deauville and for his support in iconographic research.

Thank-you to Jordan Lahmar-Martins for his research relating to Rudolph Valentino's French ancestry.

Thank-you Liam Muldowney for sharing his Douglas Gerrard research.

Thank-you to Fabrice Pacchin at the Archives Municipales de Besançon

Thank-you to Ms. Valerie Verneuille for her contribution to the Daven file.

Tank-you to Aurelio Miccoli for sharing his valuable research in local archives.

Thank-you to Nello Rassu coordinator of the multimedia Quazza lab at the CINEDUMEDIA UNIVERSITY RESEARCH CENTER of the University of Turin.

ROLF ARMSTRONG *paints*
RUDOLPH VALENTINO
in words
By Rolf Armstrong

AN ancient Chinese mask looks down from my studio wall—slant-eyed, sphinx like. Along the sunny quays of the Mediterranean, I have seen groups of swarthy, vivid Italian and Spanish sailors.

A toreador, small flat ears of an angry bob-cat, brushed my shoulder as he left the reddened bull-ring.

I can tell when a boxer first senses that his opponent is helpless. The eyes that direct the knock-out.

Valentino recalled these things to my mind, in my first glance at him. Immediately I knew that here was not merely the talented actor, nor the screen's most famous lover, but a man of unique, and subtle individuality, with strange power to stir the imagination. The oddly varied memories he stirred in me had, after all, one quality in common—intensity. And Valentino is intensity incarnate.

This, then, was the keynote of my portrait. To accentuate this characteristic, I invented a technique of severe simplicity, and a pose, and line composition calculated to climax in his smouldering eyes.

In my sketch I endeavored to indicate, not only the mere arrangement of his features, so familiar from countless photographs, but that underlying spirit that no camera can reproduce. I hope I have interpreted both his force and his sensitiveness, and some exotic tang. The portrait is unconventional; it leaves much to the imagination. Necessarily so. For that is Valentino.

The art on the cover of this book was created by Rolf Armstrong and appeared on the cover of Screenland Magazine in January 1924 Cover graphics and layout by Lucero Rabaudi

Index